Human Rights in the 21st Century

EDITORIAL BOARD

Human Rights in the 21st Century

Challenges Ahead

EDITOR
MOHAMMAD SHABBIR
Ambedkar Chair Professor of Law
Dr. Ambedkar Chair of Legal Studies and Research
Department of Law, Aligarh Muslim University, Aligarh

RAWAT PUBLICATIONS
Jaipur • New Delhi • Bangalore • Kolkata • Guwahati

ISBN 978-81-316-0129-7

Reprinted, 2017

Published by
Prem Rawat for **Rawat Publications**
Satyam Apts, Sector 3, Jawahar Nagar, Jaipur 302 004 (India)
Phone: 0141 265 1748 / 7006 Fax: 0141 265 1748
E-mail: info@rawatbooks.com
Website: www.rawatbooks.com

New Delhi Office
4858/24, Ansari Road, Daryaganj, New Delhi 110 002
Phone: 011 2326 3290

Also at *Bangalore, Kolkata* and *Guwahati*

Typeset by Rawat Computers, Jaipur
Printed at Nice Printing Press, New Delhi

Contents

Foreword

In present democratic world, the relationship between the citizens and the state is determined by the extent to which citizens are guaranteed with such rights as liberty, equality, fraternity, justice, fairplay, and dignity. These are today considered as important human rights. The ancient and medieval periods witnessed bloodshed for maintaining the supremacy of religion and in defence of established order, but in our age, there are revolutions, revolts and national movements for such rights.

The period after the Second World War has witnessed intensive debate on the concern for human rights. Towards the close of the middle age, with the emergence of nation-states and establishment of despotic regimes, the assertion for rights started within the national boundaries as a reaction to the repressive regimes and, consequently, history witnessed many revolutions in the late seventeenth and eighteenth centuries. Human Right Declarations and Bills of Rights were enshrined in national constitutions. The rapid industrialization led to globalization phenomenon and advocacy for standard of living have increased the complexities of current societies. It is a hard reality that any nation today is not sovereign in true sense, irrespective of its largeness and powerfulness. No country – small or big – can survive and thrive in isolation. The interdependence of the modern world is a reality. These reasons prompted a wave of interest towards the rights of human beings at national and international levels. At the present juncture, the human rights phenomenon covers a much wider area. The right to development has been surfaced recently. It is evident that the concept of human rights has to traverse a long way and numerous additions have been made to it.

The root of the contemporary conception of human rights can be traced to the period of 'renaissance and enlightenment'. The first half of the twentieth century was marked not only by the prevalence of colonial rule in the large part of the world, but also for the rise of authoritarian government and the establishment of the fascist and aggressive regimes in many countries of the world. Also, this period witnessed the rise of national liberation movements and movements for the democracy in different parts of the world. The twentieth century also experienced most devastating two world wars. The period between two world wars has been described as the 'age of catastrophe'.

To ensure observance of human rights, it is a *sine qua non* to generate awareness for human rights. This task of concretization can be achieved only through concerted efforts of individuals, organizations and officials holding aloft the banner of human rights. It appears that when an individual complains of violation of human rights and seeks remedy, he often pitches himself against the might of the state and its agencies.

No doubt, the respect for human rights has increased and its observance too; however, gross violation of recognized norms continues unabated in all parts of the world though there is difference of degree only. There are large-scale breaches of civil and political rights, as well as economic, social and cultural rights such as right to life, right to adequate standard of living, right to freedom of speech and expression, right to protection from torture and inhuman treatment, police atrocities, arbitrary arrest etc. The obligations set out in the course of international conventions and treaties for the protection and promotion of human rights accepted by the different countries are flouted flagrantly by them without impunity. The most formidable challenge to the human rights is their abuse by governmental agencies themselves.

For the observance of human rights, its knowledge is imperative. Education on human rights is of great importance and it is viewed as an essential contribution to the development of a human rights culture.

Here, observation of Mr. Justice Rangnath Misra, former Chief Justice of India and the first Chairman of the National Human Rights Commission, deserves to be quoted:

> "...Violation of human rights is widely rampant, violation of human rights is in the homes, the streets, the public offices (and) educational institution".

Here arises a question – how can such a paradox be resolved? Virtually, spread of awareness about, and protection and promotion of, human rights, respect for each other's rights and fulfilment of our obligations towards the fellow beings and the society are the only possible solutions.

The contents of this book are fascinating as it discusses constitutional jurisprudence in relation to reservation in favour of backward Muslims, extension of reservation policy in private sector, social duties and human rights, social status and legal rights of prostitutes, position of genocide in international law, human rights violation in Iraq and the role of UN, women empowerment through reservation, scheduled castes and violation of their rights, domestic violations and women's rights, good governance, human rights and the right of minorities, conversion and its implications to marriage, human rights of displaced persons, human rights of marginalized groups, Dr. Ambedkar's perspective on social justice and empowerment, need of human rights education, etc.

The book would be of immense value to the researchers, academicians, law makers, judges, lawyers, social scientists, NGOs and social activists, along with all concerned who are committed to strengthening policy, objects and understanding of human rights jurisprudence and its philosophy taking into account its relevance and potent challenges in the 21st century. It is a meaningful addition to the existing knowledge of human rights jurisprudence.

The book is being published by Dr. Ambedkar Chair Professor of Law, Professor Mohammad Shabbir, under the aegis of Dr. Ambedkar Chair of Legal Studies & Research, Department of Law, Aligarh Muslim University, Aligarh, which has already brought out a number of useful publications.

This work deserves a praise from all those who champion the cause of human rights jurisprudence. It provides the understanding of the fundamentals and objectives of human rights in the contemporary era. I am confident that this informative and objective work will be studied with keenness by all those who are committed to perceive peaceful world by observing the ethics of human rights in every walk of life.

Prof. P.K. Abdul Azis
Vice-Chancellor
Aligarh Muslim University
Aligarh

Preface

Human rights are those rights that every individual must have by virtue of being a member of the society. They are based on demand for a life in which the inherent dignity of human being aspires for respect, protection and dignity. Human rights are innate individual and are of an intrinsic factor in the quality of human persons. According to Jefferson, "inherent and inalienable rights of men come within the framework of Human Rights". The first document using the expression 'human rights' is seen in the Charter of United Nations, which declares promotion and fostering of human rights as one of the basic goals of United Nations, though it does not explain the contents of human rights. The International Bill of Human Rights, which was drawn subsequently, comprises:

1. Universal Declaration of Human Rights (1948)
2. International Covenant of Economic, Social and Cultural Rights (1966)
3. International Covenant of Civil and Political Rights (1966)
4. Optimal protocol providing the rights for individual petition.

These are accepted by the international community as human rights in the post-cold World War II. The United States and many western countries and communities are laying increasing emphasis on human rights. In 1974, the United States enacted the Foreign Assistance Act and its Section 116 was designed to prohibit or restrict assistance to any government which "engages in gross violation of internationally recognized Human Rights".

Many Asian countries, which are the signatories to the Universal Declaration, feel that western countries are using human rights as an instrument for their political and ideological hegemony. These perceptions came into sharp reaction in the United Nations Conference on Human Rights in Vienna in 1993. The Asian viewpoint was put forward by countries like China, Singapore, Malaysia, etc., which emphasized that while human rights are universal in nature and they must be considered in the context of "dynamic process of international norm setting, bearing in mind the significance of national and regional peculiarities and various historical, cultural and religious backgrounds". The hub of the Asian criticism of the western concept of human rights is that there are no universal human rights because there is no single human nature, and thus no universal moral law which appeals across cultures. There is also criticism that developed countries are seeking to impose western values on non-western societies under the guise of promoting good governance and human rights. Thus, the Universal Charter of Human Rights is being challenged by many nations of the South. It has been aggressively argued by countries like Malaysia and Singapore that the cultural matrix within which relations between individuals and states are invaded, are fundamentally different in Asia from that in the West. The communication tradition and consensus-seeking approach in Asia are considerably different from the ethos of the West. Another point of difference is in the context of economic circumstances of the Asian countries, which are not similar to the West. Nonetheless, even in the midst of controversies and clashes of western and Asian perceptions and perspectives, there is an acknowledgement of the fact that there are some fundamental human rights whose violation would be condemned by all the major faiths and cultures of the world. Abuses like racism, ethnic cleansing, torture, rape, arbitrary detention, etc., are not tolerated by any culture or faith that respects humanity.

The United Nations has launched a World Public Information Campaign (WPIC) for human rights. Knowledge and awareness of human rights is equally important. Only those people, who are educated about and aware of their human rights, can pressurize their governments to observe those rights. Knowledge of human rights is essential as a tool for the observance and the promotion of it for the creation of climate of public opinion in which violation of human rights is unbearable. However, education about, and knowledge of human rights cannot totally prevent the occurrence of violation of human rights. It can create moral and mental inhibition and a sense of shame on the part of violators and, thus, contribute to the protection of human rights.

Human rights can be defined as those basic rights, which are inherent in our nature and without which we cannot live as a human being. Fundamental freedoms and human rights help us to develop and use our intelligence, qualities, talents and conscience to satisfy our mundane and spiritual needs by the respect of human rights. We protect the inherent dignity and in return receive respect and affection. Nonetheless, the denial of human rights and fundamental freedoms not only results in personal tragedy, but also creates conditions for social and political unrest, sowing the seeds of violence and conflict. The respect for human rights and human dignity is the foundation of freedom, justice, fraternity and peace in the world. Human rights are universal and are applicable to all without discrimination. Human rights are sometimes called 'Natural Rights', 'Basic Rights' and 'Fundamental Rights'. A civilized country must respect and recognize them. The legal education should protect them. International concern for human rights is enshrined in the Charter of the United Nations.

The quality of any civilization can be measured by the respect it has for the protection and promotion of human rights. The essence of human rights is of universal concern and it virtually cuts across ideological and political boundaries. The Universal Declaration of Human Rights and the nation-states' entry into the arena of international covenants, along with the optional protocols to the international covenant on civil and political rights, marks the turning point in the development of human rights under the regime of rule of law. The important task in promoting human progress is to maintain a proper balance between the interests of the individual and the ethos of a democratic society and between individual and collective rights. The state is duty-bound to harmonize the rights of the individual with the requirements of the community. The golden thread of human rights runs through the very philosophy of the Constitution. The Fundamental Rights, the Directive Principles of State Policy, the Fundamental Duties and effective judicial mechanism for the protection of human rights underline the importance of constitutional culture in India. India's concern for the protection and promotion of human rights is also supported by the establishment of the National Human Rights Commission (NHRC). The United Nations decided to proclaim the ten-year period beginning with 1 January, 1995 as the decade for human rights education. Human rights education contributes to the development consistent with the dignity of human personality taking into account the various elements of society, such as racial minorities, disabled persons, prisoners, children, women, etc.

'Know Your Human Rights' is the message addressed by the United Nations to the citizens of all countries regardless of race, faith, colour, sex, language, creed and place of birth. A big majority of people today are not aware of their rights as human beings. Realizing this fact, the United Nations has launched a world public information campaign for human rights as mentioned earlier.

Awareness and knowledge of human rights is equally important in times of peace and war. These are essential tools for the observance and promotion of human rights and also for creation of a climate of public opinion wherein violation of human rights may not be permissible. Human rights are those rights which are inherent in our nature and without which we cannot live as human being. These are based on mankind's demand for a life in which the dignity and worth of each human being would get respect and protection. Human rights are of universal nature and apply to all persons without any discrimination. Human rights being basic, natural and fundamental cannot be taken away. The root of human rights may be traced to humanitarian traditions, religious precepts, freedoms and equality of human being. In the Hellenistic period, the Stoice philosophers evolved the doctrine of natural rights which belongs to all men in all times. They believed in universal brotherhood. Roman philosophers followed the Stoice's stressing the fundamental resemblance and the equality of men stemming from their common possession of reason. In middle ages, great philosopher, Thomas Acquinas affirmed that "unjust laws have no moral validity". However, the situation changed materially with Renaissance. The important event of this period was the signing of Magna Carta by the king which sets first milestone on the road to the liberties of the people. The Magna Carta is known as "the great charter of liberty", which provided that "no person shall be captured or imprisoned, outlawed or exiled or destroyed, nor will go against or send against him except by law and full judgment – under the law of the land". During this period, Hugo Grotious in Holland and Thomas Hobbes and John Locke in England provided the necessary wings to the movement of freedom and liberty on the strength of the Bill of Rights, 1689, the great charter of liberty and on the call of Rousseau, the men united for the preservation of their rights of freedom and equality. In 1789, the French Declaration of the rights of men and of the citizens asserted: "Men are born and remain free and equal in respect of rights. These rights are of liberty, equality, fraternity, property, security and resistance to oppression." In 1814, by the treaty of peace between British and French governments, it was agreed to cooperate in the abolition of slave trade. This practice was condemned by several other countries such as Australia, Portugal, Spain, Sudan and Russia at the Congress of Vienna in 1815. The treaty of peace "between the allied and associate powers of Germany was endeavouring the instrument which dealt with a number of political, legal, humanitarian and economic issues". The international concern for human dignity found expression in covenant of the League of Nations.

The fundamental duties are the charter of human duties which helps in promoting the human rights. India is also a party to the Universal Declaration of Human Rights and does rectify the International Covenant on Civil and Political Rights as well as the International Covenant on Economic, Social and Cultural Rights.

In this backdrop, the key questions to be answered are to what extent the UN Charter shows its concern for human rights? What has been the impact of Universal Declaration of Human Rights and other major covenants relating to human rights on the protection and promotion of human rights at the national and international levels? To what extent the Constitution of India is aimed at protecting and promoting the human rights of the people? Has India been able to achieve that target or not? What has been the role of judiciary? What role the National Human Rights Commission is playing? And, what is the position on the issue of the imperativeness of human rights education through colleges and universities in India? On all these questions this book accepts the challenges. Observance of human rights is posing problems almost everywhere and there is not a single country whose record is flawless. In the countries which have obtained independence recently, the problems are more aggravated. Many are victims of poverty, ignorance, disease and inertia. Western commentators generally underestimate the importance of illiteracy and ignorance. Conference held in Kabul could do meaningful exercise on numerous human rights issues in many countries where economic resources stand as obstacle and the bulk of population lives on the margin of poverty. Arguments were advanced in such matters as the development of the economy and the improvements in sectors like health, education and housing, the state needed necessary powers to implement plans even though, meanwhile, the rights of individual or groups might be temporarily curtailed. Some participants astonished, nonetheless, whether the governments of developing countries did not show excessive concern for the internet and extra security and apply unnecessary instructions on human rights. The scarcity of competent and efficient public officials is also an obstacle to progress in the sphere of human rights. Specific problem of underdeveloped world arises in the service area of labour mobilization. Neither the human rights provisions of United Nations Charter and the Universal Declaration of Human Rights, nor the other treaties and declarations, have brought about any material change.

In 1952, 1957, and again in 1962, the General Assembly of the United Nations repeated that notwithstanding the obligations arising from the UN Charter and Universal Declaration of Human Rights, violation of human rights continues to occur in various parts of the world.

India got independence in 1947 having a Constitution which guaranteed to all its citizens liberty, equality, justice, social and political, irrespective of the caste, colour, creed, sex and place of birth.

The fundamental rights are recognized as the basic rights of individuals. These also promise the removal of all kinds of inequities from the lives of people. Likewise, hosts of Directive Principles of State Policy promote the concept of human rights. Till date, many amendments have been made and many laws have been enacted to realize the objective of human rights. Despite such arrangements, we find the picture as a mix of many successes with occasional failures. India has not only incorporated an elaborate Bill of Rights in its Constitution but effects have been made to translate these into reality. The contents of Declaration of Human Rights, 1948 are incorporated in the Constitution of India.

It may be pointed out that initially the attitude of judiciary in India towards Directive Principles was not favourable as it had nullified many important legislations embodying socio-economic reforms, but with the passage of time, there has been a shift in the attitude of the Indian judiciary towards socio-economic rights. Basically, the Directive Principles intend to promote social welfare in consonance with basic objects of the human rights which acclaim global perspective and are enforced at national level. The framers of the Constitution of India adopted American pattern of incorporating the Bill of Rights in the Constitution itself. The Swaraj Bill of India, 1895 stated about the freedom of speech and expression, right to equality, etc., and it was felt that the human rights should be given priority. Human rights have been incorporated in the Constitution on the pattern of the Constitutions of United States and Switzerland.

On the issue of human rights, the observation of Justice Chandrachud (as he was then) in *Keshavananda Bharti* v. *State of Kerala* is relevant to be reproduced: "...it is really the poor, starved and mindless millions who need the court's protection for securing to themselves the enjoyment of Human Rights. In the absence of explicit mandate, the Court should abstain from striking down a constitutional amendment which makes and endeavour to wipe-out every tear from every eye".

The judiciary has been in a position to achieve success in terms of protection of human rights more particularly, through Social Action Litigation (SAL), also popularly known as Public Interest Litigation (PIL), by providing relief to poor, downtrodden, exploited and victimized categories of people.

In India, the National Human Rights Commission was initially constituted on 12 October 1993, under the Protection of Human Rights Ordinance. It is devoted to protecting and promoting human rights.

Violation of human rights is a global phenomenon. The difference is only of degree. When the people, like in India, are illiterate, ignorant, poor and exploited ones, the violation is bound to be more, but when the people are educated and advanced, they are likely to be less prone to inhuman treatment and exploitations.

Women's rights are integral to human rights. The human rights of women should be considered as collective rights of women accepted as a person with the capacity to act on her behalf. Also, children are entitled to rights as much as any section of the society. A civilized and a sensitive society will accord dignity to its young citizens by evolving conducive conditions in which they can develop their full potential and look forward to a full and satisfying adult life.

Developmental rights are hub of human rights discourse. They are interdependent and indivisible. Right to development is based on the premise that all individuals are entitled to enjoy economic, social, cultural and political development. In the absence of human rights and fundamental freedoms, duties cannot be realized. The rights of indigenous people have to be understood in the context of developmental rights. The struggle of the indigenous people all over the world is centred around the issue of economic survival and recognition of dignity.

Refugee movements are involuntary movements of population. Today, more than 13 million people are refugees on account of human rights violations. Refugees in South Asia constitute approximately about 12 per cent of the global population. Besides 1951 United Nations Convention for Refugees, there are many international and regional documents which lay down rights for refugees.

In the contemporary era, global terrorism has emerged as one of the most destructive instruments of any international, national, internal, ethnic and religious conflicts in the form of organized violence. It has infected almost all continents – Europe, America, Asia and Africa – and has emerged as a serious challenge to the national and international human rights regimes. To combat a problem of this magnitude calls for evolving a cooperative framework at the national, regional and international levels.

Now-a-days, environmental issues have become a significant factor in national and international politics. There is wide environmental degradation which affects human activity and its threat to the essence of human rights. The causes of environmental degradation are basically demographic and economic, the remedies often have to do with industrial activities, internal regulation and international cooperation touching on matters to remedy the situation. Nonetheless, environmental problem can be a source of political conflict amongst states and can contribute to violence within and amongst states leading to violation of human rights.

Today's civil society is characterized by an increasing level of ethnic conflicts and socio-political violence. The rise of this phenomenon is largely an outcome of socio-political and economic process. When politicized social groups fail to manoeuvre, negotiate and bargain within the political sphere, they resort to violence, which has a direct bearing on human welfare and human rights. Government policies always have significant effect on the course and trajectory of socio-political violence.

Violence is spreading faster than culture and this tendency is in need of curb. The violence is a killer of human rights. The National Human Rights Commission is making use of all the channels including education to spread a message of human rights. Cumulative efforts have to be made to reduce violence. To develop a culture of human rights is the ultimate goal to the National Human Rights Commission. The Commission desires universities to have course on human rights at graduate, post-graduate and research levels. The Commission recently insisted University Grants Commission (UGC) and Ministry of Human Resource Development (HRD) for the inclusion of human rights in curriculum of graduate, post-graduate and research levels.

Ignorance, poverty, illiteracy, violence, terrorism, discrimination, inequalities, inequities, police atrocities, custodial deaths, denial of dues to Muslims as minority community, non-participation of Muslims in administration and law-making, due to discriminatory approach, communal violence, corruption, exploitation of children, exploitation of women and injustice to them, female infanticide, nominal representation of women in legislatures and other evils and ills are hugely rampant, while our Constitution promises otherwise. There are a few potent questions: What went wrong? Why went wrong? And, how went wrong? And what is needed to carry forward human rights movement successfully to achieve the desired goals?

This book: *Human Rights in the 21st Century: Challenges Ahead* discusses constitutional jurisprudence in relation to reservation in favour of Indian backward Muslims, social duties and human rights, extension of reservation policy in private sector, social status and legal rights of prostitution, genocide in international law and Indian state practice, women in governance through empowerment by reservation, Dalit and violation of their human rights, domestic violence as an aberration in women human rights, good governance, human rights and the rights of minorities, the need of communal harmony in India with reference to the Hague Peace Agenda, conversion and its implications to marriage, human rights of displaced persons, sanitization and marginalization of manual scavengers in India: human rights perspective, Dr. Ambedkar's perspective on social justice and empowerment, denial of reservation benefit to the converted people, Article 22 and requirement of human rights standard under the International Covenant on Civil and Political Rights, need of human rights education, quest for women empowerment and directive principles of state policy v. contemporary development.

A group of noted human rights activists, academicians, legal luminaries and social scientists have endeavoured to analyze causes responsible for the sordid state of affairs and challenges to human rights advancing solutions in the selected areas of human rights as specified above. This volume would be of immense value to the researchers, social activists, social scientists, academicians, lawyers, judges, law reformers and legislators along with all concerned who are committed to strengthening policy, objects and understanding of human rights philosophy taking into account its relevance and potent challenges with which it is confronted in the 21st century. Of course, it is a meaningful addition to the existing literature of human rights jurisprudence.

Dr. Ambedkar Foundation, Ministry of Social Justice and Empowerment, Government of India, deserves praise for its initiative to accomplish this volume successfully. I hereby do register my sense of gratitude to Rawat Publications, Delhi/Jaipur, for its excellent publication maintaining world class standard.

Mohammad Shabbir

Dr. Ambedkar Chair of Legal Studies and Research, Department of Law, Aligarh Muslim University, Aligarh

An Introduction

MOHAMMAD SHABBIR

The sub-committee on education, set up for centenary celebrations of Baba Saheb Dr. Bhim Rao Ambedkar, a great leader, law-giver, constitution-maker, social reformer, scholar, thinker, philosopher and jurist in one of its recommendations in the year 1992, suggested for setting up Dr. Ambedkar Chairs in different disciplines in different institutions/universities. In pursuance of this recommendation, Dr. Ambedkar Chairs were set up for undertaking study and research on various aspects of the philosophy, thoughts, ideologies, missions and ideals of Dr. B.R. Ambedkar, by Dr. Ambedkar Foundation, Ministry of Social Justice and Empowerment, Government of India, New Delhi.

Dr. Ambedkar Chair of Legal Studies and Research, created in the Department of Law, Aligarh Muslim University, is one such Chair. The prime objective of setting up of the Chair is to provide necessary facilities to undertake studies and research by intellectuals, academicians, scholars, researchers and students to understand, assess, analyze and disseminate ideas, ideologies, thoughts and missions of Dr. Ambedkar, and also to provide opportunity to develop appropriate methodologies and strategies to translate them into practical propositions. The study and research under the Chair should focus on the socio-legal and economic status of the Scheduled Castes (SCs) and Scheduled Tribes (STs), minorities, weaker sections and other marginalized groups of Indian society concentrating on the impact and outcome of various measures, strategies and programmes adopted by the various agencies of the government from time to time. The entire research exercise should focus on bringing out meaningful outcome to suggest remedial measures and facilitate the relevant organizations to adopt these measures for the formulation of meaningful policies and programmes.

Dr. Ambedkar Foundation allocates thrust area for study, research and various other activities and programmes. To achieve the objectives, the Chair undertakes research in the allocated thrust area. The thrust areas include: Personal Laws and Uniform Civil Code, Human Rights, Law, Constitution, Weaker Sections, Minorities, Scheduled Castes and their Development, Dr. Ambedkar's Role and Contributions in Law and Constitution Making, Social Justice, Gender Justice, Women and Law, Role of Judiciary and its Limitations, Jurisprudence and Criminal Justice System. It organizes seminars, workshops, symposia, conferences, lectures and penal discussions. It provides a forum to academicians, intellectuals, researchers, scholars and students for undertaking theoretical and empirical research in the allocated thrust area by applying the appropriate research methodologies. It assigns short-term and long-term research projects to under-graduate/ post-graduate students and research scholars. Post-graduate dissertations and doctoral theses leading to PhD are allocated by the Chair. Productive activities of the Chair includes publication of books, journals, articles, research papers, research studies, research outcomes, case studies and monographs in the allocated thrust area. The Chair undertakes any other studies and research projects assigned by the Dr. Ambedkar Foundation from time to time according to its laid-down terms and conditions. Such research studies can be entrusted by the Chair to other relevant institutions with the approval of the Foundation. The Chair provides research guidance to post-graduate, MPhil/LLM and research scholars. The Chair, with the prior approval of the Foundation, may enter into national/international collaborations for undertaking study and research on subject(s) relevant to the objectives and functions of the Chair and its allocated thrust area. To carry out these objectives and to execute the functions of the Chair, the Foundation has provision for human resource to assist the institution wherein the Chair is created.

Dr. Ambedkar Chair Professor is obligated to promote study and research activities in concerned discipline wherein the Chair is created in general, and in allocated thrust area, in process of carrying out the objectives and functions of the Chair. The Professor handles the case studies, short-term and long-term research projects satisfying the objectives of setting up the Chair in the discipline, undertakes the publication of books, journals, articles, monographs, case studies and research projects in the allocated thrust area. He is also mandated to supervise and provide guidance to post-graduate students' dissertations, MPhil dissertations and doctoral theses leading to award of PhD/LLD in allocated thrust area. He also organizes seminars, symposia, conferences, workshops, lectures and penal discussions out of the topics/themes/issues of the allocated thrust area in discipline of the Chair. The Chair Professor, besides his normal duties as Professor of Law in the Department of Law, also handles the academic, administrative and financial responsibilities associated with the Chair. He is assisted by the Research Officer and other supporting staff of the Chair in process of carrying out the objectives and functions of setting up the Chair. Research Officer, Research Fellows and Research Assistants are assigned study and research by the Chair Professor out of the thrust areas in the assigned discipline of the Chair.

Dr. Ambedkar Chair of Legal Studies and Research, Department of Law, Aligarh Muslim University, Aligarh was created recognizing its contributions in the field of law, on 10 March 1992, as a constructive homage to the memory of Bharat Ratna Baba Saheb Dr. B.R. Ambedkar, the messiah of the suppressed segments of the society. It is a matter of honour and distinction for which the University rightly deserves, due to its matchless contributions in the field of legal studies and research.

Acknowledgements

I express my deep sense of gratitude to Professor Dr. Abdul Azis, Vice-Chancellor, Aligarh Muslim University, Aligarh, India for enriching the book by contributing his learned 'Foreword'.

Dr. Ambedkar Foundation, Ministry of Social Justice and Empowerment, Government of India deserves commendation for its initiative to accomplish this volume successfully.

I am thankful to Rawat Publications, New Delhi/Jaipur for utmost concern and professional devotion in publishing this book fulfilling the world class standard.

Mohammad Shabbir

1

Constitutional Jurisprudence Affirms Reservation for Indian Backward Muslims

Advocacy for the Motion

MOHAMMAD SHABBIR

The caste system is pervasive in India; and it has become almost a feature of all the religious groups. The Hindu society is divided in four social strata: Brahmin, Kshatriya, Vaish and Shudras by divine sanction. Out of its impact, the Indian Muslims admit their social division into two: (1) Ashraf, and (2) Ajlaf. Ashraf means 'noble' and it includes all descendants of foreigners and converts from high caste Hindus. All other Muslims, including the occupational groups and all converts of lower ranks are known by the contemptuous term 'Ajlaf' which means the 'mean people'. Within these groups there are castes with social precedence of the same nature as one finds among the Hindus. This division is unique and has been practised and perpetuated in the Indian sub-continent, while elsewhere, in the rest part of the Muslim world, no such gradation of Muslim community is found because Islam does not sanction such gradation and division.

The Census reports, district and state gazetteers prepared during the British regime provide detailed information about various population characteristics including the caste and information on the divisions and sub-divisions of Indian society. The Census of 1921 had a special report on castes among Muslim population. Discussion about the caste among the Indian Muslims, their place in the social hierarchy and educational status, was not to the liking of the intelligentsia, mostly to Ashrafs (nobles) who argued that a discussion of castes stratification among the Muslims was uncalled for; since it was against the Islamic principles of equality. However, caste has been a social reality and social scientists on the basis of empirical research have come to the conclusion that caste divisions exist in Muslim society. The basic difference between the Muslims and the Hindu caste system is that the Muslims have caste division and have practised it, while among the Hindus one finds not only the practice but also the theory of caste with approval of religious philosophy.[1]

The study of Muslim caste in Uttar Pradesh discusses the origin and existence of caste, caste structure and organization and inter-caste relationship among the Muslims. Study about the Awadh region of Uttar Pradesh upholds: The region is well known for majority of Muslim Zamindars (landlords), the cultivators and serving castes are derived from the lower ranks of both Hindus and Muslims. The Ashraf (nobles) have been associating themselves with the high status of the feudal system – the Zamindars, while serving castes of the villages have been regarded as people of inferior or of low birth. Birth alone decided an individual's social status. Even if persons of low caste, such as Nai (barber) or Gaddi (grazier) acquired some property and thus they raised their economic status. They would never rank equal with those born as Ashraf, no matter how poor these Ashrafs might be. In the rural areas, the caste impact is great and the Ashraf (Sayyed), Sheikh, Moghal and Pathan) are clearly distinguishable from the rest of the serving castes namely; Julasha, Kabaria, Dhunia, Nai, Qassab, Teli, Gaḍdi and others.[2]

Studies performed by Imtiaz Ahmad, Zarina Bhatti and M.K.A. Siddiqui on caste and social stratification among the

Muslims have further supported the findings noted above. It is obvious from these studies that the Muslims of lower social ranking were not having opportunity of education and are denied upward mobility.[3]

Political leaders and social reformers amongst Hindus like Gandhi, Phule, Periyar and Ambedkar were not only concerned about the plight of Dalits, but they actively fought against the evils of the Hindu caste system, nonetheless, it is hard to find such example where Muslim political leaders, social reformers and, religious preachers have made any such effort to get free from this social evil which is opposed to the tenets and teachings of Islam. The observation of Dr. B.R. Ambedkar, admirably sums up the realities of Muslim society in India:[4]

> The existence of the evil (caste system) among the Muslims is disturbing enough. But far more distressing is the fact that there is no organized movement of social reforms among the Musalmans of India on a scale sufficient to bring about their eradication. The Hindus have their social evils, but some of them are conscious of their existence and a few of them are actively agitating for their removal. The Muslims, on the other hand, do not realize that there is evil. Moreover, like the Hindus, among the Muslims also, the high-ranking castes have their settlements near the city center whereas those placed at the bottom are to be found close to the periphery of the urban settlement.

The Constitution of India envisages an egalitarian society. It promises equality of opportunity to all the citizens of the country. However, it is not possible to eradicate age-old inequalities simply by adopting doctrines and principles in the Constitution. It, therefore, becomes imperative to adopt special measures in order to at least maximize, if not to bring to an end the inequalities of the past. Affirmative action or positive discrimination is aimed at reducing the levels of inequalities where people are segregated and denied opportunities of education and upward mobility. Equality of status and proper progress of the nation is not possible unless all sections of the people are not represented. The Constitution sanctions that the state may take such steps as are needed to safeguard the interest of the socially and educationally deprived groups. Such groups fall into thee broad categories: (i) Scheduled Castes, (ii) Scheduled Tribes, and (iii) Other Backward Classes. The basic argument in favour of reservation for socially deprived; has been that special opportunities should be created for this section over and above the general provision to satisfy the spirit of equity of opportunity for all. Dr. B.R. Ambedkar while placing before the Constituent Assembly such a proposal argued that the aim of providing equal opportunities to all irrespective of caste, creed and community is very important. However, he was of the view that special opportunities must be created for those sections of society, which have been deprived and disadvantaged. One of the Directive Principles of State Policy directs state to adopt measures for the benefit of other backward classes without specifying what these measures should be and who the 'other backward classes' are. Kalekar Commission in 1953 and Mandal Commission in 1980 were set up to identify castes and communities and to place them in the category of 'Other Backward Classes'.

The 'castelessness' among Indian Muslims is a complete myth. No non-tribal Indian community is free of the evils of caste system. Imtiaz Ahmad's work on social stratification, caste and kinship among the Muslims has shown that conversion to Islam could not break the caste structure. It perpetuated discrimination, inequalities and its removal requires affirmative action and positive discrimination in prevailing scenario. The Kalekar and Mandal Commissions took into consideration this fact and included low caste Muslims in the list of 'other backward classes' on the ground that they are as socially and educationally backward as the Hindu backward classes, and recommended the need of the benefit of reservation. The Muslim backward classes are satisfied and feel that their deprivation, which is based on social ranking on grounds of birth, has been realized for the benefit of reservation. Under the Government of India Act, 1935, a list of extremely backward castes was drawn up and was known as Scheduled Castes. Some of these castes such as Dhobi (washerman), Mochi (cobbler), and Halalkhors (sweepers) had both Hindu and Muslim members and special provisions were made for their special benefits, but it was made available to Hindu Scheduled Castes only. Thus, non-Hindu Scheduled Castes were denied the benefits under Government of

India Act, 1935. By an amendment in 1956, the reservation benefit was extended to the Sikh Scheduled Castes and in 1990 this was extended to Neo-Buddhists. Despite Muslims' backwardness, they have not been extended the benefit of reservation. The exclusion of Muslim Scheduled Castes and backwards from the benefit of reservation is unfair and contrary to the spirit of the Constitution and its principles of secularism and equality.[5]

Much is also being made out of the advantages, which have come to the backward classes because of the implementation of the Mandal recommendations. It should be noted that dealing with the implementation aspect, the Supreme Court in 1992 not only limited the volume of reservation to the extent of 50 per cent; but also inserted an economic exclusion clause under the name of 'creamy layer' among backward classes for the advantages of affirmative action. It is said that such rider jeopardizes the cause of social justice.

Diverse opinions have emerged on the recent initiative of Andhra Pradesh government to provide five per cent reservation to the Muslim community in educational institutions and government jobs. Pandemonium over the issue has eclipsed the genuine concerns, which Government Order 33 seeks to redress. Reservations made on religious basis may give rise to fissiparous tendencies and would result in disparaging the ideals of secularism and non-discrimination, but going into the historicity and sociality of pathetic condition of the Muslim community, one may come to the logical conclusion that providing reservation to them would strengthen the concept of equality. The dominant philosophy of Equality revolves round the premise that equality should be among equals and unequal be treated differently. Law may be enacted for unequals treating them as a separate class. The entire reservation policy hinges on this rationale.

A pertinent question arises here when SC/ST, a majority of whole belong to the Hindu community or its derivatives, reap benefits of reservation, why no accusing finger is raised and why defenders of Hindutva come out to protest that these caste-based reservation pose a serious danger to the soul of secularism. Why no hue and cry was raised as the reservation for the last 60 years is creating conditions favourable for the establishment of a state where every seat of power will be controlled by persons belonging to the Hindu majority (either through reservation or otherwise). The most questionable part of the whole controversy vis-à-vis Muslims' reservation is the partisian attitude of some pressure groups.

Muslims are not better off today than any other oppressed segments of the society, socially, educationally and economically backward, and have also been the victim of the gross neglect of successive governments, especially over the last 60 years. Statistics show a grim and sorry state of affairs with regard to the social, educational and economic advancement of the Muslim populace in this country of vast diversities. What to talk about whole India, in Andhra Pradesh itself 66 per cent of 6.4 million Muslim population lives below the poverty line. The total Muslim literacy rate is eight per cent, while a negligible four per cent women are literate. The data applies to other states too. It was for this reason that the Saxena Commission recommended a fixed percentage for Muslims in educational institutions and government jobs to improve the lot of the most neglected and deprived sections of the society.

The opposition to the demand of Muslim reservation is based on the claim that they had been the rulers of the country for centuries, and hence, cannot be victims of historical oppression and suppression. This brings us to an important point: "is the reservation to the SC/ST logical on the ground that their ancestors were subjected to social and economic suppression centuries ago, so that the offspring who have not even dreamt of the stigma and effects of those atrocities be given reservation?" This logic of applying ointment to the wound affected to the forefathers is illogical and without any merit today. But by the law these victims of history are enjoying the fruits of the constitutional affirmative action. It will be erroneous to presume that mere belonging to the religion of the ruler would make you socially, economically, and educationally well off. In those days, Muslims also were suffering from the agony of poverty and exploitation at other hands of the rulers who happened to be Muslims just as Dalits are persecuted today at the hand of those who too are Hindus. The long journey of India from 1947, towards establishing an egalitarian and non-communal nation, has been marred by the biases and prejudges against the Muslims community. It has suffered irreparable losses during the last 60 years with regards to its social, economic, educational, religious and political status. The strength of the community has gone down to negligible figures in the years that followed. The 33 per cent of Muslim employment in government jobs in 1947 has drastically and unfortunately registered a decline of 31.5 per cent, reducing to approximately 1.5 per cent.

Nationalism and nation-building need to be harmonious. Reservation to Muslims would certainly increase their participation in nation-building resulting automatically in the development of the feeling of patriotism and nationalism in the Indian Muslims. A good and evolving democracy is that, which protects the interests and the well-being of the minorities. The phenomenon of employing affirmative actions for the benefits of minorities is not new to world democracies. Even in US, the policy of affirmative actions is deep-rooted. It has been the consistent policy of the America to give reservation to its black-American minority in educational institution. US Supreme Court upheld the admission of a black-American boy in the Department of Law, Michigan University, USA, where he was admitted on a low merit. This resulted in denial of admission to an American having higher merit. When this matter finally reached the Supreme Court, it held the admission of black-American valid and constitutional on the ground of affirmative action. In India, minorities are not given their due share which they deserve in the policy making and governance of the action. Several Commissions have recommended reservation in paramilitary and police forces too on the basis of religious leanings so as to reduce the communal biases and prejudices in the forces too against people of a particular religious identity. This, if done would have proved to be a protective wall to prevent Gujarat-like situations from raising their deadly heads now and then.

The concept of equality and equal protection of laws in its natural spectrum encompasses social, economic and political justice in democratic set-up.[6] Equality before law is correlative to the concept of rule of laws for all-round evaluation of healthy social order.[7] Equal protection of the laws would mean that among equals, the law should be equal and equally administered, that is like should be treated alike; thus equal protection requires affirmative action by the state towards unequal by providing them facilities and opportunities.[8] It means the right to equal treatment ought to be in similar circumstances both in the privileges and in the liabilities imposed by the laws.[9] No one should be favoured and placed under any disadvantage, in the circumstances that do not admit of any reasonable justification for a different treatment. Nonetheless, when there is any reasonable basis for classification, the legislature would be entitled to make a different treatment. Constitutionally, legislature is competent to exercise its discretion and make classification.[10] It is for the legislature to identify the class, caste and community by adopting a mechanism to determine the entitlement for extending protection specifying the basis of such protection. In such matters court cannot interfere.[11] The guarantee of equal protection is an assurance of equal treatment of persons placed in 'equal circumstances', permitting differentiation in different circumstances. Equality does not mean that every law must have universal application for all persons who are not by nature, attainment or circumstance in the same position as the varying needs of different classes of persons often require separate treatment.[12] The principle of equality does not take away from the state the power of classifying persons for the legitimate purpose. In order to be legitimate and reasonable, classification must not be capricious and arbitrary, rather must be rationalistic. In order to pass the test of reasonableness, two conditions must be fulfilled, i.e., first, the classification must be founded on intelligible differentia which distinguishes these that are grouped together from others, and secondly that differentia must have a rationale relation to the object sought to be achieved.[13]

Constitutionally it is an established fact that state shall not discriminate between citizens on grounds only of religion, race, caste, sex, place of birth or any of them.[14] The significance of the word 'only' is that if there is any other ground for consideration for the differential treatment besides those prohibited by this article, the discrimination or preferential treatment provided situation will not be unconstitutional,[15] provided situation demands.

The prohibition of discrimination indicated above would not preclude the state from making special provision for the advancement of any socially and educationally backward classes of citizens. Such citizens for their progress and for the progress of nation require special protection and hence any legislation which is necessary for making of special provisions to give protection to people or persons of these classes would not be violative of the constitutional mandate.

As a matter of caution, reservation would not be unreasonable, excessive or extravagant and also must not go beyond the permissible and legitimate limits, otherwise, it may be challenged as a fraud on the Constitution.[16]

A nine-judge bench of the Supreme Court in Indra Sawhney's case[17] (popularly known as the Mandal Commission case) has laid down the following principles which summarize the law of reservation:

1. Backward class of citizens is not defined in the Constitution. There is intimate connection between caste, occupations, poverty and social backwardness. A caste may by itself constitutes a class.
2. The backwardness contemplated by Article 16 (4) is mainly social. It need not be both social and educational.
3. 'Means-test' signifies imposition of an income limit for the purpose of excluding persons from the backward classes. Those income which is above that limit are referred to as the 'creamy layer'. Income or the extent of property can be taken as a measure of social advancement and on that basis the 'creamy layer' of a given caste can be extended.
4. To get reservation a class or caste must be backward and should not be adequately represented in government jobs and educational institutions.
5. Reservation limit should be up to 50 per cent of available posts.
6. For purpose of reservation, identification of backward classes is subject to judicial review.

Surveys by the National Sample Survey Organization (NSSO) have shown that deprivation in jobs, education and consumption is more widespread among the Muslims. In 1999-2000 surveys, the unemployment rate among Muslims was higher. Data on literacy tells a similar story among Muslims. The higher incidence of deprivation of Muslims holds for town as well as countryside, men as well as women. Now, there is need for special policies and programmes that should address the extreme economic and educational backwardness encountered within the Muslim community.[18] Sachar Committee's report is due, and by this the acute social, educational and economic backwardness is sure to surface even surpassing the backwardness of the Scheduled Castes and Scheduled Tribes. Caste has been operative condition for reservation, but this is not the first time that the members of religious community have been given quotas. By the rules of state governments, Muslims are already covered by reservation facilities in Tamil Nadu, Kerala and Karnataka. In Tamil Nadu, they are entitled to reservation under 30 per cent category earmarked for 'other backward classes'. In Kerala, 12 per cent jobs are reserved for Muslims. In Karnataka in 1994, reservation policy was introduced in favour of Muslims. The reservation rules for Muslims in Kerala and Karnataka are subject to 'creamy layer' doctrine introduced in 1992 by the Supreme Court in Indra Sahaney case. In referred states, introduced reservation policy is working well, however, there is demand for greater share of the cake; there is defect in Andhra's reservation policy introduced for Muslims because the identification of Muslims as a separate category has not been done on the recommendation by the State Commission for Backward Classes. The apex court had rightly ordered that socially disadvantaged groups entitled to reservation on each state must be identified by such a body upholding the spirit of Article 15(4) of the Constitution. Also, the doctrine of 'creamy layer' was not applied in case of Andhra Pradesh reservation scheme.[19]

It is the egalitarian principle that inspires the historically disadvantaged sections of people to demand reservation as their legal and legitimate right. It is essentially not asking for compensation for past sin. It is get to rid of injustices that reservation demands. The socio-religious system, and disabilities arising out of it unfortunately still continue. Under this system, the Brahmins, the upper caste have undue, unearned and unjust privileges, whereas the Shudras and Panchams caste suffer from discrimination, suppression and neglect. The graded inequality bases on mere incident of birth of a person in a caste group, the lower caste were denied educational opportunities and religious performances and share in the administration by the ruling class. Despite legal disapproval, the system and its impacts still continue making them socially, educationally and economically backward. The socio-cultural disabilities still perpetuate inequalities and injustices. Under the prevailing conditions how could there be fair opportunities, free, fair and equal competitions among unequals. Reservation is demanded as a right to set right the wrongs and disabilities arising out of the unequal caste structure. The wrongs and consequent disabilities are historical as they originated in past, but they are not the thing of past, rather realities of even today.

The Election Commission objected to timing of the Union Cabinet's 29 September, 2004's decision to set up a Special Commission for the "Socially and economically backward among religious and linguistic minorities". To apply the model code of conduct to a mere decision to appoint a Commission for the welfare of minorities on the ground that the assembly election were on in Maharashtra and Arunachal Pradesh was patently unreasonable. Affirmative action for all religious and linguistic minorities was a promise of the Congress Party made in 2004 election manifesto. This was reiterated as a commitment in the National Common Minimum Programme and it was included by the United Progressive Alliance (UPA) government in the presidential address to Parliament.[20]

The recent verdict of the apex court that upheld various provisions of the reservation in the Constitution of India, it places SCs/STs on par with the other backward classes which include backward Muslims too, for which the creamy layer was introduced by the recommendations of the Backward Commission. The Constitution provides for preferential treatment for socially and educationally backward classes, namely the SCs/STs and OBCs. Only these three categories are mentioned in the Constitution and they are treated separately and exclusively and not at par with one another. Article 16 (4) states:

> Nothing in this Article shall prevent the state from making any provision for the reservation of appointment or post in favour of any backward class of citizen which, in the opinion of the state, is not adequately represented in the services under the state.

It is pertinent to point it out that the present generation may not be responsible for the past but this cannot disown the past. The principle for distinguishing OBCs from SCs and STs is the inhuman practice of untouchability and outburst of rigid caste system prevalent in India. Dr. B.R. Ambedkar argued untouchability out of Hindu rigid caste system was worst than slavery. It is argued that one of the consequences of excluding creamy layer from the benefits meant to SCs and STs is that it will create a vacuum in the fight for justice. No doubt the reservation policy played a vital role in creating a small layer amongst the SCs and STs comprising doctors, engineers, professors, diplomats, bureaucrats, politicians, and artists, who happened to be leading the struggle for the dignity of these communities in one area or other. This creamy layer in the prevailing circumstances may not be able to retain its status over a period of time which may be more damaging to the entire community in the long run.[21]

Promoting the welfare of millions of non-privileged Indians is a solemn duty cast upon the state by the Supreme Law of the land. The founding fathers treated it as part of egalitarian philosophy incorporated in the Constitution of India. This duty was first mentioned in the historic Objectives Resolution adopted by the Constituent Assembly in 1947, and later incorporated in the preamble of the Constitution. Since then 'equality' and 'justice' have been held to be the twin concerns of the state. It forbids discrimination only on grounds of race, religion, caste, sex, or place of birth. Article 15(4) and 16(4) empower the state to make special provisions, including reservation, for the advancement of "socially and educationally backward classes" in addition to the Scheduled Castes and Scheduled Tribes. It is a potent question whether religious and linguistic minorities do come in the category of 'backward classes' as envisaged by the Constitution? Some objective criteria should be evolved to exclude 'creamy layer' to be counted in the category of 'backward classes' to be beneficiary of affirmative action. Backward must be established by applying well-defined criteria. The proposed Commission will have access to a wealth of data including its own strategy for determining the deserving persons from backward classes. Data comes from the National Sample Survey Organization (NSSO), the National Family Health Survey-II (NFHS-II) and also from the Census of 2001 are relevant. "Incidence of socio-economic and educational backwardness among India's million Muslims is significantly greater than among any other minorities or Hindu as a population category." The 1999-2000 NSSO survey reveals that Muslims face greater deprivation in jobs, education, and consumption than any other population groups demarcated by religion. The latest Census provides evidence that the literacy in 2001 was 59 per cent among Muslims compared with 65 per cent for Hindus, and work participation rate for Muslims was 31.3 per cent compared with 40.4 per cent for Hindus. Such data will help Commissions propose to recommend reservation in favour of Muslim backward classes.[22]

Our Constitution has provisions, which can come to the rescue of Muslim community and to the Government of Andhra Pradesh. Article 15(a) of the Indian Constitution provides that state can make special provisions for the advancement of any socially and educationally backward class of citizen. Constitution encourages the state to make special provisions for the advancement of that sections. Muslims are, no doubt, educationally and socially backward and, therefore, they are legally entitled for beneficial measures like the one bestowed by Tamil Nadu, Kerala, Karnataka and Andhra Pradesh governments. Not only this, Article 16(4) of the Constitution even goes further to help out these sections which due to certain reasons out of their control, could not find state employment. Under this Article, state is empowered to make affirmative measures like reservation in appointments in favour of any backward class of citizens, which in the opinion of the state, is not adequately represented in the services under the state. This Article even dispenses with the precondition of being educationally and socially backward as is the case with Article 15(4). One need not be educationally or socially backward, but the conditions of inadequacy of representation in the state employment is a dominant factor. Muslims by no stretch of imagination be considered to be adequately represented in the state employment. If recent move of Andhra Pradesh government for reservation is seen with the legal eyes focusing on constitutional mandate, one would not find any incongruity. The state is under constitutional duty under Article 46 of the Constitution of India to promote the educational and economic interests of the weaker sections of the people and to protect them from social justice and all other forms of exploitation.[23]

Parliament has passed with unanimity 93rd Amendment Act in order to achieve this goal. 93rd Amendment Act of 2006 of the Constitution introduced changes in Article 15 by inserting Clause (5) in it, which is now Article 15(5). The amendment reads as follows:

> (5) Nothing in this article (Article 15) or in sub-clause (g) of clause (1) of Article 19 shall prevent the state from making any special provision, by law, for the advancement of any socially and educationally backward classes of citizens or for the Scheduled Castes or the Scheduled Tribes in so far as such special provisions relate to their admissions to educational institutions including private educational instructions, whether aided or unaided by the state, other than the minority educational institutions referred to in clause (1) of Article 30.

There is no denying the fact that reservation, as a tool of advancement of a community cannot be used perpetually. It must be a temporary measure, which should be discontinued if the purpose is achieved. Muslim reservation should also be made on this premise. The benefit of reservation should be restricted to those Muslims who deserve and thus by applying exclusion clause of 'creamy layer' this rich Muslims must be discouraged for reaping the benefit of reservation. The fruits must go to the deserving ones only. It should not be like SC/ST reservation, where all the advantages are for those who do not need them now. It is high time that, when people are demanding reservation even in the private sector, it will be quite immature, unreasonable and improper to preclude and discourage Muslims from getting it in the public sector and state-run educational institutions, jobs and legislative houses.[24]

Recent Andhra Pradesh High Court's quashing of A.P. government's sanctioning of 5 per cent reservation to Muslims in government jobs and educational institutions has resulted in a debate on the issue of desirability of reservation for a backward community like Muslims on the basis of religion. At the outset, it should be clarified and that rejection of Andhra Pradesh government's order by Andhra Pradesh High Court is purely based on technical ground. Virtually, the Court has upheld the constitutionality of reservation for Muslim as a backward community. The Court instructs the Andhra Pradesh government's to adopt necessary legal measures to reconstitute Andhra Pradesh Backward Class Commission to identity the backward classes and the 'creamy layer'. As pointed out earlier, the Constitution of India in its preamble specifies for creation of an egalitarian society, which should ensure justice: social, economic and political to every citizen, and by extension to every community – religious, ethnic or linguistic. It also emphasises the necessity of securing equality of status and of opportunity, without any distinction of caste and religion. Article 15(4) provides that state can make special provisions for the advancement of any socially and educationally backward classes of citizens. The Census 2001 data and National Sample Survey Reports establish that Muslims as community are socially, educationally and economically backward and are in need of support from the state for alleviation of their deprivation and backwardness. Under the circumstances, it is the need of the hour that the central and state governments must fulfil their constitutional and legal obligations and are urged for judicious use of relevant constitutional provisions and remove hurdles to make necessary arrangement of reservation of Muslims so that they can become equal and dignified citizens and play their participatory role in the task of nation-building. By such gesture, the doctrine of representation and participation shall be translated into action ensuring the contributory role of biggest minority constituting second number population for the building of nation. By the marginalization of Muslims, the square development of nation is not possible. It may be pointed out that the communally tainted BJP and Sangh Parivar along with the 'Secular' Congress have to be blamed for denying the fair share of Muslims in government jobs, their representation in legislative houses and their due share in educational institutions on one pretext or another. It is heartening to note that a sense of objectivity and fairness motivated present UPA government, which has constituted a Commission under the chairmanship of Justice Rajendra Sachchar, former Chief Justice, Delhi High Court to look into the relevant issues for considering the viability and modalities of reservation for Muslims and the Commission is mandated to submit its report within a time frame which it has done successfully. Its recommendations are appreciated widely, but the government is not coming forward whole heartedly for its implementation under the refuge of political expediency.

Objection to reservation for Muslims is based on the contention that religion cannot and should not form the basis for reservation in a secular dispensation. It appears to be a strange logic. Dalits, Scheduled Castes, Scheduled Tribes and others who are the beneficiaries to reservation policy are generally part of Hindu religion and yet they are given reservation despite being the part of Hinduism, i.e., the religion of the majority community. Muslims, who fulfil the required standard, well-equipped universally or nationally, are backward in India being a largest minority, and are being denied the facility of reservation because they happened to be adherents of a particular religion. The Muslims deprivation in government and semi-government jobs is more than 80 per cent. Observe railway station, post office or any government departments or semi-government institutions, Muslim faces are rarely seen as employee. Hence, mariginalization is rampant.[25]

Establishing justice for all and nation-building is an onerous duty on the part of our Welfare State. Narrow minded policies are based on injustice and hatred, and are patronized by petty minds, spoiling the spirit of harmony which is the life blood of the nation. If due share is given to Muslims in decision-making and responsibility sharing, it would help in the creation of egalitarian and equitable society. Also, it would be a bulwark against communal elements in society who obstacle the onward march of democracy, justice and satisfaction of the genuine citizens of India. Muslims are 13.4 per cent of Indian population. Every eight Indian is a Muslim.[26] His deprivation is a national problem, which must be tackled at national level to ensure him to play his constructive role in the task of national building. It is a matter of satisfaction that this need is being realized and recognized by the people and political parties. States like Tamil Nadu, Karnataka, Kerala and Manipur have long back given reservation to Muslims. The Andhra government has done concrete work in this direction.

Recent assertion of Prime Minister, Manmohan Singh for fair share for minorities in education, jobs and legislative houses touches the core of the findings of the Sachchar Committee which finds Muslims much worse than the general population including the Scheduled Castes and Scheduled Tribes in terms of education, incomes, jobs and access to public and private services. It is underlined that the certain indices such percentage enrolled in educational institutions, Muslims are worse than SC/STs generally considered to be at the bottom of the social packing order. Out of the findings of the Sachchar Committee two voices are bound to emerge: First those are aligned to the left will advocate reservation as the remedy to systematic discrimination against Muslims by the state institutions, second the right will blame conservative Muslim clergy which has vested interest in keeping the community backward. Both are correct to a considerable extent in their approaches.[27]

On the basis of legality, reality and legitimacy, reservation in favour of Indian backward Muslims is need of the hour. The present UPA government is mandated to discharge its constitutional obligation to the effect. It is heartening to note that the present government has taken up the issue of reservation seriously and it has already constituted time-bound Commission to look into the matter and to recommend the modalities for extension of reservation in favour of Indian backward Muslims. Constitutional provisions affirm that the constitutional jurisprudence favours the reservation for the Indian backward Muslims. Our government is constitutionally obligated to take up the matter of reservation of backward Muslims to ensure the square progress of the nation. It is heartening to note that the recommendations of Sachar Committee is prompting the UPA government to formulate various policies, schemes and programmes including reservation in favour of backward Muslims. It is buttressed emphatically that the government is under legal and moral obligations to design mechanism for ensuing the participation and progress of Indian backward Muslims.

Notes

1. K.Z. Amani, "Dalit Muslims Demand Reservation", *Basic Problems of Backward Muslims*, edited by A.H. Ansari, p. 85, see also *Census of India United Provinces and Audh*, Vol. XVI, Part II, Table pp. 136-37.
2. Ibid.
3. Ibid., et al., p. 86.
4. See B.R. Ambedkar, *Pakistan or Partition of India*, Vol. VIII (ed. 1, 1990), Education Department, Government of Maharashtra.
5. Ibid.
6. Supra, Note 1 et al., p. 90.
7. See *Dalmia Cement (Bharat) Ltd.* v. *Union of India (1996)* 10 S.C.C. 104.
8. Ibid.
9. *Panchayat Varga Shramajivi Saudaik Saka Kari Khedut Cooperative* v. *Harisbhai*, AIR 1996 SC. 2578.
10. *State of West Bengal* v. *Anwar Ali* (1952) S.C.R. 289.
11. *A.C. Pradhan* v. *Union Govt. of India (1997)* S.C.C. 104.
12. D.D. Basu, *Introduced to the Constitution of India* (ed. 19th, 2001, New Delhi) p. 89, see also *D.C. Bhatia* v. *Union Govt. of India (1995)* 1 S.C.C. 104.
13. *Dhirendra* v. *Legal Remembrance (1950)* S.C.R. 869.
14. *Chiranjit Lal* v. *Union of India (1950)* S.C.R. 869.
15. See Article 15 (2) of the Constitution of India.
16. *Yusuf* v. *State of Bombay (1954)* S.C.C. 321.
17. See *Balaji* v. *State of Mysore (1963)* S.C.C. 647.
18. *Indira Sawhney* v. *Union of India* (1999) Supple (3) S.C.C. 217.
19. See "Reservations Controversy", *The Hindu*, Aug 2, 2004, New Delhi.
20. Ibid.
21. Bhalchandra Mungekar, "Blow to Justice", *Times of India* (31 October, 2006), New Delhi.

22. See "Minorities And Backwardness", *The Hindu*, 12th October, 2004, New Delhi.
23. Ibid.
24. See A. Hafiz, "Reservation for Muslims is a Constitutional Need", The Milli Gazette, 109, Vol. 5, No. 15, 1-15 August, 2004.
25. See "Reservations for Muslims" (Editorials) *Radiance Views Weekly* (New Delhi) dated 10-16 October, 2004.
26. Ibid.
27. See editorial captioned: "Muslim Empowerment can be Win-Win Game for All", *Times of India* (4 November, 2006), New Delhi.

2

Social Duties and Human Rights

A New Perceptive

S.K. VARSHNEY

This cosmos is 'Garbh-Kumbah' uterus for life to germinate and flourish. Life, we study as animal and plant kingdom on planet earth. In the words of a saint 'Brahm Gyani', life is a relationship between self and the universe (१ ॐ). Self (life) is created by God the Almighty (Immutable Energy from the Cosmos; we call cosmic energy). The five elements of life are space, water, fire or heat, earth or soil and air. Life element survives in the presence of these, is the eternal truth.[1]

Man is born with an obligation to discharge and that is, he has to love himself as well as all life around him. It is due to this obligation he has to acquire certain inherent rights, where there is an obligation to discharge there shall be a right to be honoured and accepted. These rights are against each other (natural born persons) as well as against organizations, associations, companies, etc. (legal persons). Rights are there for natural born person as well as legal persons, therefore the distinction between private and public rights is just for convenience, nothing more. This duty-right relationship is the basis of human existence in the society. Therefore, first and foremost, social duty of man is to preserve and protect life on the planet earth. Man as a sovereign is an undisputable identity. Self has the total concept of the universe, as we say self (soul) is infinite and invisible. Soul and super-soul connection is the very essence of human life. Through this route we shall reach the realm of positivity from where we may acquire the bliss for positive actions. God has provided us with highly technical and most effective system of control we call 'mind'. Our nervous system is the effective network to approach the ultimate power which provides us with the strength to conduct self in the society. The link with immutable energy must continue consistently and regularly. This uninterrupted flow keeps us alive, agile and active throughout our lives. The human machine which has been finally operated by the Almighty is temporarily put to the control of self through various energy power wheels.[2]

Body power wheels from *muladhar* are for us to encash our strength in various activities for the body to remain in most active form as long as possible therefore we say that public policy is health and morality. Any act against public policy shall not be accepted. Love for life means care and concern for the protection of public health and morals. For this purpose, positive law as clear, effective and conducive ought to be created for spiritual well-being. Spirit and substance are the two partners in this world who should never part. The integration of soul, mind and body is the first obligation to be discharged as soon as possible. In the present state of affairs we are unnecessarily raising our voice for our human rights. Human rights are turning it, to unwanted propaganda which is injurious to mankind. Along with this craving for right, we must be conscious about the divine obligation with which we are born. We ought to protect inner and outer of the self. We are born with an obligation to love and be loved. Welfare concept of state has projected the image of inherent rights more than the inherent duties. Duties shall always precede rights, because God has given us energy to survive, and that is coupled with an absolute duty which has no corresponding right. Right and duties in this world are always correlative. We ought to comply with socio-legal duties which the state has to enforce and an individual has to comply with. This is how the state sovereignty concept emerged in nineteenth century. Emergence of state provided us with an analytical mind to analyse the metaphysical concept scientifically. Spiritual legalism is a new science of the 21st century. Theory of love, life, law which deals with the science of life as spiritual legal process is no less difficult than the Pythagorus Theorem where square of life plus square of love and God is equal to law; an extensive sphere of human activity and wisdom known as spiritual legalism.

Whenever someone asks for his respective rights in a Court of Law, he must be asked whether he has fulfilled his corresponding obligation closely akin to the right he is asking for. Moral obligations are added to the Constitution as fundamental duties next to the chapter of fundamental rights. Its love for man and love for nature which shall inculcate best values in us to survive in a best possible atmosphere. Human relations are strengthened when there is compassion. We are all governed by our selfish desires which compel us just to think of ourself. Just take a step towards the virtuous realm of Divinity where divine dictate awaits you.[3]

Go for introspection before you enter in verbal discussion about the human rights. Individualism had led us to collectivism and the result we have witnessed in welfarism. The wheel of time and nature never stops. From welfarism we have reached the era of cyberism. Spiritual legalism theory of love, life, law which emerged in the 21st century shall lead to the world of infinite, to the cosmos of reality where inherent human rights shall get its due. The Almighty God has the great power of creation and can only balance the two of them the man and the nature. He has provided us a 'mind' to act on His behalf to solve the conflicts and confusions of life in the same manner as He is doing. Therefore, we shall be using our discretion as per His dictate. Human mind is the most judicious concept on the planet earth therefore it has realized its potential as poet, philosopher, scientist, jurist and so on and so forth. This potential has given birth to multi-disciplines of life. For centuries human mind remained in the fold of search and research. Now the time is ripe enough for micro-research. The unending reaches of mind has taken us to infinite heights. Present era highlights the creation of silicon valley which has come to be known as a State Art Technology.

The obligation to love and be loved dictates us not to harm anyone. This dictate is for the prevention of wrongs which are causing disastrous impact on humanity. All moral wrongs must be stopped as they are the sins. It is sin we should detest not the sinner. The two broad categories belong to moral and legal wrongs. The wrongs are further categorized into 'tort' and 'crime'. Violence makes the behaviour of man most serious and we call them crimes. As we all are born with inherent rights and obligation, we ought to interfere with liberties, privileges and powers of each other. In case of clash and conflict it is we who have to adopt some balancing technique to resolve our differences. Judicial organ of the present day state has assumed this duty of balancing of conflicting interest. American realistic school of jurisprudence exerts a great influence of this approach. Preet philosophy of spiritual legalism is an extensive treatise on human behaviour in the civilized world of silicon.

Human relationship
Not at all a manipulation
It's not control even

It's unconditional Love
He loves me because
I am beautiful

No
I am beautiful
Because he loves me

God has passed a precious gift
Gift of care, concern and compassion

Oh dear
Love is my passion
My eyes are as dark as raven
We two love in heaven

Love is to create beauty
That's the obligation
Best of all duty.

Right and duty are the coverage supreme, therefore never ask for the right which is not due to you. First of all fulfil the obligation pertaining to life and liberty by performing your duty, then ask for the right. If you do your duty, rights will automatically follow you. You need not struggle for the right as they are inherent. Remember to comply with the obligation Divine. The sun shines over you to give energy, power and strength. Human rights are the evidence of patience, sincerity and confidence.

Divinity a New Dynamics for Human Rights
(Age-old Concept of Divinity Explored)

Human 'mind' is the divine source of all discipline. It is the sound ethics relating to good and bad which is the very basis of all philosophies of the world. It is with tremendous efforts and effective coordination that we shall achieve the goal set by the humanistic trend of mind all over the globe.

How the Mind works
Creation of the Idea
Vibration in the media
Positive and negative nodes
One button on switchboard

Your conscious accelerates
To open the wisdom gate

Current and undercurrent
Are the various events
Sometime consent

Coupled with this
Facts are put against rules

Ruler has the tool
Laws are not for fools

A decision when arrived
Wisdom is the price.

The two significant aspects of human life are: sunrise and sunset. From both an 'idea' emerges to govern us with tremendous love. Love therefore is the global impact we all as individuals feel. So we assume all energy emanating right from the sun at the start of day we call 'sunrise'. So is the influence of sunset. By that time all is set for the day which we had planned for the day. Each day is to assist you to enhance your potential.

For observation of duties
For realization of rights
Spread a message of Love
Never ever use might.

It is 'love' which shall provide you infinite energy as it puts you on right track of positivity where you are governed with good consciousness. Just put a stop on unconsciousnable acts and enjoy the fruits of human rights philosophy. Use love as force and might, instead of bombs and explosive is the Preet's dictum of 'Love-Life-Law'. Centuries are moving around us like innumerous stars on the extensive sky, so we must trust God with utmost faith as He is not controlling just one universe but under His eternity there are unknown number of universes therefore never loose the divine conscience within self.[4]

Let us all possess a sound mind where apart from intelligence, reason and logic there lies an emotional power supported by spiritual quotient to control all selfish desires. Aggressive behaviour of human beings need to be controlled. Lust is the first step towards love. It is an inherent quality of a human mind to possess the desired object. Eyes behold the beauty, immediate actions proceed towards the desire to catch and grab the beautiful object. This craving may culminate in lust and the lover of beauty may become a rapist, a criminal of worse kind; control this evil and be virtuous to have the bliss, to capture the aroma of love-eternal around you. Your desires are the tools of mind, which assume and control the total self. Let us fight for the wisdom which leads us to the man-made realm of 'Human Rights'. Let us be the responsible members of the global world. Let us be the fearless members of the global society. Let the memories of our lives, works and our deeds, continue in others. We shall take the first step together for the promotion of one and the only inherent right 'to love and be loved'. Preet spells out the dictum of love in a small poem of her life as 'Preet Purana' with the earnest prayer "Oh Lord bless us with your sacred, virtuous power which makes you omnipotent and

Almighty". The bliss is our best human right to ensure the survival of the mankind.

Globalization for Preet

Where the whole world
One country
Of the twenty-first century
We the citizens
Are all living being
Love shall spring
Man, animal, bird and plant
Are to supplement not to supplant
Let us wish luck to Preet
Her love for the planet
Is a big treat.

Life is a big bonanza which gradually proceeds towards the good to avoid evil. Its your concentration with consistency which shall fast carry us towards positivity of action as per planning of your mind. The sound base on which you have to construct the future well-being of the globe is faithfulness towards humanity. Humility and simplicity is the great virtue of man. Acquire and retain as much as you can. If the seed has to sprout, it should go beneath the soil with the attitude, "I am nothing", cultivate humility and develop sincerity. Let your ego bow low in front of the Supreme and His creation. Visualizing everything as Him, our real nature unfolds. An egoless person cannot die, because he is not a body any more. He is consciousness. Our desires compel us to identify self with the body. Self, when free of egoistic tendencies, it immediately finds the path of positivity. Positivity gives the discretion to decide for good and against evil. With super self you are always intensive, open and receptive. Mind and intellect becomes full. The beginner is able to bow down with humility, and due to this the true knowledge flows in. A person full of mere information becomes egoistic which is a great hurdle in the way of assumption of divine obligation.

Various actions of Man
Categorized
As legislative
Administrative and judicial
Good and real
State emerged
With three organs
As great search
Activism of the state
Became man's fate
A new revolution
State Art Technology
A new philosophy
Preet's spiritualogy
A science and archaeology.

'Preet' is a nascent 'idea' which throws light on purity of human mind to acquire peace and tranquillity. Preet as a noble 'idea' which gets into the fold of sacred thought. Let us possess and create a clear and clean environment which is conducive to all beings.

Philosophy

Human minds discipline
With psychology
And lot of law
Spiritual legalism
A product of intellect
Between logic and emotion
Mind has to select
Selection my endeavour
Election a democratic flavour
Oh dear remain sober
Avoid being too political
Police, politics and law
When integrated
Best world was created
Assume duties global
Possess rights noble.

Constitution and Computer

We all are fast leading towards global aspect of rights and duties in today's corporate world. Today's world is working on human relation issue internationally. Constitution and computers are the two new guides which will equip human mind to maintain human relations all over the world.

Constitutions of the world are the unique documents consisting of 39 constitutions of the world from Albania to the United States of America. It covers a wide spectrum of rights and obligations of the state and individual. There are constitutions, the text of which runs into hundreds of pages. At the same time there are others which are quite brief. For example, the Constitution of India is reputed to be the largest whereas the Constitution of the United States of America is the shortest. Some of the constitutions like US. Constitution were framed in "horse and buggy" days by a touch of dynamism of the machine age by their interpretative process, otherwise it would have been difficult for the nation to cope with the problems arising out of the industrial and commercial revolution of which the constitution makers could not have dreamt at the time of framing of the constitution.

The principles under the provisions of the constitution are not to be interpreted and applied strictly according to the literal meaning of words used by the framers of the constitution. Interpretation of constitutional principles is a matter of reasoned application of rational precepts of conditions of time and place. Constitutional law cannot be expounded with the aid of dictionary. In ascertaining the meaning of words used in a constitution, their origin and line of growth must be kept in view. The provisions of the constitution are not to be taken as mathematical formulas, having essence in their form, their significance is vital and not formal. Creative role of the US Supreme Court is a pious pledge of the judges to rely on the spirit of people which has been well infused in the substance of the written document as a guiding angle for all times to come. The wide judicial interpretation by the Supreme Court of the broad power of the federal government like the commerce power, taxing, spending, and war powers has largely met the needs of the growing nation.

Supreme Court of United States has done a great deal of law making during the first hundred years. Unfortunately, Indian Constitution was interpreted as an ordinary statute right from the beginning. Constitution of any country is the very mind and spirit of the people to protect inherent human rights and obligations. Constitution is an extraordinary, divine aspect of human existence on the globe. To speak the truth, judiciary as well as the government must have abiding faith in the adaptability of this sacred document of human dignity and the human faith in divinity. Amendment after amendments have poured in only with a view to negating the supreme court decisions. There was a sort of battle royal between the judiciary and executive; if anything has suffered badly, it is the Constitution itself. Constitution ought to be saved at any cost is the zealous efforts undertaken by the Preet's spiritual legalism theory. It is we the people of India who have solemnly resolved to constitute India into a sovereign, socialist, secular, democratic republic with justice, liberty, equality and fraternity. This goal set in the preamble must be carried on uninterruptedly and continuously. Judiciary in India has adopted fast activism methodology to save the spirit of the Constitution in the last few decades.

This judicial activism has paved the way of spiritual legalism philosophy in the social democratic fabric of the Indian society. Directive Principles of the State Policy are fast finding their way to enter the realm of fundamental rights. Right to wholesome environment and right to education have become the part of Article 21 of the Constitution through this judicial activism, where the judges have paid serious attention towards the very spirit of the Constitution. First and foremost principle of Preet philosophy is that it is the spirit which shall rule the substance and not the vice versa.[5] Justice Krishna Iyer often talks about the soul of the Constitution and its protection.

Part IV of the Constitution relating to fundamental duties comprises of eleven fundamental duties which are equally important for the sanctity of human rights incorporated in Part III of the Constitution and the Directive Principles of State Policy (as incorporated in Part IV). Every citizen has to abide by these clauses of Article 51A. These fundamental duties encourage us to move towards excellence in all spheres of individual and collective activity so that the nation constantly rises to higher level of endeavour and achievement. To promote harmony and the spirit of common brotherhood amongst all people of India transcending religious, linguistic and regional or sectional diversities; to renounce practices derogatory to the dignity of women. Preet philosophy and Indology integration has lead to value and preservation of the rich heritage of India's composite culture.

Let us uphold and protect the sovereignty, unity and integrity of India. For this we shall have to protect and improve the natural environment including forests, lakes, rivers and wild-life and to have compassion for all living beings. We all are born with the obligation "to love and be loved" and is the Preet's motto of Love-Life-Law. We have to save self and property in a manner where we shall always avoid violence; we shall develop the scientific temper, humanism and the spirit of inquiry and reform.

Activism

Activism, a noble sentiment

Judicial activism
An endeavour
Oh dear, this mind is clever
Logic and reason is the intellect
Between the two you can't select
Both are equally significant
The two together are one unit
Logic reason is your mathematics
Your mind knows
All the tricks
We are blessed with reason
That leads us to have
A sound discretion
Judicial activism
A noble task
After all man is smart
Judge and the judgment
The two weaving unit
Social fabric we have to knit

Set the fabric right
Is the Preet's idea bright.

Activism of mind makes the human mind agile. This agility leads to all kind of activities of this world. A reasonable mind with its average intelligence, strength, vigour and wisdom, conducts itself well in the society. Extra intelligence and strength should always be honoured.

Human life is full of day-to-day confusions; therefore we are continuously undergoing conflicts. This ever-increasing stress on mind is the cause of death and disease. Before we cure the outer environment we need to be careful about the inner consciousness, which must remain clean and intact.

Human confusion and conflicts result in the everyday clashes which endangers life on the planet. Legal process and its effectiveness all depends on the conscience of the human race. In the present global world, it must be realized that we are governed by two important aspects of human mind. One is computer and another is constitution.

Constitutions of the world brew with the 'Idea' pertaining to human rights and obligations. A man is born free therefore, freedom, liberty, equality, fraternity and morality all have become judicial concepts. These are to be deciphered in the purview of the various interests prevailing all over the world. This endeavour of the present-day society has enhanced human potential, which the man has utilized to attain the climax in state art technology for globalization. Computers (with various other supports like laptop) mobiles, etc., have almost changed the pattern and given a new corporate world to us. In this world, natural born persons are coexisting with legal persons effectively and sincerely.

Act and Action

All minds plan
Computer
We have created another mind
When you desire consequence
This is known as intention
Motive you may have

Either good or bad
It's only sometime relevant
But intention shows the consent
Why do we cause harm
Is it that injury
Always actionable
No,
There must be a legal injury
Where there is an injury
There is a remedy
A culprit
Shall have to face trial
A dispute between the two
The judge will resolve
Relevant questions are to be solved
Learn to know the law
Offender or the wrongdoer
Both shall be booked.

What has the court to decide? To deliver a sound judgment is the court's pride. The judge is the guide. The jury, a thought to retain. Judiciary must catch the fame, words of the enactments, provisions of law books governing human conduct in the society is the significant concern of the human beings as well as the lawyers and judges.

Legal philosophy and the legal ethics of the whole system revolves around the spiritual legalism of the Preet philosophy as discussed in Love-Life-Law, Freedom, Tribute to Humanity, Spiritual Prudence in Legalism, Mind, Sex, Success, Cosmos, Universe and Stars, Law and Indology, Apkritya Vidhi: Naya Niti Shashtra, Divine Dictate, Preet Yog A Cure, Woman, Religion and Law, etc.[6]

Let it not become
Extremism
Collect self
To know and practice
Spiritual legalism
Know the spirit of law
Get into the science of soul

Have a scientific temper
Preet's body is a temple
Metaphysics to physics
Journey was tedious
Its love eternal
Which was true and real.

Love knows no end, therefore it has no beginning either. Love is care, concern and compassion. Love is a great sensation. Above referred work of S.K. Varshney speaks volumes about the care, concern and compassion woven in the social fabric of present global society. Let us stop talking about social duties. Let us talk more about global obligations. All living beings on the planet earth are created by the supreme source of cosmic energy. This energy is known as the God Almighty. Protect it fast.

The body is not the real man, neither is the mind, for the mind waxes and wanes. It is the spirit beyond, which alone can live for ever. The body and mind continually changing and are, in fact, only names of series of changeful phenomena, like rivers whose waters are in a constant state of flux, yet present the appearance of unbroken streams. Every particle of the body is continually changing; no one has the same body for many minutes together and yet we think of it as the same body. So with the mind, one moment happy another unhappy. State of mind changes every moment. And this is called human attitude.

One thing which never changes is the infinite Divine Energy of the cosmos which is the eternal aspect of love for all His creations. Every particle in this universe is in constant state of flux. But taking the universe as a unit as one whole, it cannot move, thus it cannot change. Give your self (soul) a chance to connect with the super-self (God) within us. An inner retreat shall provide you with a return to eternal peace, superb silence. This silence is Preet's supreme 'Bliss' which once found is never lost. All negative traits shall disappear soon. Your heart shall be filled with joy, a rare kind of ecstasy. Presence of God the Almighty radiates spirituality which mends our mind in such a way that we start moving towards positive direction to assume our pious duty to attain sainthood of rarest kind. And on this platform all virtues shall assemble. Soul, mind and body all shall be so aligned to fight all evil. Our inner self will remain free from negative thoughts of the devil.

Computer and Mobile Sting Operation

Amendment in Cyber Laws

May gag press
To whom we shall address
Let us talk to the government
Who make amendment
Sting operation
Must not stink
Between individual
And the society
There is fine link
Privacy of individual
A grave situation
A great question
Give me some suggestion
Can you reach an individual bedroom
The answer is yes
But when
There is danger to decency and decorum
National security
Public order remain in doldrums.

In the last few years, we have seen an increased number of sting operations; Tahelka case being the most popular and prominent of them all. The right to conduct a sting operation is part of the overall right of freedom of speech and expression of the press. The press owes a responsibility not just to the public and its readers, but to the nation at large to uncover the truth. For this, the media and press can resort to various methodologies, sting operation being one of them.

Preet philosophy will never be in favour of unregulated and uncontrolled right to conduct sting operations on each and every issue. Somewhere down the way, a line has to be drawn. Any sting operation is necessary if it has an impact upon the security of the country, friendly relations with foreign nations, public order, decency, or is necessary to prevent the commission of any cognizable offence and can be justified legally and under the public policy. It is not the case, if the sting operation targets all limits of individual privacy.

The recent sting operation Duryodhan has however demonstrated that if it is for the national good, it will be well received, not withstanding what the victims of the sting operations say. Since sting operations are conducted using sophisticated technologies in digital form, they are therefore covered by the provisions of the Information Technology Act 2000.

The Indian Cyber Law, has no specific provision relating to sting operations. This can be attributed to the fact the India lacks a strong law on privacy and violation of an individual's right to privacy by private entities and leaves the victim without any effective remedy.

The Government of India has proposed certain major amendments to the Information Technology Act, 2000 in order to protect the privacy of individual 'Right to Privacy' to develop and establish as a specific wrong must pay attention to the spirit of people as propounded in the theory of Love-Life-Law.

Here I would suggest that the Indian media/press should not remain quiet and indifferent to the aforesaid issue regarding proposed amendment by the government. As for the government rather than coming up with the proposed amendments, it will be more prudent to stipulate guidelines for sting operation. There is unanimity all across that at no point of time can a sting operation enter the bedroom or private life of an individual, even if they be the most prominent public faces. These kind of sting operations need to be made illegal soon through legislation. However, legitimate sting operations must be an integral part of fundamental rights and liberties of the media/press. The government needs to come down with a strong hand against sting operations which capture the sex escapades of couples and sell the CDs in the open market. There is no reason to legislate in haste and repent at leisure.

The law relating to negligence started its journey in the mid-nineteenth century and attained maturity and by the end of twentieth century it got merged with the absolute liability tort. Right to privacy as tort has a recent origin in the later half of the twentieth century. Right to privacy is closely related to State Art Technology era. Right to privacy is a global issue.

Under the existing provisions of the Indian Cyber Law, the concept of a network service provider has been defined so as to include any intermediary. If you provide an electronic procurement platform, you are providing a service on the network and to some extent you act as an intermediary. In all such cases, you are likely to come within the ambit of a network service provider. Since you will be dealing with all third party information or data, you will be made liable under the Indian Cyber Law for the same.

Our country has already seen a couple of litigations concerning the e-procurement space and these litigations are currently pending in different courts. It is important that you do exercise appropriate due diligence to limit liability for such potential third party data or information made available on your e-procurement platform.

Top Products

Top products
Ethics and philosophy
Born out of mind's factory
Self is the principle secretary
What is academic
Is ethics
What you have to administer
Is the philosophy
What mind delivers is psychology
Academic must be administrative
Try to learn
What the state is
Today's state is art and technology
Law shall add another feather
Wear the cap of multi-discipline
Today Preet provides a new clipping
As a self discipline.

Theories and philosophies can only control State Art Technology system when it is well equipped with the spirit to have desired impact on the substance. Today's corporate world is comprised of two kinds of person one natural born person and another legal person. All philosophies of mind with its reason and logic pertains to smooth functioning of the global system. Global obligations of the aforesaid two kinds of persons shall have to be considered in details and for that an effective legal science shall have to be applied to solve the various problems of individual, associations and nations. Preet's spiritualogy the new legal science has wide-opened the door of legal ethics and psychology.

'Preet' an idea
For the legal science
As a institution
Soon Preet was known
To give perfect solution
All mysteries are unearthed
Full of life is the planet earth
Preet a freedom from negativity
Preet carries you toward completeness
A superb positivity
Negativity
Is an imprisonment
Get released soon
'Preet' is a boon
Excel in self with courage
This is true for all age.

Just be a 'Preet' devotee and achieve physical and mental health. Preet is the unification of two forces, one materialistic another divine. Preet shall cure ailments of inner and outer as good wine. Have the solace, get rid of ailment with grace.

Wisdom shall never yield to self interest. Divinity as eternity shall always control life on this planet. Evil activities of the man if not controlled shall lead to disaster Preet philosophy is the one and the only discipline of the twenty-first century which has given a new life to the planet. Spiritualogy as a legal science will have a full control on State Art Technology system.

Scratch the Border

Nothing extraordinary
Never stick to boundary
Never draw imaginary lines
Between rights and obligations

Between the two nations
Self is my soul I call it
'Preet' soul is invisible
Dignified soul
Is not controlled
By the geography
Just read
Preet's autobiography
Dance and sing
God a great unifying force
Integrate self with superself
That is 'Preet Yog'
A new method
A novel 'Prayog'.

Yog is union and Prayog is experiment. Therefore, love as a union is the first and the foremost experiment which a scientist should carry on to develop a new science of life as propounded by the doctrine found in the theory of Love-Life-Law. This legal science shall open wide the doors of humanism in the present day society.

Concept

To move towards success
We must have a right access
Our approach
Must be positive
Use logic and reason
To analyse self
Self help shall be
Best kind of help
Remedy is the redress
For the injury
You have suffered
Injury and remedy
The two judicial concepts
Which we have to accept.

Conceptual yet actual. Judicial thinking is the nucleus of learning around which we shall develop the theory of

Love-Life-Law. Movement from metaphysics to physics and the vice versa shall enable us to grasp the true meaning of self and the super self.

Cosmic Mind

Man only possesses
Never owes
We write so much of prose
We just possess
Mind and body
Soul, subtle
With vibratory waves
Which mind has to chase
God created all
Soul, mind and body
He is the owner
God the super self
Man just the possessor
Who needs God's help
Preet suggests
Go, beyond body
To enter the centre
Called Mind
Brain a hardware
Consciousness operated as software.

All minds are parts of one cosmic mind; neither brain is mind nor mind is located in brain. This mechanical approach of the traditional science is already been shattered. As it lies outside the parameters of time and space. Journey to the centre of mind is beyond body, therefore personal consciousness of the individual is connected with collective consciousness which is universal. Preet philosophy is an effort to relate self-consciousness with God the Almighty.

Where there is ignorance
There shall be knowledge
Where there is war
There shall be peace
Where there is money

There shall be poverty
Nonsense shall bring all sense
Nuisance shall culminate in good sense
Any solution, for pollution
Mind needs good tuition
Get rid of ignorance
To breed endurance
Law is a pure science
You may call it a legal science.

Logic and reason; all science. Emotion and intellect a divine sign. Proceed towards divinity with the help of a novel concept as embedded in Preet's spiritualogy. Look into the spirit first then to the substance and form. Love-Life-Law all the three 'L' are equally significant for the biological coexistence of all the species of the plants and animals. Therefore, rights of the living beings are much more important than the human rights. To put it in one word, its the 'social obligation' of the human being which is most important in the context of present-day society.

Both are man's tutor: constitution and the computer. Self has overpowered substance and the net result we find in a new wave where materialism culminates in spiritualism. This perception is unique. Infinite is the upright future for the present day society in the silicon era. Let us interpret constitution with eternal and spiritual wisdom as found in Preet's spirituality of Love, Life and Law. The two together: computer and the constitution shall certainly lead us towards the better global society with superior divine obligation (positivity).[7]

Notes

1. See *Cosmos*: S.K. Varshney.
2. See *Love-Life-Law*: S.K. Varshney.
3. Refer to *Divine Dictate*: S.K. Varshney.
4. Refer to "Universe and Stars", *Cosmos* by S.K. Varshney.
5. Refer to Bhopal Gas Tragedy case and *M.C. Mehta* v. *Union of India*.
6. S.K. Varshney.
7. Refer to *Sing a Song*: S.K. Varshney.

3

Extension of Reservation Policy in Private Sector

Possibilities, Impediments and Consequences

C. CHELLAPAN

The Constitution of India has provided necessary provisions for reservation for the Scheduled Castes and Scheduled Tribes. As regards the Government of India services the percentage of reservation for the SCs is 15 per cent and for the STs it is 7.5 per cent. As a result of the Mandal Commission report the Backward Classes also have been given the benefit of reservation in the initial recruitment. In respect of the state services each state government reserves the posts to the SCs, STs and BCs depending upon the percentage of the population of these communities in their respective states. It is true that as a result of the reservation the individuals belonging to these communities have been benefitted. However, there is no provision in the Constitution to provide such reservation in the private sector. There has been a growing demand that reservation should be made applicable in the private sector also. The political parties also have taken up this issue as one of their promises during the last electioneering. The United Progressive Alliance government in the National Common Minimum Programme has stated, that their UPA government is very sensitive to the issue of affirmative action including reservation in the private sector and have promised to initiate immediately a national dialogue with all political parties, industry and other organizations to see how best the private sector can fulfil the aspirations of scheduled castes and scheduled tribes youth.

In pursuance of this statement the UPA government has already started discussions on this subject with the various political parties and experts to ascertain their views. There was a conference on "Reservation in Private Sectors" convened by the Ministry of Social Justice and Empowerment on 24, August 2004 in New Delhi.[1] This subject has evoked lot of discussions in the electronic media and press. Conferences and seminars are being organized on this subject in different parts of the country. Therefore, I am happy that Dr. Ambedkar Chair of Legal Studies and Research, Department of Law, Aligarh Muslim University has decided to hold a National Seminar on this subject. I thank the organizers of this seminar for having invited me to present a paper on this subject.

Before taking up the main subject it is better to have a little look back into the past history. After independence, India opted for mixed economy with the pubic sector as the principal instrument for faster planned growth and social justice. The Second Five-Year Plan, the Industrial Policy Resolution in 1956 and the adoption of socialistic pattern of society laid the foundation of the public sector. Prime Minister Jawaharlal Nehru assigned to it the role of commanding heights of economy. The Second Plan said "the basic criteria for determining the lines of advance must not be private profit but social gain and the pattern of development and the structure of the socio-economic relation should be so planned that they result not only in appreciable increase in the national income and employment but also in greater equality in incomes and wealth". Later on, the concept of joint sector was enthusiastically pursued by the state governments, wherein the government undertakings and private entrepreneurs joined together in the equity participation, etc., with the private partners having greater say. But Indira Gandhi as Prime Minister gave importance to public sector and initiated several measures to better the lot of the weaker sections particularly the Scheduled Castes and Scheduled Tribes.

Nationalization of banks and bank recruitment boards have given greater opportunities for employment of these disadvantaged people, besides contributing to economy growth. V.P. Singh and his government through Mandal report have given reservation for the backward classes in central government services. Rajiv Gandhi described the public sector as the core of our economy: "Government's commitments to the growing role of the Public Sector is unflagging".

During these periods the emphasis was on public sector and on accelerating the process of the advancement of the Scheduled Castes and Scheduled Tribes and other backward classes. Then came the debate about privatization of public sector enterprises. One point emerged clearly. Several public sector enterprises came up because the private sector was not coming forward to take risks and invest capital in basic, key and strategic industries when planned development process was initiated after independence. We need not go into the merits or demerits of privatization of public enterprises, except the issue of role of private sector in espousing and assisting the weaker sections particularly the Scheduled Castes and Scheduled Tribes.

When the economic situation was deteriorating in the country it was the present Prime Minister, Manmohan Singh (as Finance Minister under the Prime Ministership of Late P.V. Narasimha Rao) who had shown pragmatism and consummate ability. He ushered in economic reforms to restore health, sustained growth and development of economy and the country as evidenced in his budgets. While doing this he was aware of the need to take care of the poor. While addressing the Indian Institute of Management (IIM) Ahmedabad on 3, April 1994, he said "any package of economic reforms which does not pay sufficient heed to the needs of the poor can give rise to unmanageable social, economic and political problems". Again at a conference at the Indian Social Institute in Delhi, Manmohan Singh reiterated that economic reforms would always be with human face and social justice. At a meeting of the CII Annual Session in Delhi on 19 April, 1994, he said "that there was a growing apprehension that as the role of the public sector diminishes the employment opportunities for

Scheduled Castes and Scheduled Tribes would shrink". "If this thought acquires momentum it will hurt the process of reforms." He warned: "the private sector must address these issues and ensure that in the vocational training these sections of the labour force are not neglected".

The Vajpayee government had initiated several measures for liberalization, privatization and globalization. Separate ministry for disinvestments of public sectors enterprises was also created and the process of disinvestments and privatization was continued with full vigour.

After 2004 Parliament elections, the UPA government is in place with its National Common Minimum Programme. This programme inter alia states "the UPA government is very sensitive to the issue of affirmative action including reservation in the Private Sector. It will immediately initiate national dialogue with all political parties, Industry and other organizations to see how best the private sector can fulfil the aspirations of Scheduled Castes and Scheduled Tribe youth". While conceding that private sector has an important role to play in the national economy and development requiring needed encouragement and assistance, the UPA government has also reminded the private sector about its role and responsibility in assisting the Scheduled Castes and tribes in their quest for advancement and progress.

It has been stated that when the entrepreneurs want to put up any industry or start business they have to invest huge amounts of money for this purpose. Therefore, while investing such huge sums of money, one would like to have his own trusted people in running the industry or business so that they do not result in loss. It is true that one has to invest huge amount to start any industry in these days. However, almost all the entrepreneurs or promoters get financial help from the commercial banks as loan. This money advanced by the banks is public money. Moreover, such enterprises also receive lot of concessions extended by the central or concerned state governments. These state governments in order to get their states industrially developed are vying with each other to woo them to put the units in their states. Therefore, while enjoying such benefits from state and central governments these entrepreneurs or promoters are obliged to employ suitable candidates from other communities also such as the Scheduled Castes and Scheduled Tribes and backward classes.

Liberalization, privatization and globalization are new phenomena and likely to grow rapidly in the changed economic scenario, The ostensible purpose is to increase economic growth and face the highly competitive world and market forces. In India, public sector industries which at one time were to have commanding heights of economy are disinvested. Socialism which still adore the Preamble to the Constitution of India has gone. Economic growth by itself is of no use. Inequity should be reduced if not eliminated. More equitable distribution of benefits of growths to people is necessary. Economic reforms with social justice should be our cardinal principle. Otherwise through privatization and liberalization and globalization there will be islands of opulence and accumulated wealth and divide between rich and poor will be sharper. These are anti-Dalit and anti-poor. Private sector has social obligations to perform in actively helping to improve the socio-economic conditions of the people, particularly Dalits and other weaker sections. This sector gets more financial support from governments and banks.

The Advisory Panel on Pace of Socio-economic Change and Development under the Constitution with Justice. K. Ponnayya as Member-in-Charge and Justice K. Ramaswamy as Chairman has observed:

> "In the changed economic scenario private sector is likely to grow rapidly. The private sector enterprises by and large draw substantial support from government bodies and banks, which handle public funds. Large investments in their enterprises come from the public funds. Public sector has therefore social responsibilities to perform. It needs actively to help in the improvement of socio-economic conditions of the people especially those belonging to the weaker sections of the society, so as to build a conflict free and caring society without which no enterprise either public or private can hope to flourish. At present Scheduled Caste and Scheduled Tribe employees in the private sectors are believed to be numerically insignificant except at the shop floor level. There is an increasing apprehension that the employment

opportunity of the Scheduled Castes or the weaker sections would shrink with the reduction in the role of the government."

"Areas of the social obligation of the private sector need to be identified. Private sector should contribute in the areas of advancement of education, health and in provision of employment opportunities of weaker sections of the people including the Scheduled Caste and Scheduled Tribes and Other Backward Classes. Policy framework for active involvement and participation of private sector for socio-economic development of the people needs to be evolved after a meaningful, purposeful and result oriented debate with the leaders of Indian industry, trade and commerce."

Sukhadeo Thorat says: "faced with caste related discrimination against and deprivation of social groups, the state has used the reservation policy in employment, education and other spheres. Despite discrimination in the private economic domain, reservation is confined to the minuscule government sector – the vast private agriculture and industry sectors where more that 90 per cent of SC/STs are employed remain untouched by the reservation policy." Due to the rapid narrowing of the state sector on account of the privatization and the withdrawal of the state from many spheres under the liberalization regime, the little space that the discriminated groups has gained in public employment is now being compressed further. If the prevalence of economic discrimination is the justification for reservation in the public sector, why can it not be the reason for reservation in the private sector? In countries such as the US, Northern Ireland, Malaysia and others in Latin America, affirmative action was developed from the very beginning both in the public and the private sector.

Therefore, it is high time that we introduced reservation in the private sector and provided long-withheld justice. Economists now have enough evidence to show that markets are not neutral, but do discriminate against so called 'untouchable' and other low castes. Some strands in mainstream economics, which form the theoretical supportive base for affirmative action in the West, believe that market discrimination not only brings about unequal income distribution, but also adversely affects economic growth by bringing imperfection in the labour market. Further, by inducing income inequalities, discrimination creates a situation of potential inter-group conflict. Affirmative action as a remedy for market discrimination is thus justified, on grounds of both equity and growth.

India must enact an Equal Employment Opportunity Act (as in the United States) so as to provide legal safeguards against discrimination. This could be supplemented by affirmative action in terms of reservation in some categories of jobs and other markets (*Economics Times*, 26 March, 2004). Besides market discrimination, there is also the view that in India kinship, clan, caste and class are factors that perpetuate inequalities through the system of linkages, leading to 'Institutionalization of inequalities'.

It may be appropriate to point out that in a capitalist country like the US the minority communities have adequate percentage employment compared to their percentage of population. The minorities in the US, i.e., African American, American Indians/Alaska natives, Asian/Pacific Islanders and Hispanics who form 27.30 per cent of the total population are having employment ranging from 12.95 per cent in official/managers level to 44.53 per cent in labourer's category. The share of these minorities is 14.09 per cent in the enterprises and business in the US. In General Motors, 23 per cent of its employees belong to minorities. So also in the Ford Motors, the minorities form 18.2 per cent of the total employees. Out of the total employees of IBM 21.56 per cent of them are racial/ethnic minorities. In managerial/official and professional category the minorities account for 14.66 per cent. Could IBM have ever achieved its pre-eminent standing in world IT business by compromising on merits and competitiveness?

If the minorities in the US have the appreciable percentage in the employment and business and enterprises it is because of the affirmative action taken by the people of the US. Perhaps it may be true that in order to compensate the injustice done to these minorities during the past, the people have provided them jobs in an appreciable manner. Therefore, it can be said about India also. In order to make good or compensate the injustice meted out to the SCs and STs and backward classes the managers of the private sector should agree to provide employment to these people. There are people who are well qualified and educated belonging to these communities. Therefore, the private sector need not have any inhibition in this regard.

The former President, K.R. Narayanan said "It is forgotten that the reservations have been provided not as charity but as human rights to a big chunk of our population who actually contribute to agriculture, industry and services as landless labourers, factory and municipal workers. There are signs that our privileged classes are getting tired of the affirmative action provided by constitutional provisions. On this Golden Jubilee I would like to say that let us not get tired of what we have provided for our weaker sections; for otherwise as Dr. Ambedkar pointed out, the edifice of our democracy would be like a palace built on a dung heap".

In India, political democracy has come to stay as seen from successive elections. But social and economic democracy is still a dream despite five decades after Independence. The civil society should have harmony, liberty, equality and fraternity. Efforts of the government to improve the conditions of the Scheduled Castes and Scheduled Tribes have not yielded the desired results. The policy of reservation providing special priorities and special facilities to elevate them on par with developed sections of the society has not been implemented effectively and properly. Socio-economic measures for their benefit need to be reviewed and restructured to ensure that benefits are accrued to them.

The Constitution of India rests firmly on the principles of Liberty, Equality, Fraternity and Justice. It has great concern for the poorest and weakest in society. Special provisions and mechanisms have been provided for the advancement of the Scheduled Castes and Scheduled Tribes and Other Backward Classes. Article 17 abolishes untouchability. Article 14 enumerates 'Right to Equality'. Article 335 provides for appointments in services. Article 38, 39, 39A require the state to ensure a creation of social order with justice and to strive to minimize inequalities in income, status and opportunity to bring about an equitable distribution of resources. Article 46 directs the state to provide with a special care, the education and the economic interests of the weaker sections especially those of the schedule caste and schedule tribes.

It has been stated that India has to compete in an international arena now as a result of globalization and liberalization. The Indian industries cannot do so with the people employed as a result of reservation. Again the sectors that are showing growth today are IT, business process outsourcing (BPO) and services. These are places where people with deportment skill and mental agility are needed. This kind of criticism shows that if individuals belonging to SC/ST and other backward classes are recruited as a result of the extension of reservation, they may not be having these abilities and capabilities and will not rise up to the expectation. It is very unfortunate that some people have such biased views against the SCs, STs and OBCs. They are not for a moment prepared to accept that as a result of good education there are well qualified and eligible persons in large numbers in these communities also. There are so many individuals belonging to these communities who have excelled themselves and done creditable work in different areas. If necessary facilities and opportunities are provided, there is no doubt that they will also prove their mettle. After recruitment, if necessary training is imparted they will be able to rise up to any situation. Therefore, even without giving any chance to show their ability it is unjustified to make such sweeping criticism. It may also be pointed out that there are large number of industrial units which have been provided with all necessary concessions, etc., have become sick. For this state of affairs, there are ever so many reasons like mismanagement, wrong decisions being taken, etc. This happened even while these industries and business were being handled by their own kith and kin.

The individuals who are having money power are able to put up industries and thereby get economic power. However, these entrepreneurs are not still free from the age old misconceptions about the socially disadvantaged people. Though there are a few forward looking individuals, their main concern is to run the industries successfully. They do not have any social responsibility towards the socially disadvantaged people.

The laws pertaining to production are not pro poor and the socially disadvantaged. The economic policy of the government lays stress only on production and not concerned with social justice.

Mandal Judgment favoured the Other Backward Classes and not the Scheduled Castes and Scheduled Tribes. In fact it has done a great injustice to these people. Some of the concessions enjoyed by them have been taken away as a result of this judgment. After great deal of representations some of these concessions have been restored but not fully. It is very clear that the cleavage between the haves and have-nots is widening. Among the have-nots the lot of the SCs and STs is becoming miserable. Therefore it is right time that this trend is stopped by taking some urgent ameliorative measures. Otherwise as Dr. Ambedkar pointed out "the edifice of democracy would be like a palace built on dung heap".

As stated earlier the Ministry of Social Justice and Empowerment has been discussing this subject with all concerned. It is ascertained that a meeting was held with the leading industrialists and business houses also in September 2004. In pursuance of these discussions a statement was issued by more than dozen industrialists and corporate houses. A letter was also addressed by Ratan N. Tata on behalf of the signatories and addressed to the Minister of Social Justice and Empowerment.[2] In their statement they have stated the following:

> "We welcome the move by the UPA government to have a dialogue with industry on Affirmative Action to address the aspirations of youth from the disadvantaged sections, particularly the Scheduled Castes and Scheduled Tribes. Social justice requires all sections of society to work together to reduce disparities among different groups and to offer all young people equal opportunities to become productive members of society and lead a life of dignity. This is a right that members from the Scheduled Castes and Scheduled Tribes have been historically denied for social, cultural and economic reasons."
>
> As individual representatives of Indian industry, we fully support the government in addressing this important social goal. We recognize that in a liberalized and decontrolled economy, the

benefits of reservations for members from the Scheduled Castes and Scheduled Tribes in government and public sector undertaking need to be complemented by affirmative action by industry. We are reassured to learn from the government that it has no intention of resorting to legislative action to impose a statutory obligation of reservations on industry.

The imperatives of a competitive economy require that industry place a premium on merit. However, we also recognize that merit is not a natural phenomenon but shaped by social circumstances. We must therefore create an environment where youth from the Scheduled Castes and Scheduled Tribes can become as meritorious as any other youth when they enter their economically productive years. The need is not just to provide jobs but also incubate the emergence of a robust entrepreneurial class of youth from the Scheduled Castes and Scheduled Tribes.

We believe that providing quality education, facilities for skill development and creating a culture for entrepreneurship among the youth from Scheduled Castes and Schedule Tribes are key to creating this environment. Such initiatives can be propelled with the innovative use of modern management systems and IT tools to help the disadvantaged expand their economic opportunities. This is a long-term endeavour which needs commitment now and cannot be delayed.

Many large companies in India have for long selected employees on the basis of merit and practised equal opportunity employment policies. Taking that spirit forward, all of us in Indian industry commit ourselves to making our due contribution to Indian society in wiping out social and caste discrimination and dedicate ourselves to playing our part in building a new set of values in India where every citizen, irrespective of religion or caste, will have an equal opportunity for education, employment and earning a livelihood.

More specifically, we commit to expand our current activities for disadvantaged persons with regard to scholarships, company-run private schools, partnership with government schools, vocational training in-house as well as in partnership with IIT's vendor development programmes, etc. We will do this through credible NGOs and Self-Help Groups. In these, and other ways, we shall implement in letter and spirit a programme of affirmative action to empower persons who are socially and economically backward."

As may be seen from the above statement these leading industrialists have agreed to provide scholarships to the youth belonging to the disadvantaged society and also provide necessary vocational training in-house as well as in partnership with IITs, etc. Therefore, it is now for the Ministry to take further action on the offer made by the industrialists. It is appreciable and a welcome suggestion on the part of the industrialists to have come forward and offered the facilities like scholarships, in-house training, etc., to the youth belonging to the disadvantaged society so that after undergoing the necessary training they can be absorbed in the industries or can be helped to put up their own industrial units.

In view of the fact that the industrialists have come forward with the above suggestions the government can take action on either of the following:

(i) To enact a legislation introducing the reservation in the private sector also and watch its implementation by the private sector, or
(ii) In the circumstances explained by the industrialists and business houses, allow them to implement the reservation by themselves by giving some time and thereafter bring legislation, if necessary. The government should take necessary further action in this regard expeditiously.

To sum up:

(i) The private sector is largely government and bank-assisted sector with public funds.
(ii) Private sector is part of the society and cannot work in isolation without taking the social realities and dynamics into account.
(iii) Social and economic democracy with emphasis on equality and equality of opportunities for the deprived and the depressed, i.e., the Scheduled Caste and Scheduled Tribes is the very foundation of the Constitution of India.

(iv) Private sector is one of the major instruments for social and economic transformation envisaged in the Constitution.

(v) Private sector has social responsibility and commitment to the nation's progress and objectives. It is not mere economic growth.

(vi) The state intervention, if not controlled is a necessity to ensure that 'privatization' does not lead to islands of opulence and wealth with vested interests making the divide between the rich and the poor sharper.

(vii) Uncontrolled and unregulated private sector will further aggravate the social tensions and confidence, which the country is already facing.

(viii) The private sector in India is largely influenced by kinship, clan, caste, etc., creating institutionalized inequalities.

(ix) It has to reorient its outlook, attitude and approach.

(x) It has to join hands with the government to bring in a social order based on equality and equity by providing all possible avenues and opportunities to the Scheduled Castes and Scheduled Tribes including training, employment, etc.

(xi) A suitable mechanism/enactment has to be formulated to give effect to the affirmative action including reservation in the private sector as in the USA and other countries.

(xii) A 'National Monitoring Commission' should be set up to oversee and monitor the progress in the implementation of the reservation in the private sector.

(xiii) In view of the letter addressed to the Minister of Social Justice and Empowerment, by some leading industrialists and business houses, a decision has to be taken by the government either to pass a legislation introducing the reservation in the private sector also, and watch the implementation or allow the industrialists to implement the reservation on their own and bring necessary legislation later, if necessary.

Notes

1. Reservation in Private Sector – Address by A. Padmanaban, I.A.S. (Retd.), Former Governor, Mizoram at the conference on 'Reservation in Private Sector' convened by the Ministry of Social Justice and Empowerment, Government of India on 24 August, 2004 in New Delhi.
2. Correspondence of A. Padmanaban, I.A.S. (Retd) to Ratan N. Tata and others about affirmative action and reservation in private sector.

4

Social Status and Legal Rights of Prostitutes

Mauryan Period to Present Day Scenario

ABHA KULSHRESHTHA

Prostitution is the ultimate degradation of a woman. This word pictures shame, exploitation, misery, torture and ill-health. Several sayings are there about it, one of which is that it is one of the oldest professions of the world! In Indian history we find enough mention of it. Ancient Sanskrit literature indicates existence of prostitutes. In the *Rgveda, vra,* a she elephant denoted the same as *ganika.*[1] In *Mahabharata* and *Ramayana* both the word *ganika* and *vesya* were used for the designation of prostitutes. Ganika, according to these epics were in high esteem.[2] The *Mrcchakatika* and the *Daridracarudatta* referred to *Vasantasena* as a *ganika* but loosely the word *vesya*, *panastri* and *prakasanari* denote the same meaning. In *Sukasaptati* it was stated that there were several kinds of prostitutes namely *ganika*, *vilasini*, *rupajiva*, *arthavrttika* and *darika*. In *Kathasaritsagara* the word *ganika* was loosely used besides *varavanita*. In the *Jatakas* the word *ganika* in the meaning of a highly esteemed person, was very often used, besides *nagarasobhini* and *varnadasi*. In *Milindapanha*, *ganika* and *kumbhadasi* were mentioned to explain about those who came to the town to find residence there.[3] All these references suggest that prostitutes existed in Ancient India.

By sixth century B.C. in India big kingdoms came into existence. There are several contemporary sources which describe social condition of this period. From those sources it becomes clear that prostitutes enjoyed a social standing not accorded to them anywhere else in the world except Athens. The great prestige which these women had is clear from the story of Amrapali in the Vinaya Texts of *Mulasarvastivada*.[4] Many suitors, including princes having sought her hand, her father brought the matter to the notice of the Licchavi *gana* and it was discussed by the Assembly. When the members saw Amrapali they decided she should not be for one person but become a public property. Amrapali agreed provided she was granted five boons. King Bimbisara was also charmed by her. One day Buddha came to Vaisali and Amrapali invited him to her house for a meal. When the Licchavis came to know of the acceptance of the hospitality of Amrapali by Buddha, they thought themselves humiliated. They requested Amrapali to give up the idea of bringing Buddha in her house and offered her money. But to their astonishment Amrapali refused money and would have even refused kingdom of Vaisali, if it was offered to her. Amrapali would not sell her chance to offer a meal to a man, who in his lifetime only had come to be regarded as saviour of mankind. The nobles then approached 'Buddha' and pressed him to accept their invitation. As the leaders of the town they claimed the privilege of honouring the great master. But 'Buddha' would not withdraw his word. Next morning 'Buddha' went to the house of Amrapali with his disciples. The woman had nicely arranged for lord's meal; afterwards she sat at his feet and dedicated her all to him, renouncing the world.

Thus, it is clear that prostitutes were not looked down upon by the kings, religious teachers or the society in general. Some of them were highly accomplished in fine arts.

In the subsequent period, the prostitutes kept on enjoying a strong place in society. Compared to our present times, there was no shame and degradation attached to their profession. In Kautilya's *Arthasastra* we find several rules and regulations which protected them from exploitation and misery.

According to *Arthasastra* a 'ganika' was a government servant who was supervised by *ganikadhyaksas.*[5] Ganikas were appointed by the state to perform several duties, like, to amuse the king and the courtiers in the royal court at the time of festivals and festivities, accompany the king and the army during the wars or huntings, to hold the umbrella, the golden pitcher and the fan or attend the king seated on the throne or chariot. They could receive customers if not engaged in these works.

The 'ganikadhyaksas' carefully supervised the work of ganikas. They fixed the salary of one thousand *pana* per annum,[6] there was a second or middle level category of ganikas who received two thousand *pana;* the top category received three thousand *pana.* This classification was based on the beauty, wealth and jewellery of a particular female.

A ganika was highly accomplished person, well-versed in sixty-four arts,[7] bold and cunning. They were heroines of many contemporary dramas written with them as centre point. In these dramas they speak in Sanskrit, whereas other women speak in *prakrta,* which indicates towards their high place in the society. Even the foreign travellers noticed their high position in the society. Thus, prostitution was not considered a shameful occupation, rather it was elevating. When the kings returned victorious from wars they had to see prostitutes and other insignia of royalty.[8]

Arthasastra mentions another word *pratiganika* who was probably a substitute ganika, that is a government servant, with whom a contract was concluded for a short duration only. She could become in future a ganika but as long as she was only a pratiganika she received only half of the salary of the ganika for whom she substituted.

There were other types of prostitutes besides the state appointed ganikas, like *rupajiva, vesya, pumscali,* etc. A *rupajiva* was a woman who lived on her beauty, she had to pay monthly to the government a tax amounting to twice the amount of her daily earning.[9] '*Rupajiva* was a higher kind of prostitute but not as high as *ganikas* were. Vesya was a general term for all kinds of prostitutes according to the *Kamsastra.* Kautilya has used this word in connection with those prostitutes who served as spies. *'Pumscali'* seems to be the word used by Kautilya for a very low kind of prostitute; it meant a profligate woman, a woman who ran after man.[10] Anyone who was seen constantly in her presence was considered a suspected person. A pumscali could also be used as a spy. There was prevalence of the system of *devadasi* too. The temple prostitutes had to be attached to a temple and if they were unable to perform their services due to illness the king had to support them.[11] Such girls were kept at the great temple of Mahakala at Ujjayini in Kalidasa's time and at a shrine of the Sun-god in a city east of Sindh in the time of Hiuen-Tsang.[12]

Kautilya in his *Arthasastra* mentions various ways to overcome the enemy; we hear of *visa-kanyas* or poison girls, who were fed on poison since childhood and were used by the king to incite love in any of his undesirable foe, which would lead to his death in the arms of the poison girl. It seems that prostitutes were used as spies. The prostitutes were not poison girls but because their presence was not respected in many places, they were used for getting information about many things. They could be used to spy upon thieves as they were in each other's company often; foreign travellers who came into the kingdom, leader of enemy's army or chief of corporation *(srenis)*, etc. Prostitutes were also used to spy on military men and for kidnapping princes.[13] Though ganikas were not asked to be spies but they were supposed to inform the *ganikadhyaksa* about any *'purusa'* who was of uncertain credentials.

The appointment of ganikas as state servant was done carefully, according to Kautilya's *Arthasastra.* Any woman who was beautiful *(surupa),* young *(yuva)* and was endowed with sixty-four arts could become ganika. Usually daughters of ganikas became ganika. Poor parents gave their daughters to ganikadhyaksa, as prostitution was not considered a shameful occupation in Mauryan times and a ganika was a highly esteemed person. But in the later period only highly placed ganikas enjoyed such positions. Along with the general decline in the condition of women during later period, we hear that prostitution came to be looked down upon.

In a model town, special dwelling places were designed for prostitutes in the south of the city. In the *Agnipurana,* similar rule is followed that to the south of the town dancers and prostitutes *(vesyastri)* shall live.[14] A description of these quarters of prostitutes is also found in the *Dasakumaracarita.* We find many instances in Sanskrit literary works in which it is shown that *devadasis* dwelt on special streets near the temples and that the prostitutes occupied special quarters.

The ganikas were wealthy women. The three types of ganikas along with their salary have been mentioned earlier; besides salaries they received income in the form of gifts like garments, gold, silver, brass, iron and copper objects, perfumes, cattle, etc. However, the ganikadhyaksa exercised control over financial affairs of the ganikas under them. Since ganikas received monthly salary and were appointed by the state to increase king's treasury, their expenditure was taken into account and all extra earnings were to be remitted to the state, barring personal inheritance. Ganikas were trained under competent teachers, maintained by the state in the art of dramatics, singing, dancing, playing on musical instruments, painting, writing, act of entertaining, conversation and shampooing. Kautilya refers to ganikas who in accordance with their quality, youth and beauty were appointed as personal companions of the king and could play dice with him and were paid highly.[15]

Prostitutes *(vesya* and *rupajiva)* had to pay taxes to the state. According to Kautilya, the government servants did not pay taxes on their salaries, and since ganikas were government servants, while others were taxable on their income, they paid twenty-four times their fee for one day; yearly.

The prostitutes enjoyed several rights in ancient times. Ganikas being government servants, had the right to a pension scheme in case they lost their beauty, became old, or incapable of earning any money. If a ganika lost her beauty and popularity she had to accept a lower post of becoming a gatherer of fresh ganikas or work in the storehouse or the kitchen of the king.[16]

A ganika was not free. She was a government servant and so she was totally under king's orders. She could not refuse anybody if king ordered so, unlike rupajiva and vesya who were prostitutes but not government employees. If she defied the orders of the king she was to receive a thousand lashes with a whip.

A ganika could however buy her freedom from the king, who was her master, by paying the redemption *(niskraya)*. Her son could also regain freedom. But the redemption charges were quite high. Kautilya mentions it as: *"nis krayascatun, bhsatisahasro ganikayah"*; which means the redemption of a ganika amounts to 24,000 pana. The son of a ganika was also not free and from his eighth year onwards he had to work as a bard *(kusilava)*, actor *(rangopajivin)* or dancer *(talavacara)*.[17]

Ganikas had property rights over their own jewellery and those things they had bought out of their income. Anyone who deprived a ganika of her jewellery had to pay as a fine eight times the value of such jewellery.[18] From the story of *Mrcchakatika* it is clear that like Ganika Vasantasena, other ganikas had the full right of ownership of jewellery and had the right to pledge it. It follows then that the ganikas had inheritance right too. If a ganika died, her daughter or her sister inherited her household and if any one of them was not available, then the king inherited from the deceased ganika.[19]

A ganika had several professional rights too. For example if she made a contract with a prospective partner and could not fulfil due to her illness she was to be excused.[20] Otherwise she had to pay the person twice the amount which was to be given to her for her services. Offences committed towards a ganika by any person was punished severely as it could harm king's interest too. The penalties for keeping under confinement, abducting or disfiguring a ganika amounted to one thousand *pana*.[21]

Though it is true that ganikas were not looked down upon and enjoyed several rights but there are several literary evidences which suggest that ordinary men were advised to keep away from them:

"Like fuel burning in a blazing fire, they burn the man whom they serve for gold."[22]

"They attract men by their tempting figure and voice, perfumes and touch and by their dalliance in stratagem. They assume different poses to allure weak-minded people and cause them to fall a prey to their sinful snare."

"The prostitutes love not the man but his money. Being moved by their greed or carnal appetite they consumed the rich men in whom they were interested."[23]

The *Dhammapada* Commentary presents interesting story about keeping morals:

Sirima was a very beautiful courtesan of Rajagrha and was the daughter of Silavati. She was celebrated for her skill as a dancer and musician and her fee was one thousand *kasarpanas.* In the same city a rich man named 'Sumana' lived who was son of a treasurer. His wife 'Uttara' was devoted to Buddha, while her husband was not. Uttara engaged the services of Sirima for her husband so that she might be free to attend to her religious duties. When Sirima died, king Bimbisara at the request of Buddha, had to keep her body, so that it could be seen by the people. By a royal proclamation all the citizens were compelled to see Sirima's dead body under penalty of a fine. After seeing the corpse daily, the monk and the people realized how transitory is a human body. Such a lovely body which was coveted by kings and princes, became rotten, worm eaten and at last nothing but the bones were left. It proved that beauty is but skin deep.[24]

Thus, it can be concluded that prostitutes were an integral part of society during the age of Buddha. State appointed prostitutes were called ganikas who were well-versed in sixty-four arts, who enjoyed a high place in the society because of their beauty, proficiency and state patronage. They had several legal and humanitarian rights. Besides them there were many categories of prostitutes called *rupajiva,* who were not government servants but worked for themselves, *kumbhadasi, paricanka, nati, pumscali, devadasi, bandhaki,* etc., were low kind of prostitutes who could be used by the state in the services of a spy. Their numerous activities are amply described in various contemporary Sanskrit and other literary works.

"Frailty, thy name is woman", was the ignominy heaped upon women of Victorian era by William Shakespeare in his great work *Hamlet*. The history of sociology has, however, established the contrary, i.e., 'fortitude', thy name is woman; 'caress', thy name is woman; 'self-sacrifice', thy name is woman; tenacity and successful pursuit, their apathetical is women. Indira Gandhi, Margaret Thatcher, Srimovo Bhandarnaike and Golda Meir are few illustrious women having proved successful in democratic governance of the respective democratic states. Amids, them, still, a class of women is trapped as victims of circumstances, unfounded social sanctions, handicaps and coercive forms in the flesh trade, optimized as 'prostitutes', 'fallen women'.

Prostitution in society has not been an unknown phenomenon; it is of ancient origin and has its manifestation in various forms with varied degree unfounded on so called social sanctions, etc. The victims of the trap are the poor, illiterate and ignorant sections of the society and are the target group in the flesh trade; rich communities exploit them and harvest at their misery and ignominy in an organized gangsterism, in particular, with police nexus. It is of grave social concern, increasingly realized by enlightened public spirited sections of the society to prevent gender exploitation of girl children. The prostitute has always been an object and was never seen as complete human being with dignity of person; as if she has had no needs and aspirations of her own, individually or collectively. Their problems are compounded by coercion laid around them and torturous treatment meted out to them. When they make attempts either to resist the prostitution or to relieve themselves from the trap, they succumb to the violent treatment and resultantly many a one settle for prostitution. Prostitute is equally a human being. Despite that trap, she is confronted with the problems to bear and rear the children. The limitations of trade confront them in bringing up their children, be it male or female. Their children are equally subjected to inhuman treatment by managers of brothels and are subjected to discrimination, social isolation; they are deprived of their right to live normal life for no fault of their own.

We find Devadasis, Yogins and Venkatasins in particular families, are offered as Devadasi or Jogin or Venkatasin, by whatever local name they are called. They are making the lives of the girl miserable; in the guise of prosperous future and custom, the girl is detained in prostitution for no fault of her. This is prevalent in particular in six districts of Karnataka, viz., Raichur, Bijapur, Belgaum, Dharwar, Bellary and Gulbarga where their number is identified as 21,306. In Andhra Pradesh, in five districts, namely

Medak, Karimnagar, Nizamabad, Nalgonda and Warangal, such girls are known as Jogins. Nizarnabad District has the largest number of Jogins as per the survey conducted in 1996, as many as 16,300 Jogins were found in that state. Similarly, in Maharashtra, they are found in large number, in particular in Marathawada and Vidarba regions. The common feature of such women is that predominantly they are from Scheduled Castes, Scheduled Tribes and Other Backward Classes. The eldest girl in every family is being offered as Devadasi, Jogin or Venkatasin. Sometimes, they do redeem the pledge made to the gods or goddesses, etc. Original families of these Devadasis, Jogins or Venkatasins were by and large poor.

The full development of personality and fundamental freedoms and equal participation by women in political, social, economic and cultural life are concomitants for national development, social and family stability and growth – cultural, social and economical. All forms of discrimination on ground of gender is violative of fundamental freedoms and human rights. Eradication of prostitution in any form is integral to social weal and glory of womanhood.

Therefore, it is the duty of the state and all voluntary non-government organizations and public spirited persons to come in to their aid to retrieve them from prostitution, rehabilitate them with a helping hand to lead a life with dignity of person, self-employment through provisions of education, financial support, developed marketing facilities as some of major avenues in this behalf. Marriage is another object to give them real status in society. Acceptance by the family is also another important input to rekindle the faith of self-respect and self-confidence. Housing, legal aid, free counselling assistance and all other similar aids and services are meaningful measures to ensure that unfortunate fallen women do not again fall into the trap of red light area contaminated with foul atmosphere. Law is a social engineer. The courts are part of the state steering by way of judicial review. Judicial statesmanship is required to help regaining social order and stability.

Mahajan Committee was constituted by Hon'ble Supreme Court.[25] The Committee submitted its report touching all aspects of miseries of prostitutes and their children and has also recommended their rehabilitation.

The prohibition of Devdasi System – The Andhra Pradesh Devdasis (Prohibition of Dedication) Act, 1988 is in existence wherein it is clearly mentioned that dedication as "Devadasi" is unlawful. Penalties are provided under the Act for violation of provisions of the Act.

We are aware of Immoral Traffic (Prevention). Act, 1956. We are also aware of Constitutional Provisions. Convention on the Elimination of All Forms of Discrimination Against Women (CEDAW) is known to all of us.

There are penal provisions in Indian Penal Code (Ss. 372 and 373) as well.

Inspite of penal provisions, imprisonment, fine, etc., we find that call-girl rackets are flourishing in metros as well as small towns. Prostitution is most common in Thailand and China where minor girls take up this profession and die very early. Money has become the need of the day for everyone. It is easy money by prostitution and therefore we find more and more cases of prostitution. Police, political leaders, judiciary, NGOs, welfare organizations inspite of best efforts are not able to combat this social evil.

'Janmat' channel on television very recently had discussion on prostitution and many prostitutes gave their comments as to how they were forced into prostitution and inspite of best efforts, could never come out of the same. They also shared their feelings that society has never accepted them and always called them 'fallen women'. The discussion was anchored by Shekhar Suman. Many people, specially males opined that prostitution should be legalized in India as has been done so in many other countries.

We all know prostitution is a curse and all of us should contribute to its eradication.

Notes

1. F. Rosen, (ed.) *Rgveda,* London, 1893, p. 123.
2. R.T.H, Griffith, trans. into English, *Ramayana,* Benaras, 1915, p. 389.
3. L. Sternbach, *Juridical Studies in Ancient Indian Law,* Delhi, 1965, p. 211.
4. B.C. Law, trans. *Mulasarvastivada,* Vol. 1, London, 1923, p. 218.
5. R. Shamasastry, *Kautiliya Arthasastram,* Mysore, 1924, p. 179.
6. Ibid., p. 123
7. Pandit Durgaprasada, (ed.) *Kamasutra of Vatsvayana,* Bombay 1900, p. 160. The sixty-four arts may be divided into eleven main groups, e.g., general education (14), domestic science (4), toilet (4), dressing (2), music and dancing (5), fine arts (8), physical culture (3), games (4), art of entertaining (4), professional training (14), pet animals (2).
8. M.N. Dutta, (English trans.) *Agni-Purana,* Calcutta, 1901, p. 230.
9. R. Shamasastry, op.cit., p. 129.
10. Ibid., p. 184.
11. L. Sternbach, op.cit., p. 208.
12. R.C. Majumdar (ed.), *The Classical Age,* BVB Vol. III, 4th Ed., Bombay, 1988, p. 573.
13. *Satrinasa yudhiyanam vesyah karu* s *kusilavah dandavrdahasca janiyuis saucasaucam atandritah,* R. Shamasastry, op. cit., p. 249.
14. M.N. Dutta, op. cit., p. 239.
15. A. Thakur (ed.), *The Comprehensive History of Bihar,* Vol. 1, Part-1, Patna, 1974, p. 655.
16. *Vidha-vanyanga-kanya-pravrajita dandapratikarinibhl rupajiva-matrkabhir vrddhara-jadasibhir vyuparatopasthana-devadasibhisca kartayet,* R. Shamasastry, op. cit., p. 113.
17. *Ganikjaputram rangopajivinasca mukhyan nispadayeyuh sarva-talavacaranahca,* Ibid., p. 124.
18. *Ganika bhasana apaharato stagunodandah,* Ibid., p. 125.
19. *Nispatitapretayor duhita bhagini va kutumbam bhareta. Tan mata va pratiganikam sthapayet tasam abhave raja nasets* – when a ganika goes abroad or dies, the daughter or sister should get the household or the mother shall give a substitute ganika. In the absence of them the king should take it. Ibid., p. 192.

20. L. Sastri Panasikar (9th ed.) *Mitaksara* of Vijnanesvara, (4th ed.), Bombay, 1936 *"Yada tu sulkam grhitva svasthapi arthapatim necchati toda dvigunam sulkam dadyat"*.
21. R. Shamasastry, op. cit., p. 124.
22. *Jataka* – (ed.) v. Fausboll, Vol. 11, p. 330, London, 1877-97.
23. Ibid., Vol. V, p. 452.
24. *Dhammapada* Commentary – English trans. (Buddhist Legends by E.W. Burligame, 3 Vol., Cambridge 1921. pp. 106-109.).
25. AIR 1997 (SC) 3021.

5

Genocide in International Law and Indian State Practice

A Comparative Panorama

B.C. NIRMAL

Genocide may be a new name, but the thing itself is as old as humanity.[1] History is full of horrendous accounts of mass killings by governments of their own peoples, acts of extermination of enemies and brutalities heaped on the adversaries and their people in all ages and all places of the globe. Instances of genocide from antiquity are recorded in Homer's writings. Examples of extermination of adversaries also include large scale destruction and devastation of adversary cities and towns at the hands of Assuranasiripal-II (853-859 B.C.), massacre of rebel Babylon in 689 B.C., destruction of Thebes in 668-622 B.C. and conquest of Babylon (648 B.C.). The numerous slaughter stories of conquered people in the Old Testament testify the fact that even Jews resorted to policy of extermination and genocide when they were in power. The other instances of genocide from the past include the deliberate mass extermination of Christians by the imperial government of Rome, the complete extermination of Tasmanian aborigines by White Australians, the killing of the Caribbean Arawak Indians by Columbus, of the Aztec of Mexico by Cortez, of the Incas of Peru by Pizzaro and of other Indian tribes, the infamous massacres committed by Chenghiz Khan and his successors over a period of about 200 years involving killings of millions of Arabs, Prussians and others. Persecution and mass killings of Armenians in Turkey in 1915, genocidal massacres committed in the name of ideology in the old USSR and mass killings of people in Ukraine in a government sponsored and engineered famine crime are some of the instances of the crimes of genocide from the preceding century. Thus, the history of genocide is as old as the civilization itself. It is believed that acts of genocide along with epidemics or natural disasters or independently of these and other factors such as war were responsible for the disappearance of some of the civilizations in many parts of the world.

At all periods of history genocide had inflicted great losses on humanity. It is more reprehensible and catastrophic than wars and has caused four times more deaths than all the wars in history. According to Rummel about 40 million people were killed in all the wars and 13 million killed in genocides up to the beginning of the 20th century and around 37 million were killed in wars and 170 million killed in genocide during the 20th century. Man's genocidal tendencies along with weapons of mass destruction threaten the very existence of *Homo sapiens* as species. While the international community has responded to the challenges of prevention and punishment of genocide by recognizing genocide as a crime under international law, which is contrary to the spirit and aims of the United Nations and by developing appropriate normative and institutional responses, the second half of the preceding century witnessed at least 25 instances of genocide and the UN could do little to control, let alone prevent. What is worrisome is the commission of the crime of genocide despite the recognition of prohibition against genocide as *jus cogens* under international law and the obligation of each state to prevent and punish the crimes of genocide.

Mass killing and ethnic cleansing of Croats and Bosnian Muslims in the Serb dominated areas in Croatia and Bosnia and Herzegovina in 1991-92 and mass killing and expulsion of ethnic Albanians from Kosovo during 1998-99 and massacre of over 8,000

Tutsis in Rwanda in 1994 and other cases of genocide from other parts of the world brought into sharp focus the inadequacies of the existing international law instruments and the United Nations system in averting genocide and protecting the victims of genocide. While the indictment and trial of perpetrators of crimes against humanity in former Yugoslavia and Rwanda, the adoption of the Rome Statute and operationalization of the International Criminal Court and the establishment of special prosecution institutions in several states (such as Ethiopia, Rwanda and Uganda) are certainly positive developments towards the prosecution and punishment of the perpetrators of the crimes of genocide and crimes against humanity, they are apparently not enough to combat and eliminate the crime of genocide. Besides complementing international efforts to deal with the problem of genocide with national efforts, particularly the enactment of anti-genocide laws, governments of nation states should work together for development of an integrated early warning and early response system. There is also an urgent need to undertake a systematic review of existing international conventions and institutional mechanisms and strengthen them further in order to liberate mankind from the odious scourge of genocide. Against this background, this essay discusses and examines the efficacy of international rules relating to genocide and suggests measures for improving their implementation and enforcement. An attempt is also made hereunder to give a brief account of the Indian state practice on the subject and underline the need of enacting a specific legislation on prevention and control of genocide.

Meaning and Definition of Genocide

The term 'genocide' was for the first time coined by Raphael Lemkin in his book *Axis Rule in Occupied Europe* published during Second World War.[2] It is derived from the Greek word '*genos*' (race) and Latin word '*cide*' (killing). Thus "genocide is an act which is committed in order to exterminate fully or partially, a national, ethnical, social or religious group". In other words, genocide is the deliberate and systematic extermination of an ethnic or national group. According to Chalk "genocide is a form of one-sided mass killing in which a state or other authority intends to destroy a group".[3] Although genocide has now a specific connotation in modern international law different from one attributed to it by Lemkin, his pioneering study has played a significant role in increasing an understanding of 'genocide' and its various dimensions. Under his definition, genocide was the coordinated and planned annihilation by variety of actions aimed at undermining the foundations essential to the survival of the group as a group. He conceived of genocide as a "composite of different acts of persecution or destruction". In his view not only attacks on political and social institutions, culture, language, national feelings, religion and the economic existence of the group but even ruthless acts that undermine the liberty, dignity and personal security of members of a group would constitute genocide provided they contributed to weakening the viability of the group. In his opinion, acts of the state involving destruction of a culture without the killing of its bearers would also qualify as genocide. In his study Lemkin classified actual cases of genocide on the basis of the intent of the perpetrator under three categories: (i) genocide related to wars of extermination in antiquity and the middle ages; (ii) cultural genocide characterized by the destruction of a culture without an attempt to physically destroying its bearers, and (iii) Nazi-style genocide which combined ancient and modern forms of genocide.

In its first resolution on the subject the UN General Assembly significantly narrowed Lemkin's definition of genocide by downplaying ethnocide as one of its components, but broadened the definition by adding a new category of victims – political and other groups to Lemkin's list.[4] The General Assembly's definition was based on the notion of denial of the right of existence of entire human groups. But subsequently, political and social groups were excluded from the definition of genocide enshrined in Article II of the Genocide Convention.[5] As despite its various omissions and imperfections, this definition has been retained in subsequent international instruments like the Statutes of Ad-hoc Tribunals and the Rome Statute,[6] a brief discussion of its characteristics and essentials becomes necessary.

Article II of the Genocide Convention defines genocide as any of the following acts committed with intent to destroy, in whole or part, a national, ethnical, social or religious group, as such: (a) Killing members of the group; (b) Causing serious bodily or mental harms to members of the group; (c) Deliberately inflicting on the group conditions of life calculated to bring about its physical destruction in whole or part; (d) Imposing measures intended to prevent births within the group; (e) Forcibly transferring children of the group to another groups. Several points need to be noted here. First, the presence of the specific intent to destroy the group in question in whole or in part is a critical element of genocide.[7] It is this element which distinguishes genocide from extermination or mass murder. In genocide acts of killing are directed against groups defined in terms of nationality, ethnicity, or religion. Second, the crime of genocide involves a wide range of actions, including not only deprivation of life but also the prevention of life (abortion and sterilization) devices considerably endangering life and health (artificial death in special camps), deliberate separation of families for depopulation purposes and so forth. Third, the definition makes no distinction between lethal and non-lethal attacks on members of a target group; killing members of the group and deliberately inflicting conditions of life calculated to bring about its physical destruction in whole or in a part are co-mingled in the definition with "causing mental harm to members of the groups" and "forcibly transferring children of the group to another group". Fourth, the groups protected do not include political or social groups.[8] Fifth, cultural genocide does not expressly feature under this definition.[9] It is only when one of the four protected groups is denied its right to exist in the future by means of the forcible transfer of children to another group that some protection is accorded to the cultural identity of the group and to its right to continued cultural existence under the system of the Genocide Convention.

In view of the requirement of the existence of a specific intent to destroy, in whole or in part, a national, ethnical, racial or religious group to sustain the charge of genocide many cases of large scale massacre or mass killing are likely to go unpunished as it is possible for states to deny genocidal activity by noting that such intent was in fact absent.

The exclusion of political and social groups from the protection of the Genocide Convention is its another blind spot. Governments have exploited this omission in the Convention definition with grave human consequences for the victims of extensive killing programmes. Scholars like Pieter N. Drost have rejected the notion that the victims of genocide are limited to racial, religious, national and ethnic groups and instead have suggested that the UN redefine genocide to cover the deliberate destruction of physical life of individual human being by reason of his/her membership of any human collectively as such. In the same vein, Whitaker recommended expanding the definition of genocide in the Genocide Convention to protect political, economic and social groups. In the era of ideology he observed, "people are killed for ideological reasons". In Hermitz's view genocide is "a structural and systematic destruction of innocent people" by a state's bureaucratic apparatus.

Social scientist, Jessie Bernard viewed genocide as the ultimate weapon for resolving a conflict in a racial and ethnic society. For Vahhan Dadrian, genocide is a successful attempt by a dominant group, vested with normal authority and/or with preponderant access to the overall resources of power, to reduce by coercion or lethal violence the member of a minority group. In the eyes of the perpetrator the ultimate extermination of the minority group is desirable and useful and the vulnerability of the latter is a major factor contributing to decision for genocide. Israel Charry too has set aside the UN definition and like Hermitz and Dadiran has proffered a new definition of genocide which equates genocide with the mass killing of substantial number of human beings under conditions of the essential defenseless and helplessness of the victims. The only caveat in his definition is the killing of the enemy military forces that does not amount to genocide. The concept of genocide, according to Steven T. Katz, applies only when there is an actualized intent, however successfully carried out to physically destroy an entire group and such a group is defined by perpetrators. For Barbara Harp and R. Gurr, genocide and politicides are the promotion and execution of policies by a state or its agents which result in the deaths of a substantial portion of a group.

In view of the above discussion it is clear that the UN definition of genocide is not only narrow but is deficient in various respects. Yet, this definition has been retained in the Statutes of Yugoslavia, and Rwanda tribunals and the Rome Statute. While the International Criminal Court is yet to develop its jurisprudence on the definition of genocide, ad-hoc Tribunals have refined the definition of genocide and clarified its essential elements. Several points need to be noted here with regard to major contributions of these tribunals. First, ethnic cleansing, sexual violence and rape may amount to genocide, when committed with the necessary specific intent to commit genocide.[10] Second, genocide may be committed by omission as well as by acts.[11] Third, sexual mutilation, enforced sterilization, forced birth control, forced separation of males and females, prohibition of marriages are examples of measures intended to prevent births within the group. Fourth, forcible transfer of children from one group to another means not only indirect action of forcible physical transfer, but any act or threat of trauma which would lead to the forcible transfer of all children from one group to another. Fifth, the subjection of a group to a subsistence diet, the systematic expulsion from their homes and the deprivation of essential medical supplies below a minimum vital standards are examples of the deliberate infliction on the group of conditions if they are calculated to bring about its destruction in whole or in part, which is an act enumerated in Article II-C of the Genocide Convention. Sixth, considering the difficulties in establishing the critical element of intention recourse may be had in the absence of confessions to inferences from facts.[12] And finally, while in *Akayesu*, the trial Chamber of the Rwanda Tribunal leaned towards the objective definition of membership of groups,[13] the importance of subjective elements has been emphasized in other cases.[14] By making gradual but progressive shift from an objective position towards a subjective approach these tribunals have made a significant departure from some notable precedents created by the World Court in *Minorities in Upper Silesia Case*[15] and *Nottebohm Case.*[16] This shift in approach is welcome for it taking into account the particular political, social and cultural context and also giving more weight to the perception of the perpetrators of the crime of genocide than the authentic ethnicity of the victims.[17]

As noted earlier, genocide is distinguishable from extermination. The former has prohibitely high standard of *mensrea* (criminal intention) than the latter and further its scope of applicability is limited. This is explained in *Krstic* case:[18]

> Extermination distinguishes itself from the crime of genocide by the fact that the targeted population does not necessarily have any common national, ethnical, social or religious characteristic, and that it also covers situations where some members of a group are killed, while others are spared. For this reason, extermination may be... when the crime is directed against an entire group of individuals even though no discriminatory intent nor intention to destroy the group as such on national, ethnical, racial or religious has been demonstrated, or where the targeted population does not share any common national, ethnical, social or religious characteristics.

Genocide: An International Crime

Genocide is a heinous crime and as such has been condemned by the civilized world. Horrors of the holocaust and brutalities heaped on 6 million Jews and their massacre outraged the conscience of the humankind to such a great extent that the UN. General Assembly by its Resolution 96(l) of 11 December 1946 declared genocide to be a crime under international law, contrary to the spirit and aims of the United Nations and adopted two years later on 9 December 1948, Convention on the Prevention and Punishment of the Crime of Genocide, i.e., one day before the adoption of the international *Magna Carta* of Human Rights in the form of the Universal Declaration of Human Rights, in "order to liberate mankind from such odious scourge". Article I of the Convention confirms that, "genocide, whether committed in time of peace or in time of war is a crime under international law".

It is important to note here that although the Nuremberg Charter, 1945 did not expressly use the term 'genocide', the definition of the crimes against peace covered many acts today regarded as constituting genocide. And the indictment of the defendants expressly charged them with the genocide, and the prosecution used the term during the proceedings. The definition of Crimes against Humanity under Article 6 of the Nuremberg

Tribunal Charter referred to "persecutions on political, racial or religious grounds". Article 6(a) of the London Charter defined crimes against humanity as murder, extermination, enslavement, deportation and other inhuman acts committed against civilian population before or during the war.

But as we have seen earlier, genocide has certain specific characteristics which distinguishes it from mass killing or extermination or from other crimes. As noted by the International Court of Justice in the *Genocide Case*, the crime of genocide "shocks the conscience of mankind, results in great losses to humanity ... and is contrary to moral law and to the spirit and aims of the United Nations".[19] For this reason whether it is committed in time of peace or in time of war it is equally reprehensible and condemnable and Article III of the Genocide Convention makes not only genocide but even conspiracy or attempt to commit genocide; complicity in genocide and direct and public incitement to commit genocide punishable. All those who commit genocide or any of the other acts enumerated in Article III shall be punished irrespective of their official position. Article V imposes an obligation on the contracting parties to enact, in accordance with their respective constitutions, the necessary legislation to give effect to the provisions of the present Convention, and, in particular to provide effective penalties for persons guilty of genocide and the other acts enumerated in Article III. In the fulfilment of this obligation a number of countries have made genocide punishable under their respective penal laws.[20]

The Genocide Convention also provides in Article VI that "persons charged with genocide or, any of the other acts enumerated in Article III shall be tried by a competent tribunal of the state in the territory of which the act was committed". George Schwarzenberger, however, states: "Hardly any of these alleged crimes have been committed spontaneously by irresponsible individuals. Yet the whole Convention is based on the assumption of virtuous governments and criminal individuals, a reversion of the truth in proportion to the degree of totalitarianism and nationalism practised in any country". In any event even if this assumption were correct, the criminal law of every civilized state would have provided sufficiently against any individual act of the kind, which are enumerated in the Convention. While there is much substance in this argument, the accused of genocide have been tried and convicted by domestic courts of a number of countries such as Ethiopia, Bolivia, Colombia, Haiti, Austria, Israel, Denmark. Rwanda's national courts have also convicted some members of the Hutu ethnic group of genocide under the local law. In this context it is important to note that trials for the crime of genocide by the national courts are often only known in the country or region where they occur. In some cases the accused persons were prosecuted for international crimes of genocide which have been incorporated into domestic law. In other cases, the accused were prosecuted for domestic offences such as murder because of non-incorporation of international crimes into domestic law even though that nation had ratified the Genocide Convention. The importance of these trials needs not to be underestimated because international tribunals are designed to judge only the most serious cases of genocide. Further, in many cases it may be preferable for a competent national tribunal to decide such a case. It must be recognized that domestic trials of perpetrators of the crime of genocide can play a crucial role in establishing legal justice in the aftermath of such horrific and heinous crimes. For these reasons it is necessary that states besides ratifying the Convention should incorporate its provisions into their domestic law by enacting a suitable legislation on genocide. This is all the more necessary in view of the fact that most perpetrators of genocide never stand trial for their crimes.

Genocide is such a serious crime that for the purpose of extradition it is not to be considered as a political crime. Article VII provides: "Genocide and the other acts enumerated in Article III shall not be considered as political crimes for the purpose of extradition. The Contracting Parties pledge themselves in such cases to grant extradition in accordance with their laws and treaties in force".

As aptly observed by the International Court of Justice in the *Bosnia* Case,[21] 'it was followed from the object and purpose of the Genocide Convention that the rights and obligations contained therein were rights and obligations *erga omnes* and that the obligation upon each state to prevent and punish the crime of genocide was not dependent upon the type of conflict involved in the particular situation (whether international or domestic), and it was not territorially limited by the Convention".[22] The type of state responsibility envisaged under Article IX of the Convention does not contain any clause the effect or object of which is to limit the scope of its jurisdiction *ratione temporis* so as to exclude events prior to a particular date.[23] Further, the Convention provides for the submission of dispute regarding its interpretation and application to the International Court of Justice. But this provision has been invoked only once in the entire history of this important treaty. In the case concerning *Application of the Convention on the Prevention and Punishment of the Crime of Genocide* (*Bosnia and Herzegovina* v. *Yugoslavia, Serbia and Montenegro*), Bosnia claimed that Yugoslavia had violated the Genocide Convention.[24] The Court in its order of 8 April 1993 on the request for the Indication of Provisional Measures held that Article IX of the Convention provided a valid jurisdictional basis.[25] The Court called upon both parties not to take any action that might aggravate or extend the dispute over the prevention and punishment of the crime of genocide. The Court requested the Government of Yugoslavia to take all measures within its power to prevent commission of the crime of genocide. The Yugoslav government was specifically called upon to ensure that "any military, paramilitary or irregular armed units which may be directed or supported by it, as well as any organizations and persons which may be subject to its control, direction or influence do not commit any acts of genocide".[26] The Court subsequently reaffirmed these provisional measures in its Order of Provisional Measures of 13 September 1993 as measures which should be "immediately and effectively implemented".[27] In a recent judgment the International Court of Justice has ruled that although what occurred in 1995 in Srebernica was indeed an act of genocide, the Serbian State was not directly complication in it. The decision is ambivalent and unfortunate and raises several larger issues relating to prevention and punishment of the crime of genocide. It is more so because Slebodan Milosevic's death deprived the ICTY of the possibility of ruling in the responsibility.[28]

The first time an international trial for genocide took place in Europe when on 6 July, 1998 the Yugoslav Tribunal began the trial of a Bosnian Serb on the charge of genocide. But it came to an abrupt halt when the defendant died in his cell of an apparent heart attack. The Rwanda Tribunal is also trying dozens of defendants on charges of genocide. A former prime minister of Rwanda pleaded guilty to charges of genocide. The Tribunal has also found a Mayor in Rwanda guilty of genocide.

Under the Rome Statute the International Criminal Court (ICC)[29] has jurisdiction over the crime of genocide. But the exclusion of political, social or professional groups from the definition of genocide in Article VI and the requirement of proof of a specific intent to destroy a group in whole or in part, besides an intent to commit any of the acts enumerated in the Article will considerably restrict the ICC's jurisdiction in the matter. So while the establishment and operationalization of the Court is a significant step in the march towards universal respect for human rights and the rule of law, to expect that the Court will prosecute and punish an increasingly higher number of perpetrators of the crimes of genocide and crimes against humanity is to ignore several limitations that the Rome Statute has imposed on the Court. As we have noted elsewhere, the existence of several preconditions for the exercise of jurisdiction coupled with the principle of complementarity, rules of admissibility and limited *ratione materiae* and *ratione temporis* of the court are severe limitations on the working of the court.[30] In addition, the challenges facing the Court are far greater than its predecessors encountered not only because unlike its predecessors, it is an *ex ante* and not *ex post* tribunal but also due to the fact that it has no police force of its own, no power of enforcement and no soldiers. So, for its success it depends not only on the effective, speedy, unreserved and ongoing cooperation of states parties to the Rome Statute but also on the support and active cooperation of the United Nations, regional institutions like African Union and even the goodwill of the non-party states like the United States.[31]

In view of the foregoing, to guarantee lasting respect for and the enforcement of international justice states should not only extend their full support to the ICC but also strengthen their national criminal justice systems. Strengthening national justice system for this purpose is in fact an overriding obligation of every state under international law. If domestic law and courts are equipped enough to prosecute and punish the perpetrators of the most serious crimes of concern to the international community, there will remain very little need for trials by an international tribunal. This is indeed the very philosophy of the Rome Statute and this is what the ICC is expecting states to do.

Genocide has been declared to be a crime in Article 19 of the Draft Code of Crimes against Peace and Security of Mankind. As for state responsibility for the commission of the crime of genocide, ILC draft Articles on State Responsibility, 2001 no longer provide for the concept of 'state crimes'. However, Draft Article 40 refers to international responsibility of state for a serious breach of an obligation arising under a peremptory norm of international law.[32] A breach is to be considered serious if it involves a 'gross or systematic failure'. Article 41 deals with the particular consequences of such a serious breach and imposes a duty on states to cooperate to bring the serious breaches to an end through lawful means. Further, there is also the duty of non-recognition of the situation 'created' by such a serious breach and not to render aid or assistance in maintaining the situation. Since prohibition of genocide is recognized as an peremptory norm of international law, these provisions will be of crucial importance in respect of the international responsibility of the state in a serious breach of it. Draft Article 49 which deals with counter-measures provides that such measures could be taken only to induce the responsible state to comply with the obligation and not as a measure to punish or seek vengeance.

Genocide as A Human Rights Problem

Genocide is a most serious and grave violation of a series of human rights and fundamental freedoms set forth in the Universal Declaration of Human Rights, 1948; Human Rights Covenants, 1966, the Torture Convention, 1984, the Racial Discrimination Convention, 1965, the Convention on the Elimination of All Forms of Discrimination Against Women, 1979, Convention on the Rights of the Child, 1989 and regional human rights treaties and declarations.[33] Genocide involving killing being a violation of the right to life is of very serious nature in view of the special and protected place of the right to life in the human rights jurisprudence. To use the words of the Commission on Human Rights, "right to life is the most fundamental of all rights".[34] According to Manfred Nowak, "the right to life has properly been characterized as the supreme human right since without effective guarantee of this right, all other rights of human being would be devoid of meaning".[35] This is a non-derogable right "having a peremptory character at all times, circumstances and situations".[36] Genocide may also involve violations of freedom from torture, freedom of thought, conscience and religion and freedom from slavery and servitude. Interestingly, these rights also have the character of *juscogens*.

While genocide is a serious international crime independent of war crimes and crimes against humanity, many of the constituent elements of genocide like willfully killing, torture or inhuman treatment, willfully causing grave suffering, or serious injury to body or health, unlawful deportation or transfer, or unlawful confinement of protected persons when committed in time of war will constitute grave breaches under the Geneva Conventions, 1949 to be governed by the rules of international humanitarian law. Accordingly, even when these acts do not constitute genocide, their perpetrators may be tried as war criminals. Murder, extermination or mass killing when committed as part of a widespread or systematic attack directed against any civilian population with knowledge may amount to crimes against humanity.

In view of the foregoing prevention of genocide and mass violence should become a key task for the UN. Human Rights Council and other international human rights bodies in the present century.[37] Global monitoring of gross human rights violations and integrated and coordinated efforts of all human rights bodies are of crucial importance in any international efforts to combat and eliminate the menace of genocide and other forms of mass murder. As the task is a stupendous one, it cannot be accomplished without an active involvement of NGOs, civil society institutions and media. Human Rights Watch, Amnesty International and NGOs coalitions should develop a rapid and broad system for protection of possible victims in conflict areas. Amnesty International and other similar bodies should also accord top priority to genocide prevention and make meaningful interventions in monitoring risk areas and protecting minorities at risk of extermination.

There is also an urgent need to develop an integrated early warning and early response system to genocide. A new mechanism for rapid reaction in cases of genocide in the form of red genocide alert should be established within the UN Secretariat. As the development of an early system requires identification and specification of indicators of genocide, a working theory about the genocidal process on the basis of the comprehensive study of the cases of genocide will be necessary. Institutes of peace research may play an important role in this regard by undertaking research projects on violence prevention and confidence building measures. The international community can learn many lessons from the past traumatic experiences of genocide as well as from relevant experience of genocide free regions of the world.

It has been observed that the identification of some people as 'us' und hence as human and of others as 'them' and therefore to be dehumanized plays a decisive role in the formation of a genocide plan and its eventual execution. Hence, factors responsible for this common human tendency need to be identified and addressed. Steps should also be taken for promoting amity, goodwill, religious tolerance and communal harmony among people should be given top priority. It is humbly submitted that in order to avert the commission of the crime of genocide in the future, United Nations and national governments should take all possible steps for the promotion of democratization, respect for basic human rights and minority rights, rule of law and good governance.

Indian State Practice

India's tradition in international law and human rights dates back to ancient times. Its overall record as a torch-bearer in enhancing the ideas and principles of international law has been very much impressive. The role it has been playing in the pre-colonial era and in the post-independent phase in promoting the rule of law in international relations has been remarkable. Its commitment to the purposes and principles of the UN. Charter and its sustained efforts to promote multilateralism and create a universal world order are well known. All these are in accord with the constitutional mandate which requires the state to foster respect for international law and treaty obligations.[38] Consistent with its adherence to the rule of law and respect for human rights and fundamental freedoms, India has played an active role in the conclusion of human rights treaties, covenants and conventions and taken a number of legislative, administrative and other measures to give effect to the provisions of these treaties. In addition to its obligations under human rights treaties to which it is a party the sovereign, democratic, socialist and secular Indian Republic is mandated by its own Constitution to promote and protect human rights and fundamental freedoms guaranteed under Part III of the Constitution. As the crime of genocide involves violations of a series of human rights including the right to life, the state is duty bound to save the lives, property and dignity of individuals living within its jurisdiction without discrimination as to race, religion, sex, language, political opinion, descent or status, from different categories of crimes including international crimes like genocide, war crimes and crimes against humanity.

In this context it is also important to note that India is a party to the Genocide Convention, 1948 and as such is under a treaty obligation to prevent and punish the acts of genocide. As already noted, the Convention makes all persons committing genocide punishable whether they are constitutionally responsible rulers, public officials or private individuals. It is also to be recognized that the *jus cogens* obligations outlawing genocide and rules of customary international on the subject are not only internationally binding on India but may also be deemed to be incorporated in our domestic jurisprudence.

Despite the above mentioned constitutional and international obligations, India forgot the Genocide Convention after its ratification in 1953 and did not care since then to enact a specific legislation to prevent and punish genocide which is in a clear violation of Article V of the Convention. It has made reservations to Article IX which runs as follows: “Disputes between the contracting parties relating to the interpretation, application or fulfilment of the present Convention, including those relating to the responsibility of a state for genocide or for any of the other acts enumerated in Article II, shall be submitted to the International Court of Justice at the request of any of the parties to the dispute.”

It is true that the state is already armed with a plethora of criminal legislations to deal with mass killing and acts enumerated in Article III of the Convention which when committed against an ethnical, racial or religious group in certain circumstances will tantamount to genocide but existing laws hardly capture the seriousness and gravity of the crime of genocide, especially horrors, brutalities and an intent to destroy, in whole or in part of a target group. As we have seen, genocide is the most serious crime of concern to the international community as a whole and threatens the peace, security and well-being of the world. Hence, laws designed to deal with traditional crimes will not be adequate to prevent and punish the acts of genocide. To say is not to deny that the criminal justice system seems to be by and large effective to deal with crimes whether they are serious or minor provided it is allowed to work without any interference from the ruling party and persons at the helm of affairs. But what happened in Gujarat and in similar carnage elsewhere is a great reminder that all is not well with our criminal justice system and if people, civil society institutions and human rights institutions do not remain continuously vigilant, the administration and even the judicial system is susceptible to be hijacked by the politicians and vested interests for serving their selfish ends. That this is not just a mere possibility but has already occurred on a few occasions requires a firm resolve on the part of the government and the people alike not to allow the same to happen in the future.

It must be recognized that, what happened in Gujarat and in similar carnage elsewhere, earlier, were not merely a matter of law and order, each of these were all organized crimes targeted against targeted groups, the state governments either actively conniving with the minority group, or remaining as bystanders, resulting in a total collapse of the rule of law and the justice system altogether. In a severe indictment of the police, public prosecutor, and the state government, the trial court, the High Court, the Apex Court also noted this distressing fact in the *Zahira Sheikh Case* and lamented that the justice delivery system was being taken for a ride and utterly allowed to be abused, misused and mutilated by subterfuge.[39] The Court, while giving a warning against the hijacking of the judicial system at the behest of the state government observed: "Criminal trials should not be reduced to mock trials or shadow or fixed trials. Judicial criminal administration system must be kept clean and beyond the reach of whimsical political will or agendas and properly insulated from discriminatory standards or yardsticks of the type prohibited by the mandate of the Constitution."[40]

It is gratifying to note that even in those cases where a total collapse of the rule of law and the judicial system occurred, the state governments, the politicians and the police were made accountable as a result of the tenacity of human rights groups, the National Human Rights Commission, NGOs and most significantly the Supreme Court of India. But this fact does not dispense with the need of a dispassionate and objective nationwide debate on the essential elements of an effective judicial system after taking into account the public perception about its performance and nature and direction of needed reforms in the judicial system to enable it to meet the needs and challenges of times. In the *Zahira Sheikh Case* the Apex Court sought to provide some relief to the victims by transferring the trial of the case to a Mumbai court. But the problem of hijacking of the judicial system in the cases of mass killings and programmes cannot be dealt with by the transfer of cases from one state to another alone. What is needed, therefore, is strengthening of the criminal justice through the adoption of a series of corrective and remedial measures. The government will do well to learn lessons from the traumatic events of the past. It is true that the public at large continues to hold our judiciary in high esteem and the system has served us well over the last five decades. At the same time it is equally fair to state that in the public perception the judicial system has been of late showing signs of stress and today, and doubts are being raised by a section of society about the efficiency and effectiveness of the system.

Any national strategy regarding the prevention and punishment of genocide should also take into account the public perception of the Indian police force as an organization to be a violator of human rights.[41] While it would be wrong to consider every personnel of the force consisting of nearly of 2.2 million people violators of human rights it would also be unfair to ignore the public perception in this regard altogether. The Apex Court has also time and again expressed grave concern by persons who are supposed to be the protectors of the citizens but commit violence under the shield of uniform and authority in the four walls of a police station or lock up, the victims being totally helpless. As the Apex Court observed in *D.K. Basu's Case*, experience shows that worst violations of human rights take place during the course of investigation, when the police with a view to secure evidence or confession often resorts to third degree methods including torture.[42] The increasing incidence of torture and deaths in custody has assumed such alarming proportions that it is affecting the credibility of the rule of law and the administration of criminal justice. In this distressing scenario the UPA government's policy to prevent the Godhra and post-Godhra type riots by enacting a new law on communal violence, especially when not less than 18 legislations on the subject are already adorning the statute book, will not be enough. While enacting a new legislation on the communal violence is welcome, Parliament should go one step further and enact a legislation on genocide and crimes against humanity. There is also an urgent need to adopt measures to insulate police machinery from political/executive interference to make it more efficient and effective and to strengthen and preserve the rule of law.[43]

The establishment and operationalization of the International Criminal Court also provides an immediate and appropriate occasion for us to consider the need of enacting a legislation on genocide and crimes against humanity. It is high time that the Government of India reconsider its position on the ICC and change its negative attitude towards it. As more than 100 states have already acceded to the ICC statute, the reluctance on the part of India to join the Court is bewildering. As we have argued elsewhere, familiar accusations directed against and criticisms of the ICC seem to be exaggerated and without much firm foundation. While it is for the Government of India to take appropriate decision on the accession of the ICC Statute, it should be based on sound policy considerations and in conformity with its past glorious record as a respector of international rule of law, multilateralism and its significant contribution to the codification and progressive development of international law. Accession or no accession, India is duty bound to prosecute the perpetrators of the crime of genocide to the best of its ability by reforming and strengthening its national criminal justice system.

Conclusion

Core international crimes like genocide threaten the peace, security and well-being of the world. To put an end of impunity for the perpetrators of acts of genocide and thus to contribute to their prevention international efforts should be complemented by reforming and strengthening of national criminal justice systems. UN Human Rights Council and other human rights bodies should coordinate and integrate their efforts towards the prevention of extermination, genocide and mass murders. Huttington's Clash of Civilizations Theory and similar other ideas which have tendency to widen cultural gap between different parts of the world and different civilizations should be discouraged and projects like 'The Alliance of Civilizations' need to be strengthened further. Every government must do more to outlaw violent religious intolerance and xenophobia. This will require extensive education and development programmes, a stepped-up inter-faith dialogue, more open societies, cultural networking, etc. Conscious and concerted efforts are also needed to tackle the problems of poverty, illiteracy, WMD proliferation. The prohibition of inhuman ideologies and terrorism, an early warning system and rapid response system to genocide may be established within the UN Secretariat. Governments must do more to promote an apt management of religious and ethnic conflicts to prevent them from evolving into open hostilities. Genocide constitutes *juscogens* and creates obligations *erga omnes* for member states of the international community. Consistent with the current global trends to deal with the problem of genocide India should also enact a legislation on genocide and crimes against humanity.

Notes

1. Frank Chalk, *History and Sociology of Genocide* (1990).
2. R. Lemkin, *Axis Rule in Occupied Europe* (1944).
3. Chalk, n.1. at p. 23.
4. UN General Assembly Resolution 96(1), 11 December, 1946.
5. UNGA Res. 260 A(III) of 9 December 1948, N. Robinson, *The Genocide Convention* 1960. For scholarly discussions on genocide in international law, see: L. Kuper, *Genocide* (1981), B. Whitaker, *Revised and Updated Report on the Question of Prevention and Punishment of the Crime of Genocide*, 1985, E/CN 4/sub.2/1985/6; W. Schabas, *Genocide in International Law* (2000); Antonio Cassese, *International Criminal Law* (2003), pp. 96-109.
6. ICTY Statute, (Article 4), ICTR Statute (Article 2), ICC Statute (Article 6).
7. States may deny genocide activity by arguing that the relevant intent to destroy in whole or in part was absent. See, Kuper, n. 5, at pp. 32-35. N. Ruhasyankika, *Study on the Question of the Prevention and Punishment of the Crime of Genocide*, 1978, E/CN.U/Sub.2/416, p. 25.
8. Kuper, n. 5, at pp. 25-30; Robinson, n. 5, at p. 59, Ruhashyankika, n. 7, at p. 21.
9. Kuper, n. 5, at p. 31, Robinson, n. 5, p. 64.
10. *The Akayesu Case*, ICTR – 96 – 4 – T, para 731.
11. *The Kambanda Case*, ICTR – 97 – 23 – S, para 39.
12. See The *Jelisic Case*, IT – 95-10, para 66 (importance of the specific intent), The *Akayesu Case*, ICTR-96-4-T, 1998 para 523. With regard to relevant facts, see *Kayishema and Ruzindana* case, ICTR – 95 – 1 – 7, para 93.
13. *The Akayesu Case*, ICTR-96-4T, paras 511-515.
14. See, e.g. *Kayishema and Ruzindana Case*, ICTR-95-I-T, para 67 and *Rutaganda*, ICTR-96-3-T.
15. P.C.I.J. Series A, No. 12.
16. *Nottebohm* (*Liechtenstein* v. *Guatemala*), (Merits) (1955) ICJ Reports, p. 4.
17. G. Verdirame, "The Genocide Definition in The Jurisprudence of the Ad Hoc Tribunals", *ICLQ*, 49 (2000), 578, at pp. 588-94.
18. ICTY, Trial Chamber, decision of 2 Aug. 2001 Case No. IT-98-33-T. In the case the Trial Chamber has made a considerable contribution

in various respects to the definition of *mens rea* as well as *actus reus* of genocide.

19. ICJ Reports, 1951, pp. 5, 23.
20. To mention a few of them are Canada, Romania, Bolivia, Yugoslavia (now defunct), Ivory Coast, Ethiopia, Ghana, Rwanda, Seychelles, Antigua and Barbuda, Bardados, Tuvalu, Albania, Austria, Belarus, Bosnia-Herzegovina, Bulgaria, Croatia, Brazia, Colombia, Cuba, Guatemala, Paraguay, El-Salvador, Panama, Mexico, Nicaragua, Czech, Denmark, France, Georgia, Hungary, Ireland, Italy, Lithuania, Poland, Luxemburg, Peru, Australia, Bahrain, Fiji, Hong Kong (China), Israel, Kirabati, Kyrgyzstan, Solomon Islands, Portugal, Spain, Russia, U.K. and Sweden.
21. ICJ Reports (Preliminary objectives) ICJ Report 1996, pp. 595, 615.
22. Ibid. at p. 616.
23. Ibid. at p. 617.
24. In the case concerning *Application of the Convention on the Prevention and Punishment of the Crime of Genocide (Bosnia and Herzegovina: Yugoslavia (Serbia and Montenegro)* Bosnia claimed that Serbia had violated the Genocide Convention, ICJ Reports, 1993, p. 3 and 325. The court in its order of 8 April 1993 on the Request for the Indication of Provisional Measures held that Article 9 of the Genocide Convention provided a valid jurisdictional basis, ICJ Reports 1993, pp. 3, 16.
25. ICJ Reports 1993, pp. 3, 18.
26. Ibid. at pp. 3, 24.
27. Ibid. at pp. 325, 350. Yugoslavia subsequently withdrew the counter-claims that it had introduced against Bosnia, while introducing an application in April 2001 for revision of the 1996 judgment. It reasoned that a new fact had appeared since that state had become a new member of the UN during 2002. See ICJ order of 10 Sept. 2001. For the court's order on the Application for Revision of the Judgment of 11 July 1996 in this case, see ICJ Reports, 2003, pp. 15, 67.
28. "Ambivalent Justice", *The Times of India*, New Delhi, Saturday, March 3, 2007.
29. See, M.H. Arsanjani, "The Rome Statute of the International Criminal Court", *AJIL* 93 (1999), pp. 22-28; Darryl Robinson, "Defining 'Crimes against Humanity' at Rome Conference", *AJIL* 93 (1999), 43; David J. Scheffer, "The United States and the International Criminal Court", *AJIL*, 93 (1999), pp. 12-18; Arsanjani and Reisman "The Law-in-Action of the International Criminal

Court", 99 (2005), 385; Hans-Peter-Kaul, "Construction Site for More Justice: The International Criminal Court After Two Years", AJIL, 99 (2005), p. 370.

29. See B.C. Nirmal, "Jurisdiction of the International Criminal Court", *ISIL Year Book of International Humanitarian and Refugee Law*, Vol. 3 (2003), pp. 116-134.
30. See B.C. Nirmal, "Crimes within the Jurisdiction of the International Criminal Court", paper presented at International Conference on Recent Trends in International Criminal Law. *ISIL*, New Delhi (2005).
31. For further details, See M.N. Shaw, *International Law* (2003), p. 720.
32. See generally, H. Steiner and P. Alston, *International Human Rights in Context* (2nd ed., 2000); A.H. Robertson and J. Merills, *Human Rights in the World* (4th ed. 1996). For study of human rights in the Indian context see B.C. Nirmal, "Ancient Indian Perspective of Human Rights and Its Relevance", *IJIL* 43 (2003) 445; Nirmal, "Human Rights and Their Derogation under the Indian Constitution", *Current Legal Issues* (2003), 1-27; Nirmal, 'Poverty and Human Rights: An Indian Context", *IJIL*, 46 (2006), pp. 187-280.
33. See para. 1 of General Comment No. 6 (16th Session) adopted by The UN Human Rights Committee on 27 July 1982, UN Doc. HRI/GEN/1 Rev. 3, 6-7.
34. See Manfred Novak, *UN Covenant on Civil and Political Rights: CCPR Commentary* (1993), p. 104.
35. See Kurt Hendel, Foreword to *The Right to Life in International Law*, edited by B.G. Ramcharan XI (1985). According to the Human Rights Committee the right to life found in Article 6 of the International Covenant on Civil and Political Rights is the "supreme right from which no derogation is permitted even in time of pubic emergency", UN Doc E.CN.4/1983/9. The UN Commission on Human Rights report on Chile (18 February 1983) stated, "The International community therefore considers the right to life in the context of *jus cogens* in international human rights law. See, Theodore S. Orlin, "The Right to Life/The Right to Die: The Rights, Their Relationship and the Jurisprudential Problems", in Orlin et al. (eds.) *The Jurisprudence of Human Rights Law: A Comparative Interpretive Approach* (2000), 73 at 75.
36. By resolution 60/251 of 15 March, 2006. the UN General Assembly has established UN Human Rights Council to replace the UN Commission on Human Rights.
37. Article 51(c) of the Indian Constitution.

38. *Zahira Habibullah H. Sheikh* v. *State of Gujarat*, 2004 Cri.L.J., 2050 at 2062 (SC).
39. Ibid.
40. A research paper, "Political and Administrative Manipulation of the Police" published in 1979 by the Bureau of Political Research and Development had warned that excessive control of the political executive and its political advisors over the police had the inherent danger of making the police a tool for subverting the process of law.
41. The violation of fundamental and human rights of citizens if generally in the nature of non-enforcement and discriminatory application of the laws with the result that the police personnel having clout are not held accountable even for blatant violations of laws and, in any case, not brought to justice for the direct violations of the rights of citizens in the form of unauthorized detentions, torture, harassment, fabrication of evidence, malicious prosecution, etc. See the averment of the petitioners in the case of *Prakash Singh and others* v. *Union of India*, (2006) 8 SCC 1.
42. *D.K. Basu* v. *State of West Bengal*, (1997) 1 SCC 416.
43. While issuing a number of directions in respect of police reform the Apex Court in *Prakash Singh and Ors*. v. *Union of India and Ors*., held: "The commitment, devotion and accountability of the police has to be only to the rule of law. The supervision and control has to be such that it ensures that the police serves the people without any regard, whatsoever, to the status and position of any person while investigating a crime or taking preventive measures. Its approach has to be service oriented, its role has to be defined so that in appropriate cases, where on account of acts of omission and commission of police, the rule of law becomes a casualty, the guilty police officers are brought to book and appropriate action is taken without any delay." (2006) 8 SCC 1, p. 12. The directions of the Apex Court pertain to establishment of State Security Commission, Police Establishment Board, Police Complaints Authority and National Security Commission, separation of investigating police from the law and order police, selection and minimum tenure of DGP and minimum tenure of IG of Police and other officers.

6

Women in Governance Through Empowerment by Reservation

An Overview

LALITA PARIHAR

The author of Indian Constitution, Dr. Ambedkar seems to have emphasized that among other things the Indian males shall have to give up prerogative of parenting and hence admit that both men and women are equal and have one principal roles that of being people. He perhaps anticipated that a day would come when women would no longer have the exclusive "right to choose" between home and the career, that both men and women would have the same option and same obligation towards themselves and the society. For the same reason chose political democracy as a means to achieve social democracy.[1] The authors of the Constitution attributed the socio-economic inequality and discrimination against Scheduled Castes, Scheduled Tribes and women to the cultural conditioning of the people which had to be addressed to make the newly born nation to progress and develop so that it can compete with the developed nations of the world. For these reason certain constitutional measures were couched in proverbial but crisp language that its enumerative in construction and composition, liable to yield calculable results. Also was a duty imposed on the legal luminaries to write appropriate postil that would weld the social reality with the constitutional objectives and guarantees? The United Nations Organization rose to the occasion and declared as late as 1986 that the world nations have a high stake in development underlining the relevance to Dr. Ambedkar's vision for his people in the 3rd millennium.

Women and Constitutional Perspective of Governance

The Constitution in its preamble declares the country to be a democracy, essence of it being equal participation of men and women in shaping the destiny of nation. The same promise is being reiterated by way of the recognition of right to life which has no meaning if bereft of dignity, unless it treads on the path of equality in matters – social, economic and political.[2] Given the demographic nature and cultural conditioning of the country, the authors of the Constitution looked at political democracy as a means to protect weaker sections like Scheduled Castes, Scheduled Tribes, women and children. It would primarily secure equal participation to both women and men not only in political process, but also in power sharing and governance of the country. As a sequel to it, the Articles 14, 15, 16, and 21 found a rightful place in the Part III which has emerged as hub of the Constitution. Also were put some major indicators in the form of objectives laid down in Articles 37-51A in Part IV of the Constitution which the states are obligated to achieve.[3] Thus was incorporated Benthamite principle to ensure greater happiness of greater number as a sole guide to built an egalitarian society.[4] At the height of it the nation is made bound to renounce practices derogatory to dignity of women. Notwithstanding these guarantees and promises women continue to remain deprived of their fair share in the governance of the country, though having excelled in education and entered into professions monopolized by men. Yet they fail to find proper share in decision-making institutions like parliament and legislatures respectively because democratic process, being based on political party system, is exclusively manipulated by men who prefer to choose a few women than to allot them a fair share in elections. Women on the other hand (Indian women) do not like to go alone and follow the Swedish model,[5] perhaps just to avoid confrontation and endanger social solidarity that may widen the gap between men women. As a result, their role in democratic process is limited to mere participation in elections and no more. They do not find berth in the committees of the parliament that generally author the policies for the country. Women are not associated with budgeting of the country either. Though women happen to be the ideal managers of the household economy and practically bear the brunt of male budgeting system yet they are ignored. This policy is equally visible in the composition and constitution of the judiciary since practicing women lawyers, not to speak about their due share in judiciary, are rarely appointed as presiding officers of the court either at central or state level. As and when masculine policies show cracks, masculine norms and cultural conditionality hits women below the belt; that too when a woman is pitched against a man like in restitution of conjugal rights,[6] guardianship,[7] etc.

Judicial Creativity and Exposition

Women are denied their due share in governance either by monopolizing professions or where they succeed to enter such professions, their stay is made difficult under normative procedures and rules. Where both fail, they are struck by masculine norms of the workplace. Notwithstanding non-representative composition of the judiciary, the courts have tirelessly been fighting gender bias. The Allahabad High Court while levelling the status of male and female nurses held that the latter need not to resign on marriage.[8] So did Orissa High Court rescue the married women district judges.[9] Lamenting about the gender bias, Justice Krishna Iyer observed "in these days of nuclear families, intercontinental marriages and unconventional behaviour one fails to understand the naked bias against the gender of species even in third century after freedom". C.B. Muthama had to bear the cross had not Supreme Court come to her rescue.[10] This policy has been for long followed in corporate sector as well. Justice Fazl Ali expressed concern regarding the policy floated by Air India requiring and air hostess to resign on first pregnancy or marriage within four years of service. The learned judge observed about it saying "such a course of action is extremely detestable and abhorrent to the notion of civilized society and is not only a cruel and callous act but also an open insult to Indian womanhood the most sacrosanct and cherished institution.[11] Where all this is absent the masculine and non-conducive environment of the workplace takes toll of women. This amply shows that there is great deal of difference between the norms of decision and the norms of conduct as the cases before the court presents only the tip of iceberg. To address, it the protagonists of female cause finally addressed this problem at the grass-root level.

Women and 73rd Amendment of the Constitution

Despite the fact that 73rd Amendment shows a serious desire of the government that women should be associated in governance and the same should be achieved at grass-root level. But there have been occasions when cover attempts are made to defeat the benign purpose of 73rd Amendment. For example the states of Uttar Pradesh, Orissa, Tamil Nadu, and Bihar deferred Panchayat elections beyond the period of five years, that a Dehradun-based NGO namely Rural Litigation Entitlement Kendra filed a PIL to attract the attention of the Apex Court in 1995 against the aforementioned states and the Union of India with regard to deferring of the Panchayat elections and successfully secured a direction against the erring states.[12] An analysis of the causes behind such an attitude on the part of states it seems has been to defeat the right of women to claim one-third share in governance in local bodies as per Article 243(D) of the Constitution. Unlike male Panches, women Pradhans and women members of the Panchayats have proved to be the dedicated workers possessing ability and vision to restructure rural India. In the states that had deferred election to Panchayats, it is found that the elected women Panches have not generated only awareness about importance of gender equality but have proved the utility of such awareness. These Panches and Pradhans worked together as a pressure group and exposed the malafides both of legislature and the executive, albeit bureaucracy.[13] In some cases they have demanded 50 per cent share of the village revenue and secured the same.[14] They have even saved the thousands of the wage earners and while doing so exposed the influence group in some of the states. In these states women Panches have succeeded to combat alcohol related violence against women by making administration to pounce into motion and close the alcohol shops.[15]

In some states, women Pradhans have introduced the community forestation schemes and changed the very texture of their villages.[16] In some states women Pradhans have been innovative to the extent that they have successfully managed to settle age-old disputes between the forest department and local population by taking resort to Alternate Dispute Settlement mechanism – thus proved their ability to protect the interests of villagers without trenching on the interests of the state.[17] All this appears to have humiliated male Panches and Pradhans who did not achieve fraction of this for full six decades in office after independence. In view of this it is natural to see the man in action. Consequently efforts are made by men to dissuade women to contest elections to local bodies at the grass-root level. They do not mind to obstruct the elections to the Panchayats even if it endangers social solidarity; it should be stopped because it exposes and humiliates them, has therefore been the only cause to defeat the Article 243-D of the Constitution. Why has the state failed to go beyond 243-D? We need not to remind that mere participation of women in political process does not mean political democracy because social democracy which is a corollary of political democracy cannot be achieved unless weaker sections progress and develop in general and the women in particular receive a fair share in the governance of the country. This bespeaks of the urgency to take Article 243-D beyond the realm of Panchayat to the state and central level.

The expressions may fail to sum up the contribution made by Dr. Ambedkar towards developing an indigenous legal thought that could weld diverse strands of India legal culture without injuring the susceptibility of any of its constituents, as he knew that India has to wake up to join the nations of the world in its race for progress and development. As an author of the Constitution, it seems he was deliberate to use proverbial but crisp language to encapsule rights of the Indian people irrespective of their caste and creed, and sex because he could very well understand the psychology of his people. In the process he imposed a great onus on the legal luminaries of India to write suitable postil on his work provided the same is mathematically calculable and does not change the essence of fundamental aspects of the Constitution, wherein the right to equality and right to life would no more be susceptible to lopsided interpretations, which could scuttle the progress and development of the nation as a whole. It appears that the same theme received extraordinary attention and attraction at international level when the United Nations in its Declaration in 1986 emphasized that the world nations have a high stake in 'development' which is a continuous process aiming not only at the well-being of the people but ensuring their active, free and meaningful participation in political processes. As such 'development' in the present context has to achieve a significant perceptible goal. In the context of women, a corresponding duty is cast on the state in terms of assuring that the meaning of development does not include only the psychological empowerment and economic development but also an assurance to them as to their security both within and outside the family, which is impossible to achieve without their participation in governance of the state. This would enable women to live with self-assurance so as to enjoy the constitutional guarantees as to their right to life which includes right to live with dignity.[18] The same may in turn, call for allowing the national system of governance to be run democratically with participation of all in a manner consistent with the expectations both of men and women. This would not be realized unless a commune in political sense of the word comes into being. In absence of it mere association of women in governance would appear to them to be merely as a zero sum game. Even if they are associated in governance but so long they continue to remain least protected by an appropriate normative framework which hitherto has been masculine in its orientation, women would continue to remain deprived of the dessert of democracy and the Constitution. The absence of gender neutral normative framework does not only obstruct the women's understanding of the essence of development but might also disable them to grasp the basic issues related with it. Where we talk about women in governance it is to be assumed that women have achieved substantive freedom and possess capacity to lead the life that they value and could even enhance and reshuffle their choice in the course of realizing goals. Such is the heart throb of total developmental economics. Any talk about the women in governance would be suggestive to presuppose that women are already in governance or they are halfway in their achievements but in real terms that is not the case. It is true that women have proportionately progressed in claiming major share in academics and intellectual pursuits, even they have made gate-crash entry into certain occupation hitherto monopolized by men, yet they cannot claim to be holding to reins of governance under their control. This brings to light the paradox of a welfare state like India where women are in essence devoured in the name of equality which has by and large been pivoting around male value system than being women friendly. As such, constitutional guarantee as to equality appears to point at "equality before law (for men) and equal protection of law (to men)". This becomes aptly visible where a female is pitched against male be it the matter of restitution[19] or her claim to guardianship.[20] It is true that a great deal for women welfare has been done and the state is probably gearing up to do a great deal more but that does not mean women have been given their proper share in governance. Whatever the case, the same shall be made available to them within the framework of existing institutional framework. Despite the general perception of women in governance about men's right to get more loving, is fine but challenges that go to the very essence of male ordered society hit them below the belt. As a result women feel disappointed because the things are going so slow that they are apprehensive of a backlash even from men who are ostensibly reasonable.

Woman and Constitutional Perspectives of Governance

The Constitution in its preamble declares India to be a democracy and the essence of it being equal participation of men and women in developing and shaping the nation. The same promise is reiterated by way of guarantees in Articles 14, 16 and 21. The protection of dignity being the lifeline of this right. While it is correct that Article 21 protects right to life but one feels like enquiring about the kind of mechanism that has been devised by the drafters of the Constitution to make democracy functional. In this regard objectives have been outlined in Chapter IV that the states shall strive for and achieve as the same constitute the active obligations of the state. The whole scheme is geared around the principle that task of laws should be to bring about the maximum happiness of each individual, for the happiness of each would result in happiness of all.[21] The Articles 35-51 were accordingly incorporated to work as levers of social change. In order to create an egalitarian society the constitution makers sought to promote social, economic and political development so as to secure the dignity of an individual.[22] True it may be that the constitution makers intended to ameliorate the position of laity in general – has it been so in case of women too needs an evaluation. The question assumes significance because a woman happens to be doubly in disadvantageous position. Theoretically, much has been achieved in terms of Constitution taking more care of the women and her rights. For example Article 39(d)(e) and (f) protects gender equality in terms of equal pay for equal work, their health and strength so as not to fall prey to moral and material abandonment and other exploitative forces bearing a nexus with economic necessity.[23] Feeling quite concerned for sustaining the economic rights of women the constitution makers laid down that state shall make provision for securing just and humane conditions of work and for maternity relief.[24] At the height of it Article 51-A, of the Constitution declares that it shall be the duty of every citizen of India to renounce practices derogatory to the dignity of women. All these Articles theoretically do not only aim at empowering the women but equally seem to ensure that their fair share in the governance especially when the same is juxtaposed with Article 14, which guarantees equality before law and equal protection of laws, is both allowed and protected. Given the fact that Benthamite principle does not support absolute equality, the guiding principle has been that all persons and things similarly circumstanced shall be treated alike both in privileges and rights conferred on them under the Constitution. Furthermore to promote the egalitarian social order the Constitution permits the state to make a resort to affirmative action and for the same Article 15(3) has been purposefully enshrined in the Constitution only to promote gender equality. This per se is sufficient to emphasize that the Constitution in aggregate desires to ensure protection to political rights of women so far as their participation in political processes is concerned. Also has been guaranteed the equality of opportunity in the matters of employment under Article 16 of the Constitution. Thus, it may be said that the theoretically the stage was all set for promoting women's right to claim share in governance of the state. But have they received a fair share is not only intriguing but also exposes the conditions reflective of the ground reality? It may be legitimately asked whether women have representation in the Parliament proportionate to their size. Do they find representation in various committees of the Parliament which are generally found to be responsible for shaping the future of the nation, be those committees evolving the guidelines determining the sphere of activity either of the parliament or that of the executive? The issues like these have divided our elite into two distinct groups apart from the group that has generally remained immune towards these issues and accept the things as their fait accompli. The protagonists of gender cause may genuinely claim that the neglect of women, by men who have traditionally controlled power, amounts to denial of their civil rights and indignation of female folk. To empower women and ensure them their genuine share in governance is impossible to achieve unless men are disempowered first and redistribution of power takes place. This may be the application of pure Benthamite principle to ensure women their share in governance. In their opinion the failure of political system to accommodate women's interest has been on account of male reluctance to shun power. The denial on their part virtually results in indignation of women, which is also a case of denial of right to life to them and constitutes violation of the duty cast under Article 51-A, that binds every Indian citizen to honour the dignity of women. The antagonists contest these views admitting that India is a Democratic Republic that has its roots in political party system and women should carve out a place for themselves within the political parties. But protagonists may genuinely contest such views by arguing that the political parties or for that matter the National Parliament is also dominated by men. Jawaharlal Nehru while realizing the same, lamented that "we are in fact to be blamed for this injustice as laws are man made, our society dominated by men manipulated by men and most of us naturally take a very lopsided view of this matter".[25] and hence these political parties share with their hand-picked few women the desserts of political process. They ignore the basic responsibility towards womenfolk in the sense they are not accommodated and allotted a share proportional to their size and encouraged to contest elections. The question is whether women should go alone and form political parties to bridge the gap, thus go the Swedish way where women floated political parties and participated in election process independently.[26] Or they should go with men and work shoulder to shoulder with them. Perhaps the latter is preferable because it suits India's ethos and cultural heritage. Going alone means pitching against men and in the prevailing conditions it would result in drawing the lines which is likely to endanger women's cause. The male psyche of ownership has dominated even the political process as they are reluctant to shun power; so are they least prepared to give up their control over the purse, otherwise called budgeting. One wonders why do women fail for find representation, not to speak of an adequate one in the formulation of budget proposals in the Parliament bearing in mind that woman in every respect has to bears the brunt of ill-conceived budgeting as she is the person who ultimately has to manage the economy of the household? Keeping women away from the budgeting process without any justification is not understandable. If they can manage very well the economy of the household they can equally tender a highly valuable advice in the preparation of a national budget. In fact, budgeting should be the sole prerogative of the women as times have shown that they are the best managers and possess natural tendencies to construct the household. For example Margaret Thatcher the Prime Minister of Britain, built up economy of her country at a time when its economy was in shambles, thus proved her ability that a woman can control and manipulate the numbers.

It is true that this nation has a colour-and sex-blind Constitution so it is equally correct that only a few women could find a berth in the Constituent Assembly but this was owing to various reasons inter alia due to lack of education and the same could be to some extent justifiable. But women have since excelled in education and so they have managed to join professions generally monopolized hitherto by men yet they are ignored and not preferred in various disciplines and professions without any understandable reasoning. The most glaring example being failure of the High Court and Supreme Court to appoint practicing lady lawyers as judges proportionate to their size in Bar at state and central levels to make judiciary an aptly representative body in its constitution and composition.

Judicial Creativity and Exposition

Notwithstanding the non-representative composition of judiciary, the courts have generally exposed the gender bias working behind the law and at the same time appreciated the mettle, ability and courage shown by women to enter different professions at the cost of fighting legal battles against the government and its policies towards women. This happened within the first three decades after the nation became independent, registering an adverse impact on the psyche of women who usually had to fight conventional norms on one hand and on the other hand make preparations to compete with men. In this regard one may recall the observations of Justice Krishna Iyer who lamented that "in these days of nuclear families, intercontinental marriages and unconventional behaviour one fails to understand the naked bias against the gender of the species even a third of the century after freedom."[27] The policy like this was in ordinary circumstances sufficient to deter women to enter the administrative services.[28] The situation in corporate sector was never better, yet the women preferred to join and fight for their rights than leaving the whole cake to be eaten by men. In this regard the *Air Hostess Case* assumes the significance of a beacon light that would guide women in their struggle against discriminatory policies and trends.[29] Justice Fazl Ali expressed his concern regarding the policy floated by Air India vis-à-vis its married female employees who were required to resign on first pregnancy of marriage within four years of service whichever occurs earliest and observed that "such a course of action is extremely detestable and abhorrent to the notion of a civilized society and is not only a callous and cruel act but also an open insult to Indian womanhood the most sacro-sanct and cherished institution". In view of the governmental policies being discriminatory, the workers in private institutions dare to adopt different ways and means in order to keep women away from their workplace. Women have long been fighting or facing silently the hostile environment that is impressively masculine; so are the workplace norms and procedures. Apart from this the practical behaviour of workmen towards their co-women workers is not generally palliative too. The same was noticed by the Supreme Court of India in *Vishaka* v. *State of Rajasthan*[30] and issued directions to make environment at workplace ideal and conducive for women workers, which may be viewed as an honest and earnest endeavour to protect the dignity of woman and womanhood and at the same time exposed the masculine qualms of parliamentarians and legislators.

The cases like the above reflecting discriminatory texture are only a tip of the iceberg that came before the Apex Court for adjudication. According to Ehrlich, only a minute fraction of social life comes before courts and even then it usually represents some from of breakdown of social life. The reality being that much of the discrimination flourishes unnoticed and to understand the same one needs to search the cause for divergence outside the confines of legal literature because there would always remain a gap between the norms of decision, which correspond to that which is traditionally understood to be laws and norms of conduct which govern life in society.[31] The cumulative impact of this contradiction has adversely effected the psyche of women in this country and has been not less than a double edged weapon in the sense that women have been deterred to join the professions monopolized hitherto by men and those who enter such professions have to face norms and procedures authored by men only to suit masculine psyche hence protect their interests. It is therefore natural that their share in governance has remained the minimal. The same was realized of late by the protagonists of the women's cause and they finally resolved to address this problem at the grass-root level.

Women and 73rd Constitutional Amendment

The need for recognition of the 'identity' of woman, dawned upon the lawmakers, was the sine qua non to usher in an era of women empowerment. Perhaps it was realized that any change from the top would prove meaningless unless the male psyche at the grass-root level was changed. Although no miracles could be expected in the beginning, yet it was the only course open to elevate women and enable them to claim a share in the governance of the country, as such make it a meaningful proposition. To achieve such an objective, it was felt that participation making processes could be meaningful provided the same was not only guaranteed but also implemented. A modest attempt in this attempt in this regard was made in the form of 73rd Amendment Act, 1992 wherein one-third total number of seats under Article 243(d) are reserved for Scheduled Castes and Scheduled Tribes as the case may be in every Panchayat. Secondly under Article 243(d) (iii) not less than one-third (including the number of seats reserved for women belonging to the Scheduled Castes and Scheduled Tribes) of total number of seats to be filled by direct election in every Panchayat shall be reserved for women and such seats may be allotted to different constituencies in a Panchayat. Under Article 243(d) (iv) the office of the chairperson in the Panchayat at the village or any other level has been reserved for women apart from the same being reserved for Scheduled Castes and Scheduled Tribes. The seriousness of the matter can be ascertained from the fact that not less than one-third of the total number of offices of chairpersons in the Panchayat at each level has been emphasized to be reserved for women. The spirit being the amendment has certainly been to allow women to emerge in governance at the grass-root level. The seriousness of the matter can be ascertained from the fact that the reservation shall cease to have any effect on the expiration of the period of fifty years as specified in Article 334 of the Constitution vis-à-vis Scheduled Castes and Scheduled Tribes but the same shall not apply to the women in general. As such the office of the chairperson in the Panchayats at the village or any other level for the Scheduled Caste, Scheduled Tribes and the women has been made to be a permanent feature of the Constitution.[32]

Notwithstanding the constitutional directives, one feels astonished to investigate as to why does masculinity occasionally surface on the face of the rulers of the constituent federal units as and when elections to the local bodies become overdue. Earnest attempts are made to delay these elections so as to thwart the election of women to Panchayats. For example, in order to keep women away and be deprived of empowerment at grass-root level, some of the states as early as in 1993 attempted to extend the term of Panches beyond their normal lifespan. As such, apart from the state of Uttar Pradesh, Himachal Pradesh, Orissa, Tamil Nadu, and Bihar had also deferred Panchayat elections beyond the period of five years.

One feels constrained to investigate and unveil the policy behind such deferment so as to underline reasons behind reluctance to hold elections as per schedule? Do they defer it only to defeat the right of women to claim share in governance in local bodies to the extent of minimum one-third representation in Panchayats? Or the rulers are alarmed over dedicated style of functioning of the elected women Panches, and have begun restructuring of the rural India which the male Panches could not achieve during six decades after Independence. Or they are not prepared to take humiliation any more as women have exhibited extraordinary ability towards generating awareness about gender equality which the rural man is least prepared to accept? Or reason behind such resistance being that women in these states have excelled beyond male expectations and they have shown this by bringing about change on the ground level through their collective effort as these elected women observe that their strength lies in 'okkattu' (togetherness), as such they had become a pressure group in these states with joint action for gender empowerment where "earlier individual EWRs (elected women representatives) found themselves unable to make a dent, the okkattu had proved its worth".[33] It has enabled them to show better performance. This apart, their pressure lobbies have not only succeeded in influencing bureaucracy but have even exposed the policy makers, that they have found okkattu to be the sine qua non towards sustaining both the struggle for effective decentralization and devolution of power to grass-root level and execute developmental programme that alone would bring about gender equality. All this has contributed to male apprehension to lose their regalia to women and some of the states consequently torpedoing election of women to Panchayats by way of their deferment is natural. After all hitherto it has shown unbelievably better results that even rustic, illiterate and poor women like Sona Bai of Bangalore once empowered would show their ability to bring about magnificent transformation in them. Sona Bai emerged bold, reassured and confident so as to speak about her experiences and the experiences of her sisters.[34] In view of this it is likely that the politicians in aforementioned status realized the danger to their monopoly, therefore preferred deferring the elections. They had in front of them the extent to which women could go to campaign for bringing about a change in man dominated environment and gradually usher in an era of gender equality. As in Tamil Nadu, the Federation of Women Presidents of Panchayats (representing over 38,500 elected women representatives in the state including 4,264 women residents) secured 50 per cent of village revenue to their Panchayat, soon after sending a resolution in this regard to the state government demanding prompt response to their representations imposing a ten day limit for government orders to reach villages. They succeeded to get it and were assured about the same.[35] Likewise women have shown considerable interest towards protection of environment and employment of the villagers. In the course they have fought politically influential contractors who operated an illegal sand mining quarry in the district that endangered livelihood of thousand of residents.[36] Similarly in the state of Karnataka in the Navalakal area of Raichuri district women have successfully been able to combat the problem of alcoholism related domestic violence by organizing a traffic blockade *(rasta roko)* with two thousand women till the District Commissioner and the police got the liquor shops closed.[37] In the same vein several villages of Uttaranchal have been transformed by some women Pradhans by changing the economic profile of these villages. As of this some villages have managed to overcome the problem of fodder. They have even solved the age-old disputes between the villagers and forest department through alternate methods of dispute settlement. The community forestation scheme introduced by women Pradhans in these states has been a great success story that has changed the texture of these villages.[38] Women have not as yet overcome male resistance to their power sharing to the elected bodies at the grass-root level. Diverse means are tested to dissuade women so that they give up their resolve to contest for Panchayat membership. In certain cases men do not mind even boycotting women candidates and their families, including depriving them of their means of sustenance only to ensure that just men alone to the exclusion of women contested election. In this regard men do not mind to win at the cost of endangering social solidarity no matter the contestant is a 70-year old male with worn out energy and perseverance that too when he may have remained a Pradhan for 20 years.[39]

Why has the state failed to go beyond this concession? The women's share in political power is a major step towards achieving their say in governance. This they can achieve it seems, by pleading for change in normative procedures which in effect would require the identity of women to be recognized as an equal partner in the governance, that too not by courtesy of oblation but as per their rights so that governance is a win-win game for both men and women. This bespeaks of the urgency to carry the spirit of Article 243(d) beyond the realm of Panchayats to the state and central level.

Unless the women receive their share in legislative houses besides in all those committees and commissions constituted by the centre as well as by the states, there is no possibility that such normative procedures would change that have hitherto devoured women in the name of equality authored by man.

Notes

1. Dr. B.R. Ambedkar, "Constituent Assembly Debates", November 25, 1949; also see: B. Shiva Rao, *Framing of India's Constitution, Select Documents* Vol. II, p. 5 (1967).
2. *Keshvananda Bharti* v. *State of Kerala* (1973)4 S.C.C. 225.
3. Article 39(d) (e) (f) of the Constitution deserves special attention.
4. Jereny Bentham, "An Introduction to the principles of Murals and Legislation", para VI cited in: R.W.M. Dias, *Jurisprudence*, p. 427 (1994).
5. Generally see: Hilda Scott, Right to be Human, (U.K., 1982).
6. *Harvinder Kour* v. *Harminder Singh*, AIR (1984) S.C. 1562; *Saroj Rani* v. *Sudershan*, AIR (1984) S.C. 1956.
7. *T. Sareetha* v. *Venkata Subiah*, AIR (1983) A.P. 356.
8. *Githa Hariharan* v. *Reserve Bank of India*., AIR (1999) S.C. 1149.
9. (1973) I Serv, L.R., 909 (All) *Radha Charan* v. *State*, AIR (1969) Ori, 237.
10. *C.B. Muthamma* v. *Union of India* AIR (1979) S.C. 1868.
11. *Air India* v. *Nargish Meerza & Others*, AIR (1981) S.C. 1829.

12. For details see: Radhakrishna Rao, "Decentralization of Power Role of Women in Local Governance", *The Kashmir Times*, p. 9 (16 December, 2005).
13. Shakuntala Narsimhan, "Changing the Lives of Villages Women", *Grass Roots*, p. 4 (August, 2003).
14. Ibid.
15. Ibid.
16. C.K. Chandramohan, "Women Pradhans bring Winds of Change", *Grass Roots*, p. 6 (August 2002).
17. Ibid.
18. *Francis Coralie* v. *Union Territory of Delhi*, AIR (1981) S.C. 746; *Bandhua Mukti Morcha* v. *Union of India*, AIR (1984) S.C. 802.
19. *Harvinder Kour* v. *Harmander Singh*, AIR (1984) S.C. 1562; *Saroj Rani* v. *Sudhershan*, AIR (1984) S.C. 1956; *T. Sareetha* v. *T. Venkata Subiah*, AIR (1983) A.P. 356.
20. *Githa Hariharan* v. *Reserve Bank of India*, AIR (1999) S.C. 1149.
21. Jeremy Bentham, "An Introduction to the Principles of Morals and Legislation", para. VI cited in: R.W.M. Dias, *Jurisprudence*, p. 427 (1994).
22. *Keshavnanda Bharti* v. *State of Kerala* (1973) 4 S.C.C. 225.
23. Article 39(d) lays down: The State shall, in particular, direct its policy towards securing that: there is equal pay or equal work for both men and women; (e) that the health and strength of workers, men and women, and the tender age of children are not abused and that citizens are not forced by economic necessity to enter avocations unsuited to their of strength; (f) that children are give opportunities and facilities to develop in a healthy manner and in conditions of freedom and dignity and that childhood and youth are protected against exploitation and against moral and material abandonment.
24. Article 42 lays down that the state shall make provision for securing just and human conditions of work and maternity relief.
25. G.B.K. Hooja, "The New Education Policy and Women's Development", in Dr. (Mrs.) L. Devasia and Dr. V.V. Devasia, (eds.), *Woman in India*, p. 108 (1990).
26. Hilda Scott, *Right to be Human*, (U.K. 1982).
27. *C.B. Muthamma* v. *Union of India*, AIR (1976) S.C. 1868.
28. In C.B. Muthamma case a senior member of Indian Foreign Service invoked the constitutional remedy in respect of Rule 8 (ii) of the Indian Foreign Service Rules 1961 which provided that "a woman

member of the service shall obtain permission of the government in writing before her marriage is solemnized and even after marriage she would be required to resign from service that her family and domestic commitments are likely to come in the way of due and efficient discharging of duties".

29. *Air India* v. *Nargish Meerja & others*, AIR (1981) S.C. 1829.
30. AIR (1997) S.C.
31. Ehrlich, *Fundamental Principles of Sociology of Law* (tr. Moll) cited in: R.W.M. Dias, *Jurisprudence*, p. 425 (1994).
32. Article 243-D (iv) second proviso lays down that not less than one-third of the total number of offices of chairpersons in the Panchayats at each level shall be reserved for women and sub clause (v) further lays down that the reservation of seats under clauses (1) (ii) and the reservation of office of chairpersons (other than the reservation for women) under clause (iv) shall cease to have effect on the expiration of the period specified in Article 334.
33. Sakuntala Narasimhan, "Changing the Lives of Village Women", *Grass Roots*, (August, 2003).
34. Sakuntala Narasimhan, "Changing the Lives of Village Women", *Grass Roots*, (August, 2003) p. 4.
35. Ibid.
36. Ibid.
37. Ibid.
38. C.K. Chandramohan, "Women Pradhans' Bring Winds of Change", *Grass Roots*, (August, 2002).
39. Rinku Pegu, "Putting Her Foot Forward", *Hindu* (4th May 2003).

7

Dalits and Violations of their Human Rights

An Introspection

RATTAN SINGH

Even the world has entered in the phase of liberalization, privatization and globalization (L.P.G.) but the Indian society is still based on the historically deep-rooted Varna[1] ideology mediated through its pollution and purity norms. The origin of the Varna and Jati is usually associated with the coming of the Aryans on Indian soil. There is no evidence that they existed earlier or within the Dravidian society.[2] The Indian caste system based on the notion of purity and pollution believed that the Scheduled Castes were impure and polluted. As a result, they were forced to live outside the village/town proper and suffered from discrimination in all walks of life. In the 20th century, Dr. B.R. Ambedkar, who was the first highly educated and active leader from within the community, focused the attention of the world to the awful position and plight of the Indian Scheduled Castes,[3] variously known as Panchamas, outcastes, Anthyayajas, depressed classes, Achut and finally rechristened as 'Harijan' by the Mahatma Gandhi.

It is necessary to mention that the first serious effort against the social religious and economic discrimination was started by

Dr. Baba Saheb Ambedkar in early 1920. The major beginning was made with the agitation in the town of Mahad in Kolaba district of Maharashtra to get entry to untouchables to public water tank. The agitation was started in 1927 and finally through the legal battle the untouchables got the right ten years later in 1935. This agitation also went for almost 10 years. It is important to recognize that in 1920s and 1930s entire Maharashtra was covered by the social movement of Dalits for acquiring civic rights. It is because of Dr. Baba Saheb Ambedkar's constant struggle that the problems of untouchables was brought on the national scene and as a result Gandhi, the Congress and the British government had to accept the problems of Dalits. It is because of Dr. Baba Saheb Ambedkar's struggle that the provisions were made in the Indian Constitution and the law against unsociability was passed in 1955.[4]

Deeply concerned about the historical injustice faced by certain sections of the society, the founding fathers of our Constitution enshrined The ideas of justice – social, economic and political – in the Preamble of Constitution, and included far reaching protective provisions under the Chapter on Fundamental Rights and Directive Principles of the State Policy. Due to some provisions made in the Constitution, a little progress was made by Dalits in some spheres of their life.

A Brief Profile of Dalits

There are more Dalits in India than the people in Pakistan. The report of 1981 Census reveals that the population of Scheduled Castes has gone up from 80 million to 100 million in 1981. The population of the Scheduled Castes according to 1991 Census has reached up to 1382.23 million. Therefore, the population of Scheduled Castes has increased to 16 per cent further of the country's population in 1991. According to the Census report of 2001, the Dalit population is nearly about 16.20 per cent of India's people. Their contribution to society in terms of the freedom moment, social reforms, labour, art and culture is enormous, but in the country's economic resources it is disproportionately lower.[5] They account for one sixth of India's population, but not of its land. They hold a tiny fraction of one sixth of land owned by the

Indians. As much as 77 per cent of the Dalit workers are in the primary or agricultural sector of the economy. Only 16 per cent of the Dalits live in urban areas, remaining 84 per cent, in rural areas of India. People confronted by seemingly untraceable problems brought on by millennia of exploitation, enforced poverty and deprivation.

Constitution Scheme of Social Reconstruction

The Constitution of India is a charter of a peaceful democratic social revolution. Such a social revolution is meant to get India out of medievalism based on the birth, religion, custom and community and reconstructs her social structure on modern foundations of law, individual merit and secular outlook. Obsessed with this desire, the framers of the Constitution laid down a scheme, which is enshrined in the Fundamental Rights and Directive Principles as follows:

Fundamental Rights

Article 14 enunciates the right to equality, which provides that states shall not deny any person equality before law or the equal protection of law within the territory of India. Article 15 operationalizes the concept of equality in a manner, which specifically touches upon the conditions of the Scheduled Castes and Scheduled Tribes. It prohibits discrimination on grounds of religion, race, caste, sex or place of birth. Article 17 of the Indian Constitution forbids the practice of the untouchability in any form. The enforcement of any disability arising out of the untouchability has been made an offence punishable in accordance with laws. Article 23 prohibits traffic in human beings and beggar and forced labour in any form and contravention of this provision has been an offence punishable in accordance with law. Article 24 provides that no child below the age of 14 years shall be employed to work in any factory or mine or engaged in any hazardous employment. Article 25(2)(b) assures all classes and sections of Hindus access to Hindu religious institution of public character. The Article provides the Hindu religious institution of public character shall be open to all classes and sections of Hindus.

Directive Principles

Part IV of the Constitution relates to the Directive Principles of State Policy. Directive principles serve as guidelines for the state in making laws, contain specific provisions, viz., Articles 398, 39 and 39-A, which enjoin on the state the duty to ensure the creation of a just social order, and Article 42 and 46 ask the states to promote with special care the educational and economic interests of the weaker sections especially the Scheduled Castes (Dalits). Here, it will be worth to mention some of the legislative steps which are taken under the shadow of Fundamental Rights and Directive Principles of State Policy but proved redundant to protect the Dalits. Some of them are:

1. The Untouchability (Offences) Act, 1955.
2. Protection of Civil Rights Act.
3. Scheduled Castes and Scheduled Tribes (Prevention of Atrocities) Act, 1989.
4. The Employment of Manual Scavengers and Construction of Dry Latrines (Prohibition) Act, 1993.
5. Bounded Labour System (Abolition) Act, 1973.
6. Minimum Wages Act, 1948.
7. Equal Remuneration Act, 1976.
8. Child Labour (Prohibition and Regulation) Act, 1986.
9. Inter-State Migrant Workmen (Regulation of Employment and Conditions of Services) Act, 1979.

Some of the government and non-government watchdog agencies are also working for the welfare of Dalits, i.e., National Commission for SCs and STs, National Human Rights Commission, National Commission for Women, National Commission for Safai Karamcharis, etc.

International Standards Applicable to India

Apart from the constitutional and legislative provisions, there are various International Human Rights Conventions for the welfare of Dalits. These conventions are ratified by India, namely:

1. Universal Declaration of Human Rights, 1948.
2. International Convention on Civil and Political Rights, 1966.

3. International Covenant on Economic, Social and Cultural Rights, 1966.
4. International Convention on Elimination of all forms of Racial Discrimination, 1965.
5. Convention on Elimination of all forms of Discrimination Against Women, 1979.
6. Convention on the Rights of the Child, 1989.
7. ILO Convention No. 29 – Forced Labour Convention, 1930.
8. ILO Convention No. 111 – Discrimination (Employment and Occupation) Convention, 1958.

The true aim of providing constitutional safeguards is to bring a societal balance between the enhancement of status of Dalits and general social good. It embodies the philosophy of Distributive Justice with a strong determination to build up a new and independent nation, which will ensure the triumph of justice, liberty, equality and fraternity. Therefore, our Constitution is a very strong document. Dr. B.R. Ambedkar showed his reluctance on the implementation of the Constitution on November 26, 1948. He said, "Here I do not enter into the merits of the Constitution. However good and faultless a Constitution may be, but if those who implement it are incompetent and useless, that Constitution results in an evil. Similarly, however defective a Constitution may be, but if its executors are good the same Constitution results in the good of the people."[6]

It becomes clear from the vision of Dr. Ambedkar that the Indian Constitution is not a weak one but its executors are weak. Even after about 60 years of independence, the Dalits are facing various challenges to their life. Inspite of having numerous reform movements, constitutional provisions and legislative measures, the levels of discrimination against untouchables are far from encouraging. Caste prejudices and the practice of untouchability continue in rural as well as urban areas of India. The welfare state which guaranteed access into government jobs and education has been withdrawn and Indian economy has been liberalized and opened to the private sectors. National Human Rights Commission in its report observed that despite elaborative provisions in the Constitution and other laws, it is an unfortunate reality that social injustice and exploitation of Dalits and other weaker sections persists. The humiliation which Dalits suffer even today, more than half a century after India proclaimed itself to be a republic, is a matter of shame.[7]

Dalit's Human Rights

Though widely used in recent times among civil society actors, it is hard to define the term 'human rights'. Technically, 'human rights' means the rights relating to "the life, liberty, equality and dignity of individuals guaranteed by the Constitution or embodied in the International Covenants and enforceable by courts in India".[8] To put it simply, "human rights constitute those very rights which one has precisely because of being a human. They are inherent in our nature and without which we cannot live as human beings. They are not earned, bought or inherited nor are they created by any contractual authority".[9] Human rights address every human being, however reality shows that plight of many human beings, more so of Dalits, has not changed much and therefore there is a focus on Dalit's human rights. It is argued that in India, the Constitution has done away with caste discrimination and there are provisions for protection of these violations and therefore, mention of caste discrimination in human rights documents is not called for.

However, in recent years an increasing number of human rights organizations and bodies are coming up to recognize untouchability and caste discrimination as a gross human rights violations. Many international organizations like Human Rights Watch, Amnesty International, Minority Rights Group and Anti-Slavery International are making Dalit's human rights a priority issue and are concerned to raise the issue internationally in United Nation bodies, governments and the public at large.[10]

Since caste still operates as a defining condition in establishing marriages, social relations and access to employment, millions of Dalits and other former low-caste people remain behind in education, employment and access to wealth. Although untouchability and casteism is banned in India, discrimination is widely practised and statistics draws the logical conclusion that there is a broad correlation between one's economic state and one's position within the caste hierarchy.[11]

Reasons for the Dalit's Human Rights Violations

The following are some of the reasons responsible for the violation of the human rights of Dalits:

1. Dalits and their share in Agricultural Land.
2. Dalits and Poverty.
3. Dalits and Education.
4. Dalits and Places of Worship.
5. Dalits and Bounded Labour.
6. Dalits and Burial Grounds.
7. Dalits and Dalit Colonies.
8. Dalits and Social Discrimination.
9. Dalits in Private Sectors.
10. Dalits and Panchayat.
11. Dalits and Police Atrocities.
12. Dalits in Indian Judiciary.
13. Dalits and Basic Civil Amenities.
14. Dalits and Status of their Women.
15. Dalits and Development

Dalits and their Share in Agricultural Land

Dalits account for one-sixth of India's population, but not of its land. At best, they hold a tiny fraction of one sixth of land owned by Indians. What is not disputed by anyone, is that they are mainly landless and where they own land at all, it is marginal and usually of low quality. The importance of their position in relation to agricultural economy is enormous. As much as 77 per cent of the Dalit workforce is in the primary or agricultural sector of the economy. But very few of them own land. They form, instead, the bulk of agricultural labourers in this country.

Land has a great deal to do with both economic and social status but Dalits are the first categories who are suffering in agricultural society. The importance of land was recognized right at the time of drawing up the Constitution. S. Nagappa expressed a significant point of view in those discussions. He said, "I am prepared for the abolition of reservations, provided every Harijan (Dalit) family gets ten acres of wet land, twenty acres of dry land and all the children of Harijans are educated, free of cost, up to the university course, and give one-fifth of the key posts either in civilian or in military departments."

The implementation of land reforms in the country as a whole has been termed as largely a failure except for slogans of success. The implementation of land reforms has been subverted by the absence of political will and bureaucratic commitment, loopholes in the laws, tremendous manipulative powers of the landed classes, lack of organization among the poor and excessive interference by the courts. Therefore, the intended benefits to the poor in general failed to materialize.[12] Even rural landlordism has been abolished; strong feudal features, however, still govern the rural structural ethos. Rural elites still endeavour to maintain their hold on various sectors of society. The upper castes, the traditionally privileged beneficiaries of rural social order, still attempt to exploit the weak and the vulnerable. Their apprehensions of decline of power often lead to mounting of social tensions. There have been attempts on their part to enforce the continuation of their old tyrannical practices.[13] The demand for minimum wages by Dalit agricultural labour is another source of atrocities on them. The wage disputes relate to failure to pay minimum wages, non-payment of wages, delayed payments and demand for higher wages. These disputes have arisen mostly between landlords and Dalits. In the vent of these disputes the landlords and other employers have adopted violent methods to suppress the demands of Dalits.[14]

Dalits and Poverty

While poverty affects many communities across the spectrum, it would be correct to say that the Scheduled Castes and Scheduled Tribes are amongst its worst victims. Those millions and millions of Dalits working as agricultural labourers earn between Rs 12 to Rs 30 in many parts of the country. This is usually in violation of laws relating to minimum wages for agricultural labourers who produce this country's food, get a little share of it.

We have been pleased to congratulate ourselves on being a 'self sufficient nation' in food production. We have even had food surpluses. This self-sufficiency, however, is very fragile. It is based on the reality that 400 million people go to bed hungry every night. If they got their minimum calorie requirements, our great surpluses would vanish and our level of production seem very inadequate.[15]

Dalits and Education

The rate of literacy among Scheduled Castes, as per 1991 Census, was 37.41 per cent as compared to non-SC and ST communities. For Scheduled Tribes, it was even lower (29.6%). Female literacy among the Scheduled Castes was 23.76 per cent as compared to 44.82 per cent in respect of non-Scheduled Castes and Scheduled Tribes, while for Scheduled Castes it was 49.91 per cent as against 69.53 per cent for non-Scheduled Castes and Scheduled Tribes males. As per indication available from the 2001 Census, there is marginal increase in the literacy rate of SC and ST population. In some of the areas, Dalits are not allowed to sit along with other students and if they are followed, they become subject to discrimination. Whether it is in private employment, school drop-out rate, literacy rate, access to higher education or even government jobs, they are at the wrong end of the spectrum.

Dalits and Places of Worship

In some parts of India, Dalits are still banned entry into temples. Indeed, this practice has been one of the issues in some of the conversion controversies that erupt from time to time. Still, the government prefers to keep silent about this.

Dalits and Bonded Labour

A huge section of bonded labourers in this country are Dalits. They are amongst the most debt affected people in India. Dalits pay a huge price for this. It is the class who labour from day to night to pay off a debt that will never end. They are bonded against debts that they incurred either for marriage or day-to-day expenses. Some of these bonded labourers work for the same master for several years or even for life and live a wretched life.[16]

Dalits and Burial Grounds

They have no access to the burial grounds/burning ghats in many villages in this country. In some of the areas, they are not allowed to burn their relatives in the common burial grounds. Therefore, separate burial grounds and burning ghats are marked for them which is a clear sign of discrimination.

Dalits and Dalit Colonies

The official programmes of the Government of India practise their own forms of exclusion. The Indira Aawas Yojana, for instance, reinforces the pattern of building homes for Dalits away from the rest of the village. Historically, in many places, Dalit colonies were settled to the south of the village, on the outskirts. This is apparently based on a principle of 'Vastu' which says that Lord Yama dwells in the south. So the elites of the Hindus social hierarchy were advised not to even sleep with their heads facing south. In some of the states, Dalit colonies are kept on the east and south of village settlements because they have been condemned to work in traditionally so-called 'polluted' professions; scavenging, skinning of carcasses, disposal of the dead, curing of hides and so on. So in this state, they have been positioned in a direction away from the winds that blow across the main city. This way, the smell of their labour may not disturb the sacred nostrils of the upper castes.

Dalits and Social Discrimination

Across this country, in most of the major states, Dalits are now allowed to draw water from common wells and, in some places, even from hand pumps. This state is no exception. There are reports from some parts of our country that Dalits are served tea in different cups in the shops. The dominant castes continue to perceive the Dalits as dirty, cunning, lazy and good for nothing.[17] Sometimes they are made to sit separately when they are being served their mid-day meal.

Dalits in Private Sectors

Liberalization, and opening up of the economies to the private sector, is widening the gap between the rich and poor. Therefore, liberalization, globalization and privatization have to be deftly steered appropriately, with extreme care and due caution, to ensure that they serve the social aspirations, needs and development of the people.

Dalits in Indian Judiciary

While the legal system works for them the most, their access to it is the least. Under-representation in the legal fraternity is very marked. The maze of the legal system is extremely hard for Dalits.

Dalits and Panchayat

Even in the Panchayats, Dalit sarpanches are routinely deposed by fraudulent means. Often, at the end of their first year in office, they are removed by rigged votes of 'no confidence' which then leave the upper caste sarpanch in de facto powers for years. The illiterate ones are often made to put their thumb prints on some documents – and then charged with embezzlement by the very persons guilty of it. Dalit women members are precluded from attending crucial Panchayat meetings simply by holding these late at night in the upper caste basti. So half of them will not dare to enter that basti, and the ruling elite in such a meeting can pass almost any vote.

Dalits and Police Atrocities

During the British period, Dalits were treated as a community of criminals and separate laws were enacted to deal with them. After 60 years of independence, the mindset of the police still operates in their behaviour that Dalits are criminals. If offence is committed anywhere in some area, police target the entire Dalit community with offensive behaviour, search and seizure, physical abuse and assault. But if case is register by a Dalit then police adopt various mechanisms to discourage him for adopting the legal course of action. Generally, police use the following methods to deflect the objectives of law:

1. Not registering the case.
2. Pressurising the victim complainant to seek compromise to help perpetrators.
3. Foisting of false cases against victims at the behest of perpetrators to pressure them to compromise.

4. Refusing to register case under Scheduled Castes and Scheduled Tribes (Prevention of Atrocities) Act, 1989 so as to avoid strong punitive measures against the accused.
5. Not citing proper sections of the Scheduled Castes and Scheduled Tribes (Prevention of Atrocities) Act, 1989 so as to dilute the seriousness of the offence and help the perpetrators in getting minor punishment, if convicted.
6. Registering FIR but not arresting the accused; shielding public servants from arrest.
7. Delay in investigation and filing charge sheet.[18]

No other groups are so systematically criminalized by the police as Dalits are. The ruling classes have simply found this the best way of dealing with these sections – to criminalize them. Almost any single action of a Dalit can lead to their being charged with some crime. Their own legal access is the worst for any sections. The number of criminal cases for Scheduled Castes under IPC, Protection of Civil Rights Act and Scheduled Castes and Scheduled Tribes (Prevention of Atrocities) Act, is negligible. If we watch specifically, as for the nature of crimes like murder, grievous hurt, rape, arson and other such offences is concerned this is 486, 3298, 1034, 260, 18,664 and 23,742 respectively in the year 2000.[19] Even these data show gradual decline in the total number of reported cases of atrocities against Scheduled Castes, but still Dalits are humiliated because under-reporting is a very common phenomenon and therefore the decline in the number of registered cases does not provide a true picture of the incidence of atrocities.[20] There is a huge amount of under-reporting cases of atrocities. In the year 2000, number of cases of atrocities, instituted under the SC and ST (Prevention of Atrocities) Act, 1989 were 1,43,505. Out of this number 9,996 ended up in acquittal and only 1,241 ended up in conviction. From this, it is evident that only 7.83 per cent of the total cases were disposed of during the year and only 11.04 per cent of the disposed cases ended up in conviction with 88.96 per cent of cases ending in acquittal and 92.17 per cent cases pending with courts which is an alarming situation for our welfare country.[21]

The problem starts with the registration of cases itself. Police resort to various mechanisms to discourage Dalits from registering cases, to dilute the seriousness of the violence, to shield the accused persons from arrest and prosecution and, in some cases, the police themselves inflict violence.

Dalits and Basic Civil Amenities

State has the responsibility of ensuring that the citizens have basic civic amenities. These basic amenities include the facilities available to its citizens like water, electricity, housing, education, health and transport. In India, Dalits are such people who are deprived of these basic civic amenities. Since they are 'lesser human beings' they have lesser influence on the socio-political and economic system of the area and country at large. Dalits, victims of years of exploitation and exclusion of all kinds have internalized their situation as given and therefore take the situation for granted as their fate.[22] In India, it is a common thing that where Dalits live there is a shortage of water, electricity, streetlights, sewage, road, transport, etc. Another aspect of their life is that they are denied their rights to live a human life.

Dalits and Status of their Women

Ironically, the practice of untouchability and women's liberation have both ignored the plight of Dalit women. These movements, were hardly ever interested in tackling the concerns or oppressions perpetuated with such brutality on Dalit women. Even the Human Rights debates failed to make a dent. Culturally misrepresented, historically misplaced, politically mute and socially faceless, Dalit women's experiences and grievances go unrecorded even at the dawn of new millennium. She is humiliated even in the schools, where she cooks food for children of the school in mid-day scheme.[23] Two Dalit girls who were the helpers of a family were chained on charges of stealing their dog.[24] Number of reports are published in the newspapers stating the tales of Dalit women that they are paraded naked. What is important to note there is that, Dalit women grapple with the area of brute caste violence, caste driven gender violence and even caste-enforced prostitution.[25] It is the Dalit women who are on the frontline, suffering hunger, deprivation, indignity and sexual violence.

In rural areas, Dalits women are raped as part of an effort by their caste leaders to suppress movements to demand payment of minimum wages, to settle share-cropping or to reclaim lost land.[26] Thus, Dalit women are easy targets for many perpetrators because upper caste considers them to be sexually available and because they are largely unprotected by the state machinery.[27] This has led to early marriages among the Dalits as once a girl is raped she becomes unmarriageable.[28]

Dalits and Development

Dalits cannot freely participate in human rights of developments in India according to UN development project. Development is a comprehensive economic, social, cultural and political process. It aims at the constant improvement of the well-being of the entire population and of all the individuals who derive from their participation. But the Dalits cannot participate in India's economic development because they are landless labourers and divine slaves. They cannot aspire to become landowners. They have no upward social mobility under the caste Hindu system. Because they are untouchables, they have no development as they are systematically discriminated against. As an example, the greatest Dalit politician of India, Dr. Ambedkar, who attended three Round Table Conferences in London during 1930, 31 and 32, the record of the first RTC of 1930 shows that it was he who demanded from the British government, political freedom for India. Mahatama Gandhi, Nehru and their colleagues did not attend that conference. Nevertheless, the upper caste media has fairly raised Gandhi to the skies and have completely suppressed Dr. Ambedkar's political contribution to freedom because he was a Dalit. He stood for 'Akhand Bharat', i.e., undivided India.[29]

Conclusion

Discrimination, deprivation, exclusion and exploitation are endemic to every society, which leads to frustration, anger and aggression. Those who are subjected to injustice and oppression tend to rebel and revolt. These reactions culminate in an assertion which gives rise to people's movements. But social movements are not an everyday phenomenon. Discrimination and deprivation always do not lead to protest and aggression. Only when people become conscious of these inequalities and injustices and mobilize and organize themselves to struggles against those who subject them to servitude and bondage, people's movements takes place. Moreover, when the disadvantaged and the downtrodden see that another alternative is both possible and viable, they try to overthrow the existing social order.

The question of Dalit's human rights is not just a matter of addressing the atrocities, but at large it corroborates to the affirmation rights of Dalits, resisting the forces of globalization, communalism, casteism, patriarchy and so on. This paves the way for collective action. Collective action leading to people's movements results in social change. This is the ethical course of addressing Dalit's human rights.

The entire philosophy that revolves around the policy of protective discrimination is that there is need for the adjustment of political balance of communities as well as for the amelioration of the conditions of the lowly. It is a temporary measure to be used only for the purpose of mitigating the inequalities. The entire aim of incorporating national and international safeguards to Dalits in our Constitution is to bring peaceful political and socio-economic revolution with a view to balance the conflicting interests in Indian society securing the satisfaction of maximum of wants with minimum of fraction. Although the government for the welfare of Dalits in India has done much, yet Dalits are still sharing the plight of the poorer section in the general population. The various welfare programmes started by the government result in poor achievements. Therefore, there is utmost urgent need to execute the positive policies with a positive mind.

Notes

1. Varna literally means the colour, which refers to one of the four main categories (Brahmans, Kshatriyas, Vaisya and Sudras) into which the Hindu society is traditionally divided and was the basis of differentiating peoples.

2. Shail Singh; *Reservation Policy and Social Justice*, Y.K. Publishers, Agra (2002), p. 1.
3. Scheduled Castes is a nomenclature given to the cluster of castes and sub-castes which are listed in a schedule that does not necessarily carry attributes of untouchability but in fact colloquially it has come to imply exactly the same.
4. Report of the Proceedings of International Conference on Dalit Human Rights, Shri Guru Ravidass Community Centre, London, 16-17 September, 2000 p. 29.
5. P. Sainath; "Dalits and Human Rights: Battle Ahead", (www.puch.org/index.htm).
6. National Human Rights Commission's Report on "Prevention of Atrocities against Scheduled Castes (2004)", p. 9.
7. Ibid., p. (vii).
8. Section 2(d), Protection of Human Rights Act, 1993.
9. Altaf Alam; *Human Rights in India: Issues and Challenges*, Raj Publications, Delhi (2000).
10. Goldy M. George; "The Question of Dalit Human Rights", (www.countercurrents.org).
11. Ibid.
12. National Human Rights Commission's Report on "Prevention of Atrocities against Scheduled Castes (2004)", p. 85.
13. Premlata Sharma; *Problems of Dalits and OBCs*, Book Enclave, Jaipur, (2002), p. 134.
14. Ibid., p. 136.
15. Goldy M. George; "The Question of Dalit Human Rights", (www.countercurrents.org).
16. Ghanshyan Shah (ed.); *Dalit Identity and Politics*, Sage Publications, New Delhi, (2001), p. 19.
17. *The Tribune*; 3 October, 2004.
18. National Campaign on Dalit Human Rights, National Public Hearing, April 18-19, 20 (x), Chennai, Vol. 1- Summary: Jury's interim observation and recommendations, p. 314.
19. Report of National Commission on Scheduled Castes and Scheduled Tribes (1999-2000 and 2000-2001).
20. National Human Rights Commission's Report on Prevention of Atrocities against Scheduled Castes (2004), p. 33.
21. Seventh Report of Ministry of Social Justice and Empowerment (2000), p. 8.

22. Jimmy Dabhi; "Dalit Human Rights: Issues and Perspective", *Social Action*, Vol. 54, January-March, 2004, pp. 33-46, p. 38.
23. *The Tribune*; 20 October, 2004.
24. *Hindustan Times*; 8 October, 2004.
25. Afroz Alam; "Untouchables: The Unequal Citizens of India", *Indian Journal of Politics*, Department of Political Science, GNDU, Amritsar, Vol. XXXVIII, No. 2 and 3, April-September.
26. "Broken People: Caste Violence against India's Untouchables", *New York Human Rights Watch, 1999* (www.hrw.org/report/1999/-india994-04htmP550-2244).
27. Ibid.
28. Ibid.
29. Report of the Proceedings of International Conference on Dalit Human Rights, Shri Guru Ravidas Community Centre, London 16-17 September, 2000, p. 52.

8

Domestic Violence

An Aberration in Women's Human Rights

SHAVI SHARMA

Human rights and fundamental freedoms are the birthright of all human beings; their protection and promotion is the first responsibility of governments. The universal nature of these rights and freedoms is beyond question. The promotion and protection of all human rights and fundamental freedoms must be considered as a priority objective of the United Nations, in accordance with its purposes and principles, in particular with the purpose of international cooperation. In the framework of these purposes and principles, the promotion and protection of all human rights is a legitimate concern of the international community. The international community must treat human rights globally, in a fair and equal manner, on the same footing, and with the same emphasis. The Platform for Action reaffirms the importance of ensuring the universality, objectivity and non-selectivity of the consideration of human rights issues. The Platform for Action reaffirms that all human rights – civil, cultural, economic, political and social, including the right to development – are universal, indivisible, and interdependent and interrelated, as expressed in the Vienna Declaration and Programme of Action adopted by the World Conference on Human Rights. The conference reaffirmed that the human rights of women and the girl child are an inalienable, integral and indivisible part of universal human rights. The full and equal enjoyment of all human rights and fundamental freedoms by women and girls is a priority for governments and the United Nations and is essential for the advancement of women. Equal rights of men and women are explicitly mentioned in the Preamble to the Charter of the United Nations. All the major international human rights instruments include sex as one of the grounds upon which states may not discriminate. Governments must not only refrain from violating the human rights of all women, but must work actively to promote and protect these rights. Recognition of the importance of the human rights of women is reflected in the fact that three-fourths of the states members of the United Nations have become parties to the Convention on the Elimination of All Forms of Discrimination against Women (CEDAW). On December 18,1979, the United Nations adopted the Convention on the Elimination of All Forms of Discrimination Against Women, 'The Women's Convention' or 'CEDAW'. The call for a Women's Convention emerged from the First World Conference on Women in Mexico City in 1975. Until 1979, when the General Assembly adopted the Convention, there was no document that addressed comprehensively women's rights within political, cultural, economic, social, and family life. Often called an international 'Bill of Rights' for women, CEDAW is the culmination of more than thirty years of work by the United Nations Commission on the Status of Women. As of November 2001,168 countries have ratified the Convention. The creation of this treaty was the first critical step in developing appropriate human rights language for women. This language addresses abuses (physical, sexual, economic, and political) of women and promotes women's full enjoyment of their rights and well-being. The gap between the existence of rights and their effective enjoyment derives from a lack of commitment by governments to promoting and protecting those rights and the failure of governments to inform women and men alike about them. The lack of appropriate recourse mechanisms at the national and international levels, and inadequate resources at both levels, compound the problem. In most countries, steps have been taken to reflect the rights guaranteed by the Convention on the Elimination of All Forms of Discrimination against Women in national law. A number of countries have established mechanisms to strengthen women's ability to exercise their rights. In order to protect the human rights of women, it is necessary to avoid, as far as possible, resorting to reservations and to ensure that no reservation is incompatible with the object and purpose of the Convention or is otherwise incompatible with international treaty law. Unless the human rights of women, as defined by international human rights instruments, are fully recognized and effectively protected, applied, implemented and enforced in national law as well as in national practice in family, civil, penal, labour and commercial codes and administrative rules and regulations, they will exist in name only. In those countries that have not yet become parties to the Convention on the Elimination of All Forms of Discrimination against Women and other international human rights instruments, or where reservations that are incompatible with the object or purpose of the Convention have been entered, or where national laws have not yet been revised to implement international norms and standards, women's *de jure* equality is not yet secured. Women's full enjoyment of equal rights is undermined by the discrepancies between some national legislation and international law and international instruments on human rights. Overly complex administrative procedures, lack of awareness within the judicial process and inadequate monitoring of the violation of the human rights of all women, coupled with the under-representation of women in justice systems, insufficient information on existing rights and persistent attitudes and practices perpetuate women's de facto inequality. De facto inequality is also perpetuated by the lack of enforcement of, inter alia, family, civil, penal, labour and commercial laws or codes, or administrative rules and regulations intended to ensure women's full enjoyment of human rights and fundamental freedoms. Every person should be entitled to participate in, contribute to and enjoy cultural, economic, political and social development. In many cases women and girls suffer discrimination in the allocation of economic and social resources. This directly violates their economic, social and cultural rights. The United Nations in 1986 recognized the right to development as a human right. The right to development as formulated in the 1986 UN declaration is a synthesis of two set of rights. However, the distinction between the two set of rights was put to rest by the 'Vienna Declaration and Programme of Action' which affirms that "All human rights are universal, indivisible, interdependent and interrelated". There is a direct corelationship between human rights and development. Issues concerning food, nutrition, health care, shelter, employment and the like are intrinsically linked to ensure proper respect for human rights. There has to be a harmonious blending of all these rights to reach the objective, so as to provide human dignity.

Subjugation of Women

In India women constitute nearly fifty per cent of our population. Women are denied human rights from the cradle to the grave. Infanticide is rampant in certain parts of the country where the birth of a girl child is not welcome. Nearly forty-one per cent of the women abroad play an active role in the production process. In India the situation leaves much to be desired. Sexual abuse and flesh trade are gnawing evils, which threaten the existence of women as independent entities.

Violence Against Women

This violates and impairs or nullifies the enjoyment by women of human rights and fundamental freedoms. Taking into account the Declaration on the Elimination of Violence against Women and the work of special rapporteurs, gender-based violence, such as battering and other domestic violence, sexual abuse, sexual slavery and exploitation, and international trafficking in women and children, forced prostitution and sexual harassment, as well as violence against women, resulting from cultural prejudice, racism and racial discrimination, xenophobia, pornography, ethnic cleansing, armed conflict, foreign occupation, religious and anti-religious extremism and terrorism are incompatible with the dignity and the worth of the human person and must be combated and eliminated. Any harmful aspect of certain traditional, customary or modern practices that violates the rights of women should be prohibited and eliminated. Governments should take urgent action to combat and eliminate all forms of violence against women in private and public life, whether perpetrated or tolerated by the state or private persons.

Domestic Violence

Domestic violence, broadly defined, is violence within a home. Beyond this, the term has a range of definitions, some more and some less formal, which are frequently used with little awareness that a range of definitions exists. The British government, in UK Crime Survey, defined domestic violence as:

> Any violence between current or former partners in an intimate relationship, wherever and whenever the violence occurs. The violence may include physical, sexual, emotional of financial abuse.

Domestic violence is the "abusive behaviour – emotional, psychological, physical, or sexual – that one person in an intimate relationship uses in order to control the other. It takes many different forms and includes behaviours such as threats, name-calling, preventing contact with family or friends, withholding money, actual or threatened physical harm and sexual assault. Stalking can also be a form of domestic violence".[1] In the latest Indian legislation[2] the domestic violence has been defined as – any act, omission or commission or conduct of the respondent shall constitute domestic violence, in case it:

(a) Harms or injures or endangers the health, safety, life, limb or well-being, whether mental or physical, of the aggrieved person or tends to do so and includes causing physical abuse, sexual abuse, verbal and emotional abuse and economic abuse; or

(b) Harasses, harms, injures or endangers the aggrieved person with a view to coerce her or any other person related to her to meet any unlawful demand for any dowry or other property or valuable security; or

(c) Has the effect of threatening the aggrieved person or any person related to her by any conduct mentioned in clause (a) or clause (b); or

(d) Otherwise injures or causes harm, whether physical or mental, to the aggrieved person.

Explanation I – For the purpose of this section:

(i) 'Physical abuse' means any act or conduct which is of such a nature as to cause bodily pain, harm. Or danger to life, limb, or health or impair the health or development of the aggrieved person and includes assault, criminal intimidation and criminal force,

(ii) 'Sexual abuse' includes, any conduct of a sexual nature that abuses, humiliates, degrades or otherwise violates the dignity of woman;

(iii) 'Verbal and emotional abuse' includes:

(a) Insults, ridicule, humiliation, name calling and insults or ridicule specially with regard to not having a child or a male child; and

(b) Repeated threats to cause physical pain to any person in whom the aggrieved person is interested.

(iv) 'Economic abuse' includes:

(a) Deprivation of all or any economic or financial resources to which the aggrieved person is entitled under any law or custom whether payable under an order of court or otherwise or which the aggrieved person requires out of necessity including, but not limited to, household necessities for the aggrieved person and her children, if any, stridhan property, jointly or separately owned by the aggrieved person, payment of rental related to the shared household and maintenance.

(b) Disposal of household effects, any alienation of assets whether movable or immovable, valuables, shares, securities, bonds and the like or other property in which the aggrieved person has an interest or is entitled to use by virtue of the domestic relationship or which may be reasonably required by the aggrieved person or her children or her stridhan or any other property jointly or separately held by the aggrieved person.

(c) Prohibition or restriction to continued access to resources of facilities which the aggrieved person is entitled to use or enjoy by virtue of the domestic relationship including access to the shared household.

Explanation II – For the purpose of determining whether any act, omission, commission or conduct of the respondent constitute 'domestic violence' under this section, the overall facts and circumstances of the case shall be taken into consideration.

Scope of domestic violence

The term domestic violence includes within its preview a wide range of circumstances. It is also classified further into different types – sexual/non-sexual, abuse, and each of these into further sub-categories illustrated by examples in subsequent paragraphs.

Non-sexual

Abuse

- Prevented spouse/partner from having his/her fair share of the household money
- Stopped spouse/partner from seeing friends and relatives

Threat

- Frightened spouse/partner, by threatening to hurt him/her or someone close to him/her

Force – minor

- Pushed spouse/partner, held or pinned him/her down or slapped him/her

Force – major

- Kicked spouse/partner, bit him/her, or hit him/her with a fist or something else, or threw something at him/ her that hurt
- Choked or tried to strangle spouse/partner
- Threatened spouse/ partner with a weapon, such as a stick or a knife
- Threatened to kill spouse/ partner
- Used a weapon against spouse/partner, e.g., a knife, gun

Domestic violence is physical, psychological, sexual or financial violence that takes place within an intimate or family-type relationship and forms a pattern of coercive and controlling behaviour. Crime statistics and research both show that domestic violence is gender-specific – usually the perpetrator of a pattern of repeated assaults is a man; although there is evidence to suggest that in developed countries the female initiated domestic violence is more common.[3]

Factors that Perpetuate Domestic Violence

Cultural

- Gender-specific socialization
- Cultural definitions of appropriate sex roles
- Expectations of roles within relationships
- Belief in the inherent superiority of males
- Values that give men proprietary rights over women and girls
- Notion of the family as the private sphere and under male control
- Customs of marriage (bride price/ dowry)
- Acceptability of violence as a means to resolve conflict

Economic

- Women's economic dependence on men
- Limited access to cash and credit
- Discriminatory laws regarding inheritance, property rights, use of communal lands, and maintenance after divorce or widowhood
- Limited access to employment in formal and informal sectors
- Limited access to education and training for women

Legal

- Lesser legal status of women either by written law and/or by practice
- Laws regarding divorce, child custody, maintenance and inheritance
- Legal definitions of rape and domestic abuse
- Low levels of legal literacy among women
- Insensitive treatment of women and girls by police and judiciary

Political

- Under-representation of women in power, politics, the media and in the legal and medical professions
- Domestic violence not taken seriously
- Notions of family being private and beyond control of the state
- Risk of challenge to status quo/religious laws
- Limited organization of women as a political force
- Limited participation of women in organized political system[4]

Domestic Violence and Culture

Wife beating in Islam

Sheikh Muhammad Kamal Mustafa, Imam of the mosque of the city of Fuengirola, Spain, in his book *The Woman in Islam* writes on the status of violence against wives on the part of husbands in Islamic Sharia law, stating that it is permissible in some instances.

"The wife-beating must never be in exaggerated, blind anger, in order to avoid serious harm (to the woman)". He adds, "It is forbidden to beat her on the sensitive parts of her body, such as the face, breast, abdomen, and head. Instead, she should be beaten on the arms and legs", using a "rod that must not be stiff, but slim and lightweight so that no wounds, scars, or bruises are caused". Similarly, "(the blows) must not be hard".

Mustafa noted in his book that the aim of the beating was to cause the woman to feel some emotional pain, without humiliating her or harming her physically. According to him, physical blows must be the last resort to which a husband turns in punishing his wife, and is, according to the *Quran* (Chapter 4, Verse 34), the husband's third step when the wife is rebellious: First, he must reprimand her, without anger. Next, he must distance her from the conjugal bed. Only if these two methods fail should the husband turn to beating.

Sheikh Yousef Qaradhawi, head of the European Council for Fatwa and Research, has advocated "non-painful" beating of wives: "it is permissible for (the husband) to beat her lightly with his hands, avoiding her face and other sensitive parts. In no case should he resort to using a stick or any other instrument that might cause pain and injury".

Dr. Muhammad Al-Hajj, lecturer on Islamic faith at the University of Jordan (Amman) states: "Hard beatings are those that leave marks on the body or on the face. Thus, beating on the face is prohibited, because the face is a combination of the features of beauty, as it is said. It is forbidden to beat the face, it is forbidden to administer blows that leave fractures or wounds; this is what our sages have said in their books."

While some Muslims interpret the *Quran* to allow the beating of wives, many other Muslims interpret the scripture to say "leave" the wife, not beat her.

Hindu Culture

Although woman has been much eulogized in the ancient Hindu society[5] but with the passage of time the position of woman degraded in the Indian society. The evils of sati and dowry pushed the liberties of women to the dark abyss of barbaric age. Criminalization of domestic violence in India was brought about in the early 1980s after a sustained campaign by feminist groups and women activists all over the country. Great impetus was imported to this movement, especially after the much-criticized judgment of the Supreme Court in the Mathura rape case.[6] The demand for the criminalization of dowry death and domestic violence was a culmination of all these struggles ending successfully in the enactment of Section 498A in the IPC in 1983, Section 304B in 1986 and corresponding provisions in the Indian Evidence Act, 1872.

Violence against women is a global pandemic. Without exception, a woman's greatest risk of violence is from someone she knows. Domestic violence is a violation of a woman's right to physical integrity, to liberty, and all too often, to her right to life itself. When states fail to take the basic steps needed to protect women from domestic violence or allow these crimes to be committed with impunity, states are failing in their obligation to protect women from torture.

The National Coalition Against Domestic Violence (in America) defines domestic violence as a pattern of behaviour used to establish power and control over another person through fear and intimidation, often including the threat or use of violence, when one person believes they are entitled to control another.

In the past, violence against women, particularly violence occurring in the home or between intimate partners, was viewed as a private matter, not as an issue of civil or political rights. Now however, by applying these legally accepted definitions of torture to the violence that women face everyday around the world, the international community has explicitly recognized violence against women as a human rights violation involving state responsibility.

The Declaration on the Elimination of Violence Against Women issued in 1993 the United Nations, states clearly that, "States should exercise due diligence to prevent, investigate, and in accordance with national legislation, punish acts of violence against women, whether those acts are perpetrated by the state or private persons". It sets forth ways in which governments should act to prevent violence, and to protect and defend women's rights. These measures form the standard of due diligence that states are obligated to live up to.

The legal concept of due diligence describes the minimum acceptable level of effort which a state must undertake to fulfill its responsibility to protect individuals from abuses of their rights. Due diligence includes taking effective steps to *prevent* abuses, to *investigate* them when they do occur, to *prosecute* the alleged perpetrator and bring him to justice in fair proceedings, and to ensure adequate *reparation,* including compensation and redress. It also means ensuring that justice is upheld *without discrimination* of any kind. In various measures of this standard, in many countries of the world, states are failing in their due diligence and failing to protect women from violence The failure of a government to prohibit acts of violence against women, or to establish adequate legal protections against such acts, constitutes a failure of state protection. Acts of violence against women constitute torture when they are of the nature and severity envisaged by the concept of torture and the state has failed to provide effective protection.

Without exception, women's greatest risk of violence is from someone she knows. Domestic violence is a violation of a woman's rights to physical integrity, to liberty, and all too often, to her right to life, itself. And when a government fails to provide effective protection from such abuse, domestic violence becomes torture.

"No one should be subjected to torture"[7]

The Human Rights Committee, a monitoring body established by the Covenant,[8] clarifies that "it is the duty of the state party to afford everyone protection through legislation and other measures as may be necessary against the acts prohibited in Article 7, whether inflicted by people in their official capacity, outside their official capacity or in a private capacity". When states fail to provide such protections, they hold responsibility for the abuse. Such failure on the part of the state is clear in the case of Rodi Alvarado. Rodi Alvorada, a Guatemalan army officer, at the age of 16, was subjected to intense abuse, and all her efforts to get help were unsuccessful. Her husband raped her repeatedly, attempted to forcibly abort their second child by kicking her in the spine, dislocated her jaw, tried to cut her hands off with a machete, kicked her in the vagina, and used her head to break windows. He terrified her by bragging about using his power to kill innocent civilians with impunity. Even though many of the attacks took place in public, the police failed to help her in any way. After she made a complaint, her husband ignored three citations without consequence. Furthermore, the courts refused to grant her a divorce without her husband's permission.

Different Forms of Domestic Violence

From acid burning, dowry-related violence and 'honour' killings to rape, battery, and psychological abuse, women are subjected to the basest forms of abuse and humiliation. Such torture of women in rooted in a global culture which denies women equal rights with men, and which legitimizes the violent appropriation of women's bodies for individual gratification or political ends. Violence against women is compounded by discrimination on the grounds of race, ethnicity, sexual orientation, social status, class, and age, and by social and cultural norms that deny women equality also renders women more vulnerable to abuse. The common thread is discrimination against women, the denial of basic human rights to individuals simply because they are women. The Universal Declaration of Human Rights affirms the inadmissibility of discrimination and proclaims that everyone is entitled to all the rights and freedoms set forth in the declaration, without distinction of any kind, including distinction based on sex. States have a duty under international law to take positive measures to prohibit and prevent torture and to respond to instances of torture, regardless of where it takes place or whether the perpetrator is an agent of the state or a private individual. When states fail to take the basic steps needed to protect women from domestic violence or allow these crimes to be committed with impunity, states are failing in their obligation to protect women from torture.

Amnesty International considers domestic violence as torture; torture for which the state is accountable when such acts are of the nature envisioned by the international standards of torture and when the state has failed to fulfil its obligation to provide women effective protection.

Frequently, domestic violence is used to describe specific violent and overtly abusive incidents, and legal definitions will tend to take this perspective. However, when violent and abusive behaviours happen within a relationship, the effects of those behaviours continue after these overt incidents are over. Advocates and counselors will refer to domestic violence as a pattern of behaviours, including those, listed above.

Examples of Violence against Women (Throughout the Life Cycle)

Phase Type of Violence

- Pre-birth – Sex-selective abortion; effects of battering during pregnancy on birth outcomes.
- Infancy – Female infanticide; physical, sexual and psychological abuse.
- Girlhood – Child marriage, female genital mutilation, physical, sexual and psychological abuse, incest; child prostitution and pornography.

- Adolescence – Dating and courtship violence (e.g., acid throwing and date rape)
- Adulthood – economically coerced sex (e.g., school girls having sex with 'sugar daddies' in return for school fees); incest, sexual abuse in the workplace; rape; sexual harassment; forced prostitution and pornography, trafficking in women; partner violence; marital rape, dowry abuse and murders; partner homicide; psychological abuse; abuse of women with disabilities, forced pregnancy.
- Elderly – Forced 'suicide' or homicide of widows for economic reasons; sexual, physical and psychological abuse.[9]

Cause

Domestic violence is caused specifically by the choice to engage in violent or abusive behaviour against a partner, sibling or child. A variety of factors can lead to that choice, but only in the case of truly uncontrollable compulsions can those factors eliminate the potential to choose non-violent and non-abusive behaviours. Other possible causes may include behavioural changes in the individual who has a chemical dependency problem (e.g. drugs and alcohol). Mental illness may also play a role in domestic violence. Unfortunately, after domestic violence occurs both the victim and the abuser may go through a stage of denial, while other victims may choose to try to eliminate the problem by (for example) issuing a restraining order against the abuser.

Purpose

The majority view is that the purpose of domestic violence is not primarily to hurt or harm the victim. Rather, it is to gain or maintain power and control over the victim.

> It is to be noted that power in a relationship is often a matter of perception. A person may perceive themselves to be put-upon when a less involved observer would disagree.

An alternative view is that abuse arises more from an attempt to 'export' feelings of powerlessness to the victim. The purpose of an attempt to "gain or maintain power and control over the victim" is to develop and enforce a permanent channel for such attempted 'export' to the other. Since feelings are personal, and cannot be resolved via others as proxies, this 'export' is inherently impossible to achieve, hence such behaviours are inherently addictive, leading to cycles of abuse. Mutual cycles develop when each party attempts to 'pass the buck' back and forth, usually through varying mechanisms of abuse. Since preferences for abuse-mechanisms are somewhat gendered, with females strongly favouring non-physical forms of abuse, selective 'snapshots' of such interactions may create an illusion of a gendered pattern of violence. Resolution is only achieved when all parties acknowledge their responsibilities, and identify and respect mutual purpose.

Gender

It is impossible to have a discussion on domestic violence that does not include a discussion of the role gender does or does not have to play in the problem. Sometimes, the discussion of gender can overwhelm any other topic, due to the degree of emotion with which the discussion of gender can attain. The topic is also itself emotive because of the revulsion that is evoked by the idea of vulnerable people powerless and hurt at the hands of a partner, spouse or other relative.

Attention to domestic violence began in the women's movement as concern about wives being beaten by their husbands, and has remained a major focus in the modern feminist movement, particularly under the label "violence against women".[10] Erin Pizzey, the founder of an early women's shelter in Cheswick, London, has since expressed her dismay at how the issue has become a gender-political, and expressed an unpopular view in her book *Prone to Violence* that some women in the refuge system had a predisposition to seek abusive relationships. She also expressed the view that domestic violence can occur against any vulnerable intimates, regardless of their sex. Given the violence that she herself experienced in the UK for voicing her views, one might be suspicious of some of those who opposed her views, which remain very relevant. Political balance in light of pressure from the feminist movement has been helped by noting that there are women who were violent with their husbands and partners, and with the realization that where the prevailing culture ceases to be predominantly patriarchal there is no corresponding lessening in the incidence of domestic violence.[11]

Domestic violence is clearly an enormous problem. Many studies have reported the high frequency of women as victims: The Council of Europe found in a 1992 study that one in four women experience domestic violence over their lifetimes and between 6-10 per cent of women suffer domestic violence in a given year. Every minute in the UK, the police receive a call from the public for assistance for domestic violence. However, they estimate that only around 35 per cent of domestic violence is actually reported. A 2002 Women's Aid study found that 74 per cent of separated women suffered from post-separation violence. Until recently, very few studies even asked about female-on-male (or female-on-female) domestic violence; so while these figures are appallingly high, the prevalence of violence against men is typically not included in these figures. Studies based on *reported* assaults or on police records typically find much greater male-on-female violence, than the reverse. The British Crime Survey for the year 2001-02 reported, "There were an estimated 12.9 million incidents of domestic violence acts (non-sexual threats or force) against women (84%) and 2.5 million against men (16%) in England and Wales in the year prior to interview." The same report states, "Four per cent of women and two per cent of men were subject to domestic violence (non-sexual domestic threats or force) during the last year." However, men are known to be far less likely to file complaints.

Many publications claim a grave disparity in general: Women's Aid (the UK's leading domestic violence charity) say "Crime statistics and research both show that domestic violence is gender specific – usually the perpetrator of a pattern of repeated assaults is a man. Women experience the most serious physical and repeated assaults." Nearly 42 per cent of all female homicide victims compared with 4 per cent of male homicide victims, were killed by current or former partners in England and Wales in the year 2000-1. This equates to 102 women, an average of 2 women each week (Home Office, 2001). Ahimsa a UK based Domestic Violena project, says: "Research findings consistently report that over 90 per cent of domestic violence is perpetrated by men within heterosexual relationships." This, however, is simply untrue. Although it is true that many studies report only male-on-female violence because that is all they ask about, those studies that do examine prevalence in both directions overwhelmingly find little difference by gender. This is particularly true when questions are specific: for example, men typically do not report being slapped if they are simply asked about 'violence'; women do.

Martin S. Fiebert of the Department of Psychology at California State University, Long Beach, provides an annotated bibliography of 174 scholarly studies that have found significant prevalence of female-on-male domestic violence. Studies have been carried out to explore these issues, and results have seemed somewhat contradictory. A problem in conducting such studies is the amount of silence, fear and shame that results from abuse within families and relationships. Another is that abusive patterns can tend to seem normal to those who have lived in them for a length of time. Similarly, subtle forms of abuse can be quite transparent even as they set the stage for further abuse seeming normal. Finally, inconsistent definition of what domestic violence is makes strong conclusions hard to reach when compiling the available studies.

Both men and women have been arrested and convicted of assaulting their partners in both heterosexual and homosexual relationships. The bulk of these arrests have been men being arrested for assaulting women, but that has been shifting somewhat over time and clearly arrest records are not the whole story. Actual studies of behaviour show that whilst half of male/ female intimate violence is best described as mutual brawling, a quarter is the male attacking the female and the remaining quarter being females attacking their male partner. Determining how many instances of domestic violence actually involve male victims is difficult. Male domestic violence victims may be reluctant to get help for a number of reasons. A man who calls for help may even risk being arrested as the 'perpetrator' even though he was the victim.

The general consensus seems to be that male-on-female domestic violence is more likely to result in serious injury or death, whereas female-on-male (which, under the definition used by the

UK government if no others, includes preventing the father seeing the children), is more likely to result in male suicide. Men on average have more upper body strength and socialization that predisposes them to resort to violence more than women do, and that can give them a higher average lethality than women. However, women can and do use weapons to equalize whatever deficit in physical power which may be present, and can also use social constraints against men hitting women even in self-defence, to provide them with sufficient lethality to be dangerous in conflict situations.

In the United States, the bulk of the decrease in rates of intimate partner homicides is accounted for the dramatic decrease in women's murders of their male intimate partners. Murders of female intimate partners by men have dropped, but not nearly as dramatically. Men kill their female intimate partners at about four times the rate that women kill their male intimate partners. A research has found that at least two-thirds of women killed by their intimate partners were battered by those men prior to the murder. It also found that when males are killed by female intimates, the women in those relationships had been abused by their male partner about 75 per cent of the time.

Some researchers have found a relationship between the availability of domestic violence services, improved laws and enforcement regarding domestic violence and increased access to divorce, and higher earnings for women with declines in intimate partner homicide.[12]

This suggests that, ironically, male abusers have benefited from domestic violence reforms, and are less likely to be killed by their partners since women are no longer faced with murder as their "only option" to escape the violence. At the same time, men continue to kill their female partners at almost the same rate. This suggests that reforms in the civil and criminal system and social services to battered women have not impacted the fundamental causes of domestic violence. Although some presume that this indicates a gendered nature of the problem, the lack of success may itself be a result of overly simplistic gender-assumptions on the nature of violence. Gender roles and expectations can and do play a role in abusive situations, and exploring these roles and expectations can be helpful in addressing abusive situations, as do factors like race, class, religion, sexuality and philosophy. None of these factors cause one to abuse or another to be abused.

Historically, domestic violence has been seen as a family issue and little interest has been directed at violence in same-sex relationships. It has not been until recently, as the gay rights movement has brought the issues of gay and lesbian people into public attention, when research has been started to conduct on homosexual relationships. Several studies have indicated that partner abuse among same-sex couples (both female and male) is relatively similar in both prevalence and dynamics to that among heterosexual couples. Gays and lesbians, however, face special obstacles in dealing with the issues that some researchers have labelled "the double closet": not only do gay and lesbian people often feel that they are discriminated against and dismissed by police and social services, they are also often met with lack of support from their peers who would rather keep quiet about the problem in order not to attract negative attention toward the gay community. Also, the supportive services are mostly designed for the needs of heterosexual women and do not always meet the needs of other groups.

Statistics on Domestic Violence Against Women

Industrialized Countries

Canada: 29 per cent of women (a nationally representative sample of 12,300 women) reported being physically assaulted by a current or former partner since the age of 16.

Japan: 59 per cent of 796 women surveyed in 1993 reported being physically abused by their partner.

New Zealand: 20 per cent of 314 women surveyed reported being hit or physically abused by a male partner.

Switzerland: 20 per cent of 1,500 women reported being physically assaulted according to a 1997 survey.

United Kingdom: 25 per cent of women (a random sample of women from one district) had been punched or slapped by a partner or ex-partner in their lifetime.

United States: 28 per cent of women (a nationally representative sample of women) reported at least one episode of physical violence from their partner.

Asia and the Pacific Cambodia: 16 per cent of women (a nationally representative sample of women) reported being physically abused by a spouse; 8 per cent report being injured.

India: Up to 45 per cent of married men acknowledged physically abusing their wives, according to a 1996 survey of 6,902 men in the state of Uttar Pradesh.

Korea: 38 per cent of wives reported being physically abused by their spouse, based on a survey of a random sample of women.

Thailand: 20 per cent of husbands (a representative sample of 619 husbands) acknowledged physically abusing their wives at least once in their marriage.

Middle East

Egypt: 35 per cent of women (a nationally representative sample of women) reported being beaten by their husband at some point in their marriage.

Israel: 32 per cent of women reported at least one episode of physical abuse by their partner and 30 per cent reported sexual coercion by their husbands in the previous year, according to a 1997 survey of 1,826 Arab women.

Africa

Kenya: 42 per cent of 612 women surveyed in one district reported having been beaten by a partner, of those 58 per cent reported *that they* were beaten often or sometimes.

Uganda: 41 per cent of women reported being beaten or physically harmed by a partner; 41 per cent of men reported beating their partner (representative sample of women and their partners in two districts).

Zimbabwe: 32 per cent of 966 women in one province reported physical abuse by a family or household member since the age of 16, according to a 1996 survey.

Latin America and the Caribbean

Chile: 26 per cent of women (representative sample of women from Santiago) reported at least one episode of violence by a partner, 11 per cent reported at least one episode of severe violence and 15 per cent of women reported at least one episode of less severe violence.

Colombia: 19 per cent of 6,097 women surveyed have been physically assaulted by their partner in their lifetime.

Mexico: 30 per cent of 650 women surveyed in Guadalajara reported at least one episode of physical violence by a partner; 13 per cent reported physical violence within the previous year, according to a 1997 report.

Nicaragua: 52 per cent of women (representative sample of women in Leon) reported being physically abused by a partner at least once; 27 per cent reported physical abuse in the previous year, according to a 1996 report.

Central and Eastern Europe/CIS/Baltic States

Estonia: 29 per cent of women aged 18-24 fear domestic violence, and the share rises with age, affecting 52 per cent of women 65 or older, according to a 1994 survey of 2,315 women.

Poland: 60 per cent of divorced women surveyed in 1993 by the Centre for the Examination of Public Opinion reported having been hit at least once by their ex-husbands; an additional 25 per cent reported repeated violence.

Russia (St. Petersburg): 25 per cent of girls (and 11% of boys) reported unwanted sexual contact, according to a survey of 174 boys and 172 girls in grade 10 (aged 14-17).

Tajikistan: 23 per cent of 550 women aged 18-40 reported physical abuse, according to a survey.[13]

It is estimated that every year in the United States, approximately 3 million women are assaulted by their partner. Many of these incidents go unreported to authorities due to the shame and fear associated with domestic violence. In 1998, of the approximately 1.5 million violent crimes committed between intimate partners, over 8,76,000 of the victims were women, and over 8,35,000 were men. Of the approximately 1,830 murders committed against intimate partners in 1998, three out of four of the victims were women. In homes where domestic violence occurs, children in the home are at a 300 per cent greater risk of being abused. Between 3 and 5 billion dollars are spent annually for medical expenses related to domestic violence. Also, approximately 100 million dollars is lost by businesses annually through lost productivity, sick leave and absenteeism due to domestic violence.

Response to Domestic Violence

The response to domestic violence is typically a combined effort between law enforcement agencies, the courts, social service agencies and corrections/ probation agencies. The role of each has evolved as domestic violence has been brought more into public view. Historically, law enforcement agencies, the courts and correction agencies treated domestic violence as a personal matter. For example, police officers were often reluctant to intervene by making an arrest, and often chose instead to simply counsel the couple and/or ask one of the parties to leave the residence for a period of time. The courts were reluctant to impose any significant sanctions on those convicted of domestic violence, largely because it was viewed as a misdemeanour offense. This mindset of treating family violence as a personal problem of minor consequence permeated the system's response, and potentially allowed the perpetrator to continue acting violently.

Activism, initiated by victim advocacy groups and feminist groups, has led to a better understanding of the scope and effect of domestic violence on victims and families, and has brought about changes in the criminal justice system's response. In 1981, the Domestic Abuse Intervention Project became the first multidisciplinary programme designed to address the issue of domestic violence. This experiment, conducted in Duluth, Minnesota, United States; frequently referred to as the 'Duluth Project', involved coordinating the actions of a variety of agencies that deal with domestic situations. The policies and activities of diverse elements of the system, from police officers on the street, to shelters for battered women and probation officers supervising offenders, were coordinated with each other. This programme has become a model for other jurisdictions seeking to deal more effectively with domestic violence. More and more jurisdictions are mandating that suspects in domestic violence incidents be arrested if there is probable cause to believe that an assault occurred. Victim advocates are intervening directly with victims by providing them with counselling about the court process, how to obtain and use restraining orders and how to formulate and implement safety plans. Corrections/probation agencies in many areas are supervising domestic violence offenders more closely, and are also paying closer attention to the victim's needs and safety issues.

It should be noted, however, that the Duluth framework depends on a strict 'patriarchal violence' model and presumes that all violence in the home and elsewhere has a male perpetrator and female victim. Through what appears to be nothing more than circular reasoning, it explicitly rejects any concept of mutuality or symmetry in abusive relationships, and appears to have little or no basis in relation to proven principles in psychology, education or remedial therapy. Hence although the Duluth programme is widely used, anecdotal evidence indicates that its record of success has been patchy at best. It may be inappropriate for all but a relatively small number of domestic violence contexts. There is an urgent need for formal review of the Duluth framework, and development of alternative frameworks for use in other contexts.

Publicly available resources for dealing with domestic violence have tended to be almost exclusively geared towards supporting women and children who are in relationships with or who are leaving violent men, rather than for survivors of domestic violence per se. This has been due to the purported numeric preponderance of female victims and the perception that domestic violence only affected women. Resources to help men who have been using violence take responsibility for and stop their use of violence, such as Men's Behaviour Change Programmes or anger management training, are available, though attendees are ordered to pay for their own course in order that they should remain accountable for their actions.

One of the challenges for lay observers, victims, perpetrators and treatment providers is demonstrated by the tendency to describe perpetrator treatment as men's 'anger management' groups.

Comprehensive and accountable behaviour change programmes are seen as far more appropriate and effective interventions in male violence in the home than anger management groups.

Inherent in anger management only approaches, is the assumption that the violence is a result of a loss of control over one's anger. While there is little doubt that some domestic violence is about the loss of control, the choice of the target of that violence may be of greater significance. Anger management might be appropriate for the individual who lashes out indiscriminately when angry towards co-workers, supervisors or family. In most cases, however, the domestic violence perpetrator lashes out only at their intimate partner or relatively defenceless child, which suggests an element of choice or selection that, in turn, suggests a different or additional motivation beyond simple anger. Most experienced treatment providers have probably observed that for various reasons, many of which may be cultural, the perpetrator has a sense of entitlement, sometimes conscious, sometimes not, that leads directly to their choice of target.

Men's behaviour change programmes, although differing throughout the world, tend to focus on the prevention of further violence within the family and the safety of women and children. Often they abide by various standards of practice that includes 'partner contact' where the participant's female partner is contacted by the programme and informed about the course, checked about her level of safety and support and offered support services for herself if she requires them. Many of these programmes have both a male and female facilitator and follow a programme designed to highlight the impact of his behaviour, examine the attitudes, values and behaviours that lead to his choice to use violence and aim to support and challenge the man to take responsibility for his use of violence.

Work with men who use violence and abuse toward family members can be seen in Victoria, Australia where a unique combination of voluntary and mandated (court or police referred) programmes exist as well as a statewide telephone counselling, information and referral service for men exists. However, there are no equivalent services in Victoria for women who use violence or abuse, nor any support services at all for abused men. The absence of such services leads to circular claims that no such services are required, and to similarly circular claims that the available services represent proof that violence is exclusively 'male'. From the perspective of the police, who are often the first to investigate domestic violence incidents, one of the problems is that the definitions of domestic violence include 'acts' that are not by themselves crimes. The UK Crown Prosecution Service publishes guidance for prosecution in cases of alleged domestic violence. According to the Law Commission some further thought needs to be given to clauses (e) and (f) of Article 51A. Article 51A(e) desires the promotion of harmony and the spirit of common brotherhood among all the people of India transcending religious, linguistic and regional or sectional diversities and renunciation of practices derogatory to the dignity of women. It is couched in broad terms but it should be clear that attacks on minority communities or minority opinions are frowned upon. Respect for both are essential and the wording lends support to a broad humanism to cover such differences as may exist or better still, co-exist. Two thoughts can be distilled. The first is that the objective will not be reached unless there is a determined effort to restrict religious practices to the home on the justified premise that one's religion is a personal matter and is not conducive to mass assertiveness. The other is the status of women. Lip service is being paid to the doctrine of gender equality. The fact remains that generally women are still regarded as inferior both at home and workplace although the Commission has noticed an improvement, however dissatisfied it maybe with the degree of the improvement, it is necessary to separate religious precepts from civil law. Civil law as the name implies is a matter for society not for religious leaders and it would seem to us to be axiomatic that in matters of civil rights, laws of property and inheritance and marriage and divorce, although practices may differ, legal rights that accrue must be the same. For example, a marriage may be solemnized according to religious or social custom but the rights of a woman in the case of divorce must be the same no matter what her religion is. As the Supreme Court held in the *Shahbanoo Case,* an abandoned wife is an abandoned wife and it does not matter whether she professes one religion or other. Article 4(2) of ICCPR

(International Convention of Civil and Political Rights) makes non-derogable the right to life (Article 6), prohibition against torture (Article 7), freedom of thought, conscience and religion (Article 18), to name some. Similarly Indian Constitution makes non-derogable the right to life (Article 21) and personal liberty. The guiding factor is the respect for the inherent dignity of the human person which is non-derogable in any situation. In addition, the fundamental duties of every citizen covering a wide spectrum to strengthen the guarantee of Fundamental Rights is in Article 51A (Part IVA of the Constitution). The Protection of Human Rights Act, 1993 was enacted to provide for the constitution of a National Human Rights Commission, State Human Rights Commissions in states and Human Rights Courts for better protection of human rights and for matters connected therewith or incidental thereto. 'Human Rights' is defined in Section 2(l)(d) of the Act to mean the rights relating to life, liberty, equality and dignity of the individual guaranteed by the Constitution or embodied in the International Covenants and enforceable by courts in India. The functions of the Commission are enumerated in Section 12 which encompasses a wide area to enable the Commission not only to enquire into the violations or negligence in prevention of violation of human rights but also to promote the human rights culture and perform any function necessary for the promotion of human rights. The interpretation of the fundamental rights, particularly, Article 14 (right to equality) and Article 21 (right to life) by the Supreme Court, inter alia, by reading the requirements of directive principles into them, together with the impact of the *Vishaka* judgment enabling provisions in the international instruments being read into these guarantees has considerably enlarged the meaning and scope of human rights in India. The National Human Rights Commission also has interpreted its functions enumerated in Section 12 of the Act expansively to include therein monitoring of the functioning of the institutions of governance with a view to ensure better protection of human rights and to prevent their violation. The NHRC visualizes its role as that of a catalyst to improve the quality of governance with the firm belief that good governance in accordance with the Constitution and the rule of law alone can be effective for better protection of human rights. The linkage between the two is direct and clear. Emphasis on human dignity is laid not only in the UN Charter, the Universal Declaration of Human Rights and several other international covenants but also in the Constitution of India which mentions 'dignity of the individual' as a core value in its preamble. The debate on the classification of human rights based on different generations of these rights is purely academic since all of them must coexist for full development of the human personality. Empowerment of the people through human development is the aim of human rights. The Human Development Index (HDI) is the new measure of development and it is said: "a nation's ability to convert knowledge into wealth and social good through the process of innovation is going to determine its future". There is now a paradigm shift towards emphasis on intangible intellectual assets as the index of wealth.

Such distinction, however, has to be viewed from the historical context of the time when the Constitution was framed. Perhaps, in the backdrop of the then social-economic conditions of the Indian society, after about two hundred years of colonial subjugation, the framers of the Constitution evolved two sets of rights. In a way, the Fundamental Rights and the Directive Principles of State Policy are the product of human rights movement in the country. Roughly, they represent two streams in the evolution of human rights, which divide them between civil and political rights on the one hand and social, economic and cultural rights on the other. Justiciability, is essentially speaking, the basis of division between them. Whereas fundamental rights are justiciable, directive principles are not. Nonetheless, the 'founding fathers' gave a mandate in Article 37, that the directive principles, though not enforceable by any court, are "fundamental in the governance of the country and it shall be the duty of the state to apply these principles in making laws". Moreover, India, being a signatory to Universal Declaration of Human Rights, International Covenant on Economic, Social and Cultural Rights, and other international instruments, is legally as well as morally committed to ensure basic human rights to all its citizens and enact laws accordingly. As a matter of fact, the development of human rights jurisprudence in the country is basically based on the Supreme Court expanding the concept of 'right to life and liberty' under Article 21 so as to make the enjoyment of social, economic and cultural rights a reality. Both Fundamental Rights and Directive Principles of State Policy are being increasingly construed by the courts harmoniously. This trend is reflected in the opinion of the Supreme Court in *Minerva Mills Ltd*. v. *Union of India* where it was recognized that harmony between fundamental rights and directive principles of state policy was the basic feature of the Constitution.

Perhaps, realizing practical difficulties in the enforcement of directive principles by the courts, it appears that the founding fathers settled for their judicial non-enforceability but that does not mean that directive principles were in any way considered less important than fundamental rights. The resolve of the Preamble is elaborately repeated in the directive principles which, among others, specifically require, the state to minimize the inequalities in income and to eliminate inequalities in status, facilities and opportunities. The directive principles require the state to take special care of education and economic interests particularly of the vulnerable sections of the society.

Thus, both civil and political rights on the one hand and economic, social and cultural rights on the other, are indivisible and interdependent. While the former are more in the nature of injunctions against the state, the latter are demands on the state to provide positive conditions to capacitate an individual to exercise the former. The object of both is to make the individual an effective participant in the affairs of the society for full development of human personality. In his remarkable study, 'Development as Freedom', Amartya Sen observed that the achievements of democracy depend not only on electoral politics and the rules of procedure that are adopted and safeguarded, but also on the ways in which the opportunities that democracy offers are used. In particular, Sen wrote of the need to remove the major sources of three 'un- freedoms' that afflict a society – hunger, illiteracy, and early death – for democracy to have a true meaning and content. Strategies should be designed to operate across a broad range of areas depending upon the context in which they are delivered. Key areas for intervention include:

- Advocacy and awareness raising
- Education for building a culture of non-violence

- Training
- Resource development
- Direct service provision to victim survivors and perpetrators
- Networking and community mobilization
- Direct intervention to help victim survivors rebuild their lives
- Legal reform
- Monitoring interventions and measures
- Data collection and analysis
- Early identification of 'at risk' families, communities, groups, and individuals

These areas are not mutually exclusive; interventions may touch upon several areas at once. Above all, five underlying principles should guide all strategies and interventions attempting to address domestic violence:

- Prevention
- Protection
- Early intervention
- Rebuilding the lives of victim-survivors
- Accountability

It has to be kept in mind that the ultimate aim of all the human rights is "Universal acknowledgment of the equality of men and women is fundamental to peace and the survival of humanity. Implementation of the principle of equality challenges traditional practices necessitates a re-examination of the long-held assumptions underlying all human relationships from the family to society at large. Because it is so interwoven with all other facets of life, the practice of the equality of the sexes impinges on all human beings – women and men alike".[14]

Notes

1. According to the "New York State Coalition Against Domestic Violence".

2. The Protection of Women from Domestic Violence Act, 2005(No. 43 of 20051 (13, September 2005,) Section 3.
3. The UK Home Office statistics indicate that male-on-female *repeated* assaults are about twice as common as female-on-male *repeated* assaults. This is the opposite to the findings of the US National Family Violence Survey, which has consistently indicated in repeated studies for more than 30 years that females initiate domestic assault at more than twice the rate of men.
4. (Source: Heise. 1994)at Unesco.org
5. "यत्र नार्यस्तु पुज्यन्ते रमन्ते तत्र देवताः। यत्रैतास्तु न पूज्यन्ते सर्वास्तत्राफलाः क्रिया।। "meaning – thereby; in a house where women are honoured, there Gods are pleased. But where they are not honoured and are insulted nothing done in the house yields good results". Manusmriti-III-57 (quoted in J.M. Ramajois, *Ancient Indian Law*, Universal Law Publishing, New Delhi 2004).
6. *Tukaram* v. *State of Maharashtra* (1979), 2SC 143.
7. Article 7 of the International Covenant on Civil and Political Rights (ICCPR) states that "no one should be subjected to torture or to cruel, inhuman or degrading treatment or punishment".
8. International Covenant on Civil and Political Rights (ICCPR).
9. (Source: "Violence Against Women", WHO., FRH/WHD/97.8)
10. Linda G. Mills, Linda Mills, *Insult to Injury: Rethinking Our Responses to Intimate Abuse,* Princeton University Press, September 2003.
11. *supra*
12. (Laura Dugan, Daniel S. Nagin, Richard Rosenfeld, Explaining the Decline in Intimate Partner Homicide: The Effects of Changing Domesticity, Women's Status, and Domestic Violence Resources in *Homicide Studies*, Vol. 3, No. 3,187-214,1999)
13. (Adapted from Violence Against Women, WHO, FRH/WHD/97. 8, "Women in Transition", Regional Monitoring Report, *UNICEF 1999,* and a study by Domestic Violence Research Centre, Japan).
14. Janet A. Khan and Peter J. Khan, *Advancement of Women*, Wilmette, Illinois: Baha, Publishing Trust 1998.

9

Good Governance, Human Rights and the Rights of Minorities

SUSHMA YADAV

> The minorities in India have loyally accepted the rule of the majority, which is basically a communal majority and not a political majority. It is for the majority to realize its duty not to discriminate against minorities.
>
> Baba Saheb Bhim Rao Ambedkar

Development aims at creating a suitable and enabling environment for promoting long, healthy and creative lives. Governance, in any society, aims to ensure this through the exercise of economic, political and administrative authority. It is democratically organized and oriented towards the effective fulfilment of its obligations under international human rights law. The contemporary preoccupation with the issue, originated in the World Bank, for whom good governance is an instrument for sustainable growth, and where the keywords are transparency and accountability. Before proceeding, it may be useful to reflect on the ambiguity inherent in making these terms operational. To whom and for what shall the government be accountable? In the interest of whom shall transparency be ensured, and what shall be covered?

From a human rights perspective, the government should primarily be accountable to its own inhabitants. This should not exclude, as a secondary concern, accountability to external actors including transnational corporations investing on their territory. To make accountability a reality, civil society and its associations must have full and open information on the activities of the state and its allocation of resources. Transparency is required first and foremost in the interest of own inhabitants.

Equally important is to examine the substantive issue: for what should governments be held accountable? Good governance should first and foremost be tested in regard to its ability to ensure that all human rights can be enjoyed under the jurisdiction of the state. The state has the primary responsibility for the implementation of human rights. It follows that governance must be so constructed as to obtain the optimal realization of human rights for all under the jurisdiction of the state.[1]

The general logic of human rights is that everyone is free to think and act as she or he wishes except where countervailing factors requires limitations or duties. While quite obviously some limitations and duties are necessary in society, it is important that they do not interfere unnecessarily or in a disproportionate way with human freedoms. These universal human rights are meant for all individuals whether they belonged to the minorities or to the majorities. The principle of equality and non-discrimination was based on the assumption that all inhabitants of the territory, irrespective of their race, sex, language, national or ethnic origin "are endowed with reason and conscience and should act towards each other in a spirit of brotherhood".

This has been further elaborated in the Declaration on the Rights of Persons Belonging to National or Ethnic, Religious or Linguistic Minorities (hereinafter referred to as the 1992 Minority Declaration), adopted by the United Nations General Assembly in 1992,[2] which in its Article 1 calls on state to protect the existence and identity of minorities and to encourage conditions for the enjoyment of that identity. The main thrust of the rights of person belonging to minorities is to ensure the acceptance of the multicultural composition of the heterogeneous societies, to promote pluralism in togetherness based not only on reciprocal respect but also on cooperation within an overarching civil society.

The impact of a human right-based approach to good governance depends on the degree to which the values underlying the relevant human standards are shared internationally and within any given state under examination. While quite obviously some limitations and duties are necessary in society, it is important that they do not interfere unnecessarily or in a disproportionate way with human freedoms. The general guideline in international human rights law is found in the Universal Declaration of Human Rights (UDHR):

> Everyone shall be subject only to such limitations as are determined by law solely for the purpose of securing due recognition and respect for the rights and freedoms of others and of meeting the just requirements of morality, public order and the general welfare in a democratic society.[3]

In this formulation, major clues to good governance can be found. More can be added when we take into account the international conventions on human rights, to which we shall turn in a moment.

Let us start with the final words – 'in a democratic society'. There is an increasing recognition at the international level of the intimate link between democracy and human rights, most clearly articulated in a resolution adopted by the United Nations Commission on Human Rights in April 2000. It reaffirmed that good governance, including transparency and accountability, is indispensable for building peaceful, prosperous and democratic societies. In its operative part, the resolution adopted by the Commission called on all states to consolidate democracy through the promotion of pluralism and the protection of human rights with the rights of minorities and fundamental freedoms. The participation of individuals in decision-making should be maximized. Competent and public institutions should be developed or reinforced, including and an electoral system that ensures periodic, free and fair elections. The resolution spelled out in great detail the elements of democracy from a human rights perspective.

Legality is a core concern in human rights, and it is difficult to conceive of a system where legality is ensured unless there is a division between the legislative and the executive branches. Limitations to human rights, must be set by the law. Human rights instruments repeatedly use reference to law as a safeguard. The underlying concern is that any tampering with the freedoms and rights of an individual, no matter whether the individual is from a general class or from a minority group, must be based on pre-existing, general norms. Consequently, there must be a legislature, which fulfils the procedural requirements of law making, and it must be separate from the executive branch, which implements the law.

Among the measures spelled out to ensure the right of everyone to take part in the government of his/her country were free elections, steps to address the representation of under-represented segments of society, and ensuring, through legislation, institutions and mechanisms, the freedom to form democratic political parties and appropriate access to funds. Transparency and fairness of the electoral process was required, including a free, independent and pluralistic media.

While the institutional and procedural requirements are important, they are not on their own enough to ensure good governance. Every Indian state has a general duty to promote and protect the human rights set out in the UDHR. The Constitution called on all states to strengthen democracy by taking effective measures aimed at the progressive realization of economic, social and cultural rights, such as the right to education and the right to a standard of living, adequate for health and well-being, including food, clothing, housing and medical care and necessary social services. States should individually and through international cooperation take effective measures aimed at overcoming social inequalities and eliminating poverty.

Human rights provisions set limits to or give guidance to processes of governance: on one hand, the state and its agents cannot use arbitrary deprivation of liberty, denial of freedom of expression or information, or prohibition of association and assembly as part of governance, even if the majority of the population through democratic participation wanted that to be done. On the other, governments are required under human rights law to take a number of positive steps and achieve certain results. They must ensure generally healthy conditions in a society free from avoidable health risks, must ensure access to education for all, and must ensure that everyone has social insurance or social security. Good governance requires an active, agile state, which can combine, respect for the freedom of its inhabitants, with measures to ensure the economic and social outcomes required from it under human rights law.

States must, at the primary level, respect the resources owned by the individual of all classes including the minorities, her or his freedom to find a job of preference and the freedom to take the necessary actions and use the necessary resources – alone or in association with others – to satisfy his or her own needs.[4] In regard to the latter, collective or group right can become important: the resources belonging to a collective of persons, such as indigenous populations, must be respected in order for them to be able to satisfy their needs. Consequently, as part of the obligation to respect these resources, the state should take steps to recognize and register the land rights of indigenous peoples and land tenure of smallholders whose title is uncertain.

State obligations consist at a secondary level of protecting the integrity and freedom of action of all groups of people individually against other private parties. The state must protect the right to life by prohibiting and punishing homicide. It must protect freedom from deprivation of liberty and freedom of movement against third parties. It must protect the freedom to practice one's religion against aggressive religious zealots with other religious convictions. It must protect the use by it, must protect the use by individuals of their resources against other, more assertive or aggressive subjects – more powerful economic interests, protection against fraud, against unethical behaviour in trade and contractual relations, against the marketing and dumping of hazardous or dangerous products. This protective function of the state is the most important aspect of state obligations also with regard to economic, social and cultural rights, and it is similar to the role of the state as protector of civil and political rights.

Significant components of the obligation to protect are spelled out in existing law. Such legislation becomes manageable for judicial review, whether it relates to civil and political rights or economic, social and cultural rights, and therefore belies the argument that economic and social rights are inherently non-judicial. Legislation of this kind must, of course, be contextual – that is, it must be based on the specific requirements in the country concerned.

Human rights set requirements to institutions and processes of good governance, and to participation in, and outcomes of, the exercise of public power. We now turn to the more specific contents of these requirements in ethnically heterogeneous societies. A society is considered ethnically heterogeneous when different ethnic groups including the minorities coexist within the same state.

Approaches to group relation within states have differed enormously in the past. Policies can be evaluated on the basis of their content and their intended effect and, being the result of competing influences by different groups, cannot easily be classified by simple criteria. What follows is a relatively high level of abstraction from practice observed in reality, based on two dimensions of classification. The main dimension here is homogenization versus separation, with the intermediate of integration. The second dimension is equalization versus ranking (differentiation in status).

Different approaches can be found in multicultural societies, including separate schools, or separate classes for some parts of the instruction. The concern with equality in particular equal opportunities in the larger society, poses problems in the implementation even of well-intentioned pluralist policies. To find the appropriate balance between partial separateness and equality is a task of considerable complexity.

Three aspects of human rights relevant to all groups of societies will be briefly outlined: the principle of equality and non-discrimination, the right of persons belonging to minorities to express, preserve and develop their identity, and the rights of indigenous peoples of material and cultural autonomy.

Cultural coexistence, which is an unavoidable aspect of contemporary societies, can easily generate discriminations in the form of exclusions, restrictions or preference. The main thrust of modern human right is to counteract such tendencies by emphasizing equality irrespective of race, colour, religion, national or social origin and other factors. It therefore seeks to outlaw all forms of discrimination, which is defined as distinctions, exclusions, restrictions or preferences on unwarranted grounds, such as race, national background, ethnicity, or gender.

The main instruments in international human rights law to counteract challenges to the equality of human beings from different racial or ethnic groups is the International Covenant on the Elimination of All Forms of Racial Discrimination (ICERD). It has the dual objective to eliminate racial discrimination in all its forms and to promote understanding among all racial and ethnic groups (Article 2, Para. 1)

This shall not lead to the maintenance of unequal or separate right for the different groups. It might therefore appear to come into conflict with the desire by different ethnic groups to maintain their own separate identity. This dilemma can be resolved however, by distinguishing between two concerns: on the one hand, the overriding importance of equality domain, and on the other hand the possibility of maintaining a degree of pluralism in other fields of human activity.

The Rights of Persons Belonging to Minorities: Preservation of Identity

In the first period after World War II the majority of UN members gave priority the concern with equality and were reluctant to include minority rights under genre: international law. The western states, then in majority position, argued all individuals should enjoy the universal human rights whether they belonged to minorities or majorities. The principle of equality and non-discrimination was based on the assumption that all inhabitants of the territory, irrespective of the race, sex, language, national or ethnic origin, "are endowed with reason at conscience and should act towards each other in a spirit of brotherhood" (Universal Declaration Article 1).

It was broadly felt that there was very little need for space minority protection arrangements.

Over the years, however, a change of opinion has caused a gradual evolution of the normative system, arising from the demand by persons belonging to ethnic religious or linguistic groups for protection of their group, to use their own language, to be able to preserve, to reproduce and to develop their own cultural and therefore to control or have a significant impact on the content of the education of their new generations. A part of this concern is to be able effectively to influence political decisions affecting themselves.

Article 27 of the International Covenant on Civil and Political Rights provides that in those states in which ethnic, religious or linguistic minorities exist, persons belonging to such minorities shall not be denied the right, in community with the other members of their group, to enjoy their own culture to profess and practise their own religion, or to use their own language.

The special rapporteur on Prevention of Discrimination and Protection of Minorities, Mr. Capotorti, in his "Study on the Rights of Persons Belonging to Ethnic, Religious and Linguistic Minorities" stated that in order to give effect to the rights set forth in Article 27 of the covenant, active and sustained measures are required from states. A purely passive attitude on their part would render those rights ineffective.[5]

This has been further elaborated in the Declaration on the Rights of Persons Belonging to National or Ethnic, Religious or Linguistic Minorities (hereinafter referred to as the 1992 Minority Declaration), adopted by the United Nations General Assembly in 1992, which in its Article 1 calls on states to protect the existence and identity of minorities and to encourage conditions for the enjoyment of that identity.[6] It further provides that the existences and the national or ethnic, cultural, religious and linguistic identity of minorities shall be protected by states within their territories and that states shall encourage conditions for the promotion of that identity. It represents a clear trend in international law towards greater recognition of the multicultural composition of national societies in public life.

Under Article 4 of the Declaration, Paragraph 2, states are called upon to take measures to create favourable conditions to enable persons belonging to minorities to express their characteristics and to develop their culture, language, religion, traditions and customs, except where specific practices are in violation of national law and contrary to international standards. States, therefore, are under an obligation to take positive measures of special protection for minorities, in order for them to develop their culture, language and religion.

The main thrust of the rights of persons belonging to minorities is to ensure the acceptance of the multicultural composition of heterogeneous societies, to promote pluralism in togetherness based on reciprocal respect but also on cooperation within an overarching civil society. A person who objectively 'belongs' to a minority is free to use or not use the special rights of minorities. She or he is entitled to make her or his own choice of identity within the society at large.

The Minority Declaration places considerable emphasis on effective participation in the larger society of which the minority is part (Articles 2.2 and 2.3), the provisions regarding indigenous peoples seek to allocate authority to these people so that they can make their own decisions (e.g., ILO Convention 169 Article 7 and 8, Draft Declaration Articles 4, 23 and 31). The right to participation in the larger society is in the draft Declaration given a secondary significance and expressed as an optional right. They have the right to participate fully, if they so choose, through procedures determined by them, in devising legislative or administrative measures that may affect them (Draft Declaration Articles 19 and 20).

Governance in The Common Domain

In any nationwide society encompassing the whole of the permanent population of a country a common domain must exist where everybody is free to interact. It would apply to all, including members of minorities and even persons of indigenous origins, particularly those who have migrated out of the particular habitat of the indigenous population.

In the common domain, universal human rights require equality, and non-discrimination should be the overriding principle. Governance should be colour and ethnically blind, except for the adoption and implementation of transitional measures of affirmative action called for in order to create equality in fact. Such affirmative action measures must not lead to lasting differentiation.

Broadly speaking the scope of the common domain should cover nearly everything related to the common market, including access to jobs, goods and services, housing communication, transport, and health services. The market can be sustained only through the existence of a civic culture, which is over and above the separate ethnic cultures. The common domain is the space where everyone interacts, also across cultural borders.

Human rights require that everyone within the nation shall have the same rights to political representation, but in ethnically divided societies special requirements apply. While the political system should ensure a common domain, it should ideally not be controlled by a hegemonic, majority group but give incentives to peaceful group accommodation and ensure to each of the groups respect for their identity and their justified interests.

Concluding Observations

The Role of The International Community

A number of suggestions have been made above regarding criteria and guidelines for good governance in heterogeneous societies. Such recipe cannot, however, be introduced overnight, and transitional steps have to be taken at various intervals. In the transition from authoritarian or colonial rule, there is initially no civic society, which can sustain a common domain of openness, transparency and inclusiveness. In many societies there has been reversion to authoritarian rule of various kinds, in others, the process of democratization has been exploited by ethnic conflict entrepreneurs, causing, latent divisions to become open wounds, leading to violence and deep polarization. The causes are manifold. The transition often exacerbates existing ethnic problems, with conflict entrepreneurs mobilizing latent antagonisms. External factors influence the exercise of state governance to various degrees. The existence of set of international norms of human rights indicate that the international community demands or at least encourages states to ensure that their governance is in accordance with those rights, but 'international community' does not have one single policy. Some outside states pursue their own geopolitical or economic interests in affecting the policies of the country concerned. If the international community as a whole could further refine its criteria for the good of international community as a whole could further refine its criteria for good governance in heterogeneous societies and have some institution or office to act for them as a whole, the prospects for divisive conflicts in such societies would be considerably reduced.

Notes

1. The duty of states to cooperate in regard to human rights is set out in the UN Charter Article 56 through reference to Article 55, which states that all UN members pledge themselves to take joint and separate action in cooperation with the organizational perspectives.
2. See Article 29.2 of Universal Declaration of Human Rights.
3. As stated in the Article 29.1 of the Universal Declaration of Human Rights.
4. Recommended by the Committee on Economic, Social and Cultural Rights, General Comments, No. 12, 1999.
5. F. Capotorti, "Study on the Rights of Persons Belonging to Ethnic, Religious and Linguistic Minorities", UN document, E/CN.4/Sub.2/384/Rev. 1, p. 588.
6. General Assembly res. 47/135, adopted 18 December, 1992.

10

Human Rights in Azerbaijan

An Overview

JAVANSHIR MAJIDO

The Situation in the Field of Gender Mainstreaming in the Republic of Azerbaijan

As you know, Azerbaijan is a country mainly populated by Muslims and located in the south-eastern part of the Southern Caucasus with a population of more than 8 million. The Act establishing the state's independence of the Republic of Azerbaijan, which completed its legal passage on October 18, 1991, set out the basis for the statehood of an independent Azerbaijan and determined the principles of its political and economic structure. With that Act the Republic of Azerbaijan once again, after 71 years, became an independent subject of international law.

Since regaining its independence the Republic of Azerbaijan joined almost all essential international documents on the protection of women's rights. In August 1992 the Republic of Azerbaijan signed the UN Convention on the Political Rights of Women and in 1995 became a party to the UN Convention on the Elimination of All Forms of Discrimination against Women.

The Government of Azerbaijan has made certain achievements in the sphere of gender policy. The State Committee on Women's issues was established by Decree of the President of the Republic of Azerbaijan on October 14, 1998.

Main objectives and purposes of Committee are protection of the rights of women, increasing of women's participation in social and political life of the country. It is remarkable that the State Committee on Women's Issues of the Republic of Azerbaijan is the only state structure in South Caucasus in the field of gender policy.

In March, 2000 the President of Azerbaijan signed the Decree "On Implementation of the National Gender Policy in the Republic of Azerbaijan". This act envisages the ensuring of equal representation of women and men in all state structures of the Republic; providing the refugee and internally displaced women with working places by preparing the relevant state programme; reviewing the legislation with taking into account the gender aspects.

In order to launch the practical implementation of the abovementioned Decree the gender focal points were appointed in the governmental structures. According to the Decree of the Government of Azerbaijan women should be appointed as one of the Deputy Heads of the Executive Power in all regions of Azerbaijan. This decree has already been implemented in large number of the regions.

In June, 2000 the Cabinet of Ministers of the Republic of Azerbaijan adopted the National Plan of Action on Women Issues for 2000-2005. This programme was elaborated on the basis of Beijing Strategies with taking into consideration the national priorities. It covers political, social, economic, cultural, educational, health spheres, problems of refugee and internally displaced women, envisages the elaboration of the state programme 'Women and Power', implementation of the relevant measures aimed at ensuring more active participation of women in political and public life and decision-making process. The National Plan of Action includes both the participation of state structures and NGOs. The inter-agency group was established in order to implement the provisions of the National Plan of Action.

In the sphere of gender policy, Azerbaijani government cooperates closely with international organizations such as UN and other organizations. Different projects in the field of women's political participation and their involvement into policy- and decision-making are being implemented in Baku and in the regions of Azerbaijan. As result of the projects implemented by ODIHR the network of women working in governmental structures was established covering ministries, Constitutional and Supreme Courts, Baku City Hall. A number of round-tables and workshops were conducted with participation of this group of women.

However, the status of Azerbaijani women remains complicated. The processes of development are mainly going on in the capital and some of the big cities but in the rural area, the life of women is more difficult. The difficult social-economic circumstances in the regions restrict women's right to self-development.

As T.K. Arayev, the Ambassador of Azerbaijan mentioned in his speech, the hardships of transition period and the consequences of the Armenian aggression against Azerbaijan resulted in occupation of 20 per cent of Azerbaijani territory and are the main reasons of serious economic and social damages. The well-known conflict caused more than one million refugees and internally displaced persons with 54 per cent of women of their total number. At present 95 per cent of them are deprived of necessary living conditions. Only 20 per cent of employable women are provided jobs.

> Azerbaijan initiated a United Nations' resolution on the "Release of women and children taken hostage, including those subsequently imprisoned, in armed conflicts" during the 39th Session of the UN Commission on the Status of Women 1995. This resolution was extended through the years of 1996, 1997, 1998, 1999, 2000, 2001, 2002, 2003.

Another reason of the low participation of women in social, political and public life of the country is the existing traditional stereotypes of the image of woman in society, whose role is limited by the boundaries of family.

This situation demands the new approach to the building of the national gender strategy. At the moment we are in the process of building the national mechanism for developing gender strategy and incorporating gender component in practical activities within the government.

In this respect, the gender focal points in the ministries constitute the working group under the State Committee for Women's Issues which meets every month to elaborate new gender policy within each ministry and discusses what have been done in this field.

Rights of Children

Nowadays the Government of Azerbaijan is ready to accept all desirable instruments for cooperation that can help to future development of society and protect freedom of individual and human rights. In this regard Azerbaijan traditionally attaches great importance to the protection of the rights of children, who are the future of society.

The Republic of Azerbaijan ratified Convention on Child Rights with the Law No.2236 on July 21, 1992. The President of the Republic of Azerbaijan signed two optional protocols of the Convention - "Involvement of children in armed conflicts" and "Sale of children, child prostitution and child pornography" of Convention on 'Child Rights' at the UN Millennium Summit held on September 6-8, 2000.

In 1993 the Republic of Azerbaijan signed Universal Declaration on "Survival, protection and development of children" that was adopted at the high level meeting which was held for children's interests on September 30, 1990. Azerbaijan presented its first periodic report of the Convention on Child Rights at 15th session of UN Child Rights Committee in July, 1997. The Republic of Azerbaijan took an active part in Special Session (New York, May 2002) which was dedicated to the discussions about the implementation of the decisions of world meeting of UN General Assembly that was held for children's interests.

In 2004 Milli Mejlis (Parliament) of the Republic of Azerbaijan ratified the Convention No. 182 on "Elimination of the worst forms of child labour" and Recommendation No.190 of the International Labour Organization and the Hague Convention on International Adoption of Children.

In our Republic the issues concerning social and legal protection of children are regulated by a number of laws, such as Constitution of Azerbaijan Republic, Law on citizenship, Law on the legal status of foreign citizens, Law on state youth policy, Labour Code, Civil Code, Marriage Code and Family Code.

Labour Code covers such issues as employment of the children, duration of their working day, protection of interests of youth in employment and labour activity, etc.

The Civil Code of the Republic of Azerbaijan covers such issues as protection of children's interests, definition of exact maturity age, responsibility of teenagers for property and material damage, etc.

The legislative acts on child rights which were adopted by Azerbaijan are the following: Law on Child Rights, dated 19.05.1998, Law on social protection of children deprived of parental care, or those who lost their parents dated 22.06.1999, Law on Confirmation of Statute of commissions on child issues and protection, dated 31.05.2002, Law on nutrition of infants and young children, dated 17.06.2003, Decree of President on supplementary measures for assistance to the families with four or more children, dated 10.01.1992, Order of President on increasing of amount of payment for those who are on partly-paid maternity leave, dated 18.01.2001, Order of President on peace culture in the Republic of Azerbaijan and holding of an international decade (2001-2010) against torture in respect of children, dated 04.07.2001, decree of government on measures of improvement of social protection of children deprived of parental care or those who lost their parents, dated 07.11.2001, decree of government on plan of measures in connection with solving problems of abandoned and street children, dated 14.04.2003.

The Republic of Azerbaijan adopted the law on 'Child Rights' On May 19, 1998. The law on child rights was prepared in accordance with international documents such as Universal Declaration on Human Rights (1989), Declaration on Child Rights, UN Convention on Child Rights (1989), Universal Declaration on "Survival, protection and development of children" (1990). The law is directed to the political, social, economical and cultural protection of motherhood, fatherhood, family, childhood and gene pool of nation. One of its parts called 'child and family' enshrines right of child to live in family, rights and liabilities of parents, right of place of residence and inheritance right.

The part that is called 'A Child and Society' determines attitude to the protection of children from detrimental effects, children's exploitation, child labour and organization of rest.

The part about 'Protection of children in unfavourable terms' defines the following issues: orphaned children, children deprived of parental care, adoption of children, norms related to families who adopt the children and public institutions that bring the children up, the children with physical or mental disabilities and rights of those who care about them, protection of children during the period of military operations and rights of refugee.

According to Article 28 of the law, the government protects the children from all kinds of exploitation, as well as effects of dangerous, unhealthy and hard work using social, legal, economical, medical and educational methods.

> One of the issues that the government emphasizes is the education and upbringing of children deprived from parental care. The Cabinet of Ministers of the Republic of Azerbaijan, Ministry of Health, Ministry of Social Protection and Labour, Ministry of Education, Ministry of Youth and Sports prepare and realize the programs of social protection of children deprived from the parental care. The Cabinet of Ministers issued orders on "Assistance to orphaned children, children deprived from parental care, and the children who are not under the care of government" and on "Undelayable measures on improvement of living conditions and material provisions of children from boarding school type educational institutions".

The law of the Republic of Azerbaijan on "Social protection of orphan children and children deprived from parental care" defines the measures of protection of children of this category during their secondary and higher education. Among these measures there are: receiving scholarships (more than two times), full payment of salaries during the practical work, payment for buying manuals and training materials for those who study in institutions of higher education and free of charge medical services.

In our Republic a campaign was conducted for propaganda and distribution of 10 main principles of UN General Assembly's resolution 'The World Fit for Children'. In this campaign there was proper arrangement for children participation.

According to Law on Education that was adopted in 1992, the right to get an education can be applied to all children and youth, irrespective of their race, nationality, religions or property status. The law of the Republic of Azerbaijan on "People with health problems" dated 05 June, 2001 also regulates and provides special education for teenagers.

In the field of child rights protection, one of the most important issues for the Republic of Azerbaijan is the protection of child rights during military conflicts. Azerbaijan is facing the problem of more than one million refugees and IDPs, already has grown up a whole generation of children in tent camps and compact settlements who are not familiar with their native home living and who are deprived of all conditions necessary for the implementation of all legislative acts concerning child rights.

In the occupied territories of our Republic, 616 schools were destroyed where more than hundred thousand children were getting education. In general 242 infant schools, 4 technical schools, 11 vocational schools and one institution of higher education, which were covering more than 12,000 children, stopped their work. In this connection Azerbaijan signed a number of international documents on protection of child rights during armed conflict. The delegations of our Republic regularly participate in different international forums being held in this field.

Orders of the Cabinet of Ministers of the Republic of Azerbaijan (No. 128 dated 01.01.93, No. 328 dated 25.06.93, No. 403, 21.07.93) imply a number of measures on comprehensive improvement of status of those, who left their homes because of military conflict such as refugees, and internally displaced children: opening of temporary schools and infant schools, forcible payment of pensions and compensations, at the same time rendering financial aid.

Also, instructions on "Measures of strengthening public relief to families with many children" with some amendments and supplements are in force (No. 209 dated 21.04.81).

In order to coordinate work of different governmental and non-governmental organizations, for the sake of children's interests, Coordination Council on Child Issues in the Ministry of Youth, Sports and Tourism (Ministry transformed into the Ministry of Youth and Sports) was established. This Council has regularly reviewed urgent questions and given advices in connection with the protection of children for three years. Among the most noteworthy issues of street children, issues of child rest and health can be mentioned. On the last meeting with the participation of representatives of the Poverty Reduction Strategy Paper (PRSP), Save the Children and EC Food Security Programme, the Council discussed a number of measures on preventing the use of child labour and research of their status, and advised their implementation.

The implementation of Convention on 'Child Rights' implements by means of cooperation with the Office of Representative of UN Children's Fund in Azerbaijan and other international organizations. In 1996 international assistance of 8 million dollars was allocated to refugees and families in need, and 553,789 dollars to child needs by UNICEF.

Recently, a progress was achieved in the area of protection of children with specific needs. Along with the formation of legal basis in our Republic, specific steps were taken concerning children deprived from parental care, disabled children and those who live and work in the streets. In respect of children who need a specific care, following the cooperation with UNICEF, 16 experts passed training on working with 'street children'. At present, the children are being enlisted in trainings of sports sections and art studios. About 10 multi-field centres render rehabilitation services to disabled children.

The state programme on "Solving economic and social problems of talented children and youth, and development of their talent" confirmed on August 4, 2000 by the Cabinet of Ministers of the Republic of Azerbaijan has a significant effect on development of creative potential of children and youth, and indirectly helps to solve employment and recruitment problems.

In countries with transition economies, rest and proper leisure opportunities of children are extremely reduced, because of unavoidable poverty, economic and social inequality, and profit inequality. Now, effort is being put to produce a mechanism providing summer holiday for children.

There should especially be noted a growth social activity of more than 20 initiative groups that combines a few thousands of children. These groups that are supported by relevant governmental and non-governmental organizations are more active in teaching child rights.

The social and living conditions of children broken the law and sited in jails have importantly changed. With the support of the public council of tutors, competitions and tournaments between children from jails and children from normal educational institutions were conducted. Children in jails are directly getting inserted into pardon decrees of the President.

According to the Articles 18, 36 and 57 of the law of Azerbaijan Republic on "Health Protection of Population" dated 26.06.97 the children have the following rights:

- Free of charge regular medical check-up and as regulated by relevant body of executive power a right of children and youth of being treated in state hospitals.
- Right of education and labour in hygienic and sanitary conditions.
- Right for charge free medical consultations.
- Discounted nutrition and receiving of medical-social aid and social assistance at the state budget expense as regulated by relevant body of executive power.

Current Situation on Protection of Rights of Persons Belonging to National Minorities in the Republic of Azerbaijan

Azerbaijan is a multi-ethnic and multi-religious country where the national policy is planned and carried out in the spirit of traditional tolerance and harmonic coexistence of different ethnic and religious groups. The equality of all citizens without any ethnic, national, religious or linguistic definition is guaranteed by the law.

Over many centuries persons belonging to various minorities have lived in the Republic of Azerbaijan in peace and harmony with the Azerbaijani people. This multicultural, multi-ethnic heritage has been preserved in Azerbaijan even today due to the fact that Azerbaijan historically is a unique multi-ethnic society.

Despite the difficulties being experienced by Azerbaijan, due to the armed conflict with neighbouring Armenia, which occupies 20 per cent of the Azerbaijani territory and the presence of about one million refugees and forcibly displaced persons – victims of ethnic cleansing conducted by the Armenian armed forces and terrorist groups, among whom in addition to Azerbaijanis there are persons belonging to various minorities (Kurds, Russians, Jews and others), as well as problems connected with transitional period, the Government of Azerbaijan continues to pursue a consistent policy towards protection of minorities' rights.

Full-effect is given to the right of minorities to establish their own national cultural centres, associations and other organizations.

The state within its ability provides material and financial assistance to several organizations of minorities from the budget of country and Presidential foundation and assists in strengthening of mutual understanding, tolerance and respect between all persons living in its territory regardless of their ethnic, cultural, language or religious identity. Active participation of all national minorities in the life of society on equal basis, including participation in the joint events on a countrywide level, is an evidence of environment of mutual respect existing in Azerbaijan.

Dozens of newspapers and magazines are published in the language of minorities. Radio and television programmes in their languages are being broadcasted on daily basis.

In state structures of Azerbaijan different national minorities are widely represented. In areas of compact living of national minorities, representatives of local population hold leading positions in local authorities, institutions of local government and other structures. Persons belonging to national minorities work in Executive Office of the President of Azerbaijan, in Parliament, in

Cabinet of Ministers, in constitutional court, Central Election Commission, law-enforcement bodies and other state bodies. Representatives of national minorities are chairmen or deputies of chairmen of some Standing Commissions of the Milli Majlis (Parliament).

Here is a structural composition of population, languages and places of compact living of persons belonging to national minorities of the Republic of Azerbaijan.

These minorities are: Lezgins (1,78,000), Russians (14,17,000), Talyshes (7,68,000), Avars (50,9000), Turksmeskhetians (43,4000), Tatars (30,000), Ukrainians (29,000), Tsakhurs (1,59,000), Georgians (1,49,000), Kurds (1,31,000), Tats (1,09,000), Jews (89,000), Udins (41,000).

There are also 1,207,000 Armenians, who compactly live mainly in the Nagorno-Karabakh region of Azerbaijan. Reportedly, about 30,000 live outside of Nagorno-Karabakh region, including Baky city, in spite of armed conflict with Armenia and continued occupation by the latter, of the part of Azerbaijan.

The Constitution of the Republic of Azerbaijan adopted in 1995, guarantees respect for human rights and freedoms regardless of ethnic origin, race, religion, languages or other distinctions. In the constitutional act on state sovereignty of the Republic of Azerbaijan fixed that all citizens of the Republic of Azerbaijan have equal rights before the law.

The Decree of the President of the Republic of Azerbaijan on 16 September 1992 – “On protection rights and freedoms, state support of development of language and culture of national minorities and ethnic groups living in Azerbaijan” aimed at further perfection of relations between minorities and increasing of level of their involvement in building of a legal state.

Along with these legal provisions of domestic legislation, the provisions of international documents, such as the UN Convention on elimination of all forms of racial discrimination, the UN Convention on prevention of apartheid and its punishment and the UN Convention on prevention of genocide and its punishment, which Azerbaijan joined on 31 May 1996, are also being applied.

In June 2000, long before its accession to the Council of Europe, Azerbaijan joined the Framework Convention for the Protection of National Minorities. Pursuant to the Article 25 of this Convention, Azerbaijan has already submitted its national report on situation of protection of rights of persons belonging to national minorities on 4 June 2002. In the course of the examination of the submitted report, the Advisory Committee of the Framework Convention for the Protection of National Minorities has established the special working group, which with the purpose of examination of the state report visited Azerbaijan between 29 March and 4 April 2003. These steps clearly demonstrate the adherence of Azerbaijan to the international standards in the sphere of policy towards national minorities.

11

Distributive Justice and Muslims under Indian Constitution

Human Rights Perspective

IQBAL ALI KHAN

The concept of distributive justice is permeated in majority of the articles of our Constitution. Despite our Republic being socialist, it is only rarely that the Supreme Court has creatively read into the articles of the socialist thrust. In a social system built on the gross inequalities where large number of people still suffer from poverty and ignorance and are denied the human rights and basic necessities of life, thus the distributive justice is an answer.

The report on Social Economic and Educational Status of the Muslim Community in India exposes some startling facts – that Muslim are at the bottom of the development ladder, alongside Scheduled caste and Scheduled tribes and much lower than the Hindu – OBCs upper caste Hindus and other minorities. It is a cruel irony that the development process bypassed in particular Muslims who stayed back in India after the partition – those from Uttar Pradesh, Bihar and West Bengal.

The root cause of this neglect is denial of justice – social, economic and political to them. While the Constitution and the democratic framework allowed Muslims to maintain their identity and profess their faith, their representation in the political system has suffered. This impacted their participation in governance. Even as SCs and STs were identified as a target group for making policy according similar attention to the largest religious minority was considered unnecessary, if not inimical, to secular democracy. That Muslim could become easy targets of systemic religious discrimination was overlooked.[1]

All developed countries and most developing ones give appropriate emphasis to looking after the interest of minorities. In any country the faith and confidence of the minorities in the impartiality of the state is an acid test of its being a just state.[2]

The above report states that about 41 per cent of Muslims and 43 per cent of Hindus have reported themselves as OBCs. Only 0.8 per cent Muslim reporting themselves as SCs; the share of Muslims reporting themselves as STs was even lower. The Mandal Commission anticipates self-reporting by OBCs to stabilize at 52 per cent of the population; subsequent surveys seem to bear out its assessment. OBCs can be presumed to constitute 50 per cent of all Hindus and 50 per cent of all Muslims. Hence, it follows that the benefit of OBC job quotas should accrue to Hindus and Muslims according to their respective shares in the total population. However, only 3 per cent of OBC job quotas have gone to Muslims, whereas their share should have been about 14 per cent.

However, the purpose of this article is to emphasise the fact that the interest of Muslim community can be best protected and preserved by applying the principle of distributive justice. For the sake of study, the present article is divided into three parts, i.e., jurisprudential, constitutional and Sachar Committee's report and Muslims.

According to Lexicon Legal Theory, justice has been viewed from four different angles.[3]

1. Distributive Justice
2. Corrective Justice
3. Political Justice and
4. Procedural Justices.

Corrective justice is concerned with the righting of wrongs. For instance, in criminal law, the concern is with punishing crimes and in law of torts, one is focussed on the rectification of wrongfully inflicted harms. Political justice is concerned with issues such as voting rights, democracy, legitimacy and authority. Procedural justice addresses questions about the fairness of civil and criminal proceedings. Distributive justice as a rough and ready starting point, addresses questions about distribution or allocation of liberties, wealth and income.

Discussions of distributive justice usually start with the work of John Rawls – the most influential political philosopher of 20th Century.

The theory of justice developed by John Rawls constitutes another attempt to combine the values of freedom and equality in an analysis of the meaning of justice. Rawl's conception of distributive justice is composed of two cardinal principles:[4]

1. *The Equal Liberty Principle:* Each persons is to have an equal right to the most extensive basic liberty compatible with the similar liberty for others; and
2. *The Difference Principle:* Social and economic inequalities are to be arranged so that they can reasonably be expected to be to everyone's advantage, and in such a manner that the positions and offices to which they attach are open to all.

These two principles are not, however, to be accorded equal weight in social policy: the first principle has priority over the second. This means that liberty can be restricted only for the sake of liberty itself, and that the claims of social and economic equality must yield ground if their realization is not likely to lead to an increase in the total amount of liberty for all.

Thus distributive justice, economic justice, is concerned with giving all members of society a 'fair share' of the benefits and resources available. However, while everyone might agree that wealth should be distributed fairly, there is much disagreement about what counts as a fair 'fair share'. Some possible criteria of distribution are equity, equality, and need. (Equity means that one's rewards should be equal to one's contribution to a society, while 'equality' means that everyone gets the same amount, regardless of their input. Distribution on the basis of need means that people who need more will get more, while people who need less will get less.) Fair allocation of resources, or distributive justice, is crucial to the stability of a society and the well-being of its members. When issues of distributive justice are inadequately addressed and the item to be distributed is highly valued, intractable conflicts frequently result.[5]

Justice V.R. Krishna Iyer has aptly remarked about the pathetic condition of distributive justice in India. He says that the jurisprudence of distributive justice according to juristic cynics, is an essay in illusion. The basic social system is built on gross inequalities and the power lobby, and mould state policy, even judicial policy, is heavily in the hands of the proprients. The proletariat has not a dog's chance of re-orienting the system as the basis of distributive justice although such a goal is writ large in Article 38 and Article 39 (b) and (c) of the Constitution. Of course, the implications of Article 14 regarding equal justice also take us to a seeming constitutional order with social justice inscribed in print.[6]

Basically, the spirit and soul of our Constitution is to provide social, economic and political justice to the people of India. Sizable number of articles of the Constitution deal with what we call as distributive justice. It does not merely envisage a system of corrective justice in which rights and obligations arising out of the present social structure are enforced. It clearly saw that the existing social structure was unjust and needed to be changed.

There are various concepts of equality envisaged under the Indian Constitution such as egalitarian, numerical, meritarian and proportional. Right to vote has been to all adult citizens above the age of eighteen years. This is an example of egalitarian or numerical equality. The principle of meritarian equality means the right to equality guaranteed by Article 14 and prohibition of discrimination on the ground of religion/race, caste, sex, etc., included in Articles 15(1) (2), 16(1) (2), 17, 29(2) and 325 of the Constitution. Principle of proportional equality is included in the provision for compensatory discrimination for the Scheduled Castes, Scheduled Tribes and other backward classes provided under Articles 15(4), 16(4), 330, 332 and 335 of the Constitution.

The 'Objectives Resolution'[7] clearly states in unequivocal terms that the people of India have solemnly resolved to proclaim India as an Independent Sovereign Republic and to draw up for her future governance a Constitution:

1. Wherein shall be guaranteed and secured to all people of India justice – social, economic and political; equality of status of opportunity and before the law; freedom of thought, expression, belief, faith, worship, vocation, association and action, subject to law and public morality; and
2. Wherein adequate safeguard shall be provided for minorities, backward and tribal areas, and depressed and other backward classes.

The socio-economic objectives enshrined in the Constitution were appreciated and welcomed by different section of the Assembly. Referring to socio-economic justice, Dr. S. Radhakrishnan said that it intended to effect a smooth and rapid transition from a state of serfdom to one of freedom.[8]

The phrases thus used by the founding fathers clearly indicate that socio-economic justice in its realization is distributive in character. It contemplates a change in social structure in order to remake the material conditions of the society. It is rather appropriate here to mention the observation of Granville Anstin : "The Constitution was to foster the achievement of many goals. Transcendent among them was that of social revolution. Through this revolution would be fulfilled the basic needs of a common man, and it was hoped, this revolution would bring about fundamental changes in the structure of the Indian society".[9]

In this way the scheme of distributive justice as visualized in the Objective Resolution was incorporated in the Preamble, the Fundamental Rights and Directive Principles of State Policy and the other provisions (i.e., Article 332-342) of our Constitution. The gist of the scheme may be stated thus:[10]

Constitution ordains the state to promote the welfare of the people by securing and protecting as effectively as it may a social order in which justice – social, economic and political, shall inform all the institution of national life.[11]

For the establishment of social order, the Constitution has guaranteed the following fundamental rights to the people of India:

1. Right to equality[12]
2. Right to six fundamental freedoms[13]
3. Right to life and personal liberty[14]
4. Right against exploitation[15]
5. Right to freedom of religion[16]
6. Cultural and educational right[17]
7. Right to constitutional remedies[18]

Apart from the fundamental rights, the directive principles of state policy also express in unequivocal and categorical terms the ideal of distributive justice. Out of these directive principles, Article 38 catches the prime attention which requires the state inter alia to minimize the inequalities in income and to eliminate inequalities in status, facilities and opportunities, not only amongst individuals but also amongst groups of people residing in different areas or engaged in different vocations.[19] Article 39 requires the state to make available to all its citizens adequate means of livelihood; distribute ownership and control of material resources so as to subserve the common good; to operate the economic system in such a way that it does not result in concentration of wealth and means of production to the common detriment; that there is equal pay for equal work; to protect the health and strength of workers men and women and the tender age of children against abuse and that citizens are not forced by economic necessity to enter avocations unsuited to their age and strength, that children are given opportunities and facilities to develop freedom and dignity and that childhood and youth are protected against exploitation and against moral and material abandonment.[20]

The state is also required to provide equal justice through the mechanism of free legal aid in order to ensure that opportunities for securing justice are not denied to any citizen and other disabilities.[21]

Thus, it is crystal clear that our Constitution lays down the following steps to implement the policy of distributive justice:[22]

1. It declares that its objective is to usher in a new social order, where there will be justice – social, economic and political.
2. It guarantees certain rights as fundamental rights and they are made enforceable in a court of law.
3. It directs the state to bring about the necessary conditions for creating other rights, particularly social and economic rights.
4. The said fundamental rights and the statutory rights are interwoven into the design of distributive justice through the justiciable laws of social control.[23]

Concluding the constitutional aspect relating to distributive justice, it can be said that our Constitution has twin objectives:

First, to usher in a new social order ensuring distributive justice to all the citizens and; second, to protect the liberties of the people from the onslaught of autocratic and arbitrary power. These two ideas run like a golden fabric through the entire scheme of the Constitution.

But it is a pity that many of the legislative action destined at distributive justice pursuance to the implementation of the directive principles of state policy were struck down by the courts from time to time. The directives have been relegated to the position of inferiority. The mind boggling judgments of the Apex Court right from the days of *Champakam Dorairajan,*[24] *Quaresh,*[25] *Kerala Education Bill,*[26] *Golaknath,*[27] *the Bank Nationalisation,*[28] *The Privy Purse*[29] and *the Minerva Mills*[30] had shattered the hopes of the government to implement the directive principles of state policy. These decisions crippled the state machinery and paralysed the movement to the nation towards an equalitarian social order. Thanks to the 44th Amendment giving overriding effect to the directive principles over certain fundamental rights, the Supreme Court is construing the directives liberally and giving effect these directives by reading down the fundamental rights to confirm as far as possible to these directive.[31]

Equality as an aspect of justice has two phases, namely, equality as a means of doing justice and equality as an end of justice. One may accept the notion of equality, social, economic and political as an end of justice. However, it is not practicable to accept the notion of equality without 'protective discrimination', as a means of doing justice. The road to distributive justice is a two-lane highway – one requiring the equal treatment of the equals and the other requiring the unequal treatment of unequals.[32]

When it is said that injustice arises when equals are treated unequally, and also when unequals are treated equally we are stating the obvious. But to say that equals should be treated equally and unequals unequally throws no light on what is to be done by, to, and for equals and unequals. For an answer to these questions, we have to take into account the ends or purposes of action and the claims and obligations connected with them. In other words, in order to discover substance of distributive justice, it is necessary, first to establish a body of rights and duties and then to examine them in the light of the formal principle of equality, the aim being to exclude every form of invidious discrimination not justified by relevant differences.[33]

In an unequal environment where the social, economic and political inequalities are grim and large, the resort to the right to equality is often made to prevent discrimination and also sometimes to uphold discrimination. The doctrine of equality, thus envisages the idea of protective discrimination in all its manifestations. The notion of protective discrimination aims at unequal treatment of unequals, i.e., those who were the victims of man-made asperities for centuries together now need to be compensated. Mere proclamation of abstract equality will be of no use to such persons groaning under the abject poverty and the deadening weightage of backwardness. They need 'protective discrimination' or 'adventitious aids' to develop their personality and to participate in the mainstream of national life, the way, the Constitution vouchsafes and ordains for them.

It is the legitimate aspiration of citizens in a welfare state that good education and security of job should be provided to all of them. The economic interests of an individual as also distributive justice to it are twined up with its place in the educational institutions and services under the state. The pursuit of governmental jobs is looked upon as a mark of share in the state power and also to attain economic independence in the society. Moreover, with the biggest and expanding state undertakings, the employer also happens to be the state, so much so that the appointments in the public services are becoming a venue of employment and a source of livelihood. If no protective treatment is given to weaker sections in matters of education and employment they will remain as they were and our professions of distributive justice will be a dream and a teeming illusion to be vainly pursued in an agonizing atmosphere of inequality ridden society.

Much hue and cry is being made on the submission of Justice Rajendra Sachchar Committee's report regarding the plight of Muslims in India. After this report, Prime Minister, Manmohan Singh has admitted that the fruits of the development of the country are not reaching to the Muslims. He has, therefore advocated for the preferential treatment to the Muslims.

In its report the Committee has dubbed the condition of Muslim community worst than SCs and STs. The report says that Muslim community like Hindus has various castes. Although Islam does not admit any distinction among its followers on religious ground but on social grounds Muslims are also classified into two classes, i.e., upper caste and backward class. According to survey at least 20 per cent of the Muslims belong to upper caste, whereas 80 per cent population belongs to the backward class.

And the people of upper caste have a lion's share, almost 90 per cent in the field of governmental jobs including political post. Peoples belonging to the lower caste are still involved in their hereditary profession. Under such circumstances those demanding reservation for Muslim community in general are not justified on the ground that this benefit will be usurped by the those who are already in elite class. Obviously, the common Muslims will not get benefit from such policy.

The demand for reservation of seats in government jobs is not new. This is demanded through various fora. In this scenario the demand has often been for the implementation of the recommendation of Mandal Commission's report. Most of the Muslim backward castes have found place in the OBCs list prepared by the government. They are also getting benefit of 27 per cent fixed for OBCs.

Generally, the cynics of Muslim reservation argue that there are no sufficient number of highly educated candidates in the Muslim community to qualify the competition of IAS, IPS and PCS but it is submitted that there are sufficient number of Muslim candidates to be appointed at lower level jobs. But they are not. It proves that there is some sort of discrimination with them. The Sachchar Committee's report proves that there are hardly three or four per cent Muslims appointed at class III and IV level. This discrimination at all levels justices the reason for demanding reservation for Muslims.

It is to be noted that under the Indian Constitution, reservation on the ground of religion is not permitted. This Article should be amended. It is a matter of concern that on one hand Jains, Buddhist and Sikhs have been included within the definition of Hindu, on the other hand they also enjoy the benefit of being a minority. It is submitted that these communities have been admitted within the fold of minority with avid purpose of depriving the Muslim and Christian people from all sorts of principles under the Constitution. Moreover, if any SCs and STs converts to Christianity or Buddhism, he or she will be entitled to enjoy the benefit of reservation but if he or she embraces Islam, will lose this benefit simply because of being a Muslim.

In Muslim communities, there are various castes belonging to STs and they are various castes belonging to STs and they in all respects look like a STs but they are not treated as STs on the other hand persons of the same status have been recognized as STs if they are Hindus. Such type of people are agitating and making representation in different parts of UP and Bihar but of no avail.

Conclusion

It is a hard fact that in India no one would like to extend a privilege like reservation to Muslims, despite the honest truth that their condition is worse than SCs and STs. But in India where the Constitution requires to establish a welfare society based on equality of justice, this privilege cannot be denied to Muslims any more. If there is a will on the part of the government it can easily be done through 'protective discrimination'. This will very much be within the letters and spirit of the Constitution.

If the above submission is not sustainable then at least proportional representation of the Muslims should be secured in the limit of 27 per cent fixed for OBC. Moreover a new survey should be made regarding the castes falling under SCs and STs and OBCs and all castes having the status of SCs and STs and OBCs but belonging to Muslim community should be included within that list without any discrimination.

However, problems of Muslim deprivation cannot be addressed adequately through extension and implementation of reservation alone. OBC reservations apply only to public employment and now at higher levels of education. With the report detailing the nature of discrimination against Muslims, the challenge before government, political class, private sector and civil society is to create institutional mechanism to ensure the delivery of essential public goods. To begin with, Muslims should be represented in political bodies, policy-making agencies, administration and law enforcement agencies in relation to their share in the population.

Notes

1. *The Times of India*, 30 December, 2006, "A Forgotten People"
2. Ibid.
3. *Legal Theory*, Lexicon p. 49.
4. Boden Heimer, Edgar, *Jurisprudence*, 4th Indian Reprint, p. 199
5. Michelle Maies, *'Types of Justice' Beyond Intractability*, Conflict Research Consortium, University of Colorado, Boulder.
6. Justice V.R. Krishna Iyer expressed his views while writing a forwarding note of the book, *Distributive Justice under Indian Constitution* by Sudesh Kumar Sharma.
7. See B. Shiva Rao: *The Framing of India's Constitution: A Study,* pp. 121-122 (1968); See Vol. I, C.A.D. p. 59, para (5) and (6).
8. Vol. II, C.A.D. p. 269.
9. Guanville Austin; *The Indian Constitution: Corner-stone of a Nation*, Introduction.
10. Sudesh Kumar Sharma; *Distributive Justice under Indian Constitution*, p. 64.

11. Article 38(1).
12. Article 14-18.
13. Article 19.
14. Article 20-22.
15. Article 24-24.
16. Article 25-28.
17. Article 29-30.
18. Article 32.
19. Article 38(2).
20. Article 39(a) to (f).
21. Sudesh Kumar : *op.cit*. p.66.
22. See K. Subba Rao, *Social Justice and Law*, p. 21.
23. 1951 SCR 525.
24. AIR 1958 SC 731.
25. AIR 1958 SC 956.
26. AIR 1967 SC 1643.
27. AIR 1970 SC 607.
28. (1971) 1 SCJ 295.
29. (1980) 3 SCC 625.
30. See, Akhil Bhartiya Sahitya Karamchari Sangh, AIR 1981; SC 298 at 325; National Textile Workers, AIR 1983; SC 75, Woman Rao AIR 1981 SC 271. etc.
31. Sudesh Kumar op.cit. p. 71.
32. Ibid., p. 72.
33. Ibid.

12

The Need of Communal Harmony in India with Reference to The Hague Peace Agenda

D.S. SOMASHEKHAR

The Indian society is made up of Hindus belonging to thousands of castes, Christians, Muslims, Sikhs, Jains, Buddhists, Parsis and of course, hundreds of tribes. All these people speak an amazing number of languages and practise thousands of ways of life. That is why the multicoloured carpet of the Indian sub-continent is often called the "Epitome of the world". As Mark Twain has said "India land of dreams and romance – the country of a hundred nations and a hundred tongues, of a thousand religions and million Gods, cradle of the human race, birth place of human speech, mother of history, grand mother of legend, mother of traditions, the land that all men desire to see and having seen once by even a glimpse, would not give that glimpse for the shows of the rest of the globe combined".[1] This statement not only recognizes the great antiquity of India, but also highlights the pluralistic nature of our culture.

The pluralistic Indian culture which has accepted secular democracy presently is increasingly faced with the challenge of communalism and the threat of a monolithic culture. India which constitutes 16 per cent of the global population needs to maintain and continue with a peaceful society not only for her own sake, but also to maintain her stature of being "not just a nation but a vision" at the global level.

"The Indian freedom struggle was as much a social movement to establish social equality as it was a political fight against the British imperialism to secure freedom".[2] "The imagination of independent India as it was placed before the people during our freedom struggle was to be a society with the equality of castes and sexes. Democracy was the goal of our freedom struggle and people fought for it and got it. The Constituent Assembly just expressed it in writing. That is all".[3] Our Constitution also says, "It shall be the duty of every citizen of India to abide by the Constitution of India.... and to cherish and follow the noble ideals which inspired our national struggle for freedom".[4]

Despite the division of India in 1947 and our rejection of communalism as a farce ideology made it very clear that we stand for democracy and secularism.

Morality was the fountainhead of religion for Gandhiji and for years he argued that religion and politics could not be separated. "But, when he realized that communalists were using religion to fan hatred and violence against followers of other religions, Gandhiji completely changed his formulation and said in 1942 "religion is a personal matter which should have no place in politics". And he said in 1946-47: "Religion is the personal affair of each individual. It must not be mixed up with politics or national affair".[5]

Secularism

"After having won freedom in 1947, we adopted a secular Constitution. Here, perhaps it is needed to explain as to what secularism stands for. Secularism refers to worldly affairs and it is not concerned with religion and religious beliefs. As a political philosophy, secularism means keeping the state authority away from religion, and religion not interfering in the field of administration. Belief or disbelief in religion both is unimportant for this argument."

"Secularism is not opposed to religion as we see in Communist regime. It does not rule out the importance of religion in the personal life of the citizens, nor does it reject it also."[6] "Secularism neither orients people for any particular religion nor antagonizes them against any particular religion. It does not interfere in the religious celebrations of the people."

"Secularism should not accept the concept of high or low as has been accepted by religion. Therefore, in India secularism means not only 'Dharmanirapeksha' but also equal status to all religions."[7]

Even after Indian independence the problem of communalism continued. A careful observation reveals that communalism these days is assuming different proportions posing a threat to our democratic and secular fabric. Therefore, a brief explanation of the term communalism in its historical background is called for.

Communalism Before 1947

Before independence in the Indian communal problem the British imperial interest was also involved. "The strongest arm of the communal triangle was the British rulers. They were neither true friends of the Muslims nor the foes of the Hindus; they were the true friends of British imperialism and acted on the tested and tried maxim of 'Divide et Impera' (Divide and Rule). Lord John Elphinstone, Governor of Bombay (1853-60 AD) wrote 'Divide et Impera' was the old Roman motto and it should be ours".[8] Anyway, the Britishers cannot be totally blamed for what disaster the communalism brought about by 1947. What concerns us the most is the continuation of the problem of communalism and its assuming alarmingly uglier faces day by day only to cause more and more tension to the society as a whole, generating insecure feeling. So it is logical to know what communalism is in India today.

Present Day Communalism

The calculation of getting more votes as a road to power is the most crucial point in the present day communal politics. Politicians with vested interest are spreading the venom of communalism to garner votes as a path to power. "Antagonising the people of one religion against the people of another religion for the sake of political power, arguing that minorities are outsiders to the culture of the majority and the creation and enhancement of hate and contempt against minorities is Communalism".[9]

"Religion is an integral factor in the existing state of social consciousness in our society. Religion provides an identity of being part of a community to all those who believe in the same religion. It is perceived and believed that those who belong to the same religion have a certain common identity. It is this belief in commonality which is used for communal mobilization.... Communalism is the manipulation of religious consciousness to serve the interest of certain political parties."[10] "Communalism is based on spreading feelings of fear, insecurity, separateness and above all antagonism and animosity towards and among followers of different religions."[11] "Communalism draws its sustenance from religion, while it germinates in politics, it is watered by religious sectarianism."[12]

"Indian society is a composite society in cultural terms, a composite society in which various streams have joined together." This composite society is faced with reinforced communal problems. "Hindu communalism is not an upper caste phenomenon anymore. Concerted efforts are being made to incorporate the lower castes as well. In today's communalism various social, political, economic interests are converging which account for its recent resurgence."[13]

"Today most of the participants of the communal riots are poor. It is not the members of the middle class or rich who either participate or suffer in the riots. It is relatively the poor and the deprived who are the victims of riots. Perhaps the communal forces have realised that riot is the only way to communalise the poor. It is a very potent instrument because once a riot takes place the division is immediately established. The notion of 'us' and 'they' which did not earlier exist among the poor are instilled in their consciousness.[14]

Consequences of Communal Riots

Intensified communalism leads to communal riots, communal riots lead to segregation and isolation. Lack of communication between the communities leads to misunderstanding and this further leads to more communal riots even for trivial reasons. "Communalism was and has been false consciousness."[15]

Therefore, Bipin Chandra says, "In one respect communalism involves either conscious deception or unconscious self-deception; the communalist is either deceiving others or more likely he is deceiving himself as well".[16]

"From 1954 to 1993 in a span of 40 years in India 15,524 communal riots have taken place; which means in an average per year 388 communal riots have taken place in which 11,415 people have lost their lives".[17] As a result of more and more communal riots taking place, the entire society is prone to tension and uneasiness. This is not a conducive atmosphere for peace and when there is no peace, there cannot be much creativity which in turn hinders the process of progress. Of course, this is not to suggest that there are no other problems that India is facing at present. It constitutes a different argument. "Civilization begins where chaos and insecurity end. For when fear is overcome, curiosity and constructiveness are free and man passes by natural impulse towards the understanding and embelishment of life".[18]

Solutions to Right Communalism

Communalism as a menace should be tackled at every level to ensure peace and security to the people belonging to all communities. "One Communalism does not end the other, each feeds on the other and both fatten".[19] Our great nation builders like Gandhi and Nehru had realized that religion and nationality could not be synonymous. The love of one's religion is not identical with patriotism. In a multicultural society like ours if any attempt is made to build our national identity on the basis of any particular religion the result will be disastrous. "Love for one's country which is not part of one's love for humanity is not love."[20]

The following measures may be suggested in solving the problem of communalism:

1. People must be told repeatedly that "any act which leads to general good of human beings is a spiritual act" and true service to their own respective religions.

2. Well meaning individuals of all communities must enlighten people that no religion preaches intolerance and bigotry. "Tolerance or intolerance depends upon the social conditions and it is not a religious phenomenon".
3. "Today tradition is being appropriated by the communalists and, it is, in fact, the preserve of the obscurantist. The communalists claim to be the advocates of preserving the best elements of tradition and they are succeeding in making people see them in that role – Tradition can be a 'cultural idiom' which can be adopted by all".[21]
4. Religious intolerance and any attempt to communalize the situation by anyone whether Hindu or Muslim or otherwise must be opposed with equal vehemence by all sane minded people.
5. Religion should be increasingly personalized and kept out of public life.
6. Rituals should take back seat and emphasis must be more and more on spiritual and philosophical aspects of any religion.
7. The gospel that the essence of all religions is one and the same should be propagated again and again. "Truth is one, but its manifestations are different" ('Akam Sat Vipra Bhahuda Vadanti' – Upanishads)
8. Illiteracy and ignorance promote bigotry. Therefore, education must be promoted – especially secular education which helps to evolve democracy.
9. Constant and conscious efforts should be made to avoid rumours, distortions, half-truths, prejudice in understanding history which has bearing on the present life. This can be viewed in the light of communalists trying to distort Indian history. If history is not based on objective historical materials, then "history will be a pack of tricks being played on the dead".
10. At different levels of education a compulsory paper of religious tolerance – containing solid examples from the past – is taught to orient the young minds in understanding the need of harmony in the present society.
11. Especially young minds must be motivated to know the pluralistic nature of our society and they must understand that

'Unity in Diversity' is the real strength of India and not any monolithic culture or society.

12. As a token of good will, whenever possible people of one community may participate in the cultural celebrations of another community which may bridge communication gaps and promote mutual respectability.
13. The ideals of the freedom struggle which were highlighted in different forms soon after our independence must be inculcated in the present curriculum. For example a translated Kannada poem can be cited here

"We are youngsters, we are comrades,
Our hearts bouquets of flowers.
We are the nation's leaders tomorrow
Lovely and grand are our dreams.

India is the one single home
For Hindus Muslims and Christs
Our grandsire Gandhi, the apostle of Peace
The moon in the sky of our breasts.

We beat the devil of caste complexes
And tread the righteous path
We proclaim the oneness of all mankind
And our vow is to prove it a truth".[22]

14. "Religion is an important aspect of culture, but they are not identical. Religious development incorporates two components, i.e., faith and culture. Faith is religious and culture is secular. The fight against communalism can be effective only if the cultural tradition is appropriated by secular forces."[23]
15. The most important aspects of our Constitution must be highlighted to educate and enlighten people with the help of which they can be made rule minded. For example, Indian Constitution states, "No person shall be deprived of his life or personal liberty except according to procedure established by law".[24] At the same time "Secularism has to be retrieved from being a pale shadow of what is projected as religious coexistence, to a system of values and actions that come from insisting upon democratic functioning and human rights".[25]

Therefore, peace prevailing in the Indian society through communal harmony is a very important social condition not only from the point of view of India, but also in the interest of the world, because India is the biggest democratic country in the world constituting one-sixth of humanity. The concept like 'World Peace' cannot be a reality unless peace prevails in each and every part of the world. To put it differently, 'local peace' is the basis of 'global peace'. Otherwise, global peace will only be a 'Utopian concept'.

The Historic Hague Peace Conference

Realising the need and importance of world peace, civil societies, non-governmental organizations and the lovers of peace conducted an 'International Peace Conference' called 'The Hague Appeal for Peace' (The Netherlands) from May 11 to 15, 1999. One thousand different organizations from all over the world were involved in this Peace Conference. There were 10,000 delegates in the Peace Conference representing more than 100 countries. 400 different sessions on different dimensions of peace were conducted; and in the end out of consensus was evolved a peace agenda captioned *The Hague Appeal For Peace And Justice For The 21st Century.*

Madam Sheik Hasina, the Premier of Bangladesh said in the Peace Conference, "Peace is important and worthwhile for its own sake, not for what it will or will not bring about. It is a value, an ideal, and a life giving force that mankind can never abandon. We consider peace to be a fundamental human right, next only to the right to life, to be attained, protected, sustained, promoted and carried forward all the time. Peace is not in our view, a mere absence of war or conflict or violence. It is the blissful state in which all the people can lead a worthwhile and meaningful life in accordance with their wish, their talents, and ability flourishing unhindered".[26]

It was deemed in the conference that there could be no peace without hope and there could be no hope without justice. The Hague Agenda for Peace and Justice for the 21st Century consists of 50 points and the 4 major strands of the Hague appeal are:

1. Root causes of war/culture of peace.
2. International humanitarian and human rights law and institutions.

3. Prevention, resolution and transformation of violent conflicts.
4. Disarmament and human security.

Keeping in view the existing religio-communal situation of India, a few points of The Hague Peace Agenda can be discussed as under:

1. (a) The Agenda insists that peace education be made compulsory at all levels of education system.
   (b) It also insists that education ministries systematically implement peace education initiatives at a local and national level.[27]
4. (a) The Hague Appeal for Peace supports efforts to eliminate the political manipulation of racial, ethnic, religious and gender differences for political and economic purposes.
   (b) The inclusion of hate crimes in the world judicial system.[28]
8. (a) The promotion of democracy at all levels of society is a prerequisite for replacing the rule of force with the rule of law.[29]
10. Eliminate communal violence at the local level.[30] Violence in local communities paves the way for conflicts at national and international level. The Hague Appeal for Peace supports initiatives to:
   (a) Reintegrate into society the young people and some of their elders who have been marginalized often as a result of limited economic opportunities and whose marginalization has led them into violent behaviour.
   (b) Promote local peace initiatives, peace camps, and conflict resolution training.
11. Enlist world religions in transforming the culture of violence into a culture of peace and justice.[31]

Religions have been a cause of war, but, also have the potential to enable the development of a culture of peace. They may be engaged to implement paths of peace. The Hague Appeal for Peace supports:

(a) Inter-faith; inter-religious cooperation and global peace work.

(b) The promotion of religious coexistence and reconciliation.

28. In resolving conflicts local capacities can be made use of. And it is vital to maintain peace.[32]

The Hague Peace Conference believed further that, "Peace must be declared a human right and a culture of peace must be designed by which we all could live".

India the land of Buddha and Gandhi was also represented in the peace conference. The above discussed points do have relevance to the present Indian situation and they call for well-meaning individuals to strive for peace at the local level also. Because "the campaign against communalism is in fact, a struggle for the minds of people".

Conclusion

We stand committed to the cause of Indian unity and integrity. Every human soul born into any caste or religion in India should enjoy equal rights to lead a peaceful and dignified life. India can never become a 'Hindu Rastra'.

"The Judgment by the Supreme Court in 1993 on the dismissal of four Bharatiya Janata Party state governments is by far the most significant interpretation of the secular character of the Indian Constitution to date..." The Judges have observed, "If a political party espousing a particular religion comes to power, that religion tends to become the official religion. All other religions tend to acquire a secondary status which is against the scheme of the Constitution."[33]

We have to learn from the experience of Pakistan which emphasized on religion and has failed to evolve true democracy over there, In fact, confusion is worst confounded in Pakistan. The multicoloured socio-religious-cultural mosaic of India is not only beautiful but also has the seeds of creativity in its bosom right from the beginning.

I think I can conclude by referring to an anecdote related to Abdul Kalam, the philosopher-President of India. "When Jiping sought the President's message (Abdul Kalam's) to be printed in the book (the translation of *The Wings of Fire* into Chinese) Kalam recalled a homily he got from an abbot of a 500-year old Buddhist monastery during his October 15 visit to Tawang in Arunachala Pradesh. The President quoted the religious priest as saying, "First you remove 'you' and 'me' from we. Once this happens the ego will be moderated. This in turn, tames hatred, once hatred is overpowered; violence will not emerge and once that happens there will be peace".[34]

Notes

1. "Ecology and Culture interwoven with special reference to trees: A perspective", D.S. Somashekhar. *Rethinking of Indian Culture – Challenges and Responses*, Editor in Chief – Dr. Sitakanta Mahapatra. The Universe Maitree Sarani, Cuttack, 1999, p. 141.
2. "Secularism Emba Parikalpane" (Kannada) G. Rajashekhar, *Maatukathe* – 57, Neenasam, 2000, p. 39.
3. Ibid., p. 41.
4. "We the Majority", an Article by M.S. Ganesh; Shreen Ratnagar, *One India One People*, magazine, Mumbai, Aug, 2002, p. 12.
5. "The Everchanging Gandhi", *Essays on Indian Nationalism*, Prof. Bipin Chandra, Har-Anand Publications, 1993, New Delhi, p. 77.
6. "Secularism Emba Parikalpane" (Kannada) G. Rajashekhar, *Maatukathe* – 57, Neenasam, 2000, p. 41.
7. Ibid., p. 42.
8. *A New Look on Modern Indian History* B.L. Grover, S. Chand & Company Ltd., New Delhi, 1981, p. 561.
9. *Komuvadada Rajakiya* (Kannada) G. Rajashekar, K. Phaniraj, Fakir Mohammed Katpadi, Navakarnataka Publication, Bangalore, 2000.
10. "What is Communalism today"? K.K. Panikar, *Selected Writings on Communalism*, People's Publishing House, 1994, New-Delhi, p. 71.
11. "Communalism of Education", Prof. Bipin Chandra Delhi Historians' Group, December 2001, p. 12.
12. "Communalism – its facets, roots and remedies", Asghar Ali Engineer, *Selected Writings on Communalism*, People's Publishing House, 1994, New Delhi, p. 184.

13. "What is Communalism today?" K.K. Panikar, *Selected Writings on Communalism*. People's Publishing House, 1994, New Delhi, p. 71.
14. Ibid., p. 78.
15. "Communalism in Modern India", Bipin Chandra.
16. *Essays on Indian Nationalism*, Bipin Chandra, Har-Anand Publications, 1993, New Delhi, p. 23.
17. "Hindu Komuvadada Belavanige" (Kannada), K. Phaniraj *Maatukathe* – 57, Neenasam, Heggodu, 2000, p. 8.
18. *Our Oriental Heritage*, Will Durant.
19. (Jawaharlal Nehru) *A New Look on Modern Indian History*, B.L. Grover, 1981, Chand and Co., New Delhi, p. 560.
20. *The Sane Society*, Erich Fromm.
21. "What is Communalism today?" K. Panikar, *Selected Writings on Communalism*, People's Publishing House, 1994, New-Delhi.
22. *Ananda Kanda* (Betageri Krishna Sharma) Kannada poem translated into English by U.H. Ganesh.
23. Ibid., Note 21.
24. "We the Majority", an Article by M.S. Ganesh; Shreen Ratnagar, *One India One People*, magazine, Mumbai, Aug., 2002, p. 13.
25. Foreword to *Before the Night Falls* (K.N. Panikar) by Romila Thapar, published by Books for Change, 2002, Bangalore.
26. Valedictory address by Madam Sheik Hasina in The Hague Peace Conference, 15 May, 1999. The Netherlands.
27. The Hague Agenda for Peace and Justice for the 21 Century Conference edition, 1999.
28. Ibid.
29. Ibid.
30. Ibid.
31. Ibid.
32. Ibid.
33. *Before the Night Falls*, K.N. Panikar, Published by Books for Change, Nov. 2002, Bangalore, p. 48.
34. *The New Indian Express*, 16 December, 2002, Shimoga editions.

13

Conversion and its Implication to Malaysian Scenario

NOOR AZIAH MOHD. AWAL

Malaysia is a multiracial society and therefore multireligious. Even though Islam is the religion of the Federation,[1] freedom of religion is enshrined in the Malaysian Constitution.[2] Conversion from one religion is expected but not without consequences. Malaysia is unique whereby the matters relating to the religion of Islam is within the state jurisdiction and other matters are within the jurisdiction of the federal government. The Syariah Courts and the Civil Common Law courts stands side by side, whereby matters involving Muslims and Islamic law will be heard in the Syariah court and other matters shall be heard in the civil court. This was further enhanced by the amendment to the Federal Constitution in 1988, whereby according to Article 121(1A), any matters within the Syariah Court's jurisdiction, the Civil High Court shall have no jurisdiction.

However, conflict arises where one party to a non-Muslim marriage converts to Islam and the other party does not convert with him or she, the issue of custody, maintenance and matrimonial property needs to be decided. According to Section 51, Law Reform

(Marriage and Divorce) Act 1976[3] where one party to a marriage converts to Islam, the other party who so did not convert, shall apply for divorce under this section. The converted party cannot apply for divorce based on conversion under the 1976 Act because Section 3 of the Act prohibits the application of the Act to Muslims. Similarly, where one party to a Muslim marriage converts to another religion, according to Islamic law the marriage is automatically divorced but matters in relation to ancillary relief needs to be decided. The Syariah Court has no jurisdiction to hear a petition from a non-Muslim. Thus, the question that arises is which court shall have the jurisdiction to decide on all these matters. This paper intends to look at the effect of conversion to marriage in Malaysia.

Introduction

In a multireligious society like Malaysia, conversion from one religion to another is not uncommon. With Islam being the religion of the Federation as provided by Article 3 of the Federal Constitution, conversion to Islam have always been regarded as normal and acceptable, particularly where the majority of population are Muslim. Although freedom of religion is guaranteed by the Article 11 of the Federal Constitution, under Islamic law, conversion from Islam to any other religion is strictly prohibited[4] and in view of such restrictions, the Federal Constitution provides in Article 11(4) that the laws of the state or the federal territories may be passed to control or prohibit the teaching of other religion to Muslims. It must also be pointed out that under the Federal Constitution; the state legislature governs matters relating to Islamic law. It is the intention of this paper to look at the current trends in Malaysia in relation to freedom of religion and the conflict that arises from this issue.

Human Rights and Freedom of Religion

The Universal Declaration of Human Rights (the Declaration) was passed in 1948 due to the horrors, abuses and destruction caused by the Second World War. Today after 54 years, the Declaration remains the main gateway through which any quest or study of human rights begins. Many countries, including Malaysia has not ratified the Declaration.

Freedom of Religion is one of the principles guaranteed in the Declaration where Articles 2, 18 and 29, captured it. Article 2 states that the human rights as espoused under the Declaration apply to everyone without distinction of any kind, including differences in religion. Article 18 relates to religion and provides that:

"Everyone has the right to freedom of thought, conscience and religion; this right includes freedom to change his religion or belief, either alone or in the community with others and in public or private, to manifest his religion or belief in teaching, practice, worship and observance."

Articles 29 sets out limits to the scope of freedom of religion and other human rights as follows:

"In the exercise of his rights and freedoms, everyone shall be subject only to such limitations as are determined by law solely for the purpose of securing due recognition and respect for the rights and freedoms of others and of meeting the just requirements of morality, public order and the general welfare in a democratic society."

In other international declarations or conventions after the Declaration, the call to promote or protect freedom of religion has been incorporated in many forms, for example, in the United Nation Convention on the right of the child, freedom of thought, conscience and religion is provided in Article 14. This is to show that even in children, such rights are guaranteed.

Despite all the work done either by the Universal Declaration of Human Rights and many other international conventions or instrument, it is difficult to reach an agreement on the nature and extent of freedom of religion. Thus, it is not surprising that a universal view of what 'religion' is could not be worked out for either the Declaration or other declarations. For example whether the Scientologist is a 'religion' or not was decided differently in England and Australia.[5]

Freedom of Religion and Rights to Convert in Malaysia

In Malaysia, Islam is the religion of the federation as provided by Article 3 of the Federal Constitution. However, other religion may be practised in peace and harmony in any parts of the federation.

Article 11 of the Federal Constitution provides that every person has the right to profess and practise his religion. Every person has the right to propagate his religion, but state law and in respect of the federal territory federal law may control or restrict the propagation of any religion, doctrine or belief among persons professing the Muslim religion. There is however, freedom to carry on missionary work among non-Muslims. Under this Article it is also provided that no person shall be compelled to pay any tax the proceeds of which are specially allocated in whole or in part for the purposes of a religion other than his own. Every religious group has the right:

1. To manage its own religious affairs;
2. To establish and maintain institutions for religious and charitable purposes; and
3. To acquire and own property and to hold and administer it in accordance with law.

Article 11 also made a proviso that Article 11 does not authorize any act contrary to any general law relating to public order, public health and morality.

Under Article 160 of the Federal Constitution, the word law does not include Islamic law. Despite that Islamic law remains an important source of laws in Malaysia and is within the jurisdiction of the state legislature.[6] Hence, whenever an issue relating to Islam is brought before the court, Article 3 and Article 11 will be discussed or commented upon by the courts simultaneously.

Freedom of religion was raised before the court in the case of *Jamaluddin bin Othman* v. *Menteri Hal Ehwal Dalam Negeri, Malaysia and Anor,*[7] where a Malay Muslim who converted to Christianity was detained under the Internal Security Act, 1960. The reason for his detention was that he was propagating Christianity to the Muslims. On an application by the respondent for habeas corpus, the learned trial judge took the view that the minister has no power to deprive a person of his right to profess and practise his religion which is guaranteed under Article 11 of the Federal Constitution and therefore if the minister acts to restrict the freedom of a person from professing and practising his religion, his act will be inconsistent with the provision of Article 11 and thus any order of detention would not be valid.[8] The Minister of Home Affairs of Malaysia appealed to the Supreme Court where the Supreme Court upheld the High Court's decision and dismissed the appeal. According to the Supreme Court mere participation in meetings and seminar could not make a person a threat to the national security of the country. With regards to the respondent's alleged involvement in converting six Muslims, according to the court, even if it was true, it cannot by itself be regarded as a threat to the security of the country.

Freedom of religion was again raised in *Hjh Halimatulssaadiah bte Hj Kamaruddin* v. *Public Services Commission, Malaysia and Another,*[9] where in this case a woman public servant was dismissed for her refusal to observe a government circular which required public servants not to put on a veil while on duty.[10] The prohibition on veil imposed on Muslims women working in government service was justified under Article 11(5).[11]

In *Meor Atiqulrahman bin Ishak and Ors* v. *Fatimah bte Sihi and Ors,*[12] Article 3 and 11 were discussed by the High Court at full length. In this case, the plaintiffs were three male students aged eleven, nine and eight and the defendant was a headmistress of their school. The three students were expelled from the defendant school after being ordered by the defendant to stop wearing turbans to school.[13] Prior to the expulsion the defendant had issued a letter and other warnings to the three students to stop wearing turban at school. The plaintiff in their statement of claim argued that the action taken by the defendant was contrary to the Federal Constitution. In his decision the learned judge said that Article 3 of the Federal Constitution deserved a proper interpretation. According to him Islam as the religion of the Federation should extend beyond rituals and ceremonies as long as it did not deny peaceful and harmonious practice of the other religions.[14] The learned judge was actually referring to a Supreme Court decision of *Che Omar bin Che Soh* v. *PP*[15] and felt bound by that decision but eventually concluded that the issues raised by Meor Atiqulrahman were different from those in Che Omar Che bin Che Soh. It is interesting to note that in this case the learned judge went at length to explain what is meant by Article 3 and he concluded that it is not only a way of life but Islam as a religion of the Federation must take priority against other religion in the Federation. Thus he came to a conclusion that the regulation issued by the Education Ministry on school uniforms, i.e., shorts for boys and pinafore tunic for girls ignored the teaching of Islam and the given position of the Islam in the Constitution and therefore void. On the issue that Islam should be given a priority, the learned judge said that it should be considered first and foremost before other religion. It should be noted that this is the first decision of its kind in relation to supremacy of Islam in the constitutional structure even though some academicians have advanced such views.[16]

On freedom of religion, the learned judge acknowledged the fact that he was bound by the Supreme Court's decision in *Hjh Halimatussaadiah*[17] but decided that fact in Hjh Halimatussaadiah was different from the case before him. He ruled that wearing a veil at work made it difficult to identify the staff concerned and may lead to breach of public security but the same cannot be said about wearing a turban. He also said that prohibition on wearing a turban might also have an impact on Sikhs in Malaysia. It is unfortunate that the learned judge did not take the opportunity to discuss the case of *Jamaluddin bin Othman*[18] and Article 11 in great detail and precision. If the learned judge was able to distinguish *Hjh Halimatussaadiah* with *Meor Atiqulrahman*, he should have at least try to explain and understand *Jamaluddin bin Othman* and give reasons as to why he was not bound by it.

In *Kamariah Ali* v. *Kerajaan Negeri Kelantan, Malaysia and Satu lagi dan Rayuan Yang lain*[19] freedom of religion was raised in the High Court and later appealed to the Court of Appeal. In this case, the appellants were born Malay/Muslim and in 1992 were found guilty by the Syariah High Court of the state of Kelantan under Section 69 of the Majlis Agama Islam dan Adat Istiadat Melayu Kelantan, Enactment 1966. They were found guilty of conducting a ceremony contrary to hokum syarak or Islamic law. They were sentenced to 2 years imprisonment and appealed to the Syariah Appeal Court of Kelantan where the court confirmed the decision of the Syariah High Court but substituted the sentence where they were released on bond of good behaviour for three to five years and within that period, they must appear before a Kadi, in the district where they lived, once a month to pronounce their plea of repentance. This is in accordance with Section 132(1) of the Syariah Criminal Procedure Enactment of Kelantan, 1989. In August 1998 the appellants individually declared themselves to be non-Muslim and such declaration was made under the Poll Deed Act 1960. On the 5th October they were brought before the Syariah High Court of Kelantan for disobeying an order of the Syariah Appeal Court. At the trial they announced that they are no longer Muslim and showed the Poll Deed that they had made. Despite their conversion the Syariah High Court found them guilty for disobeying the Syariah Appeal Court and sentenced them to three years imprisonment. While serving their sentence and without applying for an appeal of the decision, they applied to the High Court of Malaya in Kota Bharu for the writ of habeas corpus a declaration of that they are no longer Muslim. The High Court held that since the Syariah Court had not decided the status of the appellants, i.e., whether they are still a Muslim or not, the High Court held them to be a Muslim and therefore the High Court of Malaya has no jurisdiction to hear their applications. The issue of the appellants' right to freedom of religion, the High Court held that it did not arise. The appellants appealed to the Court of Appeal.

The Court of Appeal in its judgment decided that in relation to Article 3 of the Federal Constitution, Islam as the religion of the Federation has a unique position and as such must be treated differently from any other religion. Such interpretation of the status of Islam under the Constitution had been discussed in *Meor Atiqulrahman* but the case was not even mention as it was a High Court decision. As a matter of fact, by deciding that Islam has a unique and different position from any other religion, the Court of Appeal is actually agreeing with the remarks made by the High Court Judge in *Meor Atiqulrahman*.

In relation to Article 11, the Court of Appeal looked at the meaning of the word 'has a right' in Article 11 and decided that such a right does not mean that any laws passed with an aim of punishing Muslims for non-performance of their religious obligations would be contrary to the Constitution. That, according to the Court of Appeal, would mean giving an absolute right and freedom as understood in the West. The Court went on further to state that Article 3 and 11 must be read together as the freedom of religion provided by Article 11 take into consideration of the fact that Islam is the religion of the Federation. It is through these provisions and what is provided by the Second Lists of Schedule 9 that empowered the States Legislature to pass laws that prohibit the teachings of other religions to Muslims. However, the Court of Appeal did not discuss the Supreme Court decision in *Jamaluddin bin Othman* or overruling it.

In another interesting case of *Lina Joy* v. *Majlis Agama Islam Wilayah Persekutuan and Anor,*[20] the High Court held that since the plaintiff was a born Muslim, lived as a Muslim with her family and was commonly reputed to be a Muslim, she was therefore a Muslim within the meaning of Section 2 of the Administration of Islamic Law (Federal Territories) Act 1993 and her well-being was the duty and care of the first defendant, which was the Majlis Agama Islam. In this case the plaintiff sought a number of declarations from the High Court, inter alia that she has the right to exercise her freedom of religion under Article 11(1) of the Federal Constitution and that the Administration of Islamic Law (Federal Territories) was null and void as it is inconsistent with the Federal Constitution. She as a born Muslim and at the age of 26 converted to Christianity and wished to marry a Christian. Her application to marry was turned down as her identity card still showed that she is a Muslim. She had applied to the National Registration Department to change her name and to remove the word 'Islam' from her new identity card. She applied to the High Court to order the defendant (Majlis Agama Islam) to register her name in the Registry Book as having converted out of Islam. The High Court also held that it is the exclusive jurisdiction of the Syariah Court to determine whether or not she is still a Muslim. The Court also held that by virtue of Article 160 of the Federal Constitution, the plaintiff was by definition 'Malay' and therefore could not renounce her Islamic faith at all. This is because according to Article 160, Malay is a person who professes the religion of Islam, habitually speaks the Malay language and conforms to the Malay adat. The case is now being heard in the Court of Appeal.

From the above discussion it could be seen that Islam has a special and unique position in Malaysia. Even though the freedom of religion is provided and guaranteed by the Federal Constitution, such a right is not an absolute right and must be applied carefully as Islam is the religion of the Federation.

Conversion to Islam and its Implication to a Non-Muslim Marriage

In Malaysia, non-Muslim marriages is governed by Law Reform (Marriage and Divorce) Act 1976[21] (to be referred to as LRA) where it provides that every marriage, unless void under the law, religion, custom or usage under which it was solemnized, shall continue until dissolved:

1. by death of one of the parties; or
2. by order of a court of competent jurisdiction; or
3. By a decree of nullity made by a court of competent jurisdiction.[22]

Thus if parties have been married under this Act, they can only dissolve they marriage if they satisfy one of the above requirements. Conversion to Islam is a special ground of divorce under this Act which is provided by Section 51 where it states that "where one party to a marriage has converted to Islam, the other party who has not so converted may petition for divorce: Provided that no petition under this section shall be presented before the expiration of the period of three months from the date of the conversion".

The effect of Section 51 is that after years of marriage, which was solemnized in accordance with LRA, one of the parties to the marriage converts to Islam, the followings questions arises:

1. If the non-converting party did not apply for divorce. The question that arises out of this is whether the non-Muslim marriage is still in existence or has it been dissolved by conversion to Islam by one of the party to that marriage?
2. If the party that has converted to Islam marries a Muslim woman. What is the status of the second marriage and is she entitled to his estate upon the death of her husband?

3. Who has the right to custody of the children from the non-Muslim marriage and in which court should the case be heard?
4. What happens if after many years living as Muslim and married to a Muslim woman, the man decided to convert back to his old religion?

In *Esswari Viswalingam* v. *Government of Malaysia,*[23] the appellant sought a declaration that she was a dependent as defined in Section 4 of the Pension Adjustment (Amendment) Act 1983 and also a declaration that she was entitled to a derivative pension under Section 15 of the Pensions Act 1980. Parties were married in November 1950 according to Hindu rites. In July 1978, the respondent converted to Islam. He was a pensioner under the Pensions Act and he died on the 7 January, 1985.The appellant had never applied for divorce under the LRA 1976. The High Court held that the appellant was not entitled to the derivative pension. The appellant appealed. The Supreme Court allowed her appeal and held that since her marriage to the respondent has never been terminated it remained valid under the civil law at the time of the death of respondent. Therefore she was a dependent under the pension laws and was entitled to a derivative pension. The court did not venture into the effect of Islamic law on this case or the status of marriage had the respondent contracted a marriage under Islamic law. The court held that appellant was certainly a widow of the deceased.

Section 51 has also been used by the converted spouse as an excuse not to pay maintenance. In *Letchumy* v. *Ramadason,*[24] petitioner obtained a divorce from the respondent on the grounds of desertion. After the decree was made she applied for maintenance and the matter came before the Judicial Commissioner after the decree became absolute. The Judicial Commissioner ordered the respondent to pay the petitioner $200 a month as her maintenance. The respondent subsequently applied for the order to be set-aside on the ground that he had become a Muslim and under Islamic law the petitioner has no right to claim maintenance because she has not converted to Islam with her husband during the *eddah*[25] period. The High Court held that since Section 3(1) of LRA precludes the operation of the Act to a Muslim, and as the respondent had become a Muslim, the Act cannot be made to apply to him.

However, in *Tan Sung Mooi* v. *Too Miew Kim,*[26] the decision on *Letchumy* v. *Ramadason,*[27] was overruled. In this case the petitioner and the respondent were married in 1967 under Chinese customary rights and lived together until 1982 when they decided to live apart. In 1989, the petitioner petitioned for divorce under Section 53 of the LRA. The High Court granted decree nisi and pending it being made absolute, the petitioner filed an application for an order of the division of the family assets and maintenance. The respondent then converted to Islam. He then raised the issue in the High Court that the High Court has no jurisdiction over him with respect to the ancillary relief, as he had become a Muslim. The petitioner argued that she could not come under the Shariah Court, as she is a non-Muslim. The High Court must continue to have jurisdiction in this matter otherwise it would be unconstitutional in so far as it prevented the court from granting the order for ancillary relief, as she would then have no effective remedy in law against the respondent. The Judicial Commissioner referred a number of questions for opinion of the Supreme Court. The Supreme Court held that since the legal obligations that the respondent was being sued was made while both parties were non-Muslims, the High Court would have jurisdiction to hear and determine the ancillary proceedings despite the fact that the respondent had converted to Islam after the divorce but before the hearing of the ancillary relief. Parliament clearly intended to provide ancillary relief for non-Muslims spouses and the children of the marriage as the result of the other party's conversion to Islam. In the context of legislative intent of Section 3 and the overall purpose of the Act, the respondent's legal obligations under a non-Muslim marriage could not be extinguished or avoided by conversion to Islam. Therefore, Section 3 of the LRA is not unconstitutional as has been argued by the petitioner. The Supreme Court also held that even though the new clause (1A) of Article 121 has taken away the jurisdiction of the High Court in respect of matters falling within the jurisdiction of the Shariah Court, the Shariah Court does not have jurisdiction over the petitioner who is a non-Muslim. Therefore Article 121(1A) of the Federal Constitution does not affect the jurisdiction of the

High Court to hear application under Sections 76 and 77 of the LRA. The decision of Tan Sung Mooi was well received by the non-Muslims community in Malaysia. It also dismissed the allegation that Islam can be used as an escapism by non-Muslim men to run away from their legal obligations which they contracted when they were non-Muslims by merely changing their religion to Islam.

This issue does not stop here. The wording of Section 51 has raised a number of problems. This is because according to the Act, it is not applicable to persons professing the religion of Islam. Thus, Section 51 is drafted in such a way that only the non-Muslim party to a marriage can file a petition for divorce based on conversion. It has been suggested that the wording "The other party who has not so converted..." to be replaced with "... either party to the marriage...". However, this has not been accepted because it is presumed that the probability of men converting to Islam is higher than women. The objective of the provision is to protect the rights of non-Muslim women who have been left by their husbands who have converted to Islam.[28]

This certainly creates what conflict of law term as 'limping marriages'. On one hand, a non-Muslim couple was married according to the civil laws where the marriage is monogamous. Some years later one of the party converted to Islam. According to Islamic law the marriage is terminated after the expiration of three months if the other party does not convert to Islam as well. Thus, the party that has converted is free to marry according to his or her personal law, i.e., Islamic law. In Malaysia this is what has happened. If the party that has converted is the husband, he then married another woman in accordance with Islamic law. Now, there are two marriages in existence. According to the Penal Code,[29] he shall be guilty of bigamy because he is still married under the LRA. However, this law on bigamy is not applicable to Muslims. Thus, no action has been taken on the many occasions where non-Muslim men who have converted married according to Islamic law even though his first marriage under the LRA has not been terminated because the non-Muslim wife did not petition for divorce. The conflict continues when the husband died as in the case on *Eeswari*.

Had he been married under Islamic law, his Muslims wife is entitled to his estate including his pension. Is she not a dependent too? Had they had any children, these children are also entitled to the estate of the deceased. What is their legal status? Who would be more entitled to his estate: his first wife and children from the civil marriage or his Muslims wife and children? These are common problems that have arisen out of the application of Section 51 of the LRA. Unfortunately, neither the court nor the legislature has been able to address them adequately. The common excuse was to avoid the issue because of its sensitiveness.

In *Pedley* v. *Majlis Agama Islam, Pulau Pinang and Anor,*[30] the parties were married in accordance with the Roman Catholic rites on 12 February, 1966. On 12 January, 1987 the wife embraced the religion of Islam without the plaintiff's knowledge and assumed a Muslim name. The plaintiff applied for a declaration that the conversion of his wife had not determined his marriage to her. It was held that it was clear that under the civil law a non-Muslim marriage is not dissolved upon one of the parties converting to Islam. Conversion is a ground to petition for divorce by the party who has not converted. In this case the Kadi Besar has written a letter to the plaintiff that his marriage to his wife would be dissolved according to Islamic law. According to the Wan Adnan J that assertion of the Kadi Besar did not and will not affect the plaintiff's legal position in the eyes of his own personal laws and the civil law of the country. He also held that since the declaration sought was merely an academic one and will not benefit him in any way; the court dismissed the application.

It is submitted that the learned Judge was trying to avoid the real issue in this case. The declaration sought by the husband is not purely academic. It goes to show that the wife who has converted to Islam is trapped in a marriage, which has come to an end. According to her personal law, which is Islam, since her husband does not join her to be a Muslim, her marriage to him is automatically terminated. It is prohibited (haram) for her to live with him under the same roof. She cannot apply for divorce under Section 51 because that Section clearly prohibits her from doing so. Thus, she cannot remarry. Her only option is to desert him and then apply under

Section 54 (1)(c) and base her argument on constructive desertion. But this would mean that she has to wait for another two years. The immediate question that comes to mind is whether the court will accept her husband's refusal to convert to Islam as a valid reason that forced her to leave him thus making him involved in constructive desertion? Could she file a divorce under Section 54(2)(b) that her husband has behaved in such away that it is intolerable to live with him? Would refusal to convert to Islam be considered by the court as an intolerable behaviour? He loves his wife and wanted the marriage to go on but because of her new faith he must let her go. Would court consider this as intolerable behaviour? If the court does not accept these excuses this woman shall be trapped forever in marriage, which has come to an end. Of course she may just go ahead and marry a Muslim man (like in many cases in Malaysia) but she runs the risk of being persecuted for bigamy under the Penal Code[31] (which never actually happens).

In another case of *Tey Siew Choo* v. *Teo Eng Hua,*[32] the court tried to solve some of these problems raised by Section 51. In this case the parties were married in 1982 in accordance with a Buddhist customary rites and the marriage was registered under the LRA 1976. In July 1995, the petitioner embraced Islam and parted company with the respondent. Some three years later, the petitioner petitioned for divorce under the Act. The petitioner argued that dissolution ought to be granted as her marriage had irretrievably broken down by virtue of her conversion to Islam and also by the facts as dictated in Section 54 (1)(d). The respondent did not contest the petitioner's averments.

The learned Judge in his judgment cited *Eeswari Visuvalingam,*[33] *Pedley* v. *Majlis Agama Islam Pulau Pinang,*[34] and *Tan Sung Mooi* v. *Too Miew Kim,*[35] as to show that a non-Muslim marriage will continue to exist even though one of the spouses has converted to Islam. He made no distinction between these cases with the present one before him as in all of these three cases the application was made by the spouse who were still non-Muslim. In *Tey Siew Choo,*[36] however, it was the spouse who has converted to Islam that made the application. He further held that Section 3(3) and Section 51 of the LRA are not applicable to Muslims and those married under the

Muslim law but not to those who have just recently converted to Islam. The question is whether it is true that according to Section 3 of the LRA the word 'Muslim' means a person who has been a Muslim all his or her life and not someone who has just converted to Islam? Even if statutory interpretation is being applied here, the word 'Muslim' or 'professes the religion of Islam' will be given its ordinary grammatical meaning which means that it does not make a distinction between a person who has been a Muslim all his or her life and a person who has just converted to Islam. It is therefore submitted that the line of reasoning given by the learned Judge cannot be accepted, as it is neither logical nor practical.

The judge also admitted that the reason for the application to be allowed was because the petitioner had made an application under Section 53 and the facts alleging breakdown was under Section 54(2) (d). According to the judge since the application was not contested by the respondent that goes to show that he accepted that fact. Therefore, the marriage was dissolved because marriage has broken down irretrievably, that is, not only because the petitioner has converted to Islam but also they have lived apart for a continuous period of two years. It is submitted that the decision is only correct if all parties involved are non-Muslims. Since one party to the marriage has converted to Islam, Section 53 is not applicable. The other party who has not so converted must obtain divorce. Otherwise, Section 51 shall be redundant and meaningless.

Of course, *Tey Siew Choo* is a 'God-given' decision for the many converted spouses who have been trapped in a marriage, which have irretrievably broken down due to their conversion. They are now free to apply to court for divorce under Section 54 and could be granted a divorce as in *Tey Siew Choo*. But this is not the solution to the problems raised by Section 51. It certainly does not represent the intention of Parliament. The intention of Parliament was to protect non-Muslim wives whose husbands have converted to Islam. If this intention is to be maintained, the decision in *Tey Siew Choo* is per incuriam and must be overruled.

In *Genga Devi a/p Chelliah* v. *Santanam a/l Damodaram,*[37] the couple were Hindu and married in accordance with Hindu rites in 1987. They have a son. The husband converts to Islam and on 24

April 1997 he obtained an order from the Syariah Court Alor Setar, giving him the custody of the child. The applicant wife filed an originating summons for inter alia a declaration that the order dated 24 April 1997 was ultra vires, null and void and must be set a side. The respondent raised a preliminary objection that the High Court had no jurisdiction to set the order of the Syariah Court. The High Court decided that it is clear that Article 121(1A) of the Federal Constitution that civil courts cannot interfere with the matters involving and subject to the jurisdiction of the Syariah Court. Therefore, the High Court had no jurisdiction to set aside the order of the Syariah Court. The Court also found that the applicant's application was irregular and contrary to the law.

Genga is another unfortunate case where the High Court felt found by Article 121(1A) when it should have not. What the High Court should have done was to question the issues involved in this case and what were the religions of parties when they marry and therefore Islamic law should not govern the question of the custody of a child from a non-Muslim marriage because the child was not born from a Muslim marriage. The Syariah Court has the jurisdiction when both parties are Muslims and where it involved Islamic law. It is submitted that the High Court had erred in law in deciding this case.

In *Kung Lim Siew Wan* v. *Choong Chee Kuan,*[38] parties were married in 1984 under the LRA and they have two children. They are both dentists practising in Kota Bharu, Kelantan. Since 31, July 2000 the couple has been living separately. When the plaintiff's wife made an application for the custody and maintenance of children, the husband applied for the application to be strike out, as he is a Muslim at the time of the marriage. He alleged that he has converted to Islam on the 26 November 1997. Plaintiff argued that the defendant was never a Muslim but a Buddha and the defendant never used his Muslim name and all their friends and colleagues knew him as non-Muslim.

The High Court in Kuala Lumpur held that even though there is a question on the defendant's status as a Muslim, and even if he is a Muslim, that does not exclude the High Court to hear and determine the case. According to the judge even though Section 3 of LRA states that the LRA is not applicable to Muslims or to persons who are married under Islamic law, the defendant is stopped from using his Muslim identity just to avoid his liabilities and responsibilities created under his previous non-Muslim marriage. This is due to the fact that he admitted to be a Buddha to enable his marriage to be registered under LRA and such act stopped him from going back on his word in order to avoid his responsibilities created under the civil law.

Finally in *Sharmala a/p Sathiyaseelan* v. *Dr Jeyaganesh a/l C Mogarajah,*[39] where the couple were married in 1998 in accordance with Hindu rites. They have two children aged 4 and 2 years old. On the 19 November 2002, the husband (defendant) converted to Islam and later on the 25 November converted the two children with him; the plaintiff's wife has left the defendant and went back to Kedah. On the 31, December 2002 she applied for custody of children. Trial was fixed on the 16, January but the defendant applied for postponement as he needed time to appoint a lawyer. Trial was fixed on the 25 February 2003. Meanwhile on the 7 January 2003, the defendant through his lawyer made an *ex parte* application to the Shah Alam Syariah Court for a custody order and this was not related to the High Court. On 12 April 2003 the High Court heard arguments on the issue of jurisdiction and the High Court held that it has jurisdiction to hear the application and fix trial on the 17 April 2003. Meanwhile the Shah Alam Syariah Court, based on the husband's *ex parte* application issued a warrant of arrest on the plaintiff's wife for her failure to attend the trial at the Syariah Court. On the 14 April 2003, the High Court in Kuala Lumpur turned down the application of the plaintiff to revoke the conversion of the two children to Islam as the matter is within the jurisdiction of the Jabatan Agama Islam and the Syariah Courts.

On the 17, April 2003 the High Court heard the custody application made by the plaintiff (wife) and on the 8 May 2003 the Shah Alam Syariah Court made an order giving custody to the defendant (husband). The defendant did not observe the interim order made by the Kuala Lumpur High Court and took the children out of Alor Star. The plaintiff applied for committal order. At the trial Dato Faiza Thamby Chik J held that according to Section 51 the defendant cannot apply for divorce as he has converted to Islam and he cannot apply for divorce in the Syariah Court as his wife is not a Muslim, and therefore Syariah Court has no jurisdiction. He also held that the plaintiff was not bound by the Syariah Court order and in fact the order has no effect on the interim order given by the High Court in Kuala Lumpur. This is due to the fact that the jurisdiction of the Syariah Court is within state jurisdiction. That is not the end of the case. Shamala having obtained the interim custody order took the children to Australia which is a clear act of contempt. Hence, the High Court on the 20 July 2004 when it convened to finally decide the issue of custody only decided for academic purposes as the children are no longer within its jurisdiction. The High Court held that the non-Muslim mother who is the plaintiff was entitled to care and control of the two Muslim children and as plaintiff and defendant are parents of the children, appoint them as joint custodian of the child. The decision raised eyebrows and concern amongst Muslims and it is believed that the defendant has applied for an appeal to the court of Appeal.

These cases illustrate that freedom of religion is exercised but to a certain extend also abused. Conversion to Islam does not means that one can escape from one's own obligations and responsibilities created before the conversion. It is also not a way to take away a child from his or her mother or father as in Islam, difference of religion does not severe relationship and responsibilities. Amendment to the LRA has been suggested,[40] and it is Parliament that has the power to resolve these problems.[41]

The Effect of Conversion out of Islam to Muslim Marriages

According hokum syarak, when a Muslim becomes an apostate, his or her previous Muslim marriage will be automatically dissolved.[42] However, under Islamic Family Law enactments of all the states in Malaysia, converting out of Islam does not automatically dissolve the marriage but the marriage must be confirmed by a court of competent jurisdiction.[43] Furthermore, the new enactment also inserted a new section on the criterion for deciding whether a person is a Muslim where it says that "if for the purpose of this Enactment any question arises as to whether a person is a Muslim, that question shall be decided according to the criterion of general reputation, without making any attempt to question the faith, beliefs, conducts, behaviour, character, acts or omissions of that person".[44] This enables the Syariah Court to determine whether a person is a Muslim or not on the general reputation and if he or she is not, then it should confirm that the Muslim marriage has been dissolved by the conversion out of Islam. The difficulty here is that if a wife applies for divorce because she believes her husband is an apostate, she will have to prove that on general reputation her husband is no longer a Muslim and because he does not fast during the month of *Ramadhan* or he does not observe the 5-time daily prayers. If he has changed his name and made a sworn affidavit of his conversion, it is presumed that is sufficient proof that he is no longer a Muslim by reputation. Thus, it is more difficult for a Muslim to dissolve his or her marriage based of conversion out of Islam, if no attempt can be made to question his or her behaviour, acts, etc. It is within the jurisdiction of the Syariah Court to decide whether or not a person is still a Muslim.[45]

Conclusion

Conversion to and from Islam is not unusual in a multiracial society like ours. However, having a pluralistic legal system, which, define clearly what are within Civil or Syariah jurisdiction has proof to be fatal to cases of involving conversion of only one party to a marriage. It creates too many limping marriages and uncertainty to both Muslims and non-Muslims. The problematic Section 51 may soon be amended but whether or not it will resolve the many disputes that have risen from the issue of conversion remains to be seen or proved. Even if Section 51 is amended as recommended, if either party chooses not to petition for divorce based on conversion due to certain reasons or the other, party who did not convert does not know about the conversion, the conflict may continue.

Notes

1. Federal Constitution, Article 3.
2. Federal Constitution, Article 11.
3. See Law Reform (Marriage and Divorce Act) 1976.

4. Al-Quran, Al-Baqarah 2.
5. *R* v. *Registrar General*, (1970)2 QB 697 and in *Church of New Faith* v. *Comr of Payroll Tax* (1983) 57 ALJR 785.
6. List 2 of Schedule 9, Federal Constitution.
7. (1989) 1 MLJ 418 (Supreme Court).
8. (1994) 3 MLJ 61.
9. (1994) 3 MLJ 418.
10. A veil must be contrasted with a head cover, where the former covered the head and the entire face except the two eyes, whereas the latter covers only the head but not the face.
11. This decision has been criticized by Zainur Zakaria, "Religious Freedom: Right to wear Purdah" (1993) 3 MLJ xxv.
12. (2000) 5 MLJ 375.
13. Turban is a headgear worn by male Muslim. The wearing of turban for male is not obligatory but encouraged as a practice of the Prophet SAW.
14. (2000) 5 MLJ 375 at 383.
15. (1988) 2 MLJ 85.
16. Harding, "Islam and Public Law in Malaysia: Some Reflections in the aftermath of Suzie Teoh's case" (1991) 1 MLJ xci-xcvi and Aziz Bari "Legal Education and Islamization" (1999) IIUMLJ, Vol. 7, No. 1, p. 83.
17. (1994) 3 MLJ 61.
18. Supra.
19. (2002) 3 CLJ 766.
20. (2004) 6 CLJ 242.
21. Act 164.
22. Ibid. s4.
23. (1990) 1 MLJ 86.
24. (1984) 1 MLJ 141.
25. Iddah is the 3-months waiting period after her husband has divorced a Muslim wife. It is like a 'cooling off' period where the couple may 'juju' (get back together) without going through the solemnization of marriage. After the 3 months has expired, should the couple wish to live together again, they have to go through a fresh solemnization of marriage.
26. (1991) 3 MLJ 117.
27. Supra.

28. Parliamentary Debate 4th November 1975. Parliamentary Debate (Dean Rakyat) Vol. 1, Section 11, p. 6495-6503, p. 6501.
29. Penal Code Section 494.
30. (1990) 2 MLJ 307.
31. Penal Code, Section 494.
32. (1999) 6 CLJ 308.
33. Supra.
34. Supra.
35. Supra.
36. Supra.
37. (2001) 2 AMR 1485.
38. (2003) 6 MLJ260.
39. Shamala Gets Custody of Converted Children, NST, 21 July 2004.
40. Noor Aziah Mohd. Awal, Section 51 of Law reform (Marriage and Divorce) Act 1976: An Overview, (1999) *IKIM Law Journal*, Vol. 3, No. 2, 127.
41. The Attorney General Department is believed to have drafted the amendments to be taken to Parliament early next year.
42. Al-Quran surah al-Baqarah: 222.
43. Islamic Family Law (State of Selangor) Enactment, No. 2 of 2003, Section 46.
44. Ibid., Section 5.
45. Refer to *Kamariah Ali* v. *Kerajaan Negeri Kelantan, Malaysia and Satu lagi dan Rayuan Yang lain* (2002) 3 CLJ 766, The Federal Court on 21 July 2004 held that even though the defendants have changed their religion, or become murtad, they can still be taken to the Syariah Courts because at the time they were sentenced, they were Muslims, NST, 22 July 2004.

14

Human Rights of Displaced Persons

SHAUKAT ALI

The question of human rights has never had a greater significance than in the period from 1948 to date. Not only for the intellectuals and elite, but also for the masses.[1] Universal Declaration of Human Rights opens with the statement that recognition of the inherent dignity and equal rights of all human beings is the foundation of freedom, justice and peace. Mahatma Gandhi said:

> Every human being has a right to live and therefore to find the wherewithal to feed himself and where necessary to clothe and house himself.

Article 25 of the Universal Declaration provided:

> Everyone has the right to a standard of living adequate for the health and well being of himself and of his family, including food, clothing, housing and medical care.

Article 11(2) of the International Covenant recognizes:

> The right to everyone to an adequate standard of living for himself and for his family including food, clothing and housing and to the continuous improvement of living conditions.

The expanded meaning of the expression 'right to life' as envisaged under Article 21 of the Constitution of India includes the right to live with basic human dignity and all that goes along with it namely, the bare necessities of life such as adequate nutrition, clothing and shelter over the head and facilities for reading, writing, and expressing oneself in diverse forms.

Chief Justice P.N. Bhagwati, in an address in Bombay in 1986 had emphasized:

> The right to development is one of the most important basic human rights and it constitutes the culminating point of the evolution of the concept of human rights. This 'super right', transcending the differentiation of civil and political rights and socio-economic rights into the future dimension, has been termed a "human right of the third generation". It has been recognized as an individual as well as collective right. (*Mainstream*, Vol. XXIV No. 28, dated 15.3.1986, p. 11).

Justice Bhagwati stressed the developmental orientation in its individual and collective dimensions. The individual dimension of this right he said, is concerned with the integral development of the individual in the sense of promoting his multidimensional fulfilment. If the large masses of people who inhabit the developing countries of the Third World are to achieve full and equal realization of this right to development, it is necessary that they should have effective access to:

1. tangible resources to achieve their basic needs of productive and equitable paid work, sufficient nutrition health care and hygiene, shelter, energy resources, clean water and air;
2. the necessary intangible resources, especially education and information to enable them better to utilize resources, and to participate freely in the process of development;
3. structures of production and government to assure the fair and equitable allocation of the above resources; and
4. facilities and services to organize themselves to participate, monitor, evaluate and review development programmes and processes, and to hold accountable those responsible for their implementation.

These are the necessary conditions which must be fulfilled if every one in the society is to be assured a life of basic human dignity and complete self-fulfilment which is the objective and goal of human rights. From this position it must follow as a logical corollary that the right to development includes within its ambit both civil and political rights as well as social and economic rights, and contains within it, the right to food, health and basic necessities of life; with hunger and ill health freedom can have no meaning.

What relevance do the expressions mentioned in the foregoing statements and provisions have in respect of the millions of people uprooted from their usual habitat? Millions of people have been displaced due to war, ethnic cleansing, political persecution, natural calamities, man-made disasters, developmental projects and a host of other causes. This paper aims at discussing to what extent human rights are available to these displaced persons. However, it is not within the purview of this paper to discuss the problem of refugees, international or national.

It would, therefore, be in the context to give a figurative outline of the persons and families who have been forced to leave their habitat.

Following is an account of number of families and people displaced from their homes as a result of various dams, projects undertaken by the government and various causes of displacement:

	No. of Families	*Dam/Project*	*Source*
1.	16,000 families	Pong Dam in the Bias Valley	*Surya India*, Feb. 1990
2.	18,500 families	Ukai Dam, Gujarat	*Surya India*, Feb. 1990
3.	162 villages would be submerged	Bargi Dam in Madhya Pradesh (one of the big 30 Dams to be constructed in Narmada Valley)	*Frontline*, July 30, 1993
4.	1,00,000 people to be displaced	Madhya Pradesh, 30 big, 135 medium and 3000 minor dams in Narmada Valley	*Frontline*, July 30, 1993
5.	90,000 people to be evicted	Sarda Sarovar, Gujarat	*Illustrated Weekly of India*, January 5-6, 1991

Contd.

6.	1,900 families to be evicted in Maharashtra	Sardar Sarovar, Maharashtra side	Ibid.
7.	2,00,000 families to be evicted	Both sides of Sardar Sarovar	Ibid.
8.	70,000 families to be evicted	Bisalpur Dam, Deoli, Tonk Distt. Rajasthan	*Times of India* Sept. 7, 1994
9.	37 villages to be evicted	Kishan Dam at Tons River, U.P. and H.P. Border (construction to begin in June 1996)	*Times of India* March, 3, 1995.
10.	1,10,000 people evicted	Damodar Valley Project	*Times of India* July, 17,1994
11.	6,00,000 people displaced	An assortment of industries including the Heavy Electricals Corporation, Ranchi and the Bokaro Thermal Power and Steel Plants	Ibid.
12.	1,70,000 people displaced	Coal mining in Bihar	Ibid.
13.	12,00,000	A clutch of associated industries and coal mining in Bihar	Ibid.
14.	1,00,000 people displaced	Firing range (Agni an Prithvi Misiles) Baliapal and Bhogarai blocks in Balasore district of Orissa where National Test Range Project was launched in 1987	*Times of India* Dec. 13, 1989
15.	27 villages to be evacuated	Angul-Talcher Coal fields operations	*Times of India*, Sept. 26, 1994
16.	2,50,000 people to be evicted	Netrahat Firing Range (Artillery) in Chhotanagpur area Bihar, mostly tribals	*Times of India* Jan. 17, 1994
17.	Scores of families left villages	Food crisis in Longphum, South Tripura	*Times of India* Nov. 19, 1994
18.	20,000 people affected, at the verge of eviction	Subsidence of mining area in East Singhbum	*Times of India* Nov. 7, 1994
19.	1,85,00,000 persons displaced	Various projects all over India between 1951 and 1991	*Times of India* July 17, 1994

The Problem

The foregoing chart shows figures of displaced persons only, and not their agony as a result of displacement. It is strange that the elite and the political power talk of development and at the ground reality people are faced with starvation. Faced with the spectre of starvation an exodus has begun from the remote villages in the Baremura ranges in South Tripura.[2] Though, there has been no report of any death from hunger so far, the Minister for Tribal Welfare and Tribal Rehabilitation, Aghore Deb Barma has said that it was possible that there is a food crisis in the interior hill villages. He also said that employment generation schemes were not available as the villages were situated inside the reserve forest and the hill range.

Land subsidence (cave in) in the catchment areas of Hindustan Copper Ltd.[3] has posed many problems for 20,000 people in the Singbhum area. Crack in land has been up to 100 feet, houses are collapsing, source of livelihood and water is disappearing. In the most populated area, the only source of water, a pond, has been ordered to be closed because of polluted water percolating in the pond. These people have to be evacuated from the area and a new habitation to be found. A similar problem is faced in Dhanbad coalmines catchment area. The entire area has become uninhabitable for thousands of families. The problem of livelihood and habitation is staring at them with no alternative means in sight.

Coalmines in Talcher (Orissa)

The massive coalfield operation and the consequent rapid industrialization in Angul-Talcher area in Orissa has created problems of livelihood and residence for thousands of people.[4] What is more disturbing is that hundreds of areas of land, are being acquired every year for mining. The authorities plan to evacuate 27 villages completely. A tug of war has developed between the villages and the Mahanadi Coalfields Ltd.; on the issue of compensation, rehabilitation and jobs in the coalmines.

The Jagannath and Ananta open cast mines have advanced right to the doorsteps of the villagers' houses. There is no house in the villages which has not been damaged by the regular blastings.

The threat of displacement is hanging like a Damocles' sword on all of them. In Jembu Behan village alone, 246 acres of land has been acquired, no compensation paid and authorities have asked them to leave bag and baggage. Director of the Central Cooperative Bank, Chatnya Sahoo, alleged that the MCL had asked all of the villages to leave the area by the end of 1994., But no alternative site had been provided to them. According to District Collector of Angul, Prasant Nayak, three sites had been selected by the state for rehabilitation, but villagers refuse to move. There is discrimination in aid programmes. In one part of Angul district, Kanhia, Rs 50,000 is paid over and above the compensation, no such amount is paid in Talcher in the same district.

Netrahat Firing Range

Netrahat plateau in Chota Nagpur tribal belt, a forested tribal belt area which extends across the Gumla and Palamau districts of Bihar,[5] has been used continuously for field firing practices by the Indian army since 1956. Stretching over 1471 sq. km. of traditional tribal land, the proposed Netrahat Field Firing Range will permit the 23 Artillery Brigade to perfect its battle skills. It will annihilate 245 villages and deprive 2,24,940 people of their homes and land. Of this number, 78 per cent belong to such tribes as the Oraon, Munda, Kisan, Khewar Birjia and Asur. It is a catastrophe even by the standards of the Indian republic. It is the largest single displacement of a tribal population contemplated since independence.

Besides the question of rehabilitation, the project would spell a sentence of death for the Asur and Birjia who are on the verge of extinction. When they are no more, we would have lost the oldest stream of the Indian population. The Asur were the subcontinent's first iron smelters envied for their skills by the metal questing Aryans who drove them from the Gangetiç plains into the Chota Nagpur highlands in 800 B.C. It is irony that birth of a male child in one of the islands in Andaman and Nicobar becomes a national news worthy of telecast on national hookup, but the imminent danger of extinction of the oldest tribe of India does not provoke emotion or concern.

The state has sacrificed the tribals at the alter of a so-called development programme which does not in any way benefit them; indeed, contributes to their immigration.

To assess the human cost of the nation's development programme in Bihar alone, one has only to place the displacement figures against the development projects since 1951. The Damodar Valley Project disposed 1,10,000 people; an assortment of industries, including the Heavy Electricals Corporation, Ranchi and the Bokaro thermal power and steel plants, dishoused 6,00,000 persons. A further 17,00,000 people have been displaced, by coal mining and a clutch of associated projects have turned 12,00,000 persons into refugees in their own country.

As in Bastar, Dahanu, Hirakund, Koraput, Bhakra, Malkangiri, and other project sites, the displaced become wood cutters, bonded labourers brick kiln workers, or migrate to the city, where some become domestic servants, and others turn to crimes. Propelled from a hunter-gatherer context into a monetary economy, whose workings they do not understand, they are brutally exploited. It is estimated that of the 1,85,00,000 people displaced by various projects between 1951 and 1990; only 52,50,000 people have been resettled after a fashion, the rest have been abandoned to their fate.

These mass evictions have had disastrous demographic consequences. The tribals, who constituted 60 per cent of Chota Nagpur, population in 1951, have now been reduced to a mere 30 per cent.

The tribals are brow beaten into signing away their rights by an insensitive bureaucracy which keeps them in the dark about legal and administrative procedures, so that they cannot even understand the injustices visited upon them by forces outside their control.

Sardar Sarovar and Problems

The final report of the Ram Chandra Singh Deo Committee of Madhya Pradesh MLAs demanded that the Madhya Pradesh government should stop the construction of the Sardar Sarovar Dam. Rehabilitation, the report argued, was a human problem of gigantic dimensions, and noted that oustees were living in hardship and their future bleak.

A September 1994 study, Rehabilitation of Madhya Pradesh Project Affected Families in Gujarat, carried out by the Narmada Control Authority (NCA), described the subhuman conditions oustees resettled in Gujarat were living in. At the Kukra site, most of those rehabilitated had not been given their land entitlement; others were given fragmented pieces of little value. Inadequate drainage, waterlogging, hostility and assault by local villagers, abysmal fuel, fodder and drinking water supplies: these conditions were endemic.

Impoverishment is arguably the least dangerous consequence of these conditions. During the 1994 monsoon, Gujarat newspapers reported that a cholera epidemic raged through the resettlement sites, after their poorly designed tin sheds were flooded. Crops and household materials were lost, and hundreds of tribals were hospitalized at Baroda and Vaghodia. Since no health care facilities are available nearby, this imposed a heavy financial burden on these impoverished families. Many died given that these conditions prevail when only 700 of 33,504 Madhya Pradesh families have as yet been resettled, the urgency is clear.

The Narmada Water Dispute Tribunal originally had ordered that the rehabilitation be completed at least a year prior to submergence. It needs an independent monitoring mechanism. Of the 3,100 families to have been resettled in Gujarat from Madhya Pradesh in 1992-93, land has actually been found for 1190 only. In 1993-94 of the Project Affected People (PAP) families to be shifted to Gujarat, only 986 were moved. Another problem of serious consequence has cropped up. Around 2,000 migrants from Madhya Pradesh to Gujarat, as a result of Sardar Sarovar evacuation, would not be eligible for getting benefit of reservation in view of the decision of the Supreme Court. The reason is that the caste or tribe of these people is not enumerated in the list meant for reservation benefit in Gujarat. This has created further problems leading to political implications. On the one hand political leaders are strongly advising not to leave their villages, on the other, they would be drowned if not evacuated as their villages fall under the submergence zone.

The Sardar Sarovar dam will submerge the habitants of 245 villages. Most of these are tribals. The dam is being built in Gujarat, However, the artificial reservoir created would affect large populations in the neighbouring states of Madhya Pradesh and Maharashtra.

The rehabilitation and resettlement progress has not been satisfactory by any standard. A senior member of the World Bank appraisal team, Conable, in his report dated August 29, 1989, stated that as regards rehabilitation progress between 1985 and 1989, there has been a very serious deterioration. He noted that in Madhya Pradesh 150 out of 193 villages had become openly against the dam. It was the December, 1989 report that gave details of non-implementation of 'minimum actions'. The Madhya Pradesh government was required, for instance, to provide a detailed plan, with data on land; infrastructure, time table for the first 17 villages to resettle in M.P., the written confirmation of arrangements satisfactory for resettlement of the 17 villages from M.P. to be resettled in Gujarat, a detailed plan for rehabilitation work in 1990-91.

However, the government had not even completed the bench-mark survey of the first 17 villages by 1991. Instead of collaborating with the dam affected people, the government used force when faced with non-cooperation of the tribals opposing the dam. On its part, the Government of Maharashtra sat by and did nothing. It could not identify any land for the 1,900 families of Maharashtra oustees of Sardar Sarovar Project (SSP). Despite the outward declarations of satisfactory progress on the rehabilitation front, the World Bank wrote to the three concerned states, Gujarat, Maharashtra and Madhya Pradesh and gave a deadline of May 15, 1990 to improve rehabilitation. It then took another unprecedented step: it delayed the appraisal report to 1992. This is proof, if any are required, that the rehabilitation measures had not satisfied even the elementary conditions set by the Bank. In March, 1990 Conable, one of the World Bank high officials expressed concern. He said, "we hope the SSP does not affect the quality of life in the neighbourhood of the Narmada. But it is for the borrowing government to establish its priorities".[6] He also expressed his views on the rehabilitation issue saying, "We do not govern your country (India). We only provide financial assistance". It is thus apparent that rehabilitation progress of the displaced persons was an utter failure – a disgrace to enforcement agencies for human rights.

One of the major sticking points so far has been the manner in which the resettlement of the oustees has been conducted. The Jayant Patil Committee, which was set up to review the project, found that this has been far from adequate. The land allotted to them has largely been of poor quality, under dispute and severally lacking in civic amenities. This has naturally led to many of the oustees attempting to return to their original homes which are now in the submergence zone. If this is the condition of the oustees, who at present constitute only two per cent of the total of 33,000 families who are to be rehabilitated, then the task of resettling all of them in a manner acceptable to them seems virtually impossible. At the conception stage it was agreed upon that apart from certain other conditions, rehabilitation shall be made as the construction progressed. The fact that this has not been done adequately is in direct contravention to the stipulations of the Narmada Tribunal Award.

According to one report, of the 16,000 families uprooted by the construction of the Pong dam in the Bias valley, no more than 9,000 people have been rehabilitated in Rajasthan. Many of the Bhakhra victims have not been resettled even 28 years after the completion of the dam. Out of 18,500 affected families by Ukal dam in Gujarat only 3,500 families have been resettled. The compensation provided by the government for loss of crops and land is woefully short of the prevailing rates against the prevailing rate of Rs 4,987 per acre of dry land, only Rs 932 per acre was given and for Rs 13,802 per acre of irrigated land a mere Rs 2,232 per acre was conceded, that too in instalments. The story of Narmada Project is a glaring example of negligence. In many cases the land supposed to be allotted to the displaced persons, does not exist at all. In the Bargi dam area of Madhya Pradesh there is no concrete policy for resettlement and rehabilitation, the oustees got the worst ever deal in compensation. Between 1984-89 revenue and administrative officials descended on the villages like hawks and acquired land for Rs 2000 to Rs 3000 per acre and without much ceremony, gave them marching orders. The government has set up an ideal village namely, Gorakhpur for the twice- relocated oustees of Bijasen village (one of 162 villages affected by Bargi dam in M.P.), but the experience of the people is very sore. Four starvation deaths of the resettled oustees has been reported. They were hardly provided any land, huts, and were left at the mercy of the wind to find employment. If it is the case with a small number of people in an ideal village, the agony of bulk of the oustees is not difficult to comprehend.

According to the Bilaspur Dam Submergence Coordination Committee, the farmers were not getting adequate compensation for the land acquired by the government. They are being paid at the rate of Rs 36,000 to Rs 54,000 per hectare in the irrigated area against the market rate of Rs 1,50,000 to Rs 2,00,000 per hectare. They are being paid Rs 2,000 to Rs 10,000 for every well acquired by the government while the digging expenses for every well acquired in the area was not less than Rs 50,000.[7]

In the name of development we have not only accepted displacement but have encouraged through the ideology of progress, the forced uprooting and migration of large sections of our population. The acquisition of large area of land for the National Test Range (NTR) project, in Baliapal in Balasore district of Orissa is one such example. The project NTR was formally announced in July, 1987 by the then Chief Minister of Orissa, J.B. Patnaik, who later glorified it as the 'Puja gift' for the people of Orissa. This project has displaced more than one lakh people from the two blocks of Baliapal and Bhogarai in the Balasore district. The project has acquired 55 villages, 42 in Baliapal and 13 in Bhogarai, covering 100 sq. km. Besides, we can think of the displaced people of Rourkela, Hirakund and Rangali dams, those of NILCO and BALCO projects and those who have had to leave because of the defence establishments like Chilka Naval Academy, Charbatia Air Force base, Baintala Ordnance Factory, to name only a few, Nine out of thirteen districts of Orissa have such defence establishments, most of these have displaced many people from their land.[8] Paradoxically, while all the benefits of development go to the cities like Rourkela which attracts technical knowledge, the displaced persons are employed only as casual workers or contract labourers. They are often forced to migrate being deskilled and marginalized. Additionally, rehabilitation programmes devised by the state were not evolved to encourage the reconstitution of displaced community through a conscious participatory involvement of the people by protecting their rights to the land, resources and skill. Displacement and rehabilitation in this area is creating many new problems like demographic changes, pressure on the land as a result of migratory population land decreasing, land disputes and caste hostilities.

Tihari Dam project is one of the dream projects in the series. Since its coverage area was confined to chilly area only and it was found out precisely, there was no difficulty in rehabilitating the people of ousted towns. So far as known to the author, proper measures have been undertaken by the government to put the inhabitants of the coverage area in new places almost in the same position as they were earlier. Unfortunately it does not happen in many situations.

The rehabilitation of persons displaced by the big dams prove to be the most thorny problem so far. The displacements are there to stay and permanently. The process of rehabilitation has always raised a volley of questions, not only from the displaced persons but from all conscious people also; the discrepancies are bound to be there. People who have an easy reach to the bureaucracy and politicians, get whatever is due to them and even that which is not due to them. But the poor, who are disorganized are left to fend for themselves. The rehabilitation of persons, uprooted from the command areas of dams has never been complete and it has created more problems than it has solved. The evacuees are generally transferred either to barren lands or infertile or waste land. Sensitivity to the real needs of the uprooted on whom a new lifestyle in a different socio-political milieu is being imposed is copiously lacking. The result often is an identity crisis and cultural shock. It must be realized that freedom and liberty cannot thrive on empty stomachs, and bare bodies.[9] Traditional civil and political rights, important as they are, have no meaning unless they are accompanied by social and economic rights.[10]

Right to education, be it under the UN Charter or a part of Article 221 of the Constitution of India as expanded by the Supreme Court, is non-existent for lakhs of children of displaced persons. It is the moral and legal duty of the government to establish schools for the children up to 14 years of age and only then the question of children going to school arises. In the case of displaced persons, the primary concern for them is to find an alternative source of survival. The children have been left uncared for in all the respects including education and nutrition. It is sad to say that these children have been deprived of their basic right to education whereupon, they could have built up their future course of life. They are destined to lead a life of want and misery. It is, therefore, most vital for the advancement and fulfilment of human rights promise that the policy makers and resettlement authorities must provide proper schools for the education of displaced persons so that they should not be damned for the remaining period of their lives.

Official Outlook

Strangely enough, the much infamous traditional outlook of the official machinery is mostly responsible for the agony. The implementing machinery for compensation consisting of officers from outside are totally devoid of humanitarian feeling. Files are prepared accordingly and the entire matter is treated in a mechanical way, either passing the buck or following the rut. Senior officers from the metropolis cannot encompass the problems faced by the tribals in the remote areas. Above all, when the official lethargy and incompetence or insensitivity is questioned by means of agitation and processions, it is suppressed by violent means resulting into death, serious injuries and arrests.

Prolonged litigation has led to inordinate delay in the payment of compensation in many cases. In many cases compensation has not yet been paid to Haryana farmers for the land acquired by the Central government 20 years ago for setting up Air Force Wireless Station. Around 2,000 cases are awaiting disposal in Faridabad and

Gurgaon alone. But even cases where judgment has been passed the Department of Town and Country Planning pays the compensation only after the Courts 'attach' the funds for a particular head from the treasury accounts.

Over 2,150 environmental and human right activists groups from 43 countries have sought moratorium on the World Bank funding of large dams. They have called for, the setting up of a special fund to provide repatriation for an estimated 10 million people evicted from their land by the bank funded projects without adequate compensation and rehabilitation.

There must be a moratorium on funding large dams till such time the World Bank strengthens its policy and operational procedure to, guarantee that no project entailing human displacement would be funded in countries that have not evolved a policy and legal framework ensuring restoration of the living standards of the displaced people. The affected communities should be kept informed about the project from the planning stage and their consent obtained before the implementation of the project.

The environmental and social costs of the World Bank financed projects have had a disproportionately adverse effect on the poor and marginalized sections among the displaced. Stating that public resistance from the affected communities generally led to official repression, the Manibeli Declaration said that World Bank "tolerated and thus contributed to gross human rights violations by the authorities, including arbitrary arrests, beatings and even firing at peaceful demonstrators".

Legal Position

The Fundamental Right to Property as guaranteed under Articles 19(1,f) and 31 is no more. Instead, it has been provided under Article 300A that no person shall be deprived of his property save by authority of law. There might have been controversy about the fate of the property right after the 44th Amendment. There are areas, however, where some of the decisions of the High Courts and the Supreme Court which point out towards a definite direction. In *Rakesh Prasad Tiwari* v. *Union of India*,[11] the Andhra Pradesh High Court has held that if the property is acquired for public purpose and vests in the government which claims it, such claim is illegal as long as the necessary compensations are not paid. Denying the citizen his property would be amounting to violation of Article 300A of the Constitution. State cannot claim the privilege of denying its citizens their valuable property rights. Inaction on the government in not paying the compensation even after nine years acquisition of lands, amounts to depriving a citizen his amount to infringement of right guaranteed under Article 300A.

In *Chintamani Khuntia* v. *State*,[12] the High Court of Orissa, has held that the new Article 300A must be construed to mean that the law must be a valid law and no law of acquisition or requisitioning property can be valid unless there is provision therein for compensating the expropriating owner as it is an inherent condition attached to the exercise of the power 'eminent domain' or compulsory acquisition of private property by the state. The 44th Amendment does not authorize the state to make a law depriving the property right to a citizen without payment of compensation.

The same view has been adopted by the High Court of Bombay, in *Basantibai Fakirchand Khetan* v. *State of Maharashtra*.[13] Even the Supreme Court in appeal in the Khetan case impliedly accepted the twin requirements of public purpose and compensation implicit under Article 300A in case of compulsory acquisition of property in as much as the Apex Court said that the acquisition Act complied with the conditions of the exercise of the right of eminent domain even in the sense in which it is understood in the United States where much emphasis is laid on protection of property right.[14]

A similar view, again, was taken by the full bench of the Himachal Pradesh High Court in *Mohinder Pal* v. *State of Himachal Pradesh*.[15] An Act providing for compulsory acquisition of land was challenged. It was argued by the state that such a law could not be challenged on the ground of Article 14 of the Constitution. It was held that examination whether the impugned Act was just, fair and reasonable or arbitrary in nature was not excluded. In other words, the law providing for acquisition and compensation therefore must be fair, just and reasonable. Presence of these requirements would invalidate the law providing for acquisition and compensation.

In *Tehsildar, Huzumagar* v. *V. Kenkatappa Raol,*[16] it has been held that while determining amount of compensation, reliance cannot be on the value of land in one or two purchases at small scale when acquisition of land is at large scale. The increased value in the sale of the land may be a manipulated one as the landowners on coming to know about the compulsory acquisition may create sale deeds at small scale sale, at an enhanced price and then claim it as a basis for compensation in cases of large scale requisition.

It is submitted that this judicial view may work against the landowners where acquisition is on a large scale where the entire land of a person is required, rather thousands of hectares of land is acquired and the landowners happen to be tribals, as it usually is the case. This should, therefore, not be followed in cases of acquisition of land for dams and other developmental projects in tribal areas.

The other provisions in that direction, are the judicially expanded scope of right to life under Article 21 of the Constitution of India, including within it right to education, right to livelihood, right to shelter, right to pollution-free habitat and right to a dignified life. Article 40 of the Constitution of India provides that the state shall promote with special care the educational and economic interests of the weaker sections of the people, and, in particular, of the Scheduled Castes and Scheduled Tribes, and shall protect them from social injustice and all forms of exploitation. Article 39(b) and (c) of the Constitution provides that the state shall take special care in laying down its policies, that benefits of natural resources of the country reaches to all and there is no concentration of wealth into few hands. Needless to say that these provisions of the Constitution of India embody the spirit of various clauses of the UN Declaration and the International Convention on Human Rights, particularly Article 25 and Article 11(2).

Suggestions

It is, however not only a question of compliance of conditions of exercise of the right of eminent domain in the aforesaid situations. The question of compensation is applicable only in cases of land-owners. There are numerous landless people who earn their livelihood through other means in the environment of their villages. Even in cases of compensation, it may be for the land or building acquired and not for the feeling of belonging, status, happiness and environment. The obligation of the state does not end with the payment of compensation in the aforementioned type of situations. The displaced persons must be provided at least a similar, if not better, environment in which they were living. It has been noticed in the foregoing discussion that there is not only denial of compensatory remedy, but wholesale, non-compliance of the constitutional obligation of the state.

Ironical it is, but it is apparent that the worst sufferers are the weaker sections of the people and tribals; who constitute 75 per cent of 1.85 crore displaced persons; despite the fact the constitutional mandate is an obligation on the state to take special care for their protection. For several decades there has been massive acts of trespass into the areas inhabited by the tribals. Natural resources of these areas, has gone to the elite but little sensitivity and respect for the tribals who today are on the verge of extinction as an ethnic group. In the bargain, the fact has been overlooked that development would come at the expense of poor farmers and tribals. Certainly, a high price to pay in the name of development. We are not suggesting that developmental projects should not be undertaken. We are only, saying that this development should not be at the cost of the already deprived people.

The following suggestions are made in order to provide these displaced persons human rights, i.e., the basic needs as human beings:

1. It has been noticed that even the awards by Award Tribunals in case of developmental projects are not complied with, and other remedial programmes are not fulfilled; there is an urgent need of an independent monitoring agency.
2. The National Commission on Human Rights must be empowered, in this respect to issue directions to concerned authorities for the compliance and take appropriate action in cases of non-compliance.
3. While preparing remedial measures in large-scale projects, priority should be on resettlement rather than compensation.

4. In case of resettlement and rehabilitation, priority should be on means of livelihood, shelter, health care and school for the children.
5. The would be displaced must be consulted while preparing remedial plans.
6. The National Commission on Human Rights must be involved from the very beginning, i.e., from the stage of preparing the plan for rehabilitation and resettlement.
7. As far as possible, officers in the implementation programme must be from the weaker sections, STs and SCs.
8. The project affected people must be informed at every stage, about the project, the consequences and the plans for rehabilitation and resettlement.
9. Supervision and evaluation of resettlement on the basis of participation by real representatives of the affected people may be very much helpful. These representatives may also report the NCHR.
10. Suitable agricultural land must be allotted to those who had land. At least they should be placed in similar situations.
11. In case of displaced persons, employment to at least one member of each family must be provided. This employment should not be casual worker or contract labourer.
12. Payment of compensation must be in lump sum and not in instalments.

Notes

1. P.N. Bhagwati, former Chief Justice, Supreme Court, *Main Stream*, Vol. XXIV No. 28, March, 3, 1986 p. 11.
2. *Times of India*, November, 19, 1994.
3. *Times of India*, November, 7, 1994.
4. *Times of India*, September, 26, 1994.
5. *Times of India*, January, 17, 1994.
6. "Surveyor of Doom", *Illustrated Weekly of India*, January 5-6, 1991.
7. *Times of India*, September 7, 1994.

8. Sujata Patel, "The Baliapal Struggle and Displaced Communities". *Times of India*, December, 13, 1989.
9. P.N. Bhagwati, former Chief Justice, Supreme Court, "Beyond the Human Rights Rhetoric", *The Sunday Times of India*, November, 7, 1993, p. 17.
10. Ibid.
11. AIR 1995 A.P. 75.
12. AIR 1994 Ori. 46.
13. AIR 1984 Bom. 366.
14. *State of Maharashtra* v. *Basantibal Fakirchand Khetan*, AIR 1986 SC 1466.
15. AIR 1995 H.P. 15 (F.B).
16. AIR 1994 NOC 3B5 (A.P.).

15

Human Rights Violation in Iraq and The Role of United Nations

SHAKEEL A. SAMDANI

The disastrous Second World War gave rise to an unprecedented global commitment to International Law that would presumably curtail the worst feature of human warfare, reflected in post Second World War tribunals, the UN Charter, the Geneva Protocols, and more recently the International Criminal Court set up in Rome. Ideally, all states and political actors would have strict obligations to follow moral and legal principles, including definite rules of engagement in warfare. The UN Charter, above all, clearly prohibits military forces as an instrument of statecraft except in clear-cut examples of self-defence. But all these 'noble ideals', 'hopes' and 'culture of human rights' were thrown away by US-led forces in Iraq and that too, under the supervision of UN.

Two years ago, the *Lancet* Journal published the study by researchers from Johns Hopkins University who surveyed nearly 1,000 Iraqi households in September 2004, asking how many people lived in the home and how many birth and death there had been since January 2002. The study estimated that 1,00,000 civilians have died in Iraq due to the US-led war in Iraq.[1]

Many people refused to believe the Lancet Report in 2004 from a group of American, Iraqi, and public-health scientists. Several government ministers were deployed to destroy credibility of the findings and, in large part they succeeded.

The researchers' study is based on comparing the death rate among those households during the fifteenth month before the US-led invasion of Iraq began with the eighteen months after it. As expected, the US government rejected the study. But now the denials have come back to haunt them, for the figures of Iraq have not only been confirmed by the further study but on much higher scale according to that study about 6,65,000 casualties of Iraqi people have taken place, since the invasion of Iraq in March 2003. In most of the cases the casualties are 'civilian', most of these deaths have been of men aged 15 to 44.[2]

The Johns Hopkins University team worked with Iraqi doctors, visited over 1,800 homes in Iraq, selected randomly to make sure that no bias could creep into its calculations. It identified more than 12,000 family members and tracked those who had died. The Iraqi interviewers spoke fluent English as well as Arabic, and they were well trained to collect the information they were seeking. They chased down death certificates in four of five cases to make sure that they have double check on the numbers and the causes of death given to them by the family members.[3]

The most common cause of death is as a direct result of a worsening 'Culture of Violence' mostly accused by indiscriminate US coordinated air strikes, and related military interventions, reveals the study scattered across Iraq. And the risk of violent death just after the invasion was 58 times greater than before the war.[4]

The report in the British journal is based on the work of teams from the John Hopkins University and Columbia University in the US and the AlMustansiriya University in Baghdad.

According to a report published in French newspaper *Le Maude* the Iraqi government ordered medical authorities not to reveal to UN the true figures of civilian killed in Iraq as a result of the US-led war. Ashraf Qazi, the head of UN mission in Iraq sent a telegram to headquarters in New York in these words:

"This development risk damaging the capacity of the UN Assistant Mission to report the number of civilians killed or injured."

Since July last year, the UN had been depending largely in its estimates of Iraq casualties on data provided by Baghdad, Forensic Institute and Iraqi Health Ministry. The *Telegraph* described previous US estimates as "imperfect but an indicator nonetheless the growing number of civilian victims".

The death of about 7 lakh Iraqi people is the clear indication that the human rights situation in Iraq is worsening day by day. American forces and the Iraqi forces, which are largely dominated by the Shias, are mercilessly killing the innocent people. Torture, rape, detention, deportation, night raids, extra-judicial killings, destruction of houses and massacre are a common phenomenon in Iraq. These forces are violating the guarantees given by Universal Declaration of Human Rights (UDHR), 1948 Additional Protocol 1 and 2, the Genocide Convention, and the Humanitarian Laws. Even women and children are not spared.

Role of Sanctions in Iraq

The UN sanctions against Iraq, after the war of 1981, caused grave inconveniences to the citizens of that country and also resulted in the violation of international human rights norms in a number of ways. About half a million children died due to the lack of medicine, malnutrition and food. This constitutes a great violation of Article 3[5] of UDHR, 1948. In addition, it violates Article 22[6] and Article 23,[7] in the latter domain, UN has estimated it and other studies that; due to lack of electricity and raw materials for industry, unemployment has reached its height.

After the second invasion of Iraq on 19 March, 2003, the situations had deteriorated so much so that no one is safe in Iraq. Human rights violation is rampant. The US has never published an official estimate of Iraqi casualties during the Gulf War. But Michael O'Hanlen, a military analyst at The Brookings Institution in Washington estimated there was up to 30,000 civilian casualties for a month long campaign in Iraq. On the other hand UN Humanitarian Agencies recently said that 5 lakh Iraqi had been injured only in early stage of US war. That would be counted as mass casualties, far outweighing anything that Islamic terror had wrought on America.[8]

Moreover the US-led coalition forces used chemical and biological weapons in Iraq. The US troops used chemical weapons in Falluja. The first account was unearthed in a magazine published by the US Army in March, 2005 edition of *Field Artillery*, officers from 2nd Infantry's fire support boast about their role in the attacks of Falluja in November, 2004. "White phosphorus (WP) proved to be effective and versatile munitions. We used it for screening missions at two breaches and later in the fight, as a potent psychological weapon against the 'insurgents' in trenched line and spider holes. When we would not get facts on them with HE (High Explosive), we fired 'shake and bake' mission at the insurgents, using WP to flush them out and HE to take them out".[9]

White phosphorus is not listed in the schedules of chemical weapons conventions. It can be legally used as a flare to illuminate the battlefield, or to produce smoke to hide troop movements from the enemy. Like other unlisted substances, it may be deployed for "military purposes... not depended on the use of the toxic properties of chemical as a method of warfare". But it becomes a chemical weapon as soon as it is used directly against people. A chemical weapon can be any chemical, which through its chemical action on life process can cause deaths, temporary incapicitation or permanent harm.

About the use of Napalm bomb by the American/British forces the initial reactions was that they were not used. There were widespread reports that in March, 2003 the US Marines dropped incendiary bombs around the bridges over the Tigris and Saddarn Canal on the way to Baghdad. The commander of Marine Air Group 11 admitted, "We napalmed both those approaches". Embedded journalist reported that Napalm was dropped at Safwan Hills on the border with Kuwait.[10]

The above facts narrate the civilian death due to arms and ammunition used by the occupation forces. But the death by hunger of a large number of people especially children is not being noticed by the media. According to UN report, malnutrition rate in the children under 5 has almost doubled since the US-led invasion –

to nearly 8 per cent by the end of last year. This report was prepared for the annual meeting of UN Human Rights Commission in Geneva. Zieglar, a UN specialist on hunger who prepared the report blamed the worsening situation in Iraq on the war led by coalition forces. When Saddam Hussain was overthrown, about 4 per cent of Iraqi children under 5 were going hungry; now that figure has almost doubled to 8 per cent. According to Human Rights Law the silent daily massacre is a form of murder – it must be battled and eliminated.

War Against Civilians

Contrary to popular mythology, civilian populations have always been the main victims of US military ventures and, more often than not, such victims were clearly intended. Tarique Ali, is not exaggerating when he writes: "The massacre of civilian populations was always an integral part of US war strategy." Nor is Edward Herman overstating the case when he observes, "US military policy has long been based on strategies and tactics that involve a heavy civilian toll".[11]

It was during 'Desert Storm' that the US military was first able to unveil techno war in its full glory; Iraq became a 'free-fire' zone over which 1,10,000 sorties were flown, dropping some 88,000 tonnes of bombs on a country with minimal air defences. At the very end of combat with nothing left in rubble, US planes bombed and strafed retreating Iraqi troops, killing at least 30,000 – clearly a violation of the Hague and Geneva Protocols. The bombings continued regularly after the main warfare concluded. The US employed thousands of weapons dipped, ensuring the radio active substances would be left in the water, soil, and food chain for decades.[12]

As already stated at least 5 lakh civilians were killed due to the economic sanctions enforced mainly by US and Britain under UN cover in which the embargo cruelly blocked vital imports such as medial supplies, water treatment technology, even certain food stuff that under the excessively broad definition of 'dual use', might be considered useful to the military. Sanctions policy of these sorts has been employed regularly by the US, using its economic clout, as a foreign policy tool since 1950s. The main victims have been civilian, mostly children. The 1977 additional protocol to the Geneva Conventions prohibits measures that deprived the civilian population of goods indispensable to survival, with Article 18 mandating relief operations to the civilians suffering under hardships owing to lack of supplies essential for its survival, such as foodstuffs and medical supplies.

In fact, the US alone had obstructed every humanitarian effort, mounted by NGOs as well as by members of UN Security Council, to lift the sanctions. Writing in Harper's, Joi Garden characterized the sanctions as a "legitimise act of mass slaughter". She added: "epidemic suffering is needlessly visited on Iraqis via US flat inside the UN Security Council. Within that body, the US has consistently thwarted Iraq from satisfying its most basic humanitarian needs, using sanctions as nothing less than a deadly weapon."

Human Rights Violation in Falluja

In order to deny the world the full scale of civilian deaths, and make the atrocity in Iraq palatable to Americans and Western consumers, US authorities have barred journalist and aid workers from entering the city of Falluja before the US assault and massacre began there. All Iraqi men aged between 14 to 60 years of age were prevented from leaving the city. There is no way to determine the number of civilian casualties.

Abu Gharib prison situated in south-west of Baghdad is today the most feared detention centre. Today, the building officially goes by the name Baghdad Correctional Facility. Officially there are about 8,500 detainees but the number is much more higher than disclosed. Most are being held indefinitely and without charge as 'suspected terrorist' and 'security' detainees. Family waiting outside Abu Gharib Prison say most of their relatives were picked up in indiscriminate raids.

The crime of torture, murder and rape of innocent Iraqis at Abu Gharib Prison is a sad story of human rights violation by occupation forces and Iraqi police. The pictures of systematic torture of Iraqi civilian and prisoners has exposed the myth of respect for human rights by the American-led alliance which are clearly against the Geneva Conventions and basic human values.

The Iraqi people are fighting to liberate the country from foreign occupation. There cause is noble and legitimate within international law. They are not 'insurgents', they are Iraqi men and women resisting the occupation and destruction of their country and society by foreign powers.

The destruction of Iraqi city violated the Geneva Conventions, and hence under the US War Crimes Act of 1996, the atrocities carry the death penalty. The genocide in Falluja is reminiscent to those of Serbinica and Grozney, both condemned by US administration.

The ongoing American occupation has also created worsened civil strife as well as mass environmental destructions and related public health problem that is associated with American related released radioactive and other life threatening pollutions. The American occupation has also prevailed over the neglect to the repairing of vital public services-related infrastructure, which includes US-led destruction of water system.

Role of United Nations in Iraq Crisis

As far as the role of the United Nations in Iraq crisis is concerned the UN has never been so humiliated and hijacked in its history as happened in regard to invasions on Iraq in 1991 and then in 2003. The atrocious episode began with the consideration of resolution 678 by the Security Council following Iraq's invasion of Kuwait. This was passed on November 30, 1990 and in passing this the US exercised much coercion and also used bribery. In this resolution the expert's opinion of eminent persons was that there was nothing in this resolution to authorize the US to invade Iraq with a multinational force without reference to the Security Council.

As far as the second invasion of Iraq is concerned that was also against the provisions of UN charter. The important reason given by the US for invading Iraq were that it possessed weapons of mass destruction (WMD) and that it had links with the Al-Qaeda. But so far the US has failed to give any evidence regarding these two allegations against Iraq.

Going by the resolutions passed by the United Nations especially the Security Council, we find that since 14 May, 2002 to this date[13] the Security Council and the Secretary General have tried to legitimize the illegitimate and illegal actions of the US-led alliance. For example, the UN Security Council unanimously approved Resolution 1444[14] imposing tough new arms inspection on Iraq and precise unambiguous definitions of what constitutes a 'material breach' of the Resolution. The Resolution further said that in case of non-compliance and violation of the resolution the Iraq will face 'serious consequences' which the Security Council would then determine. In this resolution, the Council decided to give Iraq which, "has been and remains in material breach" of UN Resolutions, a final opportunity to comply with a disarmament obligations. And to set up "an enhanced inspection regime". It decided that Iraq "shall provide.... accurate full and complete declaration of all aspects of its programme to develop chemical, biological and nuclear weapons, ballistic missiles and other delivery system" by December 8.[15]

It decided that "false statements or omissions in the declarations submitted" and "failure by Iraq at any time to comply with, and cooperate fully in the implementation of this resolution shall constitute a further material breach" and "will be reported to the Council for assessment". The Council decided the Iraq "shall provide... immediate, unimpeded, unconditional, and unrestricted access to any and all, including underground areas, facilities, buildings, equipment, records, and means of transport which they wish to inspect, as well as immediate, unimpeded, unrestricted, and private access to all officials and other person whom UNMOVIC or the IAEA wish to interview.... "The Council directed UNMOVIC and IAEA to "report immediately to the Council any interference by Iraq with inspection activities, as well as any failure by Iraq to comply with its disarmament obligations". In addition, the council decided that it would "convene immediately upon receipt of a report" relating to Iraqi non-compliance and recalled, "in that context, that it had repeatedly warned Iraq that it will face serious consequences as a result of its continued violations of its obligations".

On 18 November, 2002, the UN weapons inspectors returned to Iraq for the first time in almost 4 years. On 27 January, 2003,

UN submitted a formal report on Iraqi inspections. The report was critical, though not damning, with Chief UN Weapons Inspector Hans Blix stating that "Iraq appears not to have come to a genuine acceptance, not even today, of the disarmament that was demanded of it". On 28 January President Bush in his State of Union Address announced that he is ready to attack Iraq even without a mandate. On 22 February, Hans Blix orders Iraq to destroy its Al-Samoud 2 missiles by 1 March, with which Iraq complied.

Without taking approval from the Security Council President Bush on 17 March, 2003 delivered an ultimatum to Saddam Hussain to leave the country within 48 hours or else face an attack. On 19 March, the US launched attack against Iraq and called it operation Iraqi Freedom.

On 22 May, the UN Security Council approved a resolution lifting the economic sanctions against Iraq and supporting the US-led administration in Iraq. On 19 August, 2003 suicide bombing destroyed UN headquarters in Baghdad, killing 29, including top envoy Sergi Vieira de Mello and wounding more than 100. On 16 October the UN Security Council unanimously approved the US and the UK resolution on Iraq's reconstruction, which supported an international force in the country under US authority. Several countries originally opposed the resolution unless Washington agreed to a faster time table for transferring power to the Iraqis, but in the end voted for the resolution without requiring changes. On 12 February, 2004 UN envoy Lakhdar Brahimi went to Iraq on a fact finding mission and to assess the feasibility of direct elections. On 19 February, the UN Secretary General, Kofi Annan announced the results of its report about Iraq elections, concluding that "elections cannot be held before the end of June, that the 30 June date for the handover of sovereignty must be respected and we need to find a mechanism to create a caretaker government and then prepare the elections sometime later in the future." On 15 April, 2004 the Bush administration agreed to a UN proposal to replace the Iraqi Governing Council with a caretaker government when the US returns sovereignty to Iraqis on 30 June. On 27 April UN envoy Lakhdar Brahimi reported to the UN Security Council that by the end of May he will select a transitional government to run Iraq until elections are held in 2005. According to this Report the proposed government will include a President, 2 Vice-Presidents, a Prime Minister and a consultative Conference made up of 1,500 Iraqis.

On 8 June, 2004 the UN Security Council passed a resolution endorsing the appointment of an interim government in Iraq. It authorized the US military forces to remain in the country until January 2006. June 16 is a remarkable day when 9/11 Commission (formally the National Commission on Terrorists Attack) concludes in its report that there is "no credible evidence that Iraq and Al-Qaida cooperated on attacks against the United States".

In a surprising development rather we may call it admission the UN Secretary General said that the war against Iraq was 'illegal' and violated the UN Charter. The US, UK and Australia vigorously rejected his conclusion. Kofi Annan further adds that "the decision to take action in Iraq should have been made by the UN Security Council, not unilaterally by any country". Kofi Annam was one of those who believe that there should have been a Second Resolution.[16]

Moreover, a recent legal report prepared by the New York based Centre for Economic and Social Rights (CESR), a human rights organization affiliated to the UN, has turned the war as "unequivocally illegal under the UN Charter and International Law".[17]

Jurgen Habermas (University of Frankfurt) echoes views of the world-renowned intellectuals, legal luminaries and writes: Neither of the two conditions for legally permissible use of military force was fulfilled: it was neither a case of self-defense against an actual attack, or the immediate theat of one, nor was it authorized by a decision of the Security Council according to Chapter VII of the UN charter. Neither Resolution 1441 nor any one of the 17 previous (and 'spent') resolution on Iraq can count as sufficient authorization.[18]

The war on Iraq has been condemned as illegal by a panel of eminent international lawyers at a conference organized by the actor Corin Redgrave. A prominent speaker, Bums Weston, a human rights lawyer at the University of Law in the US, fears that other countries might use the American decision to wage war illegally to justify their own unlawful wars.

Sands, one of 16 prominent international lawyers who earlier this year publicly warned Tony Blair that the war was illegal, said the conflict raised two major issues. "First, did the Security Council authorize the use of force, and the answer to that is no. And (second) were we misled about the presence of weapons of mass destruction? Apparently, yes. These things are going to come back to haunt us", Sands said.

According to Robert Black QC, Professor of Scots Law, Edinburgh University, and architect of the Lockerbie trial in The Hague... It is perfectly plain that none of the Security Council Resolutions relating to Iraq authorized armed intervention.

According to Sean Murphy, Associate Professor of Law at George Washington University, Washington DC, "I think there are very sound reasons for saying that the intervention was not permitted".[19]

From the above it can be said that the role of UN, especially the Security Council is not in accordance with the purposes and principles of UN. The Security Council through its permanent members attacked a sovereign state, i.e., Iraq, which is contrary to the UN Charter. There are only two legal justifications for attacking another country:

> Self-defence, or if the Security Council authorizes to do so. It is perfectly plain that none of the Security Council resolutions relating to Iraq authorized armed intervention. The US, UK legal justification, which is based on Security Councils Resolution dating back to 1990-91, is not credible when we look closely at the resolutions and practise of Security Council, it is clear that the majority of the members of Security Council believed that further authorization was needed in March, 2003 than, in fact, existed.

There was no UN Security Council authorization, no imminent humanitarian catastrophe and no imminent threat of use of force by Iraq and that is why the US-led attack on a weak sovereign country was unlawful in the beginning and remains unlawful till date.

Moreover, the actions of the Secretary General of the United Nations also gave legitimacy to the illegal actions of the US-led alliance. The sanctions imposed on Iraq was not lifted for about 13 years due to which half a million children alone died due to the non-availability of medicines and malnutrition but within 22 days after the US declared an end to major combat operations in Iraq the Security Council lifted the economic sanctions against Iraq to support US-led administration in Iraq. What was the haste in removing the economic sanctions? Again, the Security Council unanimously approved the US and UK resolution on Iraq's reconstruction, which supported an international force in the country under US authority. On 23 and 24 October, 2003 an International Donor's Conference in Madrid was convened with the help and active support of World Bank and the United Nations.

The role of the United Nations through its envoy Lakhdar Brahmi for replacing the Iraqi Governing Council and for holding the elections in Iraq again went in favour of the aggressors. Why an illegal action was being legalized by the United Nations? The elections held in Iraq under Martial Law and the US forces are a fraud on Iraq. The present regime headed by Noorul Maliki is totally illegitimate as the elections were held under Martial Law and the Bath Party and many Sunni Islamic parties were not allowed to participate. The legitimacy of the elections is in doubt because most of the Iraqis were not allowed to participate in the elections.

Conclusion

To conclude the whole discussion, it can be said that the US-led forces have attacked Iraq twice. After the invasion of Kuwait by Iraq in 1991 and the other, on 18 March,2003. These two attacks destroyed Iraq completely, violated the sovereignty of Iraq and International Law; The Laws of Human Rights were openly violated by the US-British-led alliance. Since 1990 to this date[20] about 15 lakh people have been killed in the conflict. About two and a half lakh in 1991, about 5 lakh between 1991 to 2003 due to UN sanctions and about 7 lakh after 2003. These deaths and human casualties can only be termed as 'Genocide' by the mightiest power against defenceless civilians of Iraq. It is also very unfortunate and sad that all these deaths including human rights violations were legitimized and supervised by the UN, which was established six decades ago with the avowed object "to save the succeeding generation from the scourge of war"[21] has completely failed and belied the hopes of those leaders who had formed this organization to save the future generations from the future armed conflicts. But due to the veto power enjoyed by super powers and their selfish interests, millions of people have been killed after Second World War. And the latest example of human catastrophe and genocide committed by US-led alliance in Iraq shows that the 21st century will definitely see the World War and the massacre of millions of people. The need of the hour is to check this trend of human rights violations and force the UN to do its duties impartially. The paralysing system of veto by he permanent members of Security Council must be withdrawn and for this the members of United Nations must prevail and try their best to snatch the veto power from the permanent members. Moreover, the nation states must prevail upon the new Secretary General of UN to try for withdrawal of US-led forces from Iraq at the earliest and hold free and fair elections in Iraq in which the whole Iraqi population is allowed to participate, so that the permanent peace may prevail in Iraq and the violation of human rights may be stopped.

Notes

1. *News From India*, New Delhi, October 22, 2006.
2. *The Hindu*, New Delhi, October 13, 2006.
3. Ibid.
4. John Stokes, *The Milli Gazette*, 1-15 April, 2006.
5. Right to Life.
6. Social Security.
7. Right to Work.
8. Shadid, Anthony, "Days of Terror and Helplessness", *The Week*, March 30, 2003, p. 40.
9. *The Guardian*, November 15, 2005.
10. Ibid.
11. Call Boggs Routledge, *Master of War, Militarism and Blue Back in the Era of Empire*, 2003, p. 209.
12. Ibid., p. 214.

13. November 1, 2006,
14. (2002) The Security Council held an open debate on Iraq on October 16 and 17, 2002. During the 4 meetings, the 15 members of Council were joined by 51 UN members and 3 permanent observers in expressing their views on a number of issues related to Iraq and various options for response to President Bush's General Assembly speech.
15. Iraq submitted a 12,000 declaration on December 7, 2002.
16. *The Hindu*, September 17, 2004.
17. *Frontline*, April 11, 2003, p. 24.
18. *The Hindu*, June 5, 2003.
19. Danzing, David, Lawyers Committee Supports UN Human rights Monitors for Iraq, April, 2003, www.humanrightsdefenders/iraq/prq.hM.
20. November 1, 2006.
21. Preamble of UN Charter.

16

Stinking Existence, Tinkered Laws and Tainted Enforcement

A Study of Manual Scavengers' Fight for Human Right and Dignity in India

MOHD. ZAFAR MAHFOOZ NOMANI
AND ANIS AHMAD

> By independence we have lost the excuses of blaming the British for anything going wrong. If hereafter things go wrong, we will have nobody to blame except ourselves.
>
> Dr. B.R. Ambedkar

According dignity and human right is the foundation of freedom, justice and peace in the global and national legal regime. There is no denying the fact that the cardinal principle of international humanitarian law and human rights jurisprudence underpinned in the Universal Declaration on Human Rights and International Covenants on Civil and Political Rights, and Social and Cultural Rights[1] incorporate human rights in their national Constitutions, laws and judicial strategies for enforcement to promote socially equitable legal order. More than a decade the development of human rights appears to be quite considerable, often assuming leading role among the developing countries.[2] On the other hand the Indian Constitution as first and foremost a social document, and committed to the rule of law which is the basic to our constitutional order implies legislative protection on a large scale for the welfare of people.[3] In spite of sophistication and maturity of human rights jurisprudence in this country there are few practices such as manual scavenging which are more offensive and violative of human rights to health, environment and human dignity.[4] As happens with any social welfare legislation, the political executive and the lawmakers were oblivious of the gap between the symbolism and the substance, thus defeating the very objective of the Act and human rights jurisprudence.[5] Therefore, it is important to understand the domain of human rights discourse in a pragmatic manner to harness the symbiotic relationship between the rule of law and rule of life.[6] In this paper the authors examine the legal precepts and judicial indoctrination in realizations of the rights of marginal sections of society. It also explores the indifferent attitude of the administrative agencies for the enforcement of the existing legislations, so that social justice may be actualized to the poor people.

Problematic Overview

The menace of manual scavenging became a widespread practice with increasing urbanization in the late 19th century. It is discernable from the history that common man-centred sanitation and public health planning apparently received top priority in striking contrast to other ancient civilization.[7] The existing system of human waste disposal – manual scavenging see a deep-rooted prejudice against Dalits, on whom the hierarchical caste Hindu society has thrust this obnoxious occupation only because they are born into this segregated social group.[8] It is this caste-based prejudice that caused the beginning of the practice of manual scavenging thousands of the years ago and that now stands in the way of terminating it. According to the government statistics an estimated one million Dalits in India are manual scavengers, majority of them are women, whose work involves the removal of faeces from public and private latrines and open sewers, and the disposal of dead animals. Unofficial estimates of the actual number are much higher.[9] The data estimated that the number of manual scavengers has increased from 5.8 lakh in 1992 to 7.87 lakh. Unofficial surveys have projected that there are over 12 lakhs manual scavengers, of whom 95 per cent are Dalits who have the task thrust on them as a 'traditional occupation'. Similarly the feminist dimension of problem is notable in nature, over 80 per cent of them women. They are considered untouchables by the higher caste and are caught in a vortex of severe social and economic exploitation.[10] Further the report of Comptroller and Auditor General (CAG) was submitted, evaluating the National Scheme of Liberation and Rehabilitation of scavengers and their dependents which was being implemented by the Ministry of Social Justice and Empowerment since March 2003. The conclusion of the CAG was that this scheme had failed to achieve its objectives even after 10 years of implementation involving investment of more than Rs 600 crores. The CAG also found that although funds were available for implementation of the scheme, much of it was unspent or underutilized.[11] The CAG also noticed that there was "lack of correspondence between liberation and rehabilitation, and that there was no evidence to suggest if those liberated from the practice were in fact rehabilitated". The National Commission for Safai Karamchari, a statutory body has in its reports pointed to the continued employment of manual scavengers and the operation of dry latrines by the various departments of the Union of India, in particular the Railways, the Department of Defence and the Ministry of Industry. Twelve years after the Employment of Manual Scavengers and Construction of Dry Latrines (Prohibition) Act, 1993, was enacted, manual scavenging, one of the most dehumanizing of the occupation assigned to Dalits in their long history, remains unaffected by the legislation.[12]

International Perspective

Under the legitimated presumption that International Human Rights Conventions may best be suited as a ground norm for the municipal law relating to human rights jurisprudence.[13] The Universal Declaration on Human Rights, 1948 is the pioneering law on the subject. It deals with the basic human rights questions within the framework of health, food, housing and particularly the right to live with human decency and dignity. Under these circumstances, to map out the range of such a rights, an inquiry into the Covenants on human rights serves a logical purpose. The preamble of Universal Declaration on Human Rights, 1948 recognized the human rights facets to global human family. It runs like that "whereas recognition of the inherent dignity and of the equal and inalienable rights of the members of the human family is the foundation of freedom, justice and peace in the world".[14] This global human rights further finds a place in an article under the Universal Declaration of Human Rights,1948 which mandates that "everyone has the right to standard of living adequate for the health and well being of himself and of his family... including food, clothing, housing and medical care and necessary social services...".[15]

Further the two International Covenants on Economic, Social and Cultural Rights and Civil and Political Rights (1966) has no direct reference to the rights of manual scavengers per se, nonetheless it recognizes that: the right of everyone to an adequate standard of living for himself and his family, including adequate food, clothing and housing.[16] Affirming faith on right to health as fundamental human rights, the Covenants further encapsulates that:

> Everyone to the enjoyment of the highest attainable standard of physical and mental health....[17]

To make more substantive and logical the concept of right to life, a broad vision of the fundamental human rights approach reflected in the following words:

> Every human being has the inherent right to life. This right shall be protected by law. No one shall be arbitrarily deprived of his life.[18]

The Covenants generally requires member states to take steps to the maximum of their available resources to progressively achieve the full realization of the protected rights. It also indicates that these measures should be taken by each state separately as well as through international assistance and cooperation. The Covenant thus recognizes that the full realization of the rights may require more than domestic measures.[19]

Constitutional Conspectus

It is generally said that constitutional law is defined as basic law of a nation.[20] The Indian Constitution, in its Preamble together with Fundamental Rights Part-III and Directive Principles of State Policy Part-IV has inscribed the right to life with equality, dignity of individual and social justice to every person who is a member of the grand collective.[21] Thus, the Constitution aims at the creation of new legal norms, social philosophy and economic values which are to be effected by striking synthesis, harmony and fundamental adjustment between the individual rights and social interest to established egalitarian society.[22] The Constitution has shown concern in this behalf under Articles 14,17,19 and 21. In fact the declaration of fundamental rights in constitutional document is necessary for the welfare of the people vis-à-vis the promotion of constitutionalism.[23] Under these circumstances an inquiry into the constitutional mandate serves a logical purpose to map out the range of the rights of the people in general and vulnerable sections in particular. Article 17 emphasizes the ideology of abolition of untouchability and runs:

> 'Untouchability' is abolished and its practice in any form is forbidden. The enforcement of any disability arising out of 'Untouchability' shall be an offence punishable in accordance with law.[24]

The Article mentioned above just reflects the benign hope and promises of the Father of the Nation who vehemently opposed segregation of the Harijans and stood for the abolition of untouchability and all forms of discrimination against them.[25]

To ensure that the fundamental rights are properly protected and for its enforcement, the Constitution has conferred on the Supreme Court and High Courts of India the power to grant most effective remedies whenever such rights are violated; under the provisions of Articles 32 and 226 the court to have liberally construed the fuller exploration of the scope of fundamental rights as specially the right to life under Article 21.[26] This right is not merely lexical and legal, but expands as we conceptualize the dignity and divinity of the human personality; when we talk of the right to life as a human right, it is intended to be a legal safeguard not only against violated aggression but also against the creeping, gradually effective encroachment on vital conditions of life, conditions without which it is impossible to survive as a human being. The right to basic necessities of life is inherent in the right to life.[27] In the wake of human rights jurisprudence the ambit and scope of the constitutional rights are being amplified, which includes right to live with dignity in an evolving concept with varying contents. It can encompass not only civil and political rights but also social and economic rights.[28] In contemporary India the courts can read right to livelihood,[29] right to food,[30] right to health,[31] right to wholesome environment,[32] right to development[33] and right to access to justice and similar rights which makes life worthwhile into the ambit of Article 21 in the context of the various directive principles in the part IV of the Constitution. This is the logic of *Pavement Dweller* and *Franis Coralie Mullin* cases and derived a guarantee for the minimum needs of existence directly from the right to life.[34]

On the other hand, Directive Principles of State Policy under Part IV as fundamental charter of governance of the country, imposes a duty on the state to take positive action for socio-economic justice to all. As Granville Austin describes:

> In the Directive Principles, however, on finds an even clear state of social revolution. They at making the Indian masses free from the passivity endangered by centuries of coercion by society and by nature, free from the abject physical conditions that had prevented them from fulfilling their best selves.[35]

Dr. Ambedkar's view regarded part IV as a socialist chapter and contended that the intention of the nation was "not to pay lip-service to these principles but they were to be made the basis of all legislative and executive action that they might be taking hereafter in the matter of the governance of the country". He vehemently objected to making the Constitution any other than a mere political contrivance. He cited the Directive Principles as giving us the 'substance of a Socialistic state'. He said:

"If these Directive Principles are not socialistic in their direction, and in their content, I fail to understand what more socialism can be."[36]

In order to assess the concept of justice, social, economic and political envisioned as a pledge in preamble by our Constitution, a solemn confidence and commitment made in various Articles 38, 39,39A, 41, 43, 46 and 47are pointers to create a social order based on equality and justice through the instrumentality of law.[37] The state shall strive to promote the welfare of the people by securing and protecting, as effectively as it may, a social order in which justice, social, economic and political, shall inform all the institutions of the national life.[38] The public health and environmental values are well reflected under Article 47, which directs the state for raising of the level of nutrition, standards of living and improvement of public health.[39]

Legislative Development

In order to rescue the poor and the disadvantaged groups (Harijans, Adivasis and Dalits) from age-old exploitation, oppressive effects of discrimination and domination of the upper castes, the Dalits segregated in farflung bastees, slums and ghettos who have suffered by grinding poverty, diseases and ignorance have been provided special privileges and concession making untouchability an offence and equal access to public places and participation in democratic politics and social life a constitutional mandate.[40] In order to abolish untouchability and provide civil rights to the human beings, the parliament has formulated the policies and welfare legislations in favour of the Scheduled Castes and Scheduled Tribes such as the Protection of Civil Rights Act, 1955, Scheduled Castes and Scheduled Tribes (Prevention of Atrocities) Act, 1989 and the Protection of Human Rights Act, 1993 and more specifically the Employment of Manual Scavengers and Construction of Dry Latrines (Prohibition) Act, 1993 from social injustice and all form of exploitation.[41]

1. The Protection of Civil Rights Act, 1955: This is one of the major legislation to establish a democratic and egalitarian society and absence of all kinds of disabilities particularly the rights of Dalit's community. The very purpose of the Act is to

curb the various kind of disability while (religious and social) preaching and practice of untouchability the law provide punishment.[42] The Act provides enough measures which may be necessary for ensuring that the rights from the abolition of untouchability or made available to, and are availed of by the persons subject to any disability arising out of 'untouchability'. The state government is empowered to take all necessary action in pursuance of aims and object of the Act.[43] It also incorporates provisions that every offence under this Act shall be treated as a cognizable offence and tried summarily by a Judicial Magistrate of the first class or Metropolitan Magistrate as the case may be.[44]

2. The Scheduled Castes and The Scheduled Tribes (Prevention of Atrocities) Act, 1989: To stamp out the evil under Article 17 of the Constitution, the Parliament stepped in and made this Act with the object to prevent the commission of offences of atrocities against the members of stringent provisions to eradicate those offences, speedy trial, relief and rehabilitation of the victims of such offences; to prevent the commission of offences of atrocities against the members of Scheduled Castes and Scheduled Tribes; to provide for special courts for the trial of such offences and for the relief and rehabilitation of the victims of such offences and related matters.[45]

Identification and Rehabilitation of Manual Scavengers

In order to restore the dignity of the individual as enshrined in the preamble to the Constitution, and to the constitutional directives to the state in regard to raising levels of nutrition, standard of living and the improvement of public health of its people under Article 47 and prohibition of the employment of manual scavengers as well as construction or continuance of dry latrines and maintenance of water seal latrines, the Indian Parliament has passed a uniform law the Employment of Manual Scavengers and Construction of Dry Latrines (Prohibition) Act, 1993 under the constitutional mandate of Article 252. The Preambular assertion resolutes for the prohibition of employment of manual scavengers as well as construction or continuance of dry latrines and maintenance of water-seal latrines and matters connected therewith. To eradicate the pernicious and obnoxious practice prevalent across the country, which is deeply offensive to health and human dignity.[46] To achieve these objectives the Act employs various provisions. The state government may demarcate the areas and restrict the application of the Act in certain area, category or building, or class of persons.[47] The penultimate provisions engrafted under Chapter III of the Act, which inter alia includes appointment of executive authorities and their powers and functions,[48] power to make schemes for regulating the conversion of latrines into or construction and maintenance of water-seal latrines and rehabilitation of the persons who were engaged in employment as manual scavengers in any area,[49] issuing of directions,[50] appointment of inspectors and entry and inspection,[51] to prevent environmental pollution in certain cases,[52] financial assistance,[53] to levy fees,[54] to constitute the committees by the state government.[55] The regulatory framework of the Act is primarily based on command and prohibition principles whereby the enforcement agencies treated every offence under this Act shall be cognizable and follow fines and criminal prosecution.[56] In case of contravention with any provisions, the Act prescribes punishment up to one year imprisonment or fine up to two thousand rupees or both with an additional fine which may extend up to one hundred rupees per day of continuance for failure to comply with any orders, directions and schemes.[57] Thus, it also applies to every officer of the company as much as it does not require actual participation or mental support of the officer.[58] The cognizance of the offence could be taken on the complaint made by a person or authorized by the executive authority within three months from the date of the alleged commission of the offence.[59]

Human Rights Dimension

In order to implement the international human rights conventions and setting up of a national institution for the promotion and protection of human rights in India, of late the government has passed the Protection of Human Rights Act, 1993. The Preambular promise of the Act is to provide for the constitution of a National Human Rights Commission, State Human Rights Commissions in states and Human Rights Courts for better protection of human rights and for matters connected therewith or incidental thereto.[60]

The whole Act is divided into eight chapters. The meaning of the word human rights defined under Section 2 (d) which runs like that, human rights means the rights relating to life, liberty, equality and dignity of the individual guaranteed by the Constitution or embodied in the International Covenants and enforceable by courts of India.[61] The Act also encapsulates the Constitution of the National Human Rights Commission,[62] the State Human Rights Commissions[63] and the Human Rights Courts[64] in various districts to achieve the purposes of the Act. The Commission has discharged their functions in relation to inquiries into complaints of the violation of human rights,[65] it is also to investigate, review, study, undertake and encourage the efforts of non-governmental organizations in a number of serious cases of the human rights violations and it has submitted reports to the government wherein it has made a number of recommendations suggesting remedial measures for their effective implementation.[66] The adjudicatory provisions of the Act, engrafted in Chapter VI, which provide the establishment of Human Rights Courts in each district for the purpose of providing for speedy trail of cases arising out of violation of human rights.[67]

Role of National Human Rights Commission

It is worthwhile to note that both the enactment vis-à-vis the Employment of Manual Scavenging and Construction of Dry Latrines (Prohibition) Act, and the Protection of Human Rights Act, were passed in 1993. Therefore, the human rights initiative of NHRC created under the National Human Rights Protection Act engaged constantly to the issue of identification and rehabilitation of manual scavengers since its inception. Since the National Human Rights Commission was established on 12 October, 1993 to fulfil the mandate confessed by the protection of Human Rights Act, 1993,[68] the objective to ensure the better protection of human rights in the country. The Commission first took up the issue of manual scavenging in 1996–97. Thereafter the Commission have recounted the efforts made to deal with this issue regularly.[69] As a first step, the Commission constituted a high level committee to elaborate recommendations and to pursue plan to eradicate manual scavenging within a fixed time frame, which is deeply offensive to health and human dignity. Thereafter, the Commission has recounted the efforts made to deal with this issue. The Commission pursued this issue with his counterpart in the Ministry of Urban Development and Poverty Alleviation, which is the nodal ministry to deal the subject. The ministry in turn to emphasis that it had been impressing upon all the states and union territories from time to time, adopts the Employment of Manual Scavengers and Construction of Dry Latrines (Prohibition) Act, 1993. The ministry further urged to consult technical experts to devise workable solutions and alternative technologies, and to examine the central schemes to monitor progress in this respect.[70]

Most notably the Commission has urged all the state governments and union territories to work with greater determination to implement the Act, so as to ensure that the dehumanizing practice could be effectively stopped. So far, 26 states and union territories have either accepted the Central Law or enacted their own laws. The Commission reiterates that lack of political will and determination to end this unacceptable practice will persist in spite of laws that are enacted. There is therefore need to mobilize political cadres and social action groups to ensure that this practice, which constitutes a gross violation of human rights and an assault on the human dignity is stopped altogether.[71]

Therefore, the Commission has continued to advocate appropriate action in this matter, not only at the level of Central government but also with the state governments. In a series of action a meeting was held on 6 January, 2003 with Urban Development Secretaries of the 13 states to discuss the progress made in the eradication of manual scavenging. Certain states stressed that considerable funds were required for converting dry latrines into wet latrines. The Commission emphasized that the states and Central government needed to pool in their resources together to ensure that practice of manual scavenging is eradicated once for all.[72] Recently the Chairperson (NHRC) Justice A.S. Anand expressed displeasure with the progress in eradication of manual scavenging has been painfully slow. He called upon the state governments to set a six-month target to convert dry latrines into wet latrines and to conduct surveys in rural areas to collect data on eradication of the practice and rehabilitation of the communities engaged in it.[73] He further said that there was not enough feedback from the states on the progress in the adoption and implementation of the Employment of Manual Scavenging and Construction of Dry Latrines (Prohibition) Act, 1993. According to the NHRC, collecting data through surveys is essential to gauge the extent of the problem and to meet the 2007 deadline envisaged by the National Action Plan for total eradication of manual scavenging. According to information available with the Commission, the following states have adopted the Central Act: Andhra Pradesh, Assam, Chhattisgarh, Gujarat, Haryana, Karnataka, Kerala, Madhya Pradesh, Maharashtra, Orissa, Tamil Nadu, Tripura, Uttar Pradesh and Uttaranchal. The state of Punjab has adopted their own similar Act: Bihar, Jammu and Kashmir, Jharkhand, Manipur, Rajasthan and West Bengal, and the Union Territories of Dadar and Nagar Haveli, Daman and Diu, Lakshadweep and Pondicherry have not adopted the Act. Arunachal Pradesh, Delhi, Goa, Mizoram, Nagaland, Sikkim and the Union Territory of Chandigarh have not informed the Commission whether they abolished the practice.[74]

Judicial Recognition and Articulation

In the early 1970s the Indian judiciary particularly the Supreme Court with innovative genius have started giving a new thinking towards core democratic values and to foster socially sensitive jurisprudence to remove social injustice, caste inequality and exploitation of the Scheduled Castes and Scheduled Tribes and backward communities which has persisted over many centuries.[75] Further the emergence of the processual justice and access jurisprudence finds a new vitality with the rise of public interest litigation or social action litigation has relaxed the conservative yardsticks of the rule of *locus standi*, which brought into existence the citizens' standing. Article 32 being a Fundamental Right, is well settled that any redress for public injury arising from branch of public duty from violation of the provisions of the Constitution are always maintainable by the courts.[76] However, it is Justice V.R. Krishna Iyer who stresses on egalitarianism, social equality, and non-discrimination and access to justice are compulsive factors in our Constitution not only in the preamble but also under Articles: 14, 17, 19, 21, 38, 47 and 335,[77] being the very warp and woof of republicanism in the context of Third World traumas.[78] He also portrayed and x-rayed the utter backwardness of Harijans humanity, the struggle of the 'Father of the Nation', his fighting faith for the uplift of the manual scavengers and his assimilation on equal footing into Hindu society. He explores the soul of the Indian Constitution particularly the instrument of instructions contained in Part III and Part IV.[79] His juristic reasoning, reflects the realities of the ordinary people's life and provides a sense of justice to untouchables.[80] Of late the Supreme Court with authoritative interpretation holds that human dignity, equality of status and opportunity are integral to the right to life. For more than two decades, the judicial apparatus has been meticulously engaged in articulating the right to live with decency and human dignity out of a conventional catalogue of constitutional rights.[81] Dovetailing the issue of concession for Scheduled Castes and Scheduled Tribes the Supreme Court in a celebrated case *State of Kerala* v. *N.H. Thomas*,[82] has adopted a progressive interpretation of the relevant articles of the Constitution and by upholding special concession for Scheduled Castes, adopting a wider perspective of equalization of weaker sections as a step in aid of equality. Justice V.R. Krishna Iyer made certain insightful statements, which have a bearing on social justice and the administrative services. He ruled out:

> Social engineering – which is law in action, must adopt new strategies to liquidate encrusted group injustices or surrender society to traumatic tensions. Equilibrium, in human terms, emerges from release of the handicapped and the primitive from persistent social disadvantage by determined, creative and canny equality.[83]

This approach permeates numerous subsequent judgments of the High Courts and Supreme Court. In *Akhil Bhartiya Soshit Karamchari Sangh (Rly.)* v. *Union of India*[84] again Supreme Court speaking through justice V.R. Krishna Iyer who made certain insightful statements and dilating upon the need of justice to 'Harijans' and 'Girijans' and ruled:

In a spacious sense, equal opportunity for members of hierarchical society makes sense only if a strategy by which the under privileged have environmental facilities for developing their full human potential. This consummation is accomplished only when the utterly depressed groups can claim a fair share in public life and economic activity, including employment under the state, or when a classless and caste less society blossoms as a result of positive state action. To help the lagging social segments, by special care, is a step towards and not against a larger and stabler equality..."[85]

The court further striking that:

It is statically proved social reality in India that the depressed employment position of harijans is the master problem in the battle against generations of retardation; reservation and other solutions have made no significant impact on their employment in public services. In such unjust situations, to maintain mechanical equality is to perpetuate actual inequality. A battery of several programmes to fight down this fell backwardness must be tried out by the state.[86]

The concluding remarks of Justice Krishna Iyer was that:

Excellence and equality may co-operate fruitfully and need not complete destructively; ultimately harijan/girijan militancy must find fulfilment in effective mainstreaming and creative contribution. While they have miles to go, they have promises to keep.[87]

More ingenious and promising is the interpretation given by the Court to bring violation of The Employee's State Insurance Act, 1948 as breach of Fundamental Right contained in Article 21.The right to health as a means to achieve socio-economic justice a bed-rock to an egalitarian social order. In *CESC Limited* v. *Subhash Chandra Bose*[88] Justice K. Ramaswamy in his dissenting opinion observed that:

To the tiller of soil, wage earners, labourers, wood cutters, rickshaw pullers, scavengers and hut dwellers, the civil and political rights are mere cosmetic rights. Socio-economic and cultural rights are their means and relevant to them to realize the basic aspirations of meaningful right to life.[89]

Again in *State of Karnataka* v. *Appu Balu Ingale*[90] in which Justice K. Ramaswamy had gone into sociological and constitutional angulation of the Article 17 and Protection of Civil Rights Act, 1955, the erudite exposition of thoughts expressed:

> The thrust of Article 17 and Act is to liberate the society from blind and ritualistic adherence and traditional belief, which lost all legal or moral base. It seeks to establish new ideal for society – equality to the Dalit at par with general public, absence of disabilities, restrictions or prohibitions on grounds of caste or religion, availability of opportunities and a sense of being a participant in the main stream of national life.[91]

The court further ruled out:

> In interpreting the Act, the judge should be cognizant to and always keep at the back of his/her mind the constitutional goals and purpose of the Act and interpret the provisions of the Act in the light thus shed to annihilate untouchability, to accord to the Dalits and Tribes right to equality, social integration a fruition and fraternity a reality.[92]

Again in *Jai Singh* v. *Union of India*[93] the Supreme Court provides a progressive interpretation of the Scheduled Caste and Scheduled Tribes (Prohibition) Act, 1989 and some relevant articles of Constitution:

> Article 17 is a very significant provision from the point of view of equality before the law. It guarantees social justice and dignity of man, the twin privileges which were denied to a vast section of the Indian society for centuries together. This Article does not define Untouchability. The Untouchability Offences Act (22 of 1955)... now called 'The Protection of Civil Rights Act' also does not attempt any definition of the word 'Untouchability'.[94]

In the recent past as the hearing of a public interest petition filed by the Safai Karamchari Andolan and six other associate organization and seven individual manual scavengers in 2003,[95] pointed out that the pernicious practice existed in many states and was being continued even in public sector undertakings such as the Indian Railways. The petitioners sought enforcement of their fundamental rights guaranteed under Article 17 (right against untouchability) read with Articles 14, 19 and 21 guaranteeing equality, freedom and protection of life and personal liberty respectively. They urged the Supreme Court to issue time bound directions to the Union of India and the various states to take effective steps for the elimination of the practice of manual scavenging simultaneously with the formulation and implementation of comprehensive plans for rehabilitation of all persons employed as manual scavengers. In pursuance of this the Supreme Court Division Bench consisting of Justices S.N. Variava and H.K. Sema said the practice still continued despite a 1993 law banning it. The Court issued:

> An interim order directing that every Department/Ministry of the Union government and each of the state governments should, within six months, file an affidavit through a senior officer who would take personal responsibility for verifying the facts stated in the affidavit. If the affidavit admits the existence of manual scavenging in the particular department, public sector undertakings or corporation, then it should indicate a time bound programme within which targets for liberation and rehabilitation of manual scavengers and their ultimate eradication is proposed to be achieved".[96]

Recently the Supreme Court while dealing a special leave petition filed by Peoples Union for Civil Liberties[97] highlighting the inhuman and pathetic working condition of sewage workers who were forced to work in an unhygienic, unsecure and unsafe working environment in the capital. Further the petitioner reveals that as many as forty sewage workers had died between October 14, 1999 and January11, 2005 and several others were injured while on work. Taking into cognizance the Supreme Court has asked the Union Ministries of Labour and Urban Development, Delhi government, National Human Rights Commission, Municipal Corporation of Delhi and Delhi Jal Board to respond within a stipulated time.

Summation and Conclusion

In the backdrop of enactment of Employment of Manual Scavengers and Construction of Dry Latrine (Prohibition) Act

1993, the public campaign against manual scavenging began in 1996 in Ranpur, where Martin Macwan, a Dalit activist based in Gujarat, stumbled up on safai karamcharis who were still carrying human excreta. It is indeed India's shame that manual scavenging is a disgusting reality despite the central law forthright banning this evil practice.[98] While enforcing this law some refused to adopt the law whereas those who even complied with it, the Dalit manual scavengers live a miserable life because of marginalization.[99] Put in nutshell, after the 13 years' of enactment of Act, there has not been a single prosecution. The law seems more of a skeleton scheme than really having the sanctioning enforcement. The traditional notion of impurity and pollution still discourage people from having indoor toilets. The enforcement agencies mainly the local bodies still are having manual scavengers on their rolls reflecting the institutionalization of the practice.[100] The very definition of safai karamcharis has been expanded to include manual workers engaged in sweeping and other cleaning work to justify state governments' claim that the actual number of manual scavengers may be indeed be negligible. India has not been able to do away with a practice that is admittedly a blot on humanity because manual scavengers are rooted in caste as surely as caste is rooted in nation's psyche. Thus, the time has come that the stinking existence of manual scavengers under the tinkered laws and contaminated enforcement necessitates a judicious scanning to accord human right to dignity and well-being to Dalit scavengers.

Notes

1. Universal Declaration on Human Rights, 1948. General Assembly Resolution 217 A (III) of 10 December 1948. See also J.S. Verma *The New Universe of Human Rights*, Universal Law Publishing Co. (P) Ltd. (2004), Durga Das Basu *Human Right in Constitutional Law*, 2nd Edition, p. 57 (2005).
2. Nomani, Mohd. Zafar Mahfooz, "The Human Right to Environment in India: Legal Precepts and Judicial Doctrines in Critical Legal Perspective", V (2) *Asia Pacific Journal of Environmental Law*, 118 (2000).

3. Granville Austin, *The Indian Constitution: Corner Stone of a Nation*, 26 (1972).
4. Supra note 2 at 119.
5. V.R. Krishna Iyer, *Social Justice: Sun Set or Dawn*, 2nd Ed.14 (1993).
6. Ibid., at 38.
7. S. Vishwanathan "Exposing an Abhorrent Practice", XXIII (3) *The Frontline Magazine,* 81 (2005).
8. Ibid., at 81.
9. Ibid.
10. V. Venkatesan "A Case for Human Dignity", XXII (12) *The Frontline Magazine*, 114(2005).
11. Ibid., at 114 and 115.
12. Ibid., at 115.
13. *Supra* note 2 at 114.
14. See: Preamble of the Universal Declaration on Human Rights, 1948.
15. See: Article 25 of the Universal Declaration on Human Rights, 1948.
16. See: Article 11(1) of International Covenant on Economic, Social and Cultural Rights (1966).
17. Ibid., Article 12 (1).
18. Article 6(1) of International Covenant on Civil and Political Rights (1966).
19. Phillipe Cullet, "Intellectual Property Protection and Sustainable Development"(2005), p. 388.
20. Mohd. Zafar Mahfooz Nomani, *Natural Resources Law and Policy*, Uppal Publication, New Delhi, p. 15 (2004).
21. V.R. Krishna Iyer "Why deny education to the have-nots?" *The Hindu Daily*, New Delhi Edition, 26 November, p. 11 (2005).
22. *Supra* note 5 at 89.
23. *Supra* note 20 at 15.
24. P.M. Bakshi; *The Constitution of India*, p. 33 (2005).
25. *Supra* note 5 at 46.
26. *Supra* note 20 at 15.
27. *Supra* note 5 at 15.
28. V.R. Krishna Iyer "The Dialectics and Dynamics of Human Rights in India (Yesterday, Today and Tomorrow)", Eastern Law House, p. 282 (2000).

29. *Olga Tellis* v. *Bombay Municipal Corporation*, AIR 1986 SC 180.
30. *People Union For Civil Liberties* v. *Union of India* (2000) 5 Scale.
31. *Consumer Education and Research Centre* v. *Union of India* (1995) 3 SCC 42.
32. *Subash Kumar* v. *State of Bihar*, AIR 1991 SC 420.
33. *Supra* note 28 at.
34. *Supra* note 5 at 16.
35. *Supra* note 5 at 23.
36. Ibid., at 54.
37. Ibid., at 55.
38. See Article 38 of the Indian Constitution.
39. Ibid., at Article 47 and 48(A) of the Indian Constitution.
40. S.N. Dhyani "Fundamentals of Jurisprudence: The Indian Approach", Central Law Agency, p. 407 (2004).
41. Ibid., at 408.
42. See Preamble of the Protection of Civil Rights Act, 1955.
43. Section 15-A.
44. Section 15.
45. See Preamble of the Scheduled Castes and Schedule Tribes (Prevention of Atrocities) Act, 1989.
46. See Preamble of the Employment of Manual Scavengers and Construction of Dry Latrines (Prohibition) Act, 1993.
47. Section 4.
48. Section 5.
49. Section 6.
50. Section 7.
51. Section 9.
52. Section 10.
53. Section 11.
54. Section 12.
55. Section 13.
56. Section 16.
57. Section 14.
58. Section 15.
59. Section 18.
60. H.O. Agarwal *Human Rights*, Central Law Publications, p. 241 (2004).

61. Ibid., at 300.
62. See: Section 3 of The Protection of Human Rights Act, 1993.
63. Section 21.
64. Section 30.
65. See Chapter III of Sections 12 and 13.
66. Ibid.
67. See Chapter VI of Section 30.
68. See Preamble of the Protection of Human Rights Act, 1993.
69. National Human Rights Commission (NHRC) Annual Report (New Delhi, 2002-2003) 22.
70. Ibid., at para 8.88 and 8.94 at 133-134.
71. Ibid., at para 8.91 at 134.
72. Ibid., at para 8.92 at 134.
73. Sidhartha Narrayan "Abolition of Manual Scavenging Slow", 26 February, 2006, p.10 *The Hindu Daily*, New Delhi.
74. Ibid.
75. *Supra* note 40 at 402.
76. *Supra* note 20 at 18-19.
77. *Supra* note 40 at 408.
78. *Supra* note 5 at 119.
79. Ibid. at 69.
80. Ibid. at 49.
81. *Municipal Council Ratlam* v. *Verdhichand*, AIR 1980 SC 1662.
82. (1976) 2 SCC 310.
83. Ibid. at 361.
84. AIR, 1981 SC 298.
85. Ibid. at 324 Para 82.
86. Ibid.
87. Ibid. at 331 Para 104.
88. AIR 1992 SC., 573.
89. Ibid. at 584.
90. AIR 1993 SC 1126.
91. Ibid. at 1137.
92. Ibid. at 1138.
93. AIR 1993 Raj. 177.
94. Ibid.
95. *Supra* note 10 at 114.

96. Ibid.
97. *The Hindu Daily*, New Delhi, 7 March, 2006 p. 4.
98. Nomani, Mohd. Zafar Mahfooz, *Right to Health: A Socio-Legal Perspective*, 62(2004).
99. Nomani, Mohd. Zafar Mahfooz, "Human Right to Environment in India: From Legality to Reality" in Aftab Ahmad (ed.) *Human Right in India: Issues and Challenges* (2000).
100. Nomani, Mohd. Zafar Mahfooz, "Environment, Poverty and Law: The Symbiotic Relationship", 47(2) *Caritas India Quarterly: Special Volume on Law and Poor*, (1997).

17

Social Justice and Empowerment

Ambedkar's Perspective

ZAFAR A. KHAN

Dr. B.R. Ambedkar is remembered as one of the great sons of India. Being the Chairman of the Constitution Drafting Committee, he is respected as a founding father of the Indian Constitution. His contributions for the cause of social justice leading to empowerment have been superb. In the instant paper the relevant issues revolving with social justice and empowerment with reference to Dr. Ambedkar will be examined, taking into account the theoretical framework and practical implication.

There are varying views on the concept of social justice and empowerment. Dr. Ambedkar's debate on justice, equality and fraternity reminds us about the 'social justice trinity' embodied in the preamble of the Constitution. Ambedkar's life in the process of constitution-making was decisive because he did the professional task of drafting the provisions of the Constitution. His insights into the jurisprudence, social justice and constitutional ethos have made the Indian Constitution an instrument of import and a living reality befitting to the Indian circumstances and needs to Indian society. Dr. Ambedkar has left an indelible mark on the basic document which represents the aims and aspirations of the people vis-à-vis the ideals of social justice in which the dominant institution of our democracy is based.

'Social justice' is a vague word in the Ambedkar centenary year and has been under constitutional claptrap since 26 January, 1950 and wherever the downtrodden have sought justice on the basis of equality. In the context of terrible deprivations in the past, 'social justice' has played hide and seek with the victim sector of Indian humanity. They are in large groups suffering adversities, social and educational, economic and cultural, struggling to join the main stream. They have so far not succeeded in securing for themselves what the great preamble to the constitution has pledged to the people of India.

Social justice or distributive justice or compensatory justice, is a quest for justice. It is a challenge of equality, liberty and justice. It is in pursuit of "making law an instrument of social change and for reminding lawyers and judges that they are social engineers".[1] Empowerment means, to give lawful power to the desired object of social justice. Before discussing the views of Dr. Ambedkar concerning social justice for the depressed, underprivileged and scorned, it may be worth recalling what social justice means; what is its genesis; what is its grammar and what does it aspire. The expression 'social justice' needs correct conception as well as perception even much beyond the views concerned with public welfare or the modern 'welfare state' or "welfare as a by-product of economic action".[2]

Justice is a social virtue and the term adequately conveys the simple idea that the virtue of justice arises out of, and expresses itself in obligations towards others. Whatever may be the advantageous as well as disadvantageous arguments on the above mentioned characteristics of justice, it may be correct to say that social justice is an art which implies " just, fair and reasonable" guidance to all the dispensers that " justice according to law is necessary in the society to establish some accepted standards of common good".

The Supreme Court of India through Justice Bhagwati in *Muir Mills Co. Ltd.* v. *Suit Mills Majdoor Union*[3] described social justice as a very vague and indeterminate expression without embarking upon a discussion as to the exact connotation of the expression 'social justice' we may only observe that the concept of social justice does not emanate from the fanciful notions of any adjudicator but must be founded on a mere solid foundation.[4] In *Prakash Cotton Mills* v. *Bombay*,[5] Chagla, C.J., as he then was agreed that social justice was hard to define, but submitted that the court should import its own ideas of justice in interpreting statutory provisions; social justice was an objective of the Constitution and it was an inarticulate major premise which was personal and individual to every court and every judge, depending on the judges' outlook on life and society; and laws cannot be interpreted without reference to social justice to the achievement of which our country was pledged.[6]

Hence, social justice of distributive justice of compensatory justice, is a quest for justice. It is a challenge of equality, liberty and justice. Social justice demands to have interaction with social purpose. Social purpose requires the interpretation of the eternal principles of human freedom to meet the challenging conditions of our times and the application of the fundamental principles of justice to the problems which arise in the complex industrial and commercial life of our era.[7] Preamble of our Constitution is the culmination of securing social justice through twin brethren: Fundamental Rights and Directive Principals of State Policy, and these are directed to achieving means as well as ends of justice.[8] Thus justice devoid of social justice, that is social-economic-political is not meaningful, purposeful and result-oriented social justice does not aim at providing justice to 'haves' but equally cares for the 'have-nots', viz., underdogs, disadvantaged, scorned and underprivileged populace.[9] Social justice, therefore, means justice which is not confined to a fortunate few, but takes within its sweep, large masses of disadvantaged and underprivileged segments of society; justice which not only penetrates and destroys the inequalities of race, sex, power, position or wealth but is also heavily weighted in favour of weaker sections of humanity; justice which brings about equitable distribution of the social, material and political resources of the community; justice which the law must ensure the people that the rule of law becomes meaningful (and rule of life) and social justice a reality for them.[10]

The concepts of social justice have varied with age and clime social justice to the millions "to wipe every tear from every eye".[11] Our Constitution envisages tripartite picturesque of social justice, viz., justice – social, economic and political is directed in the preamble; socio-economic justice is procured by the Directive Principles of State Policy: justice – social and political is secured by fundamental rights.[12] Therefore the trinity – the Problem, the Directive Principles and the Fundamental Rights – the quintessence of justice, in the contemplation of the Constitution is the liberation from social-economic subjection and consists in the actualization of the goal of full and free development of every individual. Thus, in broader perspective 'social justice' is the end.

After an in-depth but a succinct as well as critical examination of the concept of social justice, Ambedkar's profile and the formative influences that shaped his life, thinking process and work, a probing into his social justice ideas may now be imperatives.

Dr. Ambedkar himself explained his social philosophy: liberty, equality and fraternity:[13] when Pandit Jawaharlal Nehru moved the objectives resolution in the Constituent Assembly,[14] it was felt that it suffered from certain lacunae and on such Dr. Ambedkar sharply reacted to the clause relating to social, economic and political justice, he opined:[15]

"I should have from that point of view expected the resolution to state in most explicit terms that in order that there may be social and economic justice in this country, that there could be nationalization of industry and nationalization of land. I do not understand how it could be possible for any future government which believes in doing justice, socially economically and politically, unless its economic is a socialistic economy. Therefore, personally, although I have no objection to the enunciation of these prepositions, the Resolution is, to my mind, somewhat disappointing".

Dr. Ambedkar dreamt India to be an egalitarian state and a casteless society. In his draft Constitution he included safeguards for the minorities. There was a lot of criticism in Constituent Assembly. He emphasized that it was a wise decision taken by the Constituent Assembly. Dr. Ambedkar had entered the Constituent

Assembly with the sole object of safeguarding the interests of Scheduled Castes and not with the ambition of drafting the Constitution.

According to Ambedkar that social justice alone could lead to social harmony and social stability, and kindle patriotic feelings. For this the depressed classes have to "educate, agitate and organize" themselves. Dr. Ambedkar's belief was that the Constitution should provide fundamental rights and equality – social, economic and political to all citizens.[16] But only this would not be enough, because the more powerful, the highly privileged higher classes may be able to deny to the lower strata of the society. Therefore, law must provide remedies against the invasion of fundamental rights. However, the term backward classes has remained to be a problematic phrase and it is still unclear as to what this is. Ambedkar clarified in the Constituent Assembly: "...A backward community is a community which is backward in the opinion of the government. It is perhaps an account of this sweeping power given in the hands of the government that this clause would not only be a paradise for lawyers but even a paradise for the government." The idea behind the protective compensatory principle is for the purpose of mitigating inequalities designed to disappear along with these inequalities; it is envisaged that society must intervene in order to ensure that the competition is fair not just free; it seeks to take needs into account, and, at the same time, to provide some cushion against the excesses of untempered competition. It will be no exaggeration to state, the emphasis of the directive principles of state policy seems to be somewhat different, that is here the state had been given the mandate to direct its policy in such a way that the objectives of social justice are realized to its full brim, and as such the state is to take into account the special needs of certain strata of society and to make special provisions for equalizing the equal condition obtaining among the different strata. Dr. Ambedkar demonstrates that it is only the political will having the testament of social justice before it under the Supreme law – which can realize the goals of social justice. If the political will hesitates to realize the social justice then judiciary will step into correct the state lawlessness. It seems that Justice V.R. Krishna Iyer rightly conceded when he made this observation: Social justice is the end, judicial justice is the means; the legislative and executive operations are human engineering and together the three branches of government have to work in comity that the Constitution may fulfil what the founding fathers designed.[17]

Dr. Ambedkar's birth in an untouchable and in a system based on graded inequality and injustice and deprivation of basic human rights to his brethren, was responsible for giving a purpose and mission to his life. The celebration of the birth centenary of this great crusader is a good occasion to recall his struggle for injustice, both in pre-independent India, and in the Constituent Assembly and more importantly to ponder over its continued relevance even today.

As regards to Ambedkar's quest for social justice in British India, he held pragmatic and uncompromising views on the amelioration of the suffering of depressed classes and the role of government in this regard. In innumerable statements, representations and evidences, he came out with flying colours in support of adequate representation and constitutional safeguards for the depressed classes. On May 29, 1928 Ambedkar submitted a statement before the Simon Commission on its arrival in India concerning the safeguards for the protection of interests of the depressed classes. Dr. Ambedkar demanded protection through adequate representation for the depressed classes. He was in favour of taking into consideration population and social status to indicate the quantum of representation. Moreover, it was the responsibility of the government to ensure the spread of education, to make no discrimination in recruitment and to provide for adequate safeguards. In 1928, Dr. Ambedkar in another statement before the Simon Commission, clarified two points, first that the terms 'Depressed classes' and 'Untouchables' were synonymous, and second that the depressed classes must be treated as a distinct minority separate from Hindu community. The Nehru Report came under Dr. Ambedkar's indictment this time. The Nehru Committee was constituted by different political parties in 1928 under the chairmanship of Motilal Nehru, to draft a Constitution. In the Nehru Report, the Committee had stated that the problem of 'untouchables' was a social problem or a religious problem, but not a political problem and therefore, it made no special provision for the representation of the depressed classes in legislatures. On May 17, 1929, Dr. Ambedkar submitted a report on the Constitution in which he stated that "there should be a provincial civil service and a provincial service commission... Indianisation of the services should be made for the fulfilment of backward classes..." A committee had been constituted by the Government of Bombay in November, 1928 to enquire into the educational, economic and social conditions of the depressed classes to recommend measures for their upliftment. Dr. Ambedkar was a prominent member of this committee, submitted its report to the government in March, 1930 in which it recommended scholarships and students hostel. For the economic upliftment of the backward classes, it stressed on the need to recruit depressed classes in the police and urged that the present bar to the recruitment of the depressed classes in the army should be removed; that a backward classes officer should maintain lists of qualified candidates from the backward classes and promote their recruitment, that hereditary services rendered by the backward classes should be enquired into, and that the housing schemes for the backward classes should be promoted.[18]

At the first Round Table Conference, Dr. Ambedkar spoke on his 'Scheme of Political Safeguards' for the protection of depressed classes. He demanded that in the future Constitution of India, the depressed classes should be given a fundamental right enacted in the Constitution which will declare untouchables to be illegal for all public purposes. "Secondly", this fundamental right must also invalidate and nullify all such disabilities and all such discriminations as may have been made hitherto. He demanded safeguards to ensure the right to adequate representation in the legislature. Speaking on the subject of joint versus electorates, Dr. Ambedkar said: "We the depressed classes, demand a complete partition between ourselves and the Hindus. We have been called Hindus for political purposes, but we have never been acknowledged socially by the Hindus as their brethren."[19] At the same conference, Dr. Ambedkar insisted on recruitment for the depressed classes in the services. On January 4, 1931, Ambedkar submitted at Round Table Conference a 'Supplementary Memorandum' in which he demanded for the depressed classes representation in proportion to their population as estimated by the Simon Commission and the Indian Central Committee. As regards the method of representation, he demanded that "the depressed classes shall have the right to elect their representation to the provincial and central legislatures through separate electorates for their voters".

Dr. Ambedkar's cumulative role in ensuring justice for the depressed classes had its desired effect upon the British authorities. On August 17, 1932, Prime Minister Mac Donald announced the 'Communal Award' creating separate electorate for the depressed classes. But unfortunately, this joy was short lived as on August 18, 1932, Gandhi announced his decision to fast unto death, to resist the Communal Award. Ultimately, Dr. Ambedkar relented and practically 'saved the life of Gandhi' by agreeing to amend the Communal Award, in a manner agreeable to Gandhi, this was the Poona Pact signed by Dr. Ambedkar, Gandhi and others on September 24, 1932 in the Yervada Prison. Dr. Ambedkar was terribly unhappy with the Poona Pact; when elections proved his misgivings true, he blamed the Poona Pact squarely for depriving the Scheduled Castes of their genuine rights. Dr. Ambedkar ultimately lost faith in the British and discounted all hopes of securing social justice for his brethren because the system of joint electorates and reserved seats has made a mockery of the right given to the Scheduled Castes to send their true representations to the legislature and is a fraud upon the Scheduled Castes. He was convinced that adequate constitutional rights for the Scheduled Castes could be secured under a free Constitution. Dr. Ambedkar's struggle was thus marked by great expectations, hopes and aspirations, as well as disappointments and frustration. Nonetheless it was a period of sustained hard work where valuable lessons were learnt. This experience was to play a major role in Dr. Ambedkar's quest for constitutional rights and social justice in the Constituent Assembly.

Dr. Ambedkar kept in mind the interests of Scheduled Castes while participating in the process of drafting the Constitution. In fact, he is quoted as saying, "I came into the Constituent Assembly with no greater aspiration then to safeguard the interests of the Scheduled Castes". But such statements should not be construed to mean that Dr. Ambedkar was blind to the existence of numerous other disadvantage and exploited sections, and was not alive to other forms of social inequality needing immediate redressal. Dr. Ambedkar had completely devoted himself to the task of securing social justice for all the backward classes in the country under the mandate of a new Constitution.

Dr. Ambedkar as the champion of the downtrodden was convinced beyond doubt as to the need for a Bill of Rights in the Indian Constitution. He had been pleading continuously for an elaborate system of fundamental rights for the minorities in particular, and for all the citizens in general. His fight for social justice was the main plank in his struggle as the leader of minorities. He was also convinced that social justice could not be secured to one and all unless it was enshrined in the Constitution itself. One of the first tasks to which the Constituent Assembly addressed itself was the formulation of a bill of rights with pride of place accorded to social justice and non-discrimination. A comprehensive charter of rights was soon evolved through various stages in the assembly and its committee. Described by Dr. Ambedkar as 'the most criticized part' of the Constitution, Part III dealing with the Fundamental Rights was discussed for as many as 38 days – 11 in sub-committee, 2 in the Advisory Committee and 25 in the Constituent Assembly. The fundamental rights in the Constitution are more elaborate and comprehensive than in the Bills of Rights or in any other Constitution.

Constitutional provisions aims at preventing discrimination and promoting social justice and the fundamental rights guaranteeing equality before the law and equal protection of law (Article 14), prohibition of discrimination on grounds of religion, race caste, sex or place of birth (Article 15), equality of opportunity in matters of public employment (Article 16), abolition of unsociability (Article 17), and prohibition of traffic in human beings and forced labour (Article 23). It is clear from the above provisions that Dr. Ambedkar and the founding fathers made genuine efforts to constitutionally guarantee equality to the disadvantaged sections of the people. Reacting to the exceptions and qualifications to the fundamental rights, Dr. Ambedkar stated that the whole of the criticism about fundamental rights is based upon a misconception. In the first place the criticism in so far as it seeks to distinguish fundamental rights from non-fundamental rights is not sound. It is incorrect to say that fundamental rights are absolute while non-fundamental rights are the gift of the law. Because fundamental rights are the gift of state, it does not follow that the state cannot qualify them. According to Dr. Ambedkar and founding fathers the objective of the Constitution was to establish and egalitarian society were rights that were guaranteed not to a few, but to all. They firmly believe that right to equality of opportunity has no meaning unless the vast disparities between rich and poor are reduced. Political liberties and individual freedoms are of little value when the year of starvation compels the vast majority of the people to the will of the few.

While the fundamental rights guarantee the rights and liberties of the individual against arbitrary state actions, the directive principles seek to emphasis economic and social goals. It was the intention of the founding fathers to incorporate into the Constitution concept and principles that should determine governmental activities. This would bring about a social and economic revolution in the country. Dr. Ambedkar categorically stated that the directive principles were not intended to be mere pious declarations. "It is the intension of the Assembly that in future both the legislature and executive should not merely pay lip service to these principles enacted in this part, but that they should be made the basis of all executive and legislative actions that may be taken hereafter in the matter of governance of the country. The directive principles strive to create a welfare state and just social order where there is no economic exploitation. Article 38 contain the essence of the people by securing and protecting effectively, as it may, a social order in which justice – social, economic and political shall inform all the institutions of national life."

Besides this, there are some special provisions contained in Part XVI of the Constitution relating to certain classes – the Scheduled Castes and Scheduled Tribes, the Anglo-Indians and the socially and educationally backward classes. Articles 330 and 332 provide that seat should be reserved for Scheduled Castes and

Scheduled Tribes in the House of the People and legislative assembly of the state respectively. Articles 331 and 333 provide for representation of the Anglo-Indian community by nomination by the President and the Governor, in case that community is not adequately represented in the Union and states' lower houses. According to Article 334, the period of such reservations is fixed as 10 years from the commencement of the Constitution. Article 335 stipulates that "the claim of the members of the Scheduled Castes and Scheduled Tribes shall be taken into consideration, consistent with the maintenance of efficiency of administration, in making appointments to services and posts in connection with the affairs of the Union or of a state". Article 336 and 337 deals with the special provision respectively for appointment in certain services, and educational grants for the Anglo-Indian Community.

Article 338 provides for a special officer for the Scheduled Castes and Scheduled Tribes to be appointed by the President whose duty is to investigate all matters relating to the safeguards provided for Scheduled Castes and Scheduled Tribes and are to be construed as including references to such OBC as may be specified by the President on receipt of a report from the Commission which may be appointed under Article 340(1). Article 339 provides for the appointment of a Commission to report in regard to the administration of the Scheduled Areas and the welfare of the Scheduled Tribes. Article 340 (1) provides for the appointment by the President of a Commission to investigate the conditions of socially and educationally backward classes within the territory of India and the difficulties under which they labour and to make recommendations as to the steps that should be taken by the Union or any state to remove such difficulties and to improve their condition, etc. There were many in the Constituent Assembly who objected to the special provisions for providing reservation, but the general consensus appeared to be in favour of reservation of jobs for Scheduled Castes and Scheduled Tribes. Dr. Ambedkar had the last word when he stressed the importance of this provision to meet the demands of communities which have not had so far representation in the state. Article 330 and 332 which provided reservation of seats in the Lok Sabha and state assemblies for the Scheduled Castes and Scheduled Tribes, was initially for a period of 10 years.

There was a practical debate in the Constituent Assembly on the desirability of restricting the concessions to a period of 10 years. Ambedkar, however, preferred a more flexible policy and made the observation: "If at the end of 10 years, the Supreme Court finds that their position has not improved or that they want further extension, it will not be beyond their capacity to invent new ways of getting the same protection which they are promised here". Thus, the observation made by Dr. Ambedkar shows his acute sense of observation and depth of understanding of social and cultural background of the society of India. He combined in himself the role of a great social reformer, a political leader and a spiritual guide of the untouchables. A unique opportunity was given to him, to give expression not only to his views on the various problems of the Indian society and policy, but also to try his hand at writing the rights of the minorities in particular and the citizens of India in general into the Constitution of India. Dr. Ambedkar's philosophy of constitutionalism revolved around social justice and change through perfectly constitutional means. He desired to create an equal society through the process of constitution-making. He dreamt of India where there would be no discrimination, no exploitation, no unsociability and no degradation. His initial strategy as long as the British were here, lay in demanding constitutional rights and safeguards. including the controversial separate electorate for the depressed classes on communal line. But with the advent of independence, Dr. Ambedkar approached the problem from the wider perspective of nationalism, democracy, humanity and justice.

It is indeed a pity that Dr. Ambedkar's view on the socio-economic justice did not prevail today, even after more than six decades of the independence and the working of the Indian Constitution. It is also a fact that economic backwardness is the primary cause for all the sufferings of the poor, the backward and the downtrodden in the Indian society.

The vital and the basic problem with which the states as well as the courts are continuously involved is the identification of the persons who are educationally and socially backward and are entitled for the constitutional benefits. This problem has not been solved from *Balaji* v. *State of Mysore*,[20] till today as the criterion adopted by the states in most of the cases were found to be based on caste which is a prohibited criterion. The Constitution aims that such identification should not be based on caste so that the vice of perpetuating caste system may be abolished that is why in Article 15(4) and 16(4) the word 'class' has been used instead of caste. Another issue of distinction between caste and class is of great legal and social significance. These two have different sociological effect. 'Class' has been included in Articles 15(4) and 16(4) because it has mobility where as 'caste' is a stagnant concept. There is no possibility of shifting a person of one caste to another. A Brahmin will always remain a Brahmin, howsoever he is ignorant. A Harijan, whether learned would remain Harijan. 'Caste' system generates feeling of separatism, a sense of superiority on religious grounds. It widens the gap in human relations and crushes the idea of fraternity and social integration where as the concept of class has opposite effects and tendencies. The poverty criterion as was indicated in Balaji was accepted by the Supreme Court in *Janki Prasad* v. *State of J&K*[21] on the reasoning that in India, social backwardness was associated with economic backwardness but the court refrained from adopting this criterion as it would make a very large proportion of population backward. But the court broke a new ground of 'education' saying that education is a cardinal element in social equipment. This criteria may pose problems when applied as the adoration of education as the basis of classification would include a vast number of illiterates. Therefore, education as basis to determine the socially backwardness could be suitable criteria as the evil of casteism could be eliminated and a simple formula for the application of protective discrimination could be evolved. Ignorance and illiteracy are great causes and sources of all social evils. Education would not only bring the downtrodden to the level of the society but enable every individual to rationalize other social and religious practices. The old rigid norms might be broken by the impact of education. Another issue attached with the problem of protective discrimination is the extent of reservation. Article 15(4) and 16(4) permit reservation but are silent on this issue. Although Article 335 controls it by enacting that the claims of Scheduled Castes and Scheduled Tribes shall be taken into account with the maintenance of efficiency of administration in appointment to services, posts in connection with the affairs of the Union or of a state. The Constitution is silent on this issue. It may be perhaps be a deliberate omission because of the fluctuating conditions of Scheduled Castes and Scheduled Tribes from one state to another. On this issue also the Balaji case may be referred in which the Supreme Court considered Article 15(4) and 16(4) as exceptions to Article 15(1) and 16(1) and held that the extent of reservation should not exceed 50 per cent of the total number of posts available. The Supreme Court in many other cases, such as from *General Manager Southern Railway* v. *Rangachari*,[22] and *Devadasan* v. *Union of India*,[23] pointed out that general efficiency of administration of general interest should not be suffered at the cost of excessive reservations. But in *State of Kerala* v. *Thomas*,[24] the court not only regarded Article 16(4) is not an exception to Article 16(1) but Justice Krishan Iyer and Justice Murtaza Ali said that the extent of reservation might be as high as eighty per cent. Thomas case can be regarded as too far fetched as compared to Balaji and ignored to maintain a balance between competing interesting and the policy of protective discrimination. Balaji case reconciled this problem in a much reasonable way. In *Chottey Lal* v. *State of UP*,[25] the Supreme Court stayed on Allahabad High Court Judgment, which had struck down the UP government order making reservations for persons belonging to backward classes in the state judicial services. The High Court upheld the reservation for the Scheduled Castes and others while striking down part of the state government order that applied to backward classes, and the court regarded Kurmis and Ahirs and other castes mentioned in the government orders as not backward classes within the meaning of Article 16(4). The Court therefore observed that the orders relating to reservation for backward classes of posts in the state judicial services were fraud on the constitutional power under Article 15(4) and 16(4). The foregoing analysis indicate the manner in which the criteria of backwardness and the problem of adjustment of competing interest was dealt with by the judiciary. In such a state of affairs the constitutional provision providing protective discrimination could not be successfully implemented because the identification of backward classes is much more important than reservation. The Central government in order to tackle this basic problem appointed a commission on 20, December, 1978 with B.P. Mandal as its Chairman. The Mandal Report being based on caste, the government deferred its implementation. The main objection to the Mandal Report was that in a county of overwhelming poverty the only criteria of backwardness should be on economic deprivation. Since poverty and caste are interlinked, it was apprehended that the acceptance of Mandal Report would amount to the perpetuation of caste system. Moreover, backwardness is not a uniform feature in any caste. Some of the castes themselves donate the economic and social backwardness and should observe maximum attention. It is said that Mandal Commission had also taken economic criteria into account in determining backwardness, but the commission used that in determining the backwardness of a caste and not of the people in general. However, the endeavour of both the commissions to dilute the system has not been successful and no workable formula for the determination of OBC could be evolved by them. When V.P. Singh became the Prime Minister in 1990, he promised to implement Mandal Report in the Manifesto released by Janata Dal. He declared in the House of Parliament to implement Mandal Report. That is to say 27 per cent jobs in government services will be reserved for OBC in addition to 22.5 already reserved for SC and ST. This declaration was so sudden that it caused a great deal of anxiety all over. It was followed by unprecedented agitation and anti-reservation stir to the whole of North India and part of Central India. The government failed to control the situation, rather the condition became more worse by the Prime Minister's speech that the government would not dilute its decision in implementing Mandal Report and in bringing socio-economic changes and upliftment of OBCs. As regards the Mandal Report, it is argued that there are grave misgiving about its methodology, its indicators, and narrowness of its field survey, its faulty deduction from the 1931 Census and its unscientific and outmoded approach and influence. Moreover, it adopted criteria for the identification of OBCs which were wholly based on caste. It used the term caste as being synonymous with class. The Commission clearly disregarded the minimum favours to the OBCs. Inspite of the flaws, the Mandal Commission deals with the constitutional ethos of social justice and equality in job opportunities. What is needed most is to assess the report in view of the present social complexities and economic status. The other important issue is the identification of backward classes of people on the present economic context. As evident from the study of case law, the judiciary and also the Mandal Commission could not evolve any criteria for the identification of the OBCs. However, the judiciary discouraged caste based criteria and adopted other criteria which dominated the daily life of OBCs and treated as socially and educationally backward for compensatory advantages. It is the matter of great dissatisfaction that inspite of exceptional and temporary measures designed for the Scheduled by our founding fathers it is seen that the mitigating inequalities between communities has not been changed. The period of reservation has been repeatedly extended four times but still it is seen that these classes of people are at the same position.[26] This is because the social, economic and political inequalities have not yet been removed and they need reservation for one time more with a view to enable them to come at par with the rest of the nation. That is true today, the lower layers of the people of the Scheduled Caste are at the same position where they were two hundred years ago barring a few who have monopolized all the benefits designed for these poor brethren.[27] The general opinion is that the benefits of reservation policy, by and large have been snatched away by the top creamy layer, thus keeping the weakest of the weak always weak and leaving the fortunate lawyers to consume the whole cake.

The Constitution wishes to establish an egalitarian society. The provisions relating to the protective discrimination in a nutshell tries to bring unequal at the levels of equal. There cannot be any equality between the people who have been unequal and who have been denied the access of education and job opportunities. Now to achieve the desired objective of bringing unequals at level of equals two possible methods can be employed: one is what may be called 'pull up method'. The other can he called 'push up method'. The strategy of pull up method results in the development and progress of only few within the disadvantaged groups, while the push-up method helps in raising the status of whole class of disadvantaged communities. In the view of this background, an attempt has been made by a PhD scholar[28] working under Dr. Ambedkar

Chair of Legal Study and Research for his doctoral thesis assessed the impact of various methods adopted for the welfare of the Scheduled Castes. The researcher had examined empirically the political, social, economic and educational impact in considerable detail. An attempt was made to find out the extent of progress, which these people have been able to achieve, by constitutional safeguards in due course of time. An effort has been made to prove the impact of reservation policy on political life of the Scheduled Castes in view of political safeguards embodied for them, to assess the impact of reservation policy on education and socio-economic life of the beneficiaries. I knew in depth the level of awareness and opinion of the Scheduled Castes with regard to constitutional safeguards and to analyse whether the benefit of reservation has really been reaped by all beneficiaries on equal footing or has gone only to a fraction of the Scheduled Castes population, i.e., the creamy layer. The study has been restricted to Aligarh, Agra and Rampur districts of Uttar Pradesh because these districts are densely populated with the Scheduled Castes population. For this, at least 5 villages were taken from each district to ascertain the upward mobility of the Scheduled Castes because of affirmative action. Similarly five localities were studied in urban areas of these districts. In addition to this, data was collected from these districts in order to find the representation of the Scheduled Castes in the respective offices. An effort is made by the researcher to make the study a good combination of questionnaire method and extensive interview method to assess the impact of reservation policy which is vital for social justice in light of the objective of study and to find out the answer to the hypothesis raised. The scrutiny of responses obtained from 300 respondents collected from the three above-mentioned districts of Uttar Pradesh had enabled the researcher to come to the following findings:

1. The execution of political safeguards in favour of the Scheduled Castes had really made the positive impact on the political life of the Scheduled Castes to the extent that they have enabled to share the political power in the light of constitutional philosophy enshrined in Articles 330 and 332 of the Constitution. The study reveals that the Scheduled Castes in

the three districts of U.P. are not politically quite aware of their political rights and are interested in sharing political power at village, state and national levels. It is well established from the fact that 218 respondents out of 300 (72.66%) are active members of the political organizations and few are constantly paying retention fee to retain their membership in the said organizations. What is fortunate is that despite their political consciousness to share political power, they have not been able to win any general seat in Lok Sabha (House of the People) and Vidhan Sabha (Assemblies). Rather, the study establishes that they have been defeated miserably. It is with this view in mind that 75.33 per cent respondents have strongly stressed that reservation of seats in the legislative bodies must continue forever. What is visible is that political awareness is growing fastly among them and they are struggling hard to find out ways and means to enable them to share political power on equal footing with higher strata of the society.

2. It has also been established that the Government of Uttar Pradesh has really evolved an adequate and satisfactory administrative apparatus for the implementation of the safeguards for the Scheduled Castes and had not been able to achieve a great deal of success in weeding out the feeling of unsociability in the society, as 72.33 per cent respondents have frankly admitted that they have been humiliated on the basis of caste feeling. Their responses have gone to the extent of establishing that the government machinery is not even helping them in safeguarding their social interests and even the police department is not sympathetic and helpful in registering their cases against the upper strata of the society as and when any atrocity is caused on them by the members of higher castes. The respondents also feel that the police are harsh and refuse them to register their cases of atrocities against the people of higher castes. Similarly 90.67 per cent respondents admit that upper castes people do not allow them to share water from the same source. Similarly, the majority of respondents admit that they have been restricted to enter the temples. Even the

practice of dinning with the people of higher castes is not prevalent in their villages.

3. It has also been well established from the responses that the Scheduled Castes have been able to change their livelihood and have virtually enabled themselves to raise their standard of living appreciably. As many as 92.67 per cent respondents do not agree that the benefits of reservation under various schemes initiated by the government for their upliftment have been reaped by them evenly. Moreover, majority respondents admit that their way of life has not undergone any change because of the impact of reservation policy. They agree that the old customs, occupations, practices in their villages are now a movement from traditional to modern society. No effort has been made by the government to remove the poverty of the Scheduled Castes.
4. It is also well found from the study that Government of U.P. is trying its best in generating a healthy educational environment in the state. This is borne out of the fact that 21.67 per cent have state in their responses that there are few educational institutions in their localities and hence they are now feeling no hardship in sending their children to school, but the problem is of higher education and they have no facility of higher education in their locality. Quite a few respondents responded that their children are getting incentives in the form of free books, copies, attendance, scholarship, uniforms, merit scholarship, etc. The truth is that the literacy rate among the Scheduled Castes is still very low. The study leads to the conclusion that the government has to put its earnest efforts to promote healthy educational environment in the state and to extend the fruits of reservation policy to those who really deserve and for whom it is meant.
5. It has been well established from the responses of the beneficiaries that the Government of U.P. is struggling hard to translate the spirit of Article 16(4) of the Indian Constitution into action. The benefits are being afforded in the form of relaxation of required experience, fee concession, pre-examination coaching, separate interviews, etc. But what is

dishearting is that despite all these efforts there appears something lacking to have healthy effect of reservation policy in the jobs of government, public sector undertakings, municipal corporations, banks and other autonomous bodies. The responses of the beneficiaries discloses that majority of the Scheduled Castes families have no representation in services. There are only 39.0 per cent families who have less than 5 members in government job and 12.33 per cent families who have more than 5 members in government jobs. But the majority that is there are 48.67 per cent families who have no member in government jobs. This is evident that the benefit of reservation in employment is being hijacked by the creamy layer of the Scheduled Castes and majority of Scheduled Castes are still being deprived of this benefit.

6. The study also reveals that the beneficiaries have a good deal of awareness about the constitutional provisions and other legislative provisions designed for their benefit. It is evident from the fact that 67.67 per cent respondents agreed that they are fully aware of the welfare legislations and constitutional safeguards, which the government has enacted from time to time. They have even stated that they know about the provisions in the national charter to knock at the door of judiciary if their rights are violated. As many as 99.33 per cent respondents claim that they know about the provisions of Untouchability Act enacted for the eradication of untouchability from the society. All this establishes that there is a great degree of awareness among the Scheduled Castes and are actively conscious to vindicate their rights and reap the benefits available to them under various welfare legislations.
7. The study reveals that the execution of the constitutional safeguards in favour of the Scheduled Castes in three districts of U.P. has enabled them to come on par with the other sections of society. The truth is that the people belonging to the scheduled castes are not ready to forgo the policy of reservation designed for them. Nearly 75.33 per cent have strongly asserted that reservation policy must be continued forever and moreover 63.33 per cent respondents have also asserted that

there is no improvement in the condition of the Scheduled Castes by the government policy in contrast to the past and 98.0 per cent do not agree that they have become so advanced that they do not need reservation any more; 82.0 per cent of the respondents suggested that the benefits should be given to the real beneficiaries and the government should give certain income criteria for the beneficiaries. It should not be given to those who are financially sound. If the government policies are properly implemented then only the backwardness will be eradicated and reservation policy will become more judicious and fruitful.

The above analysis unfolds that the social justice is the sheer anchor of the Constitution and the reservations were the means to achieve it. The Constitution of India is a twine testimony to the greatness and vision of Dr. B.R. Ambedkar. His life was an era of a great struggle against injustices and humiliations to Dalits. He comes out victoriously by giving all important rights to the oppressed in the Constitution of India. In spite of all social hurdles in his way, Dr. Ambedkar rose to the greatest heights and occupied important and prestigious position in India. In fact he came and lived like a son and gave the rights to Dalits who were living in darkness and state of slavery. Dr. Ambedkar very well knew that unless and until the reservation in jobs, legislations and education was not accorded to Dalits, they would never be in a position to be in equal proportion in the administration of the country and they would remain oppressed and slaves forever. Dr. Ambedkar as a chief architect of the Constitution made social justice a founding faith and incorporated humanist provisions to lift the level of the low Scheduled Castes to make democracy viable on equal footing for all. Dr. Ambedkar was very much conscious of the merits of equality. He would not allow the preferential treatment to eat away the non-discriminatory principle. Dr. Ambedkar was a man primarily responsible for bringing about social revolution to secure human dignity for the oppressed. The above discussion reveals that in spite of various welfare programmes and constitutional safeguards for the oppressed, the oppressed segments of the society are still where they were five centuries ago. This unchecked and uncared implementation of reservation policy is developing towards social disequilibrium instead of functioning as an engine of social engineering. It is a matter of grave concern that no government has so far conducted any analytical study to determine the real impact of reservation policy for the Scheduled Castes. The government must justify the extension of privileges on the basis of factual studies of the society. The reservation policy requires urgent restructuring so that the downtrodden get assimilated in the national mainstream with a view to give impetus to the concept of social justice. What is required is to make the policy more judicious and reasonable and to spread the benefits of reservation policy to a wide section of society. By this the unfulfilled dream of Dr. Ambedkar will come true. The educated Dalits on higher posts should realize that whatever they are today is because of Dr. Ambedkar's lifelong struggle. They should understand the importance of reservation, should educate the ignorant masses who got them the reservation, why it is required and how it will make an egalitarian society and how to make it more fruitful and judicious. They should realize that it is the key for social justice. The Dalits must realize that they are not only Hindus but the original inhabitants of this nation. Any socially educated person will like to live with dignity and identity. Just accepting the fact is not good. The Dalits should find the situation themselves since they do not have Dr. Ambedkar now. It is the responsibility of educated Dalits not only to realize the above, but also to educate the rest of Dalit masses. Educated Dalits should make it a habit to contribute one per cent of their earnings for the welfare of the backward society. They should also propagate the irrational aspect of Hinduism and never ending sufferings in it and prepare the masses towards obtaining a separate identity outside the Hindu fold. The Dalits should be educated and they should be communicated the importance of benefits of reservation policy and how it can be made more effective. Sooner the educated Dalits realize their responsibilities and act accordingly, better is for them, for their society and for the country as well. They will have to struggle to get the reservation policy extended to private sectors. Our approach should be pedantic. We must propel our energies in the right perspective, so that social justice and empowerment not merely remain a dream but becomes the reality of life. Dr. Ambedkar's vision of social justice and empowerment may be achieved in reality if a serious thought is given to actualize them by virtue of honest implementation without any social or political prejudices relinquishing the social, cultural, religious, historical and political prejudices.

Notes

1. Justice Y.V. Chandrachud, *The Challenge of Social Justice*, Supreme Court of India Publication, Third International Conference of Appellate Judges, 1985, pp. 2-3.
2. H.M. Seevai, *Constitutional Law of India*, Vol. II, 3rd ed., pp. 1599-1600.
3. (1995) 1. SCR 999.
4. Ibid. at pp. 1001-02.
5. 59 Bom, L.R. 836
6. Ibid. at p. 844.
7. Vide, Justice Y.V. Chandrachud, *The Challenge of Social Justice*, Supreme Court of India Publication, Third International Conference of Appellate Judges, 1985, pp. 3-4.
8. Vide, K.L. Bhatia, "Kaleidoscopic view of Jurisprudential Diminutions of Judicial Activism with Reference to Swedeshi Jurisprudence: Saint of Sinner", in K.L. Bhatia (ed.). *Judicial Activism and Social Change*, 1990, p. 155.
9. Ibid., p. 156
10. Vide, Justice P.N. Bhagwati, Supra note 7 at p. 21, pp. 157-61.
11. Pt. Jawahar Lal Nehru, as quoted in Granville Austin, *The Indian Constitution: Cornerstone of a Nation*, 1972, p. 26.
12. Vide, Justice V.R. Krishna Iyer. "The Judicial System – Has it a Function in our Constitutional Order", (15) 1979, *Civil and Military Law Journal*, 163, p. 168.
13. Speech on All India Radio on October 3, 1954, as mentioned in L.R. Balley (ed.) *Thoughts of Ambedkar*, 1989, pp. 73-74.
14. *Constituent Assembly Debate*, Vol I-IV, Second Reprint, 1989, pp. 57-65.
15. It must be worth mentioning here that Ambedkar as Chairman of the Drafting Committee, opposed amendment to Article 15 as providing an opening for segregated facilities, and as such the

Constituent Assembly had rejected the insertion in the original Constitution of a provision similar to Article 15(4), *C.A.D.*, Vol III, 1989 reprint, p. 661.

16. Vide, T.T. Krishnamanchari's prediction, *C.A.D.* Vol. VII, 1989 reprint, p. 699. The word backward... is going to be ultimately interpreted by the Supreme Authority (i.e., Supreme Court) on some basis, castes, community, religion, literacy or economic status... The word does not say caste. It says class, which means vide M.M. Munshi (at p. 697) economically, educationally and socially backward.
17. *Constituent Assembly Debate*, Vol. VII, at p. 41.
18. See K.N. Kadan (ed.) *Dr. Ambedkar and the Significance of his Movement*, Popular Prakashan, Bombay, 1991 at p. 30.
19. See Vasant Moon (ed.) *Dr. Baba Saheb Ambedkar: Writing and Speeches*, No.. 5, Bombay, Govt. of Maharashtra at p. 532.
20. AIR 1963, S.C. at p. 49.
21. AIR 1973, S.C. at p. 931.
22. AIR 1962, S.C. at p. 38.
23. AIR 1964, S.C. at p. 179.
24. AIR 1976, S.C. at p. 470; (1976) 2SCC 310.
25. AIR 1979, All 135.
26. See Constitution (Eight Amendment) Act, 1959; Constitution (23rd Amendment) Act, 1979; Constitution (46th Amendment) Act, 1980 and Constitution (62nd Amendment) Act, 1989.
27. Krishna Iyer, quoted in P.L. Mehta and M.G. Chitkara, "Need to Revamp Reservation Policy", *Civil and Military Law Journal*, No. 3, 171, July-September (1990).
28. Shoeb Khan "Reservation Policy: Social Justice", An empirical Study of Scheduled Caste in three districts of Uttar Pradesh with special reference to Dr. B.R. Ambedkar's (PhD thesis in Law) Submitted in the Department of Law, AMU, Aligarh in 2000.

18

Denial of Reservation Benefit to the Converted People

Constitutional Issues, Possibilities and Challenges

MUSHTAQ AHMAD

The present position with regard to the reservation benefits to the converted people is that the Hindu Scheduled Castes, converted to Sikhism or Buddhism are entitled to the constitutional benefits under para 3 of the Constitution (Scheduled Castes) Order, 1950 issued by the President of India under Article 341 of the Constitution of India. Scheduled Caste converts to Sikhism or Buddhism were given the benefit of the constitutional reservation in 1956 and 1990 respectively. This was done despite the fact that as per the Explanation 11 to Article 25 (2) (b), "the reference to Hindus shall be construed as including a reference to persons professing the Sikh, Jain or Buddhist religion, and the reference to Hindu religious institutions shall be construed accordingly". If a Scheduled Caste belonging to Hinduism, Sikhism or Buddhism converts to Christianity or Islam, he loses the reservation. Of late, there is a demand that such converts should enjoy the benefit of reservation even after their conversion. The reason given as to why only Hindu Scheduled Castes are given the constitutional reservation is that the Hinduism recognizes caste system and since Scheduled Castes' ancestors faced discrimination and social stigma for centuries and the present ones are also looked down upon, hence the constitutionally guaranteed reservation. True, Islam and Christianity do not recognize caste system, but then, the same is true about the Sikhism and Buddhism. The protagonists of continuing reservation to converts argue that though Christianity and Islam do not recognize caste hierarchy but the ground reality is that converts to these egalitarian religions too face the same problems after conversion, though in lesser degrees. It is further argued that the social stigma of being born a Scheduled Caste is carried by him wherever he goes, hence the reservational benefits should continue. The Supreme Court of India is seized of this complex issue. The demand for reservation for the Christian and the Muslim Dalits has gained momentum particularly in view of recommendations of the Minorities Commissions, etc.

Scheduled Castes vis-à-vis Religion

There are certain Articles in the Constitution of India which speak about Scheduled Castes. Article 330 (reservation of seats for Scheduled Castes and Scheduled Tribes in the House of People). Article 332 (reservation of seats for the Scheduled Castes and Scheduled Tribes in the legislative assemblies of the states), Article 334 (reservation of seats and special representations to cease after sixty years, para a), Article 335 (claims of Scheduled Castes and Scheduled Tribes to services and posts), Article 338 (National Commission for Scheduled Castes and Scheduled Tribes), and Article 341 (Scheduled Castes). Then, there are Articles 15(4) and 16(4). It is not true to say that Sikhs and Buddhists were given reservation as they were part of Hindu religion. If so, why they were not given in 1950 itself? Later, they were given the reservation because of political pressure. Religion is unconnected to Scheduled Castes in our Constitution. Nowhere in the above Articles, the word 'religion' or the name of any religion is mentioned. It follows that the status of Scheduled Castes should be determined irrespective of religion. Rather, it should be determined in relation to their actual social and economic status as obtaining today. Para 3 of the Constitution (Scheduled Castes) Order, 1950 says: "Notwithstanding anything contained in paragraph 2, no person who professes a religion different from the Hindu, Sikh or Buddhist shall be deemed to be a member of the Scheduled Caste". The vires of this order has been challenged on various grounds.

Matter in The Supreme Court

The challenge to the constitutionality of para 3 of the Constitution (Scheduled Caste) Order, 1950 on the ground of being discriminatory is pending in the Apex Court of India. Writ Petition (C) No. 180/2004 Centre, *Public Interest Litigation and another* v. *Union of India*, Writ Petition (C) No. 94/2005, *D. David* v. *Union of India*, Writ Petition (C) No. 625/2005 A. I. *United Christian Movement for Rights and another* v. *Union of India* and Writ Petition (C) No. 47/2006 *Mohd. Sadiq* and *another* (formerly Dr. Mukesh Kumar) v. *Union of India* are pending in the Supreme Court. First three petitions seek reservation for the Scheduled Caste converts to Christianity while the fourth one seeks reservation for Muslim Dalits like Mehtar and also for the Scheduled Castes converts to Islam. The author of this article is the advocate in the last case which has been filed by Mohd. Sadiq and his wife Reena Singh. Mohd. Sadiq had applied to the Allahabad University for the post of a lecturer on the Scheduled Castes quota but he was denied the same on the ground that now he was not a Scheduled Caste after his conversion to Islam. Reema Singh is a Pradhan on the Schedule Caste ticket, she, like her husband, wants to embrace Islam but in that event she will lose the post of Pradhan, hence, the Order of 1950 is violative of Article 25 also (right to religious freedom).

Constitutional Issues

The Constitution (Scheduled Castes) Order, 1950 is based on religion of Hinduism and it is a common place knowledge that the Constitution of India does not allow religion based reservation. There are certain provisions which prohibit the state from discrimination on grounds of only of religion, etc. The Reservation Order is clearly hit by Articles 14, 15, 16 and 25 of the Constitution of India. According to Article 14, "the state shall not deny to any person equality before the law or the equal protection of the laws within the territory of India", Article 15(1). "The state shall not discriminate against any citizen on grounds only of religion, race, caste, sex, place of birth or any of them". However, Article 15(4) says, "nothing in this Article or in clause (2) of Article 29 shall prevent the state from making any special provision for the advancement of any socially and educationally backward classes of citizens or for the Scheduled Castes and the Scheduled Tribes". Article 16(2) says, " No citizen shall, on grounds only of religion, race, caste, sex, descent, place of birth, residence or any of them, be ineligible for, or discriminated against in respect of any employment or office under the state". Article 16(4A) is also important according to which, "nothing in this article shall prevent the state from making any provision for reservation in matters of promotion with consequential seniority to any class or classes of posts in the services under the state in favour of Scheduled Castes and the Scheduled Tribes which, in the opinion of the state are not adequately represented in the services under the state".

Under Article 341(1) of the Constitution of India, the power to specify who are Scheduled Castes is conferred on the President of India. Exercising this power, the President of India issued the Constitution (Scheduled Castes) Order, 1950, as amended from time to time, the third paragraph of which reads. "Notwithstanding anything contained in para 2, no person who professes a religion different from Hinduism, Sikhism or Buddhism shall be deemed to be a member of a Scheduled Caste". While the Constitution expressly prohibits any discrimination on the basis of religion under Articles 14, 15 and 16. The above said Presidential Order of 1950, however, discriminates among Scheduled Castes on the basis of religion by depriving non-Hindus of benefits prescribed under the law for the scheduled castes.

The Judicial Response

That the social stigma or disability does not vanish even after conversion to other religions which do not recognize caste and untouchability was even recognized by the Hon'ble Supreme Court. The Supreme Court of India in the case of *S. Anbalagan* v. *Devarajan* ATR 1984 SC 411, in paragraph 13 has said that "in fact it may not be accurate to say that he regains his caste, it may be more accurate to say that he never lost his caste in the first instance when he embraced another religion. The practice of caste, however, irrational it may appear to our reason and however repugnant it may appear to our moral and social sense, is so deep-rooted in the Indian people that its mark does not seem to disappear on conversion to a different religion. If it disappears, it disappears only to reappear on reconversion. The mark of caste does not seem to really disappear even after some generations after conversion. In Andhra Pradesh and in Tamil Nadu there are several thousands of Christian families whose forefathers became Christians and who though they profess the Christian religion, nonetheless, observe the practice of caste. There are Christian Reddys, Christian Kammas, Christian Nadars, Christian Adi-Andhras, Christian Adi-Dravidas and so on. The practice of their caste is so rigorous that there are intermarriages with Hindus of the same caste but not with Christian of another caste. Now if such a Christian becomes a Hindu, surely he will revert to his original caste, if he had lost it at all. In fact, this process goes on continuously in India and generation by generation of lost sheep appear to return to the caste fold and are once again assimilated in that fold. This appears to be particularly so in the case of members of the Scheduled Castes, who embrace other religions in their quest for liberation, but return to their old religion on finding that their disabilities have clung to them with great tenacity.

The Supreme Court of India in the case of *Soosai* v. *Union of India and others,* 1985 (supp) SCC 590 while holding that, in principle, Scheduled Castes, converting to Christianity may continue to be regarded as Scheduled Castes, provided it can be shown that their social and economic disabilities persist, held that in that case, no material had been produced before the Court to show that in fact this is the case in paragraph 8. The Court said that "To establish that paragraph 3 of the Constitution (Scheduled Caste) Order, 1950, discriminates against Christian members of the enumerated castes it must be shown that they suffer from a comparable depth of social and economic disabilities and cultural and educational backwardness and similar levels of degradation within the Christian community necessitating intervention by the state under the provisions of the Constitution. It is not sufficient to show that they suffer from a comparable depth of social and economic disabilities and cultural and educational backwardness and similar levels of degradation within the Christian community necessitating intervention by the state under the provisions of the Constitution. It is not sufficient to show the same caste continues after conversion. It is necessary to establish further that the disabilities and handicaps suffered from such caste membership in the social order of its origin – Hinduism continues in their oppressive severity in the new environment of a different religious community. References have been made in the material before us in the most cursory manner to the character and incidents of the castes within the Christian fold, but no authoritative and detailed studies dealing with the present conditions of Christian society have been placed on the record in this case. It is, therefore, not possible to say that the President acted arbitrarily in the exercise of his judgment in enacting paragraph 3 of the Constitution (Scheduled Castes) Order, 1950. It is now well established that when a violation of Article 14 or any of its related provisions is alleged, the burden rests on the petitioner to establish by clear and cogent evidence that the state has been guilty of arbitrary discrimination."

There is another important judgment on the subject. It is pertinent to note that the Hon'ble Supreme Court in its recent Judgment in the case of *State of Kerala and another* v. *Chandra Mohan,* (2004) 3 SCC 429 para 18 said that "upon conversion a person may be governed by a different law than the law governing the community to which he originally belonged but that would not mean that notwithstanding such conversion he may not continue to be member of the Tribe". Further, in para 20, the Hon'ble Supreme Court is of opinion that "although as a broad proposition of law it cannot be accepted that merely by change of religion person ceases to be a member thereof or not must be determined by the appropriate court as such a question would depend upon the facts of each case. In such a situation, it has to be established that a person who has embraced another religion is still suffering from social disability and also following the customs and tradition of the community which he earlier belonged to".

The Current Trend and Justification for Reservation

In Chapter 3 of the Annual Report 2002-2003 issued by the Ministry of Social Justice and Empowerment, Government of India, the Ministry has implemented various schemes for the development of Scheduled Castes as the scheme of 'Post Matric Scholarships' for SC students for their economic development. National Scheduled Castes Finance and Development Corporation (NSFDC), National Safai Karamchari Finance and Development Corporation (NSKFDC), and State Scheduled Caste Development Corporation are playing a key role at national and state level. Dr. Ambedkar National Scholarship Scheme for meritorious students belonging to SC/ST has been initiated from 2003 with the objective of recognizing, promoting and assisting meritorious students for pursuing higher studies; there is centrally sponsored scheme of hostels for SC boys and girls and many others. Thus, as Scheduled Castes converts to Islam and Christianity are not considered as Scheduled Castes they could not avail those non-statutory benefits, which are implemented for the welfare of Scheduled Castes. Thus, there is no legal rationale to discriminate Scheduled Castes students and non-Hindu Scheduled Castes students.

There are some reports, which have found that caste system is prevailing even amongst the Christian and Muslims. In the case of *Indira Sawhney and others* v. *Union of India,* SCR 2 (supp) 1992 454, the Hon'ble Supreme Court in its majority judgment has said in para 17 that "The Commission next deals with OBCs among non-Hindu communities. In paragraphs 12, 11 to 12.16, the Commission refers to the fact that even among Christians, Muslims and Sikh religions which do not recognize caste, the caste system is prevailing though without religious sanction. After giving a good deal of thought to several difficulties in the way of identifying OBCs among non-Hindus, the Commission says, it has evolved a rough and ready criteria, viz., (1) all untouchables covered by any non-Hindu religion and (2) which are known by the name of their traditional hereditary occupation and whose Hindu counterparts have been included in the list of Hindu OBCs ought to be treated socially and educationally backward communities". In para 81, the Hon'ble Supreme Court says that "the Constitution was meant for the entire country and for all time to come. Non-Hindu religions like Islam, Christianity and Sikh do not recognize caste as such though, as pointed out hereinbefore, castes did exist even among these religions to a varying degree. Further, a Constitution is supposed to be a permanent document expected to last several centuries. It must surely have been envisaged that in future many classes may spring up answering the test of backwardness, requiring the protection of Article 16(4). In para 83, the Court says, "Any authority entrusted with the task of identifying backward classes may well start with the castes. It can take caste "A", apply the criteria of backwardness evolved by it to that caste and determine whether it qualifies as a backward class or not. If it does qualify, what emerges is a backward class, for the purposes of clause (4) of Article 16. The concept of caste in this behalf is not confined to castes among Hindus. It extends to castes, wherever they obtain as a fact, irrespective of religious sanction for such practice.

A Note dated 6 March, 96, prepared for the Cabinet by the Ministry of Welfare, Government of India has stated that if reservation is granted to new Dalit Christians, it will be difficult to refuse a similar demand by the Muslims. The Note has referred to 1983 report on minorities by the High Power Panel on minorities, SC and ST and other weaker sections which said "As Scheduled Castes converted to other religious also continue to suffer from the same social and educational backwardness, we recommended that the Presidential Order of 1950 be suitably amended to include all Scheduled Caste converts irrespective of the religion of their conversation so as to make eligible for all these concessions". The National Commission for Minorities has also recently recommended that all benefits available to Scheduled Castes be extended to all converts from the Scheduled Castes to Christianity and Islam. In the context of these recommendations, which apply not only to Christian converts but also to those Scheduled Caste persons who have converted to other religions, dispensation in favour of Christians alone may be open to challenge on the grounds of discrimination. The Note further says, "similar demands from other religious communities will intensify". In fact, representations have already been received by the Welfare Ministry for the inclusion of Muslim *Khatika* and *Mehtars* in the list of Scheduled Castes. In the context of reported moves to recognize Scheduled Caste Christian converts as Scheduled Castes, some members of Parliament have also written letters and tabled Questions in Parliament recently regarding a similar dispensation for Muslims of Scheduled Castes origin, or to remove altogether the nexus between religion and membership of Scheduled Castes in the existing Presidential Orders.

There are other reports also in favour of this. Various commissions appointed by the government have also recommended reservation for Scheduled Caste converts to religions other than Hinduism. The Central government appointed the First Backward Classes Commission under Article 340 of the Constitution of India on 29 January 1953. The Commission also known as Kaka Kalelkar Commission was required "to investigate the conditions of Socially and educationally backward classes within the territory of India and the difficulties under which they labour and to make recommendations as to the steps that should be taken by the Union or any state to remove difficulties and to improve their conditions". The Commission submitted its report on 30 March, 1955. In paragraph 5 of Chapter 4 it says, "Christianity has consistently refused to recognize caste. Taboo on inter-marriage, inter-dinning and widow marriages are systematically opposed in Christian Society. There is no segregation of communities as such amongst them. And yet in practice we found that segregation of converts from Scheduled Castes was not successfully overcome in certain parts of South India. We were informed that this segregation has spread even beyond the secular side of life and sometimes Harijan converts were not allowed to pray together with the upper class Christians. We were told that in some places in the South these classes are forced to have a separate cemetery for their dead". Further, para 9 says "The state should devise ways and means of helping the backward amongst the advanced communities of Christians and Muslims without forcing them to prove that caste is recognized and casteism is on the increase in their own fold. State help based on communal considerations is never without its dangers. We have accepted it as a necessity in counteracting an age-old evil. We recommend with all the emphasis that we can command that help on communal basis should not be a permanent feature". However, the Central government did not accept that report and put it in the cold storage.

The President of India by an order, in the year 1979, under Article 340 appointed the Second Backward Classes Commission also popularly known as Mandal Commission to investigate the conditions of socially and educationally backward classes within the territory of India. This Commission submitted its report on 31 December 1980. In para 10.36, it states "Prof. Madhu Dandavate stated that conversion from the faith to another did not change the socio-economic status of a person. It was, therefore, desirable that converts from Scheduled Castes to Buddhism, Christianity, etc., should be treated as Scheduled Castes. But until this change was brought about by legislation, all such converts should be listed as OBCs". In para 12.11, the report goes no to say, "There is no doubt that social and educational backwardness among non-Hindu communities is more or less of the same order among Hindu communities. Though caste system is peculiar to Hindu Society, yet, in actual practice, it also pervades the non-Hindu communities in India in varying degree". On the basis of this report, the reservation is given to socially and educationally backward classes in services under the Government of India.

The report of the National Commission for Minorities is important in this respect. The Commission in its Third Annual Report 1980 has said on page no. 31 that "the Commission has prima facie felt that since the Christians, Muslims and Buddhists of Scheduled Caste origin continue to suffer from social and economic disabilities even after their conversion, there should be no objection to their availing of the concessions admissible to them before their conversion. The Commission, however, proposes to study this subject in-depth before submitting its considered views on the subject".

The following judgments justify the demand that Christian and Muslim SCs be given constitutional reservation:

1. *AIR 1952 Madras 474*: Instances can be found in which in spite of conversion from Hinduism, the caste distinctions might continue. This is somewhat analogous to cases in which even after conversion, certain families and groups continue to be governed by the law by which they were governed before

they became converts. (*G. Michael* v. S. *Venkateswaran*, AIR 1952 Madras 474).

2. *AIR 1976 SC 1904*: "Now, before we proceed to consider this contention, it is necessary to point out that there is no absolute rule application in all cases that whenever a member of a caste is converted from Hinduism to Christianity, he loses his membership of the caste" (*The Principal, Gaunter Medical College* v. *Y. Mohan Rao*).
3. *AIR 1984 SC 411*: "The mark of caste does not seem to really disappear even after some generations after conversion. In Andhra Pradesh and in Tamil Nadu, there are several thousands of Christian families whose forefathers became Christians and who though they profess the Christian Kammas, Christian Madras, Christian Adi-Dravidas and so on. The practice of their caste is so rigorous that there are inter-marriages with Hindus of the same caste but not with Christian of another caste" (*S. Ambalgan* v. *Devrayan and, Ors*.).
4. *Supreme Court AIR 1992*: 8 out of 9 Judges said "Change of religion does not change caste". Supreme Court through the 9 Bench Judge Minority Judgment in the Mandal Case (November 30,1992 *Judgement Today*) categorically established the fact that change of religion does not change caste and disabilities of the Scheduled Castes converted to Christian continue after conversion on par with other Scheduled Castes in other religions. This view is supported by 8 of the 9 Judges.
5. Mahatma Gandhi, the Father of Nation, wrote: "Whether the Harijan is nominally a Christian, Muslim or Hindu and now Sikh, he is still a Harijan. He cannot change his spots inherited from so called Hinduism. He may change his garb and call himself a Catholic Harijan or a Muslim Harijan or Neo-Muslim or Noe-Sikh, his untouchability will haunt him during his life time". (*The Harijan* dated 26 December, 36).

There are certain other reports which are important:

Mandal Commission Report

1. *10.36*: Prof Madhu Dandavate stated that conversion from one faith to another did not change the socio-economic status of a person. It was, therefore, desirable that convert from

Scheduled Castes to Buddhism, Christianity, etc., be treated as Scheduled Castes.

2. *Para 25:* "The evidence is that the degree of segregation of the new convert from Scheduled Caste is almost as high as before his conversion. We are convinced that in practice converts from Scheduled Castes are treated as socially backward".

Minorities Commission

1. The Commission has prima facie felt that since the Christians, Muslims and Buddhists of Scheduled Castes origin continue to suffer from social and economic disabilities even after their conversion, there should be no objection to their availing of the concessions admissible to them before conversion (Third Annual Report of the Minorities Commission, New Delhi, 1980, page 31).

   The main point before the Commission is that Scheduled Castes do not find liberation from the social and economic disabilities on their conversion to Christianity, Islam or Buddhism. They continue to suffer from caste and class prejudices. Theirs converts remain unrepresented in Legislative and other bodies and their voice is never heard and thus their sufferings are not mitigated. The Kaka Kalekar Commission appointed by the Government of India, Nettoor Commission and Kumara Pillai Commission of Kerala and the Backward Classes Commission of Andhra Pradesh also recognized the fact and recommended in their reports that such converts should be regarded as members of Scheduled Castes for all practical purposes despite their conversion (Fourth Annual Report, The Minorities Commission 1981-82, New Delhi, para 55).

Ground Reality Qua Neo Muslims:

The first and the best equality principle can be traced in the following verse of *Quran* which was revealed more than fourteen hundred years ago:

"O mankind: we have created you from a single pair of male and female and made you into nations and tribes: that you know each other (not that you may discriminate and despite each other)."

> "Verify, the most honoured of you in the sight of Allah is he who is the most righteous of you. And Allah had full knowledge and is well acquainted (with all things)".
>
> "O mankind be careful for your duty to your Lord who created you from a single being and from the same created your mate and from these he caused to spread countless men and women, and be careful of your duty and be mindful of your ties of kinship, for God is ever watchful over you".
>
> The Holy Prophet thus declared at the last sermon. "No Arab has superiority over a non Arab and no non-Arab has a superiority over an Arab. No blackman has superiority over a red and no red over a black. All are born of Adam and Adam was born of the earth".

In another Hadith (tradition of the prophet), the prophet of Islam declared: "I bear witness that all human beings are brothers to each other". This concept of equality found expression much later in Article 1 of the UN Declaration of Human Rights (UNDHR), 1948, which declared "all human beings are born free and equal in dignity and right".

As per the *Quran* and traditions of the Prophet, there is no caste system in Islam. The best person is one who's conduct is good, who is virtuous and righteous and not one who is rich or belongs to a noble or higher caste. But the ground reality in the Indian context tells a different story. Scripturally, Islam does not recognize caste system but practically there exists caste system. Except congregational worships like Namaz and Haj, Muslim society too is caste ridden.

A new Muslim, even if virtuous and righteous, does not enjoy the social respectability which other Muslims do. The same social stigma of Scheduled Caste is attached to him even after his embracement of Islam, albeit the fact that he can go to any mosque and perform Namaz and dine with other Muslims of the so-called high or low caste.

After conversion, they lose the constitutional favour of reservations for the Scheduled Castes and still face the social despisement. Thus, after conversion, their social status remains almost the same and they are loser qua-reservations. They hardly gain anything on the social front; rather, they lose on the economic front which is anti-constitutional, and anti-equality.

Conclusion

The Constitution (Scheduled Castes) Order, 1950, as amended from time to time, is certainly discriminatory and violative of Articles 14, 15, 16 and 25. There cannot be religion-based reservation. The Scheduled Castes belonging to various religions cannot be discriminated. After conversion, there is hardly any change in their social status. They lose the job, which they have got by virtue of reservation. The social stigma attached to them by virtue of being born Scheduled Castes is carried wherever they go. The reservation for the Scheduled Castes should not be based on religions or on the fact that after conversion the oppression or the despisement continues with the same severity but should be based on the fact they were born as a Scheduled Castes. Last but not the least, let us wait for the Supreme Court verdict.

19

Article 22 and Requirements of Human Rights Standards under the International Covenant on Civil and Political Rights

MOHAMMAD MOMIN

What is Understood by Human Rights?

Human Rights is a package of "Rights that belong to an individual as a consequence of being human".[1] Broadly speaking human rights may be regarded as those fundamental and inalienable rights which are essential for the life of man, and are possessed by every human being cutting across his or her nationality, race, religion, sex, etc., simply because he/she is a human being. They are thus those rights which are inherent in man's nature and without which he cannot live. Human rights help us to fully develop our potentialities, human qualities, intelligence, talent and conscience. Also, they satisfy man's physical, spiritual and other needs.[2] In other words, human rights are those rights which make a man human as such and based on mankind's increasing demand for a life in which the inherent dignity and worth of each human being will receive respect and protection.

The history of man reveals that man has constantly been endeavouring to seek peace and justice through fundamental human rights which are as old as human civilization. They existed before and after Sophocles, Buddha, Christ and Muhammad *(Pbuh)*. Hinduism preaches due recognition of the dignity of man by giving importance to human soul. Buddhism and Jainism give prime importance to salvation of man.[3] Christianity upholds fatherhood of god, while Islam highlights brotherhood of man. All those ideals of great religions are meant for advancement of man. The humanist tradition of the renaissance and struggle of man for freedom and socio-economic justice is still going on in different parts of the world. The term Human Rights came into wide use after Second World War replacing the earlier phrase 'Natural Rights' which had been associated with the Greco-Roman concept of Natural Law since the end of Middle Ages. As understood today human rights refer to wide variety of values and capabilities reflecting the diversity of human circumstances and history. They are conceived of as universal, applying to all human beings everywhere, and as fundamental, referring to essential of basic human needs, which cannot be taken away by any legislature. Human rights have been classified historically in terms of the notions of three generations of human rights. The first generation of civil and political rights, associated with Enlightenment and English, American and French Revolutions, includes the right to life and liberty and the rights to freedom of speech and worship. The second generation – economic, social and cultural rights, associated with the revolts against the 19th century unregulated capitalism, includes the right to work and the right to education. Finally, the third generation of human rights, which are concerned with the political and economic aspirations of the post-war decolonized third world developing countries includes the collective rights to political self-determination and economic development. The third generation of human rights has started its journey since 1970. Following the adoption of the Universal Declaration of Human Rights in 1948 many treaties and agreements for the protection of human rights have come up with tile patronage of United Nations. Human rights appear as Fundamental Rights and Directive Principle of State Policy (DPSP) in Part III and Part IV of our

Constitution. Fundamental Rights incorporated in Part III of the Constitution are enforceable in the court of law while DPSP in Part IV are not enforceable. This part of our Constitution, i.e., Fundamental Rights Chapter in which Article 22 finds a place includes a number of provisions of the International Covenant on Civil and Political Rights (ICCPR), 1966.

With the world beginning to take the shape of a global village economically, commercially and politically, there is a growing demand from the judicial conscience, globally, that national law must be interpreted through the principle of international law. Otherwise, the preamble of the UN Charter which reaffirms faith in Fundamental Human Rights would be a "verbal vanity, semantic futility and promise of unreality,[4] Due to increasing international awareness and enterprising national judicial system, states are becoming responsible for promoting human rights. In this regard mention may be made of the *George Varghese Case*[5] where the Supreme Court of India read down the proviso to Section 51 of Civil Procedure Code by importing the International Covenant of Civil and Political Rights (ICCPR), which is a matter of great importance in a rapidly changing world. This instance obviously affords the scope and relevance of the present study: "Article 22 and Requirements of Human Rights Standards under the International Covenant on Civil and Political Rights".

Safeguards Against Arbitrary Arrest and Detention

Rights of Suspects/Accused Persons

Under the International Law Regime

The year 1946 saw the United Nations being born on the ruins of the League of Nations and more, on the holocaust let loose by world wars on their trails threatening existence of the global human civilization and the values associated with the concept of human rights hitherto cherished and nurtured by man. That is why, soon after its formation, there was a spate in the process of law-making in the international arena that culminated into adoption of a series of international declarations, conventions and covenants. Their sole object was to define, protect, enforce and ensure the basic human rights to be made available at the doorsteps of every man and woman on the planet. Simultaneously, the most sensitive, yet most neglected hitherto issues such as rights of prisoners, suspects or accused which were either ignored or received bottom-rock priority, too, attracted rapt attention of the world community. The relevant instruments were drawn up to provide safeguard and security to the victims. Therefore, before we engage ourselves to the study of their rights under the Indian national law regime it would be befitting to refer to certain important provisions of these instruments according the victims their rights:[6]

1. Universal Declaration of Human Rights (1948) (Arts. 1, 3, 5, 6, 8, 9, 10 and 11).
2. International Covenant on Civil and Political Rights (1966), i.e., ICCPR Arts. 6(l), 7, 9, 10 and 14-16.
3. Optional Protocol to the International Covenant on Civil and Political Rights (1976), Arts. 2-5.
4. Standard Minimum Rules for Treatments of Prisoners adopted by first UN Congress on the Prevention of Crime and Treatment of Offenders (1955) (Rule no. 30-34).
5. Draft Principles on Freedom from Arbitrary Arrest, Detention and Exile (1963) Arts. 10, 22(2), 24 and 26.
6. Declaration on Protection of All Persons from being subjected to Torture and other Cruel Inhuman or Degrading Treatment or Punishment (1975).
7. Code of Conduct for Law Enforcement Officials (1979), Arts. 2, 3 and 5, 6.
8. Convention against Torture and Other Cruel, Inhuman or Degrading Treatment or Punishment (1984).
9. Body of Principles for Protection of All Persons under any Form of Detention or Imprisonment (1988).
10. Declaration on Protection of Persons for Enforced Disappearance (1992).
11. Basic Principles for Treatment of Prisoners (1990).
12. Principles of Medical Ethics Relevant to the Role of Health Personnel, Particularly Physicians in the Protection of Prisoners and Detainees against Torture and other Cruel, Inhuman or Degrading Treatment or Punishment (1982).

13. Safeguards Guaranteeing Protection of Rights of those Facing the Death Penalty (1984).
14. United Nations Standard Minimum Rules for the Administration of Juvenile Justice ("Beijing Rules", 1985)
15. Declaration of Basic Principles of Justice for Victims of Crime and Abuse of Power (1985).
16. Basic Principles on the Independence of Judiciary (1985).

It may be noted that during the years following our independence, India had participated in the drafting or adoption of some 70 international instruments regarding human rights under the aegis of UN, and it is a state party to as many as 17 human rights treaties elaborated by the World Organization.[7] So far as the catalogue of instruments enumerated above is concerned, except for the Optional Protocol (1976) and Anti-Torture Convention (1987), India has signed and ratified them all. It would be, therefore, in the fitness of things that these rights be seen incorporated in our national laws, and duly enforced.[8]

Under Indian Law: Constitution of India

According to Article 21 no person can be deprived of his life or personal liberty except according to procedure established by law. Article 22 provides those procedural requirements that must be adopted and included in any procedure enacted by the legislature. If these procedural requirements were not complied with, it would then be deprivation of personal liberty. Thus, Article 22 prescribes the minimum procedural requirements in the relevant situation. Article 22 deals with two separate matters:

1. Persons arrested under ordinary laws of crime, and
2. Persons detained under law of preventive detention on suspicion.

At one time it was thought that Article 22 was a complete code in regard to laws providing for preventive detention. After *R.C. Cooper*[9] and *Maneka Gandhi*[10] the court has applied it in relation to Article 21 also. Accordingly, a law relating to preventive detention must now satisfy not only requirements of Article 22 but also the requirements of Article 21 of the Constitution. In other words the procedure prescribed under preventive detention law must be reasonable, just and fair under Articles 14, 19 and 21 of the Constitution.

Rights of Arrested Person under Ordinary Laws

Clause (1) and (2) of Article 22 guarantee four rights to persons who are arrested for any offence under an ordinary law:

(i) Right to be informed "as soon as may be" of ground of arrest [Article 22(1)]. It is also available under Article 9(2) of ICCPR.
(ii) The right to consult and to be represented by a lawyer of his own choice [Article 22(l)]. The right also finds mention under Article 3(b) of ICCPR.
(iii) The right to be produced before a Magistrate within 24 hours, [Article 22(2)]. The right is also incorporated under Article 9(3) of ICCPR.
(iv) The freedom from detention beyond the said period except by the order of the Magistrate [Article 22(2)].

Right to be informed the ground of arrest

This right gives the arrested person an opportunity to apply for bail or to file a writ petition for his release, or to prepare any other defence in time.

This is also a very important right of the accused person under the ICCPR [Article 14(3)(a)]. In *Jaginder Kumar* v. *State of UP,*[11] the Supreme Court has laid down guidelines governing arrest of a person during investigation. This is intended to strike a balance between the need of the police on one hand and protection of human rights of citizens from oppression and injustice at the hands of law enforcing agencies. The Court has held that the person is not liable to arrest merely of suspicion of complicity in an offence. There must be some reasonable justification for effecting the arrest.

Right to consult a legal practitioner

Article 22(l) of the Constitution of India confers on the arrested person the right to consult a legal practitioner of his own choice and to be defended by him. The ICCPR also provides the same right to the accused person under Article 3(b). This right begins as soon as he is taken into police custody in relation to criminal or quasi-criminal proceedings. Later the Supreme Court extended the operation of this right "to any accused person under circumstances of near-custodial interrogation" *(Nandini Satpati).*[12] The court held that while undergoing interrogation in the police custody he has a right to have his lawyer by his side. But in the Indian Constitution there is no specific provision that provides a right to free legal aid to the accused person. In *Janardhan Reddy*[13] (1951) the Supreme Court specifically held that Article 22(l) of the Constitution does not provide accused person the right to legal services of a legal practitioner at the state cost. There is, of course, a Directive Principle of State Policy contained in Article 39 A, which requires the state to provide free legal aid by suitable legislation. However, it is not enforceable in the court of law and therefore, it does not confer a constitutional right to the accused person to secure free legal assistance at the cost of the state. The Supreme Court later replenished these constitutional shortcomings through the creative judicial interpretation of Article 22 in a number of cases. In *Hussainara Khatun*[14] the Supreme Court thus spelt out the right to legal aid to the poor accused person from the language of the Article 21, drawing inspiration from Article 14(3)(d) of ICCPR.

However, with all these constitutional provisions and ruling of the Supreme Court despite, the police usually refuses to allow a lawyer to meet and interview the accused person in custody unless the court intervenes on his behalf

Right to be produced before the Magistrate within 24 hours of arrest [Article 22(2)]

This right is constitutionally guaranteed by Article 22(2). ICCPR furnishes the provision under Article 14(3)(c). In addition to the furnishing of the grounds of arrest, the arrested person must be produced before the Magistrate within 24 hours of his arrest. It can be extended beyond 24 hours only under a judicial custody. It affords a possibility for immediate release in case the arrest is not justified. The purpose of this provision is to get the legality of the arrest and detention judicially examined without unnecessary delay, and to put a check on the police the power to arrest. Being constitutionally guaranteed, the right is inviolable by ordinary legislation.

No detention beyond 24 hours except by Magistrate's order

This means that if there is necessity of detention beyond 24 hours, it is only possible under judicial custody. It also means that if there is failure to produce the arrested person before the nearest Magistrate within 24 hours, it would make the arrest illegal. In *CBI* v. *A.J. Kulkarni*[15] (1992), the Supreme Court pronounced a significant judgment giving a detailed guideline of arrest when investigation cannot be completed within 24 hours. The Judicial Magistrate can authorize the detention of accused either in judicial or police custody from time to time, but the total period of detention cannot exceed 15 days. There can be no detention in police custody after expiry of first 15 days. If the investigation is not completed within 60 or 90 days, the accused has to be released on bail under section 167(2), Cr. P.C. The judgment is welcome. It would save many under-trial prisoners from police atrocities. It would also help speedy investigation.

In this regard, the National Human Rights Commission (NHRC) in its Annual Report, 1999-2000 observes:

> Article 22(l) of the Constitution provides that any person placed under arrest shall be informed of the ground of arrest, and shall not be denied the right to be defended by a lawyer of his choice, and the Section 50 of Cr. P.C., 1973 requires the police officer arresting any person to forthwith communicate to him full particulars of the offence for which he or she is arrested or any other ground of such arrest. *In actual practice, these requirements have been observed more in breach.*[16] Likewise the requirement to produce the arrested person before the court within 24 hours is primarily a statutory requirement under the Constitution [Article 22(2)] and Cr. P.C. Section 57. But this, too, is not strictly observed.[17]

The Report also states:

> "The Commission has continued to receive a large number of complaints pertaining to Human Rights violations resulting from abuse of police powers, particularly, in respect of arrest and

detention" and "alleged acts of commission and omission on the part of the police in course of investigation".[18]

Person Detained under Law of Preventive Detention on Suspicion

Sometimes, the country is faced with certain dangers. To safeguard the interest of the country or its parts, the Central government is entitled to enact preventive detention laws, like Preventive Detention Act, Terrorist and Disruptive Activities (Preventive) Act 1987 (TADA) etc. Article 22 imposes certain rights to the person arrested under preventive detention laws. They are summarized as follows:

(a) Article 22(4) provides that no person shall be detained for a longer period than 3 months. This period of three months may be extended if an Advisory Board has reported before the expiration of the said period of 3 months that there is in its opinion sufficient cause of such detention.
(b) The person detained under any preventive detention laws shall be informed the grounds on which he is arrested and detained [Article 22(5)].

Incidence of Detention: Flagrant Violation of Human Rights

Custodial Torture

Torture is not prohibited by our Constitution. Ministry of Home Affairs has claimed that Indian laws provide adequate safeguard for protection of human rights against police brutality and torture. However, our police system is not improved and not geared up as required by various international instruments of human rights. With accumulated powers and political reasons, our police system has become more and more cruel. The news of custodial deaths and various types of systematic, organized and institutionalized tortures have become common nowadays in police culture. According to one study an expert from a "super-intelligence force"[19] was called upon to train the policemen in the latest method of torture during 1970-71. Senior police officers, bureaucrats, politicians justify it as a necessary evil to curb growing crime rate in society. When it comes to women, they are the worst victims. They face additional and unspeakable mode of torture. *Mathura Rape Case*[19A] is a case in point. Definition of torture given by UN Convention against torture and other cruel, inhuman or degrading treatment or punishment has been practically seen in our country. Here, mention may be made of a report about torture of political prisoners in India submitted before Sub-committee on International Relations: US House of Representative, 1976. The report points out 14 modes of unspeakable torture. The Amnesty International Report mentions the harrowing incident of *Bhagalpur Blinding Case.*

Custodial Death

According to the National Human Rights Commission Report, 2002-2003 (NHRC), since the Commission was established in October 1993 it has, until now, received a total of 8,596 reports of death that occurred in police and judicial custody. An analysis of 6,552 of such cases indicates that some 80 per cent of death that occurred in judicial custody was attributed to causes such as illness and old age. The remaining 20 per cent accounted for variety of reasons such as illness aggravated by medical negligence, violence between prisoners or suicide.[20]

In the year 2002-03 the figure reported to the Commission were 183 deaths in police custody and 1,157 deaths in judicial custody making a total of 1,340 deaths in custody as against a total of 1,307 such deaths in 2001-02 of which 165 occurred in police custody, 1,140 in judicial custody and 2 in custody of para-military forces.[21] Earlier during 1997-98 the total number of deaths reported before the Commission were 1,012 of which 193 accounted for police custody and 819 for judicial custody.[22] The year 1998-1999 records a total of 1,297 custodial deaths which included 183 deaths in police custody and 1,114 deaths in judicial custody. The Commission registered, in 1999-2000 Report, a total of 1,093 deaths, break-up of which showed 177 under the head of police custody and 916 under judicial custody.[23]

The currently available Report by the Commission shows that the undertrial (U/T) prisoners constituted 75.09 per cent of the total prison population for the country as a whole, till 31 December, 2001. As of 30 June, 2002 the figure stood at 74.06 per cent. It is noteworthy that the undertrial prisoners constituted more than 80 per cent of the prison population in ten states/union territories.[24] It may be noted in passing that during 2002-2003, the Commission was informed of 83 cases of police encounter by authority of various states of which Uttar Pradesh (41) topped the list followed by Maharashtra (10) and Andhra Pradesh (7).[25]

Jail Scenario: a live inferno on earth

One of the important functions of NHRC under Section 12(c) of the Protection of Human Rights Act, 1993 is "to visit any jail under the control of state government. Accordingly NHRC paid visits to nearly a score of jails which included among most distinguished ones such as Tihar (Delhi), Lucknow, Jaipur, Sabarmati Central Jail, Ahmedabad, etc. All of them were conspicuously characterized by 'overcrowding', inadequacy of jail staff, allegation of harassment, torture, poor quality of rations, non-supply of books, periodicals and non-existence of grievance redressal systems..." A few lines from the NHRC's reports on visits to the District Jail, Guwahati (10 November, 1999) and Central Jail, Shillong (12 November, 1999) may well bring home the point:

[In the Gauhati District Jail, it was]

> "found that the overall conditions of the jail were pathetic and that the inmates were living in conditions that gravely affected their dignity and their physical and mental well-being. As against the authorized capacity of 507 prisoners, 780 were lodged in the jail, 90 per cent of whom were under-trials. Toilet facilities were grossly inadequate and in a deplorable condition. There were garbage piles in the jail premises and stagnant water as well. The kitchens and food containers were unclean, and food served was unhygienic. The prisoners complained that the jail doctors were most unsympathetic, and would not prescribe medicines even from the few that were available in the jail dispensary. The X-ray machine was out of order. Prisoners had scabies and other skin diseases owing to unhygienic living conditions and lack of medical care".[26]

Regarding the prisoners' conditions at the Central Jail, Shillong, the Commission observed:

> "Housed in a small premises, there were 374 inmates against an authorized capacity of 150 inmates. The jail had only three lavatories" (with) "an acute shortage of water for drinking, bathing and washing purposes. The food served to the inmates was poor in quality and inadequate in quantity. The supply of medicine was poor and the two blankets provided to each inmate in cold climate of Shillong, were in poor shape."

> The Commission continues:

> "what was most shocking was the presence of a girl child of about 10-11 years of age, who was an under-trial prisoner. Under the provisions of the Juvenile Justice Act, no child can be kept in a regular jail. The jail houses many under-trial prisoners who had been languishing there for periods ranging from 1-9 years. Some of the prisoners had not been produced in the court even once over periods ranging from 1-3 years. According to jail authorities the under-trials were not produced in court due to lack of escort facilities."[27]

Treatment to Foreigners at Detention Centre

The NHRC received a number of complaints on the pitiable conditions existing in Lampur Sewa Sadan, Delhi where foreigners are temporarily detained when arrested for travelling in India on forged passport, etc. Accordingly the Commission visited the centre in July, 1999 and submitted that "the coordination and supervision at the ground level were found to be far from satisfactory. The detained foreigners made requests for regular visits by medical officers. They also sought telephone facilities, separate arrangement of food and better accommodation."[28]

Overcrowding Prisons

NHRC holds an analysis of prison overcrowding till 31 December, 2001. According to the analysis, total prison population of the country was 3,00,811 indicating an overcrowding of 32.33 per cent against the authorized capacity of 2,27,313. Overcrowding ranges from 39 per cent to 189 per cent. Delhi records an overcrowding of 189 per cent followed by Jharkhand (183%), Haryana (158%), Chhattisgarh (114%) and U.P. (90%).[29]

Thus, the Commission in its various reports had brought into sharp focus both the overt and covert anomalies and aberration of the prison administration throughout India. Some of the revelations made were fairly disconcerting. Even if it is assumed that the government has woken up to the problems, the remedial measures adopted till date fell woefully short of the requirements demanded by the standards of Articles 21 and 22 of the Constitution of India, far to speak of complying the norms set by any international instrument including ICCPR. The West Bengal Human Rights Commission while assessing the status of jails has aptly remarked, "The problems plaguing the system were entrenched deep into the structure and were no longer amenable to cosmetic treatment."[30]

No Incompatibility between the Right of the State and the Right of Man in the Jurisprudence of the New World Order: The Rule of Law must be Supportive of Rule of Life

Rights and liberties are not absolute. Unrestrained liberty would lead to anarchy and disorder. Man can enjoy rights, as long as there exists order in society, That is why all rights are subject to reasonable restrictions such as public health, peace and order, decency and national security. Such reasonable ground of restriction on individuals' Fundamental Rights find place in almost all constitutions of the world including Indian Constitution. But there has been numerous assaults on people's rights and liberties in the name of national security. Such assaults include confiscation and nationalization of private property, surveillance through wire-tapping and mail-opening, arbitrary search and seizure, arbitrary arrests and detention, denial of appeal to judiciary, resort to torture, political internment, concentration camps, and even liquidation of suspects/accused in custody, so on and so forth. Thus, it looks that there exists antagonism between right of man and national security. But in fact there is a close relationship between them. Question is: how far individual's right can be sacrificed to promote national security when human rights cannot be exercised without national security? This question cannot be answered unless concept of national security can be properly understood, and is distinguished from security of regime/individual. Like individual, every state has the inherent right of self-defence. This right is available to the state when its existence is threatened. That is why the state may exercise abnormal powers during emergency and deviate from its normal obligation to protect and enforce human rights of its citizens. This right of derogation of state is acknowledged under any international instruments of human rights, including ICCPR [Article 4(l)], European Convention of Human Rights [Article 15(l)], American Convention of Human Rights. But as Human Rights and Fundamental Freedoms are not absolute, the right of derogation of the state is not also absolute one. There are certain rights, which must remain unaffected, even during the public emergency. Emergency or no emergency these rights cannot be suspended. These 'non-derogable' rights – right to life, and freedom from torture being two of them, find place in international human rights instruments including ICCPR [Article 4(2)], European Convention of Human Rights [Article 15(2)] and American Convention of Human Rights [Article 27(2)]. Considering the gravity of the situation Article 4 of ICCPR also demands that:

> "Any state party to the present covenant availing itself of the right of derogation shall immediately inform the other state parties to ICCPR through intermediary of the Secretary General of the United Nations, of the provisions from which it has derogated and of the reasons by which it was actuated. Further communication shall be made through the same intermediary on the date on which it terminates such derogation."

The state can exercise the right of derogation to meet the threat to national security. But quite often national security is falsely projected to be identical with an individual's or regime's security, and states often deviate from their obligation vis-à-vis human rights to ensure the individuals' or regimes' security. The International Commission of Jurists (ICJ) rightly notes:[31]

> "There is a tendency for some governments to regard any challenge to their authority as a threat to 'the life of the nation'. This is particularly true of regimes which do not provide any lawful means for the transfer of political power and which in consequence are inclined to regard any criticism of the government as an act subversive of political order."

The study continues:

> "Having dismantled the legal machinery for the protection of the citizens, they (individual/and regimes) frequently permit their security forces to abuse the 'non-derogable' rights, including the right to life or freedom from the torture or other cruel, inhuman, or degrading treatment or punishment. These results are such as inhuman practices of anonymous arrests, secret detentions, disappearances, extrajudicial killings and systematic practices of torture."

Therefore, one should be cautious. Individual interest should not be confused with national interest We need to identify the real agenda behind the use of force. Is it personal vendetta or is it designed to restore and maintain order, so that the citizens not challenging the state can continue a peaceable life. Force resorted to for the latter purpose needs to be judged differently from force used for the former.[32] The international law regime within its confines allows the derogation of exercisable rights for national safeguards when the situation so demands. Care should always be taken to harmonize the two apparently conflicting interests for effective functioning of the state. However, under no-circumstances, the national security shall be set up as a plea for repudiation of basic and non-derogable rights such as right to life and freedom from torture by state machinery. No non-derogable rights be permitted to derogate even in the worst of emergency.

The Constitution's 59th Amendment deals that under the state's security objectives a person can be imprisoned in the national interest. However, the modern concept of human rights, which incorporates natural law theories, is the concept of constitutionalism, which assumes that man has given up to organized government only a restricted power for interference with his rights.[33] In the words of Justice Krishna Iyer "the jurisprudence of Emergency in a restless society cannot be hyper-indulgent nor oversensitive *since the rule of law must be supportive of rule of life.* But a living link must exist between the justifications for the limited suppression of human rights and the character of the chaos and the nature of the victims so affected".[34]

The Supreme Court of India: Trends of Judicial Activism Veering Round to ICCPR

It may be submitted that the trends of judicial activism set by the Supreme Court of India in the *Maneka Gandhi Case*[35] has ushered in a concept of new jurisprudence marked by an intense interaction of two sets of legal regimes – Indian National Laws and International Laws of Human Rights. In the process new soul was breathed into Article 21 inducing Article 22 to pave the way for constitutional revolution in the post-Maneka Gandhi era where the Supreme Court steers an activist role. Although Article 21 had not to suffer the scourge of Constitutional Amendments, and still maintains its original pristine form, its meaning and content have undergone a profound transformation thanks to the *Maneka Gandhi Case,* which unveiled a new horizon for the concept of personal liberty. A number of hitherto unknown dimensions of personal liberty could be construed, and a host of unenumerated human rights read into Article 21. Undoubtedly, the Supreme Court had to be prompted by the growing global awareness of human rights to keep pace with changing world order, and drew inspiration from ICCPR and other international human rights instruments. In effect the apex court has contributed a bouquet of flowery 'unenumerated rights' the trace of which can be identified in the scheme of ICCPR. The other fundamental rights which, though unenumerated in Part III of the Constitution but recognized by the court as distinct fundamental rights and enumerated in the International Covenant on Civil and Political Rights (ICCPR) are as follows:

1. Right to travel abroad[36] [Article 12(2) ICCPR].
2. Right to privacy[37] [Article 17(I)ICCPR].
3. Right to speedy trial[38] [Article 9(3) ICCPR].
4. Right to provide legal assistance[39]
5. Right not to be subjected to torture or 'to cruel inhuman or degrading treatment or punishment [Article 7 ICCPR]. This right encompasses certain rights which have been separately recognized by the Supreme Court. These separate rights are:
   (i) Right against solitary confinement,[40]
   (ii) Right against bar fatters,[41]

(iii) Right against handcuffing,[42]
(iv) Right against delayed executions,[43]
(v) Right against public hanging,[44]
(vi) Right against custodial violence.[45]

6. Right not to be imprisoned for inability to fulfil a contractual obligation[46] [Article 11 ICCPR].
7. Right to compensation for unlawful arrest and detention[47] [Article 9(5) ICCPR].
8. Right to human dignity[48] [Article 10(1) ICCPR].

It is to be noted in this context that there is another category of unenumerated rights consisting of those of human rights which are enumerated in ICCPR but are neither enumerated in Indian Constitution as Fundamental Rights nor have yet been recognized as fundamental rights by the Supreme Court.[49] These human rights are those relating to the rights not to be subjected to medical and scientific experimentation (Article 7 ICCPR), the prohibition of death sentence for crimes committed by person below 18 years of age and execution on pregnant women [Article 6(5)], special protection for treatment of juvenile [Article 10(2)(b) and Article 14(4) ICCPR], right of self-determination [Article 1(I)] (India has made reservation about this right) and prohibition of slavery and slave trade under Article 8(l).

It has consistently been recognized by the Supreme Court that the help of ICCPR and for that matter, all other International Conventions on Human Rights which have been signed and ratified by India, can be taken in interpreting constitutional provisions relating to human rights. If there is a conflict between the provision of an international convention and the provision of the Indian Constitution or Indian law, obviously the provision of the Indian Constitution or Indian law shall prevail, But if there is no conflict between the two and the relevant provision (relating to fundamental right) are of wide amplitude to encompass the provision of the international convention relating to human rights, the provisions of international convention can be read into the fundamental rights. This has been held by the Supreme Court in several cases such as *Jolly George Verghees* v. *Bank of Cochin*[50] *(1980), Vishaka* v.

State of Rajasthan[51] *(1997)* and *Appeal Export Promotion Council* v. *A.K. Chopra*[52] *(1999).*

Coming back to the context of unnumerable rights which are only illustrative and not exhaustive in nature, it is submitted that as long as these rights remain as implied rights, they cannot be enjoyed and enforced effectively. In the last 58 years no new fundamental rights has been included in Part III of our Constitution. It is imperative to include all these rights as fundamental rights in Part III of our Constitution.

Conclusion

Preventive detention laws are neither favoured nor found in any of the democratic countries of the world as they are inconsistent with democratic constitution. No country in the world including the USA has made these laws an integral part of the constitution, as has been done in India. Only during the years of hostilities of the First and the Second World Wars, it was resorted by England strictly on temporary basis as war measures. During this time, certain regulations framed under the Defence of Realm Act provided for preventive detention at the satisfaction of the Home Secretary. In *Leversidge* v. *Anderson (1942)*[53] as also in *Rex* v. *Holiday(1917),*[54] the British Court upheld the wartime measures on the ground that personal liberty could be scarified for national success in the war. With the world wars over, they ceased to have effect.

Indian Constitution, however, recognizes preventive detention in normal times also.[55]

The judges and academics treated it as a 'draconian law', 'black law', a "black spot on the Indian Constitution', 'lawless law' and so on. It was always clouded under atmosphere of distrust and mistrust. It generated much heat and excitement both outside and inside the Parliament.

In the 339 years of history of western democracy since the Civil War in Britain, the system has been tried by more than 120 countries, but has taken firm root in barely two dozen of them. Among the 90 nation states that fell in line with the UN after 1951, not even half a dozen survived with impeccable records of unbroken democratic tradition. Even India, which is considered among a few that stand tall, suffers a serious setback during the Emergency when authoritarianism takes over as the norm rather than the exception and correspondingly, the use of force by the state against its citizens has been least bridled.[56]

In India during Emergency, right to life and personal liberty guaranteed in Article 21 of Constitution are flagrantly violated by the state. Even the judiciary seemed to be helpless. It is evident from the case of ADM, Jabalpur v. S. Sukla.[57] In this case, petitions were filed by various persons detained under Section 3(l) of MISA praying for the writ of habeas corpus. However, the Supreme Court observed that no person has *locus standi* to move any writ under Article 226 of the Constitution before the High Court for habeas corpus, or any other writ or order or direction to enforce any right to personal liberty to a person detained under the Act. According to a contemporary Home Ministry Report, nearly 35,000 people (arrests of J & K excluded) arrested under TADA were released since the Act was scrapped in 1995. Of 15,000 odd cases registered under TADA, about 11,000 cases were withdrawn altogether after UF government came to power.[58] The National Police Commission in its Third Report has pointed out that power of arrest is one of the chief sources of corruption in police. According to the Report, nearly 60 per cent of the arrests are either unnecessary or unjustified.[59] It must be noted that preventive detention is not a punitive act and it is not an alternative to criminal trial under the law. It does not empower the authority to punish a person without a trial.[59A]

It is thus imperative to either do away with or introduce reform in respect of some laws and regulations like the Police Act, 1861, a few sections of the Indian Evidence Act, 1872, Jail Manual, and to crown it all, prerogative of 'immunity' extended to the government servants, which are manifestly antique, unfair and human rights unfriendly.

It is said that power corrupts, and absolute power corrupts absolutely. The prevailing concept of 'sovereign immunity', a hangover of the past, exempts the public functionaries from prosecution for any offence committed in course of discharging of their official duties. Under Sections 132 and 197(l) of the Criminal

Procedure Code, when a public servant is accused of any offence alleged to have been committed by him while acting or purporting to act in the discharging of his official duty, no court shall take cognizance of such offence, except with the prior sanction of the government. It provides safeguards to the member of the police force guilty of torture. Likewise, Section 6 of the Armed Forces Special Powers Act, 1983 grants immunity to the members of the security forces for the alleged crime. It simply leaves a precarious imprint on our aggravated records of human rights violation. *Crime in India, 2002* issued by the National Crime Records Bureau, Ministry of Home Affairs very candidly brings out the home truth:

> "Since 1999, an attempt has been made to gather information on details of cases where Human Rights are violated due to police excesses such as 'Illegal Detention', 'Fake Encounters', 'Extortion', 'Torture', etc. During the year, 95 cases Of Human Rights Violation by police were reported throughout the country. For these Human Rights Violation, 59 policemen were chargesheeted, *but none of them was convicted.* Andhra Pradesh reported the maximum 26 (27.6%) of such cases followed by Gujarat 14 (14.7%). No case was reported from any union territories. Out of 95 cases, 14 were reported for atrocities on SC/ST, 10 for 'Indignity to women', 4 for 'Extortion', 9 for 'Illegal Detention/Arrest', 5 for 'Disappearance of persons', ind 3 for 'Torture', etc.[60]

The concept of sovereign immunity needs immediate abolition and the members of police and security forces be held personally accountable for the acts of the torture. The National Police Commission in its Eighth and Concluding Report made a similar recommendation in the case of police.[61] "Repealing of Laws providing immunity to tortures" was urged by Delhi Declaration and Programme Action on Freedom from Torture. It came as a follow-up of the Vienna Declaration and Programme of Action adopted by UN World Conference on Human Rights in June 1993.[62] However, the implementation of the recommendation is yet to be in the offing.

Alongside, the present evidence law stands in the way of fixing individual liability of police personnel responsible for custodial torture or death in police lock-up, as nobody around dare to bear witness to the incident of torture perpetrated on the victims within four walls of jail/custody premises for fear of retaliation from the jail authorities. The Law Commission has appropriately suggested to suitably amend the Evidence Act (Section 114) by incorporating rebuttable presumption that the injuries sustained in police custody has been caused by police officer-in-charge who will be made to shoulder the burden of proving his innocence.[63] In *Mari Yadamma* v. *State of A.P.*[64] (AIR 2002 AP 16), an undertrial died due to the negligence providing medical aid, and torturous act of jail authorities and jail doctors. The A.P. High Court held the government liable for wrongful action of its servants. The dependants of the deceased were given compensation of Rupees two lakh. It is submitted that in such cases the personal accountability of the guilty officials should also be fixed in pursuance of judicial activism stance adopted by the Supreme Court. Such step would motivate the police to behave humanly with the detenues at the custody. "A well-trained, sensitive, citizen-friendly, but firm police force is a necessary element of good governance and promotion of human rights.[65]

Going by the discussion of the foregoing pages it is obvious that Article 22 of the Constitution of India falls much short of requirements of human rights standard under ICCPR and other international human rights instruments. Part-III of the Constitution of India furnishes a dazzling catalogue of human rights as it accommodates most of the provisions of the Universal Declaration of Human Rights, ICCPR and other international human rights instruments. India has participated in the drafting and adoption of some 70 international instruments relating to human rights under the aegis of UN, and it is a state party to 17 human rights treaties elaborated by the world organization. However, it is yet to ratify Optional Protocol to ICCPR, Second Optional Protocol to ICCPR, Convention against Tortures, among others. It is observed with all seriousness that although ICCPR to which India is a party makes seven fundamental rights non-derogable even during state of emergency, the Indian Constitution recognizes two fundamental rights under Articles 20 and 21, as non-derogable.[66] Articles 20 and 21 of the Constitution, which afford protection in respect of conviction of offences, and of protection of life and personal liberty respectively, were made non-derogable when Article 359 of the Constitution of India was amended by the 44th Amendment Act, 1978. The NHRC has all along been insisting the Central government to proceed with ratification of the Convention against Torture and Other Forms of Cruel, Inhuman or Degrading Punishment or Treatment signed by India in 1997. However, the government, as of now, has simply stopped short at informing the Commission that the question of introducing a definition of torture in Indian legislation was being examined in consultation with the concerned Ministry and Department.[67] Right against torture has already been judicially recognized by the apex court of India as a fundamental right, making that right and corresponding obligation on the state and its agencies a fundamental entrenched right.[68] One hopes the delay in ratification ends.

It is to be borne in mind that the domestic and international aspects are intensely intertwined today. The view that Article 2(7) of the UN Charter severely scuttles UN's power to step into domestic jurisdiction of its member nations has been overtly disfavoured, particularly when it comes to implementation of the provisions of human rights covenants. Therefore, an issue is not indispensably one of domestic jurisdiction if it has become the subject of international obligation undertaken by the state. Human rights and fundamental freedoms, having become subject of a solemn international obligation and a fundamental purpose of the Charter are no longer a matter which is essentially within domestic jurisdiction of a UN member.[69]

It is time we realize that the issue of human rights is not trivialized as a mere domestic issue isolated from the rest of the world. It has assumed an international dimension, and concerns the international community as a whole in the emerging New World Order in which violation of human rights in any remote corner of the globe is viewed as a challenge before Humanity.

Notes

1. *Britannica Ready Reference Encyclopedia* (2005) p. 82.
2. J.E.S. Fawcett, *The Law of Nations*, (1968), p. 151.
3. R.K. Nayak, "Training Lawyers for Countryside in the Developing Countries" 27 J.I.L.I. 61 at 64 (1985); and also, Cairo Declaration on Human Rights in Islam, 1990.
4. V.R. Krishna Iyer, "Human Rights and Inhuman Wrongs", (1990) p. 10.
5. AIR 1980 SC 470.
6. For Text, see Ian Brownlie and Guy S. Goodwin-Gill, (ed.) *Basic Documents on Human Rights* (Fourth Edition) Oxford, 2002; "Human Right: A Compilation of International Instruments", United Nations, New York, 1998; and also, "UN Human Rights: A Compilation on International Instruments" (1983).
7. National Human Rights Commission, 7th Report (1.4.99 – 31.3.2000) p. 2.
8. R.S. Saini, "Custodial Torture in Law and Practice with reference to India", *ILI*, Vol. 36:2 (1994) p. 173.
9. *R.C. Cooper* v. *Union of India* (1970) 1 SCC 248.
10. AIR 1978 SC 597.
11. (1994) 4 SCC 207.
12. *Nandini Satpati* v. *P.L. Dhani*, AIR 1978 SC 1075.
13. *Janardhan Reddy* v. *State of Hyderabad*, AIR 1951 SC 227.
14. *Hussainara Khatun* v. *State of Bihar*, AIR 1979 SC 1819.
15. (1992) 3 SCC 141.
16. Emphasis supplied.
17. National Human Rights Commission, Annual Report 1999-2000 p. 26. I S. Ibid., I Supra note 8 p. 168. 19A. *Tukaram* v. *State of Maharashtra*, AIR (1979) SC 185 (popularly known as Mathura Rape Case.
18. Ibid.
19. Supra, note 8, p. 168.

19A. *Tukaram* v. *State of Maharashtra*, AIR (1979) sc. 185 (popularly known as Mathura Rape Case).

20. National Human Rights Commission Report, 2002-2003, 4.44.
21. Id. P55 4.40.
22. National Human Rights Commission, Annual Report, 1999-2000 Annexure 18.

23. Ibid.
24. Ibid., 4.77.
25. Ibid., 4.46.
26. Supra Note 22. p. 37.
27. Ibid. pp. 37-38.
28. Ibid.
29. National Human Rights Commission 2002-2003, 4.75.
30. West Bengal Human Rights Commission, Annual Report, 1997-98, p. 27.
31. International Commission of Jurists, "State of Emergency: Their Impact on Human Rights" (1983) as quoted by R.S. Saini.
32. P.S. Jha, "Guilty of What", *H.T.* Kolkata, Vol. V, No. 51.
33. Shimon Shetreet, "Limits and Prospects of' International Norms: The Transnational Protection of Human Rights", The General Report (Twelfth Congress of International Academy of Comparative Law) 21 August 1986.
34. V.R. Krishna Iyer, Supra note, 4.
35. Supra note, 10.
36. *Satvant Singh* v. *D. Ramarathnam*, APO, Government of India, New Delhi, AIR 1967 SC 1836 and *Maneka Gandhi* v. *Union of India*, AIR 1978 sc 597, Per Bhagwati, J.
37. *Rajagopal* v. *State of Tamil Nadu*, AIR 1995 SC 264.
38. *Hussainara Khatoon* v. *Home Secretary, State of Bihar* AIR 1979 SC 1360.
39. Ibid.
40. *Sunil Batra* v. *Delhi Administration*, (1978) 4 SCC 494, 569 (FB).
41. Ibid., and *Charles De Sobharaj* v. *Delhi Administration* (1975) 4 SCC 494 (FB).
42. *P.S. Shukla* v. *Delhi Administration* (1980) 3 SCC 526.
43. *T.V. Vatheeswaran* v. *State of Tamil Nadu*, AIR 1983 SC 381.
44. *Attorney General of India* v. *Lochma Devi*, AIR 1986 SC 467.
45. *Sheela Barse* v. *State of Maharashtra* (1983) 2 SCC 96.
46. *Xavier* v. *Canara Bank Ltd.* 1969 KLT 927.
47. *Rudul Shah* v. *State of Bihar*, AIR 1983 SC 1086.
48. *Jolly George Varghese* v. *The Bank of Cochin* AIR 1980 SC 470/
49. Dr. S.K. Kapoor, "International Law and Human Rights", (2004).
50. Supra Note 48.
51. *Vishaka* v. *State of Rajasthan*, AIR 1997 SC 301.

52. *Appeal Export Promotion* v. *A.K. Chopra* AIR 1999 sc. 625.
53. (1942) AC 206.
54. (1917) AC 263.
55. Dr. J.N. Pandey, Constitution of India (2003) p. 261.
56. Supra Note, 32.
57. *ADM Jabalpur* v. *S. Slukla*, AIR 1976 SC 1207.
58. Gokulesh Sharma, *Human Rights and Legal Remedies*, p. 773.
59. Supra note, 55, p. 258.
59A. *Annual Survey of Indian Law*, 2002, Vol. XXXVIII, 11-1, New Delhi, p. 137.
60. *Crime in India*, 2002, National Crime Records Bureau, Ministry of Home Affairs, New Delhi, p. 562.
61. National Police Commission, 8th and Concluding Report, (198 1).
62. National Human Rights Commission Annual Report, 1999-2000, p. 210.
63. *Annual Survey of Indian Law*, 2002, ILI, New Delhi; p. 134.
64. AIR 2002 AP 164.
65. Dr. Manmohan Singh at the Chief Ministers' Conference on International Security and Law and Order on April 15, 2005, New Delhi, Ministry of Information and Broadcasting, Government of India, "Violence - No, Good Governance - Yes".
66. Supra note, 7.
67. National Human Rights Commission, Annual Report, 1999-2000.
68. Ibid.
69. Dr. N.A. Noor Mohammad, "The Human Rights Programme of the United Nations and the Domestic Jurisdiction Clause", AIR 1958 Journal Section, p. 89. Also, Lauterpacht, International Law and Human Rights.

20

Need of Human Rights Education

PARMINDER KAUR

Human Rights Education declared a commitment to rights expressed in the Universal Declaration, of Human Rights 1948, the UN covenants, and the United States Bill of Rights (Nassema, 2002). It affirms the responsibility to respect, protect and promote the rights of all human beings. Human rights education promotes democratic principles. It examines the issue of human rights without any type of bias and from diversified perspectives through a multiple series of educational practices. As far as implementation of human rights education is concerned, it is still a matter of paradox. The World Conference on Human Rights consider human rights education, training and public information essential for the achievement of stable and harmonious relations among communities and for fostering mutual understanding, tolerance and peace. No doubt, the Universal Declaration of Human Rights is a considerable deed of human civilization, but its existence is an adverse one, and human rights are crumbled callously everywhere in the world and this particular education has become a fake. (Naseema, 2002). The promotion of human rights education was initiated in almost all the major countries like Europe, North America, etc. But as far as Asian countries are concerned nothing valuable has been done in regard of human rights education. But the substantial situation reveals that in India and Asian countries the problem of human rights education has multiple complexities. Particularly, in India where to acquire the basic education is a great challenge. As per 1991 Census, some 328.9 million illiterate people live in India (Census of India, 2001). No doubt, the problem is quite serious, but it can be turned into an advantage if our government adopts some new policies and programmes for the removal of illiteracy.

Complexities in Implementation

Learning about the rights of all human beings is not an inert process, so a typical authoritarian teaching paradigm prevalent in Indian society cannot be adopted. Reason being, if we overview everything in context of human rights, we will come to know that respect, dignity and freedom of expressions are also recognized as rights of pupils in class-rooms. Thus, to accommodate human rights education the most suitable technique is to place the pupils in the centre of the educational process and hegemonize them to think for themselves. Such active methods are therefore especially appropriate which are relatively different from the methods used in ordinary teaching process.

Skill for interdependent thinking, ability of expression and incentive of participation are the foremost requirement for the upliftment of human rights education. So, human rights education is chiefly substructured upon learning, conceptual clarity, knowledge and debates and discussions. Many other forms of interpersonal communication, viz., non-verbal communication, self-expression and dialogue which, to a great extent will help for the development of interdependent thinking. As in sociological terms people specifically shape a particular situation to convey symbolic meanings. These symbolic meanings perform a functional task for an individual. Pioneer of this concept is Erwin Goffman (Haralambos, M., *Sociology: Themes and Perspective*). For all these things, behaviour of the teachers might be outstanding. For example, if teacher's body language, and gestures are aggressive and on the contrary he or she talk about peace, calmness and human rights the impact upon pupils will be worse. A teacher imparting human rights education must be endowed with certain qualities which are discussed ahead.

Acquaintance to the Relative Contents

To apprehend, the terms of Universal Declaration of Human Rights and international conventions actions should be ascendant. The basic texts should be presented to pupils in a form depending upon the requirement and analysis of comparative articles that is chiefly pertinent to the personal experience of pupils. Human rights is such a worldwide term, which can also be illustrated and experienced on behalf of pupils. In this field of learning, active methods are appropriate.

Debates and Discussions

Debates about human rights education can be organized in various institutions without incurring more expenditure. But organizations of debates must be abide by certain qualities. The organization of debates should ensure respect for each participants freedom of speech and which supremely bring about the indispensability and universality of human rights. A discussion on the issue of 'human rights' is not possible without active cognition; so to impose human rights without previous discussion would reject the very notion that is, individual freedom.

Human Rights Education in Primary Schools

In primary schools, it is not reasonable to introduce the methods of debates and discussions. Because age of primary school pupils is in between 8 and 9 years. Their minds are immature, so they are not proficient enough to articulate these views. The straightforward method is to develop attitude of respect for human dignity. The pupils of primary schools, must be accustomed about the requirement to have healthy atmosphere to lead a dignified life. So tutors must incorporate pupils about the ecosystem and they can also point out how human life for its survival depends upon environment. Pupils might become aware of their interdependence with environment and concept of sustainable development which must be taught in primary schools.

Human Rights Education in Secondary Schools

In secondary schools, pupils face a transition from immaturity to maturity. In this age, they can be enlightened with human rights education by the process of debates and discussions. Compulsory subjects like history, civics and geography impart a great opportunity for organizing discussions and debates. All students must get opportunity to participate in these debates and discussions.

Human Rights Education in Colleges

In colleges, students are mature enough and they can further enforce these human rights in daily routine. In colleges subject of human rights education must be amplified as a compulsory subject. Alongwith it, different seminars must be organized to make all the individuals aware of it.

Awareness through Media

The media is the most energetic tool which can bring about more influential results in bringing awareness about human rights education. Media is a sort of reflection. It acts as a 'Catalytic agent' which leaves influential impacts on all the societies. It has always been acknowledged in providing the new direction to society. It reforms society in some or other manner. Today in the age of awareness and knowledge the mass media has become ever more predominant. It is advocating opinions and get success in substituting the mindset of human beings. It is the age of technology as well as age of media. It has always been gifted in shaping up individuals personality, a society, and in an inner way on shaping up the whole world, regardless of any limit. But now it is imperative for media to adopt an intent approach to awaken the individuals regarding human rights education.

Media can help a lot by telecasting such programmes, news, information, advertisements which is directly linked to the latest information of the issues concerning human rights education. Print media which is quite inexpensive, can also help a lot on its behalf. It can help by advertising, publishing special articles and latest information of the human rights education by making the educationalists, political leaders, famous film stars and NGOs to actively participate in promoting human rights education in society. Now it is the turn of media to assert its power and become active agent to reform the whole society regardless of any selfish motives and pressures. When media becomes participatory in such awareness, education in society will automatically be enhanced in an effective manner.

Sanctions Behind Need of Human Rights Education

Child Labour

Claiming for the need of human rights education is not a superfluous attempt, rather there are some forces which prompt us to make people aware of their basic rights.

Existence of child labour in Indian society is not a new phenomena as it is in western countries; this offense has always been there. Our nation cannot develop until and unless we do not eradicate child labour. The National Crime Record Bureau's report on 'Crime in India' has reported a rise in crime against children in recent years. Surveys by International Labour Organization (ILO) in 1990 found over 79 million children under the age of 15 years were obliged to work. In some cases, children as young as 5 years have been reported to be in paid employment. In the world, both in urban and rural sectors child labour contributes about 20 per cent of India's Gross National Product. The estimate of getting a cheap labour ranges from 20 to 100 million (Sen and Dasgupta, 2003). Studies have shown that labour at the tender ages have adverse impact on the child's development, both physical and mental. The declaration of the right of the child and our own Constitution has laid down that children and youth should be protected against exploitation. Article 45, of the Directive Principle of State Policies of Indian Constitution, now make a part of fundamental rights claim to provide free and compulsory education until they complete the age of 14 years (Singh, 2001). No doubt that government has done a lot, but not all the government schools are implementing this activity.

Major causes of child labour are poverty, unemployment, lack of education. A major issue today is to eradicate child labour and provide a provision of primary education which also occupies human rights education. Eradication of child labour is one of the fundamental necessity of human rights education as the primary need of society, required for the growth of the nation.

Domestic Violence

Violence against women is as old as human civilization. In India it was during the early 1980s, when violence against women has been recognized as an important social problem. It is really a pathetic situation that, in a nation where women have continued to be victims of exploitation in different manners since the dawn of civilization. There are records that such crimes against women (under IPC and the SL) (excluding murders) increased from 68,000 in 1990 to 74,000 in 1991, 7,90,000 in 1992, 84,000 in 1993, 99,000 in 1994 and 1,06,000 in 1995 (Crime in India, 1995). Thus in five years (between 1991 and 1995), crime against women increased by 45 per cent (Ahuja, 1998). Violence in feminine context is widely spread which involves different kinds of crimes such as sexual violence, kidnapping, dowry homicides and murders, etc. At a modest estimate, there occur around 5,000 deaths due to non-payment of dowry in India (Kewlani, 2004).

National Commission for Women has laboured hard to prepare a draft bill to deal with domestic violence, but due to certain limitations, it has not succeeded (Seth, 2001). Moreover, only law is not sufficient to bring about desired changes in the society. But to recognize the attitude of Indian society is very essential, viz., change in parents attitude, change in attitude of judiciary and more specifically police authorities dealing with the women issues.

The Plight of Old People

There was a time when older persons remained integrated in the society, they actively participate in the formulation and implementation of polices that directly affect their well-being and share their knowledge and skills with younger generations. But now, in the present age they have lost their dignity.

United Nations declared the period from October 1, 1998 to December 3, 1999 as the International Year of the Older Persons.

Occasionally one reads a report or an item in the newspaper or magazine, but otherwise there has hardly been any discussion on the problems faced by old people. In fact, most people do not realize that old persons have serious grievances and that they too need care. We like to believe that in India we have a strong tradition of family values, and that we respect our elders and take care of them. But on the contrary, with increasing industralization and urbanization, there has been a break-up in the traditional family system. At this instance old people not only suffer on aging process in the physical and chronological sense, but also suffer from acute feeling of worthlessness. The position of old women is more vulnerable. Older women, thus become victims of triple neglect and discrimination, on account of gender, widowhood and age (Human Rights Education, 1998).

The Ageing Scenario in India: Some Statistics

There are 70 million aged and neglected persons today and they are expected to increase by 177 million by 2025. As many as 90 per cent aged persons are from unorganized sectors, which means no pension no provident funds or no medical insurance is provided to them. Nearly 80 per cent such persons are particularly from rural areas and 40 per cent aged persons are below poverty line without adequate food, clothing and shelter. (Source: "The Elderly: A Society in Abeyance", Neelam Mak-Lijani in *Swagat 59*, February, 1999).

So, the situation being that grave, and with increasing graying population, there is a realization that some efforts have to be made to alienate the neglect of old people (Human Rights and India, 2006).

The Plight of Refugees

The various UN conventions define the refugee as:

- A person who is outside his/her country of nationality.
- Has well-founded fear of prosecution.
- For reasons of race, religion, nationality, membership of a particular social group.
- Because of that fear he/she cannot return to his/her country.

In January 1951, The General Assembly established the United Nations High Commission for refugees as a non-political humanitarian organization. HRC's primary purpose is to safeguard the rights and well-being of the refugees.

There are communities all over the world who are forced to leave their countries and seek asylum in some other countries. Most of them are escaping the repressive policies of the ruling state, or genocide by an ethnic group, a situation of war, or famine. The problem of refugees is not merely an international phenomenon. It can well be a domestic and caused by international disturbances. The involuntary migration of large number of Kashmiri Pandits to Jammu and Delhi is one example of such domestic forced migration.

The refugees are dealt with under of Registration the Foreigners Act (1939), the Foreigners Act (1946) and the Passport Act (1967). They are dealt through ad hoc administrative decisions and related domestic law concerning passports, entry, stay and exist from Indian territory.

So by promoting human rights education an individual would anlayse the various policies and provisions made for refugees.

Lapses in the System of Human Rights Education

Illiteracy

If we examine all the qualities that distinguish human beings from other living beings, education is definitely one of them. As people fight for scarce resources, education becomes an important facility. Some people have succeeded in taking more benefits from the educational facilities than others. It is important that those who have monopolized education as well as those who have been deprived of its know the importance of the situation. The struggle for the right to education has to be seen from two angles – one of providing education and since it is attained, people must try to make the same available to those who are still deprived. It is sometimes noticed as a tendency of the deprived, as Paulo Friero in "Pedagogy of the Oppressed" pointed out, to adopt an attitude of 'adherents' to the 'oppressor'. That is actually a tendency of the educated elite to join the league of the oppressors. Just as it is important to let no one snatch the right of education, it is equally important that those 'oppressors' do not indulge, consciously or unconsciously, in subverting this crucial right to education. All political parties irrespective of ideological differences show similar concern for education of the masses, but no party government has taken up this issue seriously. The reiteration of the obligation to provide basic education without making any effort is doubly harmful. Governments make the commitment again and again without doing anything in this direction.

A thumbnail sketch of the governments expenditure shows that 25.1 per cent of the states funds go to defence, 26 per cent to debt repayment and 18 per cent for administrative expenses. Only about 31 per cent of the funds are available for the basic needs of living which include, among others, education, health, drinking water shelter and roads.

Political parties and governments raise the issue of mass education but the essence of the problem is lost as their concerns ends by making budget available for education. So budget allocation for education must increase (Human Rights Society and Development, 2006).

Functional Literacy

We very well realized that illiteracy cannot be eliminated abruptly in the whole nation, so we should endorse some other alternatives. Textual knowledge is weaker than functional knowledge. So government must plan some cultural get-togethers or occasions, where, particularly illiterate people are socialized about human rights education through means of dramas, music shows, theme oriented programmes, etc. This will be a more beneficial effort, since people learn better if discussion or participation is stressed instead of textual imposition.

Strategies for Promoting Human Rights Education

We are going to discuss about the strategies of human rights education so it is indispensable to comprehend the acute distinction between the two relative terms providing information and promoting knowledge. Many a times, the remedies are suggested to provide only information but not knowledge. But human rights is such a term to which awareness, information as well as knowledge is equally important. Thus, the ultimate aim of human rights education is to provide knowledge along with awareness and not only merely the information.

- Commencement of human rights education is of national nature. So setting up of human education cells in schools and colleges in each state and in all educational institutions is utmost necessity. In order to make all individuals aware of human rights education, it can be initiated through well designed activities. To make the new generation aware of human rights it is essential to provide it to all students, all teachers and as well as to all parents.
- Various seminars and debates must be organized and incentives must be provided to the participants. Clarity of human rights can also be provided by organizing various questionnaire hours.
- Illiteracy at both general and particular level should be checked. General illiteracy implies total inability of a person to read and write and illiteracy in particular implies lack of knowledge of human rights.
- The most important functional act is to provide human rights education at the elementary level of education.
- NGOs, government agencies, and institutions should organize seminars, festivals on human rights, to make the public aware about their own rights of survival, but it will be more beneficial if these seminars involve the general public at large, not just the public which got the opportunity to join the academic institutions only.
- Extra and co-curricular activities should include human rights concepts. This will help in providing knowledge and information to that public, which does not have technical knowledge of human rights and their implementation.

- There must be availability of various courses on human rights education. Human right education must be introduced in the curriculum at all levels of the schools.
- University of Bombay is the first university of our country which introduced P.G. Diploma Course in Human Rights; other universities can also start similar courses to create awareness among the citizens of the country.
- Public awareness of human rights education is one of the utmost necessity. For this, multiple banners should be displayed on roads. It can also be introduced in picture forms which will be more helpful in making the illiterate persons aware about human rights education.
- Human rights education as a subject not optional but as a compulsory subject of study should be included in the curriculum of schools, colleges and universities.
- Along with all these remedies, an efficient implementation of constitutional provisions are required without which India and its states cannot expect to achieve an overall development.

Conclusion

More specifically, human rights are what each human being is entitled to; to allow her/his the freedom to live a dignified, secure life of her/his choice. Major factors responsible for the violation of human rights are child labour, domestic labour, illiteracy which are the direct outcome of unemployment, poverty, etc. So, to implement human rights in an effective manner, we should eradicate these socioeconomic constraints of development from our society by adopting various means as, by active participation of human beings, with the help of media and by promoting human rights education in the curriculum or in the courses of various academic institutions.

References

Ahuja, Ram (1998), *Violence Against Women,* Rawat Publications, Jaipur.

Census of India (2001).

Haralambos, M. with Heald R.M. (1956), *Sociology: Themes and Perspectives,* Oxford University Press.

Kewlani, Jasleen (2004), "Human Rights and Domestic Violence", in *Guru Nanak Journal of Sociology*, October, Amritsar.

Nassema, C. (2002), *Human Right Education: Conceptual India and Pedagogical Aspect,* Kanishka Publishers, New Delhi.

Singh, Dolly (2001), *Child Right and Social Wrong,* Kanishka Publishers, New Delhi.

Sen, Rajkumar and Dasgupta, Asis (2003), *Problems of Child Labour in India,* Deep and Deep Publications, New Delhi, p. 120.

Seth, Mitra (2001), *Women and Development: The Indian Experience,* Sage Publications, New Delhi, pp. 269-298.

Walia, J.S. (2001), *Education in Modern India, Education and Its Problems*, Paul Publishers, Jalandhar City.

21

Quest for Women Empowerment

73rd Constitutional Amendment Act and its Implementation

P.K. MATHUR AND FASAHAT SHAMOON

The mid-1980s saw the term 'empowerment' becoming popular in the field of development especially in reference to women. More recently, the word has entered the vocabulary of development agencies such as United Nations. Empowerment is a widely used term both in popular and scholarly literature but loosely used. Its meaning often seems hazy and unclear. In order to clarify the meaning of empowerment, it is necessary to define power. The origin of the term 'empowerment' can be traced to the concept of power to see the relevance of its use for the study of people empowerment. The concept of power in political sociology can be best understood by Max Weber who had the largest influence on the sociological study of power to which he assigned a wide significance in every major social domain. He wrote, "Now: 'classes', 'status groups' and 'parties' are phenomena of the distribution of power within a community". Weber off-quoted definition of power is as follows: "In general, we understand by 'power' the chance of a man or a number of men to realize their own will in a social action even against the resistance of others who are participating in the action"

(Weber, 1978: 926). The conception of power referred to above – power as that which some have over others, corresponds to what may be called the zero-sum approach to power. Some have power to the extent that others are without it, the more power some have, the less others have of it. The concept of empowerment becomes relevant when those in power share power with others so that they participate in decision-making.

Empowerment is derived from the word 'Power' as used above. The prefix 'em' is attached to the noun 'Power' to create a verb. According to Webster's *New World Dictionary* (1982), this prefix is used to form verb meaning "to make, make into or like, cause to be". Thus, 'to empower' is to make or cause power. Yet, the actual definition offered for 'empower' are "to give power or grant power, give ability to, enable, permit". These definitions all refer to a process whereby power is given, gained, or permitted. Yet, power must be developed or taken by the powerless themselves, as well as being granted. It is possible both for individuals or groups to empower themselves as well as being the recipients of power bestowed by others. The definition of 'empower' as a transitive verb relates back to the connection of the prefix 'em' to the noun 'Power'. This can be defined as to gain power, to develop power, to give, grant, or permit power. The noun 'empowerment' which is not listed in Webster's *New World Dictionary* (1982), refers to the process by which power is gained, developed or given as people move from a condition of relative powerlessness to relative power through the empowerment process. Those in power give power to other's who gain or develop power and so they are the recipients of power granted by the powerful. Those in power share power with others so that they participate in decision-making.

History of people's empowerment can be traced back to the period immediately after mutiny of 1857 when Sir Syed Ahmad Khan wrote a book entitled *Causes of Indian Revolt* in 1858. The shock of the Indian mutiny had forced the British government to consider ways and means of establishing closer contacts with the Indian people so that a similar tragedy may not occur again. He was of the opinion that the mutiny of 1857 was the result of the gulf between the people of India and the British government, because the British government never knew the needs and the wishes of the Indian people, and the people had no means of protesting what they might feel is not right for them, and people thought that all the laws and regulations which they passed was nothing but a source of exploitation which they never liked. So, Sir Syed wanted to fill the gap between the people and the British government by suggesting the nomination of non-official Indians on the council of Governor-General, by doing this the bond between the two will be strengthened which would avert evils such as mutiny in the future (Ghram, 1885:39).

The shock of Indian mutiny had forced the British government to consider ways and means of establishing closer contacts with the Indian public opinion so that a similar tragedy may not occur again. Sir Syed suggested the nomination of the non-official Indians on the council of the Governor-General this would lead to participation in decision-making and so a beginning was made in sharing power with the people. The then Governor-General accepted this suggestion on the condition that the non-official Indians were to be concerned only with legislative matters and the Government of India Act of 1861 was passed. These councils were subsequently to be established at the local level to form the bases of local self-government or Panchayat Raj in India (Mahajan, 1986:38).

The resolution of 18 May, 1882, of Lord Ripon, the British Viceroy led to the people undertaking the management of their own affairs and so to their empowerment. He was rightly credited with the enunciation of a new philosophy of developing the capacity of the peoples for self-help which could be done only by people's education through participation in local government. It was also necessary to share power with the growing number of educated people who would then be able to share the burden of the work and to improve efficiency. The resolution embodying this doctrine has been hailed as the Magna Carta and Lord Ripon, its author, as the father of local self-government in India (Maheshwari, 1971: 17; Venkatarangaiya and Pattabhiram, 1969:109).

Reforms projected by Ripon were ignored by government and district officers who were responsible for putting them into practice, the local Daroga and Bania were the real bosses in the villages and the local leadership was not concerned while formulating the policy but rather this policy was imposed from above. Unfortunately therefore, Lord Ripon's resolution, often described as the milestone on the roads of Indian self-government or Panchayati Raj, remained a dead letter for a long time (Purwar 1967: 46-47). The next step in the history of people's empowerment was the report of the Royal Commission upon decentralization which was appointed by the government in 1907 and published in 1909. The then Secretary of State of India, was alarmed at the gigantic stature of over centralization and he took a serious note of it, and called it a great mischief. He attributed it to a widening gulf between the officials and the people of India. The Commission recommended that it is most desirable, alike in the interests of decentralization and in order to associate the people with the local tasks of administration, then an attempt should be made to constitute and develop village Panchayats for the administration of local village affairs and became an instrument of people's participation (Malaviya, 1956: 221). The proposals and suggestions of the Commission were favourably commented by the Government of India. But the officials found some practical difficulties to implement in different parts of the country. They were not willing to share power with the people as it would weaken the hold of bureaucracy on them. The inefficient bureaucracy did not do even the little that was suggested in the report of the Royal Commission on decentralization for people's participation (Mathew, 2000: 4).

The development of local self-government institutions or Panchayat Raj got further fillip with the introduction of Montague-Chelmsford Report which made local self-government a 'transferred subject' under the scheme of Drarchy (Kazi, 2002: 69). To make local self-government really representative as well as responsible, the Montague-Chelmsford Report on the Indian constitutional reforms had suggested that there should be, as far as possible, complete popular control in local bodies, that is peoples empowerment and the largest possible independence for them of outside control (Khanna, 1972: 29). Notwithstanding this professed objective of the Montague-Chelmsford Scheme, it did not make Panchayat institution democratic and vibrant instrument of people's empowerment, due to various constraints, both organizational and fiscal. The most significant development of this period was the establishment of village Panchayats in a number of provinces. However, these statutory Panchayats covered only a limited number of villages and had, generally, a limited number of functions and did little for people's empowerment (Mathew, 2000: 5).

The Government of India, showing its willingness to practice what it preached for people's empowerment issued a resolution on the 6 May, 1918, which supported the principles enunciated long before by Ripon and decentralization commission. The resolution affirmed the policy of minimum of interference in the affairs of local-government or Panchayat Raj. The resolution of 1918, approved the proposals of establishing departments of local self-government or Panchayati Raj in the provinces. And it was in pursuance of the policy contained in the British government's famous announcement of August 20, 1917, that the Government of India Act of 1919 was passed and enforced in 1920. All the provinces passed their respective Acts to revive and resuscitate Panchayats so as to ensure people's participation in local affairs (Purwar, 1967: 53). Yet, this attempt also did not lead to the sharing of power with the people and their continued to be the concentration of power in the hands of government officials.

In this way attempts were made for people's empowerment in British regime by then Viceroy Lord Ripon (1882) through Local Self-government Act, Royal Commission, in 1909 and Government of India Act, 1919. The question of representation of different population groups such as women were not considered and was limited to the resident male. This reflects the prevalent ideology of patriarchy which did not address the questions of women's participation (Buch, 2001:8). The early twentieth century saw the birth of national movement and women's organizations. These women organizations become the part of national movement under the leadership of Gandhiji and struggled for women's participation. In 1917 a deputation of Indian women led by Shrimati Sarojini Naidu presented to the British Parliament a demand for the enfranchisement of women on the basis of equality with men (Guha, 1975: 103). In this context, the franchise committee set up by then British government deliberated upon franchise to women and left it to provincial legislatures and linked it with the issue of local culture and sensitivity on the subject. The joint committee of British Parliament in its first report on the bill for the Government of India Act, 1919, endorsed the recommendation of franchise committee on the subject of women's franchise. Hence, the Government of India Act, 1919 provided that if legislative council in any province passed a resolution in favour of women's franchise, they should be put in the electoral register of that province. The law was modified only later and power were given to the councils to pass resolutions to allow qualified women to become members by election or nomination (Buch, 2001: 8-9). The Reforms Act of 1921 extended the franchise only to wives who had property and education. The British government was reluctant on this question because it could not believe that Indian society would ever regard women as equal participants with men, nor did they regard women as a political force. The massive participation of women in the national movement led to the demand of immediate acceptance of adult franchise without sex discrimination. The demand was accepted by the Indian National Congress (INC) in Karachi session 1931 which committed itself to women's political equality, regardless of their status and qualification (Guha, 1975: 104).

In the period immediately after independence it was the Constitution of free India which fulfilled the promise made by the Congress in Karachi session in 1931 for granting equality to women in all spheres including adult franchise without sex discrimination, but did not guarantee political representation to women in decision-making. The focus this time was on the development of all sections and so in March 1950, the Planning Commission came into existence and began to plan for large-scale economic and social development. It was soon realized that no development could be achieved until it is backed by the development of villages since 80 per cent of the people live in the villages the Planning Commission, therefore, thought of shaping the village development programme, so as to attack the five giants of hunger, poverty, disease, squalor and ignorance through a self-help programme of community development (Dayal, 1970: 3).

The committee on the plan project, a high powered body constituted by National Development Council, under the chairmanship of Balwantrai G. Mehta appointed in 1957, to study after the functioning of community development programme which was started on October 2, 1952. The team toured several parts of the country to examine and assess the work and to recommend to the Government of India as to what more needs to be done to make the programme a success. The team in its report submitted at the end of December 1957, had tried to find out what needs to done to make the performance match with the promise (Dayal, 1970:9; Masheshwari, 1963: 9-10). The report revolutionized the entire thinking about the community development as well as the rural local government or Panchayati Raj. It was undoubtedly an outstanding and important landmark in the field of people's empowerment, i.e., people's participation in decision-making. (Sharma 1987: 18-19).

The establishment of first ever non-Congress government at the centre in 1977 dedicated to a belief in a polity that ensure decentralization of economic and political power has provided yet another opportunity for re-invigoration of people empowerment through Panchayat Raj Institutions (PRIs) in India. (Mathur, 1981: 169-170). The committee on Panchayat Raj Institutions was appointed by the Government of India in 1978, with Asoka Mehta as its chairman to enquire into the working of Panchayat Raj Institutions, and to suggest measures to strengthen them, so as to enable a decentralized system of planning and development to be effective. The terms of reference of the committee, inter alia, required it to examine the working of Panchayat Raj Institutions in regard to mobilization of resources as to plan and implementation of the scheme for rural development in an objective and optimal manner, and in looking after the participation of women and other weaker section of the society (Shukla, 1981: 194).

In this way attempts were made for people's empowerment in post-independence period by Constitution of India, Balwantrai

Mehta committee report and Ashok Mehta committee report. The Constitution of India guaranteed equality to women in all spheres including adult franchise without sex discrimination. There were no provisions of women empowerment, that is, it did not guarantee their representation in decision-making bodies. The Balwantrai Mehta committee report provided co-option of two women members in Panchayats. The Ashok Mehta committee report provided that two women securing highest numbers of votes among women candidates in the Panchayat election could take the seats reserved for them. Thus the reports of these two committees had provision for only token representation of women in Panchayats and no provision for women's empowerment, that is, no guarantee of their representation in such decision-making bodies (Kaushik, 1995: 3).

Empowerment of women means to give power to women particularly the increasing participation in decision-making and power sharing in the representative bodies. According to Kumar and Rani (2001): empowerment means empowering women socially, economically and politically so that they can break away from male domination and claim equality with them. Women empowerment refers to the process by which they develop an ability or capacity to become aware of rights and opportunities by sharing power and participation in decision-making so as to challenge patriarchal structure and to bring about a change. The sharing of power and participation in decision-making bodies was considered a very strong instrument to achieve the goal of women development and social change.

The 73rd Constitutional Amendment Act, 1992 and implemented on 24 April, 1993 all over India in order to give women a share in power and ensure participation in decision-making in Panchayati Raj to make women an instrument of development and social change. It marked a watershed in the empowerment of women because it brought women in large numbers in Panchayats (Mishra, 1997: 21). The implementation of 73rd Constitutional Amendment Act must be examined to find out the extent to it has empowered women in the sense that sharing power and participation in decision-making has made them aware of their rights and opportunities and has enabled them to challenge the patriarchal structure and bring about change.

In this study of the implementation of 73rd Constitutional Amendment, exploratory research design was followed to find out the extent of empowerment of twelve (12) women Pradhans of Lodha block of Aligarh district. Aligarh district consists of twelve (12) blocks and Lodha block consists of twelve Nayay Panchayats which consist of 60 Gram Panchayat and 12 were headed by women. One women Pradhan was selected from every Nayay Panchayat. The case studies method was used with the help of interview-schedule and participation observation.

Aims of the Study

- To find out the extent to which women empowerment has taken place through Panchayati Raj by determining the awareness of rights and opportunities, their ability to challenge the patriarchal structure and capacity to bring about change.
- To find out the sociological parameters which leads to women empowerment.
- Consequences of women empowerment on family and society.
- To suggest the guideline and policy implication that would form an action strategy to empower women so as to improve the working of Panchayat Raj; this will make research both empirical and paraxological.

The case studies of twelve (12) women Pradhans have shown interesting results. These case studies were carried out to find out the sociological parameters of women's empowerment through Panchayati Raj. It was found that some women Pradhans were empowered by their participation in these decision-making bodies. The analysis of these case studies reveals that education, older-age, prior experience of political participation, freedom for the performance of household chores and exposure to the world outside the family were some of the sociological parameters that led to the empowerment of women through Panchayati Raj. It was found that those women Pradhans who were educated up to high school (10th Class) or twelfth class (12th class) had no problem in handling Panchayat paper work and they did not depend on their husbands, father-in-laws and other elder male members of their family to read out for them Panchayat documents and so were able to challenge the patriarchal structure. Older age was also an important sociological parameter as it was found that those women Pradhans whose age was fifty or above were free from the household chores because their daughters and daughter-in-laws were there to look after it, so they had a lots of time for Panchayat work. Another important sociological parameter was prior experience of political participation such as, they were Pradhans, member of block development council member (BDC member) and member of Panchayat Samities. These women Pradhans who had prior experience of political participation were themselves very keen and came forward willingly to contest Pradhan election. They were very active and went door to door and argued for their candidature and most of them won the election by a comfortable margin. Another sociological parameter was the exposure to the world outside the family, such as involvement in social services like Anganvadi worker, working as teacher and ANM etc. These women Pradhans did not have any restriction on their movements and were able to talk to others and were more articulate in the meetings of block, and chaired Panchayat and Gram Sabhas meetings regularly and could meet the village secretary and could enquire about the progress of development work from the higher officials such as BDO, CDO and other higher officials of the districts. All these women Pradhans look after the development work in their respective Gram Panchayats. All these women Pradhans also went to Thana (police station) with the village people for the solution of their personal problems. These women got more respect after being elected as a Pradhan of their respective Gram Panchayats. People of their village gave them more respect and they also got more respect in the families and had more say in the decision-making process, such as education and marriages of their children, buying and selling of properties and freedom in the household expenditure etc. This showed their ability to challenge the patriarchal structure. These women Pradhans also wanted to contest election even for higher post like Zilla Panchayat member (highest body of PRIs) and MLAs (member of legislative assembly).

It was found that other women Pradhans were not empowered. The analysis of these case studies revealed that lack of education, younger age, lack of prior political participation, performance of household chores and lack of exposure to the world outside family were some of sociological parameters that prevented women's empowerment through Panchayati Raj. All those women Pradhan who were illiterate had great problems in handling Panchayat activities, even in the periods of more than three years in office they did not know anything about Panchayat work. All the Panchayats papers were sent to their homes and they just thumb marked or signed on the dotted line because of inability to read Panchayats documents. So they were unable to challenge the patriarchal structure. Younger age was also a major stumbling block for all these women Pradhans who were comparatively younger than the other Pradhans. They were having more problems with the Panchayat works. Their husbands, father-in-laws and other elder male members of their families looked after the Panchayat related activities because these women Pradhans were always busy in the kitchen and looking after the small children. Another sociological parameter which prevented women empowerment through Panchayati Raj was the lack of prior experience of political participation as such they never became Pradhan, block development council member (BDC member) and Panchayat Samiti members etc. All these women Pradhans who had lack of prior experience of political participation were forced by their husbands, father-in-laws and other elder male members of their family. So, they reluctantly agreed to contest the Pradhan election. They never went out for any election campaigning but they still managed to win the Pradhan election quite comfortably due to the efforts of their husbands, father-in-laws and other elder male members of their family. Lack of exposure of the world outside the family such as involvement in any type of social services like Anganvadi worker, working as teachers and ANM, etc. All these women Pradhans had restrictions on their movements and hardly went to the block meeting. They never went to block other than the meetings days with their husbands, father-in-laws and other elder male member of their families who spoke on their behalf. All these women Pradhans never discussed Panchayat matters with their village secretaries because they had not met them face to face and did not know their names. All these women Pradhans never chaired Panchayat and Gram Sabhas meetings because they were never allowed by their husbands, father-in-laws and other elder male members of their families. None of these women Pradhans knew about the progress of development work in their respective Gram Panchayats because all the development work was looked after by their husbands, father-in-laws and other elder male member of their families. All these women Pradhan never went to Thana (police station) when it was needed and on their behalf their husbands, father-in-laws and other elder male members of their families discharged the duty. All these women Pradhans considered themselves as dummy/name-sake Pradhans and not as a real Pradhans and they did not note any change in their lives after being elected as a Pradhan of their respective Gram Panchayats. All of them were busy in the household chores before being elected Pradhan and still now they were busy with the same. Thus, they were unable to challenge patriarchal structure.

It also emerged from the analysis of these case studies that all sociological parameters must be taken together for understanding the empowerment of women through Panchayati Raj and one or two sociological parameters alone cannot be regarded as being more important for empowerment. Some women were not empowered due to the sociological parameters such as lack of education and lack of prior experience of political participation but they were empowered due to other sociological parameters such as older age, freedom for the performance of household chores and exposure to the world outside the family. Lack of education led to the dependence on their husbands, father-in-laws and other elder male member of their families to read out Panchayat documents because of their inability to read. Lack of prior experience of political participation was also a sociological parameter which made them dependent on their husbands, father-in-laws and other elder male member of their families. They were forced by them in Pradhan election and they reluctantly agreed to contest. They never went outside for any election campaign but still managed to win the election by a comfortable margin due to the efforts of their husbands, father-in-laws and other elder male members of their families. This shows that they were unable to challenge the patriarchal structure. The other sociological parameter such as older-age makes them free from the household chores because their daughter and daughter-in-laws were there to look after the household chores and they could get enough time for Panchayat work. Another sociological parameter was the exposure to the world outside family such as they were Anganvadi worker, teachers and ANMs etc. These women did not have any restriction on their movements and were able to talk to others and were more articulate in the meetings of Panchayat and Gram Sabhas, chaired them regularly and could enquire about the progress of development work from the higher officials of the district. These women Pradhans also look after the development work in their respective Gram Panchayats. They also went to Thana (police station) with the village people for the solution of their personal problems. These women Pradhan did not considered themselves as a dummy/name-sake Pradhans and consider themselves as a real Pradhan. These women Pradhans got more respect in the villages after being elected Pradhan and they also got more respect in their families and had more say in the decision-making process such as education and marriages of their children, buying and selling of property and freedom in the household expenditure etc. It was found that these women Pradhan also wanted to contest election even for higher post like Zilla Panchayat member and even MLAs. These women Pradhans did not like their dependence on their husbands, father-in-laws and other elder male members of their families and considered them to be interfering in Panchayat matters. This shows that to some extent they were able to challenge the patriarchal structure even though they were uneducated and had no prior experience of political participation. The sharing of power and participation in Panchayats had made them aware of rights and opportunities. Thus, the others sociological parameters led to the empowerment of these women through Panchayati Raj. Participation in Panchayats enhanced the capacity of these women to bring about change in their own life and to change village lives for the better. This shows that it is not necessary for women to be educated and experienced to bring about change but the sharing of power in decision-making bring about change. This demonstrates the hidden potential of women empowerment through Panchayati Raj.

All the twelve women Pradhans considered education to be important because this was the way to become independent of their husbands, father-in-laws and other elder male members of their families to read out Panchayats documents for them. All the women Pradhans considered political support to be important because without it they could not fight the Pradhan election. All these twelve case studies revealed that they considered training programmes and experience in Panchayats to be more important for effective participation. They considered training programmes to be a substitute for education even uneducated women Pradhan could take advantage of training programmes to become independent of their husbands, father-in-laws and other elder male members of their families. They considered experience of Panchayats to be a substitute for political support because it could enable them to fight Panchayat elections even without political support. Thus, training programmes and experience of Panchayat could make even those women who were dummy/name-sake Pradhans as effective participant who could attend block meetings and could chair Gram Panchayats and Gram Sabhas meetings regularly and participate in Panchayat discussions. In this way they could also know the progress of development work in their respective Gram Panchayats and could discuss with their secretaries. This means that women empowerment through Panchayati Raj was possible for such women and they could become aware of their rights and opportunities to be able to challenge patriarchal structure and to bring about change. On the basis of the results of the study it is possible to suggest guideline and policy implication that can take the form of action strategy to empower women.

Importance of Proper Training

In order to ensure effective participation of women in Panchayati Raj it is essential that women should be trained about day-to-day procedures of Panchayati Raj and various provisions enshrined in the 73rd Constitutional Amendment Act. Women must be informed of various development policies and programmes, as well as those pertaining specifically to women and children. The study showed that training programmes could be a substitute for education so that even uneducated women Pradhans could take advantage of training programmes to become empowered.

Exposure to the World Outside Family

Women must be encouraged to come out of their families and get exposed to the world as Anganvadi worker, teachers and ANMs, etc. It is only through this exposure that women can become free of restriction on their movements and be able to participate in meetings and be articulate in discussions. This would prepare the ground for their empowerment by ensuring more effective participation in Panchayati Raj.

Need for Experience of Political Participation

Women organizations such as Mahila Mandal, Mahila Manch and Mahila welfare societies must mobilize and encourage women to participate as voters and member of Gram Sabhas. This experience of political participation will pave the way for fighting Panchayat election and getting more responsible position and lead to their empowerment. The study showed that experience is substitute for political support because it enables them to fight election even without political support.

Mandatory Participation of Women and Emphasizing on Women and Child Related Schemes

Making the participation of women representatives in Panchayats mandatoıy will lead to decision-making by women without interference of male member of the families. Emphasis should be given on development and welfare schemes related to women and child, as this would strengthen the participation of women in decision-making. They should also be free from the household chores. The study showed that dependence on husbands, father-in-laws and other elder male member of their families was a stumbling block in the empowerment of women. Mandatory participation of women in Panchayats will remove such dependence. The study showed that the participation in household chores prevents women from Panchayat work. Emphasis on development programmes and welfare schemes related to women and child will encourage women to participate in Panchayats.

References

Buch, Nirmala. 2001. "Panchayat and Women", *Kurukshetra*, Vol. 49. No. 9, April.

Dayal, Rajeshwar. 1970. *Panchayati Raj in India*. Delhi: Metropolitan Book Co. Private Ltd.

Ghram, G.F.I. 1885. *The Life and Work of Sir Syed Ahmad Khan*. Edinburgh: William Blackwood.

Guha, P. 1975. Synopsis Report of the National Committee on the Status of Women in India (1971-74), New Delhi: The Indian Council of Social Science Research (ICSSR).

Hatim, Shahida. 1998. *Empowerment of Women: Problems and Prospects*. New Delhi: Deep and Deep Publications.

Kaushik, Susheela. 1995. *Woman and Panchayati Raj*. New Delhi: Haranand Publications.

Kazi, Syed Sultan. 1998. "India's Mixed Experience", *Competition Wizard*, February.

Khanna, R.L. 1972. *Panchayati Raj in India*. Ambala Cantt: The English Book Depot.

Kumar, K. Vijaya and Rani, S. Vanaja. 2001. "Empowerment of Women – A Myth or Reality", *Social Change*. September, Vol. 31 No.3.

Mahajan, Vidya Dhar. 1986. *Constitutional Development and the National Movement in India*. New Delhi: S. Chand & Company Ltd.

Maheshwari, B. 1963. *Studies in Panchayati Raj*. Delhi: Metropolitan Book Co. Private Ltd.

Maheshwari, S. 1971. *Local Government in India*. New Delhi: Orient Longman Ltd.

Malaviya, H.D. 1956. *Village Panchayats in India*. New Delhi: Economic and Political Research Department, All India Congress Committee.

Mathew, George. 2000. *Panchayati Raj in India: An Overview*. New Delhi: Concept Publishing Company.

Mathur, P.C. 1981. *Panchayati Raj*, New Delhi: The Indian Institute of Public Administration.

Mathur, P.C. 1991. "Rural Local Self-Government in India: Ideological Nuances from Ripon to Jaya Prakash Narayan, 1882-1964", *Journal of Rural Development*, Vol. 10 (5).

Mishra, S. 1997. "Women and 73rd Constitutional Amendment Act", *Social Action*, Vol. 47.

Purwar, Vijaya Lakshmi. 1967. *Panchayats in Uttar Pradesh*. Lucknow: Tej Kumar Press.

Sharma, M.L. 1987. *Gandhi and Democratic Decentralization in India*, New Delhi: Deep & Deep Publications.

Shukla, K.B. 1981. "Panchayati Raj Revisited", in Chaturvedi, T.N. and Jain, R.B (ed.) *Panchayati Raj*. New Delhi: Indian Institute of Public Administration.

Venkatarangaiya, M. and Pattabhiram, M. (eds.). 1969. *Local Government in India: Select Readings*, Bombay: Allied Publishers.

Weber, Max. 1978. *Economy and Society*, Berkeley: University of California Press, 2 Vols.

Webster, 1982. *New World Dictionary:* Second College Edition. New York: Simon and Schuster.

22

Directive Principles of State Policies v. Contemporary Development

A Socio-Legal Evaluation

JASLEEN KEWLANI

Traditionally, development was rendered solely an economic interpretation, but with the advent of novel modes of survival its conception is changing. In modern times, a multidimensional expression is used to redefine the rubrics of progress which include human development, social development, environmental sustainability and an equity platform bestowed with gender justice. In this phenomenon of progress and development, certain facilitations and inhibitions function to direct the process in a specific direction. In Indian governance, these directions have been formalized under the heading of 'Directive Principles of State Policies'. Since the very conception of the Constitution of India, these directive principles have been incorporated, but their implementation has always been relatively executed; which in turn forwarded multiple forms of repercussions on Indian society. The paper aims at understanding the concomitance between implementation of Directive Principles of State Polices and the Development Paradigm. Civic obligation, cognition and analysis of the secondary data are the composite tools, which have been used to elaborate the discussion. The findings of the assessment

> reveal that to internalize the directive principles in letters and spirit both, especially when they are not enforceable by law; the governing agencies need to add many new dimensions and subtract the obsolete techniques for their implementation.

Part IV of the Indian Constitution relates to the Directive Principles of State Policies. Establishing social welfare state is the cardinal aim of these directives (Kumar, 1997). Ethnocentric conflicts, poverty, unemployment, lack of people's participation in social development, sex abuse, female foeticide, AIDS, etc., are such evils, which need to be eradicated if welfare is to be achieved on universal scales. The founding fathers of the Constitution were aware of some of these inhibitions, but the rest of these social evolved after a span of consummation of the constitutional privileges. To combat these pernicious issues, the administration and the governance need a directive assistance, which is proposed by Directive Principles. The 'proposing element' needs to be emphasized because Directive Principles are not enforceable by laws as that of Fundamental Rights incorporated in Part III of the Indian Constitution. These directions have capacity to propose but do not possess potential to impose. This may be called a matter of 'deprivation' instead of 'differentiation'. Dr. Ambedkar while explaining the object underlying the Directive Principles of State Policy observed that while we have established political democracy, it is also the desire that we should lay down as our ideals, economic democracy (C.A.D.,III: 494-95). This economic democracy implies socialistic spirit which cannot be attained until and unless social democracy is established.

As the world population has doubled and the global economy and social survival have grown and expanded sevenfold over the last half century, the claims of humanity on the earth and its systems have become excessive. These desires and aspirations have created a complex matrix of livelihood in some nations where demographic burdens overpower any other kind of governmental liability. India is certainly amongst these countries (Brown, 2005). To enable the government in handling this interknit phenomenon of survival in Indian scenario, Directive Principles are those elderly contents of the Constitution which need to be obeyed and adhered to. An irony of Indian governance is that these directions laid down by the Constitution are not justifiable, rather these have been expressly declared non-justifiable. Had these Directive Principles been made enforceable by law courts, the present situation would certainly have been somewhat better. At present these are the elderly contents of the Constitution which need to be obeyed and adhered to. Though the implementation of Directive Principles has always been weak, but still the efforts to internalize these directives have always been rampant. In the following course of the paper, an attempt is being made in order to assess the real implementation status of these moral guidelines of state polices. The analysis has been limited to a number of selected Articles enlisted in Part IV of the Indian Constitution. Major stress has been laid on the principles guiding the socio-economic sectors of Indian existentialism.

Directive Principles of State Policies: An Empirical Assessment

Article 38(1) provides that, "the state shall strive to promote the welfare of the people by securing and protecting, as effectively as it may, a social order, in which justice – social, economic, and political, shall inform all the institutions of national life". A drastic addition was rendered to this provision through the 44th Amendment Act, 1978 which altered the text as, "the state shall in particular, strive to minimize the inequalities in income and endeavour to eliminate inequalities in status, facilities and opportunities not only amongst individuals, but also amongst groups of people residing in different areas or engaged in different vocations". The surface meaning of these declarations sounds and seems convincing and inspiring but due to non-enforceable nature of Directive Principles, they have partially been deprived of an adequate implementation. Even after having set 'equality' as a target, it could not be avoided. In India, gender discrimination, violation of human rights, domestic violence, female foeticide, environmental degradation, illiteracy, poverty, are some of the factors which have haunted the governmental efforts to bring about a social justice to the masses; in the absence of which a balanced and sustained development cannot be achieved. Two-thirds of the world's adult illiterate are women and their number ranges about half-a-billion. Around 70 per cent of the total poor persons of the world are women. Women suffer identified traumas like domestic violence, divestment in decision-making process, etc.. Women now account for 50 per cent of those infected by HIV worldwide and in Africa that figure is now 58 per cent (Anand, 2005). It does not imply that it is only women who suffer. Handicaps, refugees, old aged people, HIV infected persons and many more other segments of humanity also suffer from undesirable socio-economic and culturally proscribed setbacks.

Certain principles to be followed by the state are enumerated under Article 39 of the Indian Constitution. Article 39 requires that "the state shall in particular, direct its policies towards securing:

1. that the citizens, men and women equally, have the right to an adequate means of livelihood;
2. that the ownership and control of the material resources of the community are so distributed as best to subserve the common good;
3. that the operation of economic system does not result in concentration of wealth and means of production to the common detriment;
4. that there is equal pay for equal work for both men and women;
5. that the health and strength of workers, men and women and the tender age of children are not abused and that citizens are not forced by the economic necessity to enter associations unsuited to their age of strength;
6. that children are given opportunities to develop in a healthy manner and in conditions of freedom and dignity and that childhood and youth are protected against exploitation and against moral and material abandonment."

Though the Indian government and specially the legislature formulated many laws and policies, keeping in mind the direction laid down by Article 39 of the Constitution, but the paradox emerges in case of their adoption process. The phenomenon of scarcity of facilities of livelihood and deprivation in context of chances to develop can be interpreted through the data provided in Table 1 given below. It shows India's global position on human and gender development. These statistics do not only reveal the real internalization of Directive Principles, rather also reflect the impact of various developmental policies in abstractions.

Table 1

Indian Global Position on Human and Gender Development

Country	*Human Development Index (HDI)*		*Gender Development Index (GDI)*		*Gender Empowerment Measures (GEM)*	
	2001	*1990*	*2001*	*1992**	*2001*	*1992**
Norway	0.944	0.9	0.941	0.911	0.837	0.752
Australia	0.939	0.886	0.938	0.901	0.754	0.568
Sri Lanka	0.73	0.692	0.726	0.66	0.272	0.288
China	0.721	0.624	0.718	0.578	0.483@	0.474
Indonesia	0.682	0.619	0.677	0.591	0.362@	0.362
India	0.590	0.519	0.574	0.401	0.240@	0.226
Pakistan	0.499	0.44	0.469	0.36	0.414	0.153
Bangladesh	0.502	0.414	0.495	0.334	0.218	0.287
Nepal	0.499	0.413	0.479	0.31	N.A.	0.315
Mozambique	0.356	0.317	0.341	0.229	0.428@	0.35
Niger	0.292	0.264	0.279	.0196	N.A.	0.205

Source: UNDP Human Development Report (HDR) 1995 and 2003.

Kindly Note – @ – relates to HDR 1999.
* – GDI and GEM were estimated for the first time for 1992.

We can notice from the above mentioned statistical references that Indian position is not truly satisfactory as far as Human Development is concerned. India ranks 127th among 175 countries in terms of UNDP Human Development Index (HDI), with an HDI of 0.590 for the year 2001 (Human Development Report on Punjab, 2004). After scrutinizing the global standards of India, the discussion of particularly Indian scenario can be carried ahead. Article 39 mainly aims at social goods like socialism in work, pay and distribution of economic resources; better health facilities to both men and women; and provisions of equal means of livelihood. The Central Plan Allocation has been enhanced for almost all segments of the social sectors. Total expenditure of general government (combined centre and states) on social services is being presented in Table 2. The data shows that the allocation of the amounts for development of Indians in terms of education, health and on other social sectors, has enhanced. Ironically, if the amounts have increased, the situation still has not proportionately improved.

Analysis of Health Sector

The National Health Policy 2002 (NHP) envisages increasing public health investment from the current level of 0.9 per cent of GDP and 2 per cent of GDP by 2010. The health care delivery system, however, has created a paradoxical situation with a plethora of hospitals but few located in areas with high morbidity. Facilities are still poorest in the most needy rural areas in the state. There are unused diagnostic facilities and drugs in some places, while others suffer from shortages. Overcrowding in some hospitals coexists with under utilization in others. Most secondary and tertiary care institutions have good facilities with skilled staff, but they face difficulties in running institutions because of changing health care needs, rapid advances in technology, obsolescence of equipment and rapid turn over of staff. The situation of malaria after 1984 has more or less remained static (annual malaria cases and pf cases over 2 million and 1 million respectively) with marginal fluctuations. Tuberculosis (TB) is a serious public health problem in India. Approximately 18 lakh new cases of which about 8 lakh are highly infectious smear positive are reported every year. About 4.17 lakh persons die of TB every year.

Leprosy prevalence rate for the country as a whole is estimated at 2.4 per 10,000 population during 2004. As compared to 3.5 million in 1998 an estimated 4.58 million men, women and children were living with HIV/AIDS in the nation at the end of 2002, with an adult prevalence rate of 0.8 per cent. India account for 10 per cent of the global HIV burden. This number is still expected to increase with consequent medical economic and social implications. Along with physical disaster, HIV/AIDS also endows the human life with a stigmatizing social attitude. Over the last two

Table 2

Total Expenditure of General Government on Social Services

Items	*1986-87*	*1990-91*	*1995-96*	*2000-01*	*2001-02*	*2002-03*	*2003-04*
Total Expenditure	1,00,470	1,63,673	30.3.586	5,95,598	6,52,928	7,51,950	8,23,642
Social Services	18,967	33,254	65.465	1,31,016	1,37,286	1,52,191	1,63,464
Education	8,650	1,7093	35.289	65,718	68,071	74,709	80,987
Health	3,049	5,317	10.179	27,903	29,799	34,358	36,803
Others	7,268	10,844	19.997	37,395	39,417	43,124	45,673
As % of the total expenditure							
Social Services	18.9	20.3	21.6	22.0	21.0	20.2	19.8
Education	8.6	10.4	11.6	11.0	10.4	9.9	9.8
Health	3.0	3.2	3.4	4.7	4.6	4.6	4.5
Others	7.2	6.6	6.6	6.3	6.0	5.7	5.5
As % of expenditure of social service							
Education	45.6	53.9	53.9	50.2	49.6	49.1	49.5
Health	16.1	15.5	15.5	21.3	21.7	22.6	22.5
Others	38.3	30.5	30.5	28.5	28.7	28.3	27.9

Source: Budget Documents of the Centre and the state governments (enumerated in Economic Survey – 2003-04, Government of India)

decades, morbidity and mortality due to cardiovascular diseases, mental disorders, cancers and trauma have been rising with increases in the number of senior citizens with higher prevalence of non-communicable diseases (NCDs) and prevalence of NCDs in younger people because of lifestyle changes, obesity, stress, exposure to environmental risk factors and use of tobacco. As far as cancer is concerned, there are about 20-25 lakh cases of cancer in the country and approximately 7-9 lakh cases come up every year. Allocation of budget and legislations are largely based upon the directions laid down in Part IV of the Constitution, but the data disposes that health sector has not improved significantly, rather in some instances the situation has worsened.

Analysis of Education Services

Education is another social sector which needs a thorough discussion if directive principles are being referred to. The statistics presented in Table 2 show that a lot of expenditure is being made to enhance the education services. Obviously, the main aim of these allocations is to eradicate illiteracy in the nation. No doubt, the literacy rates in India have improved but as evident in the statistics, female still suffer the stigma of deprivation, which shows that along with other social divestments, women suffer from a biased approach in educational scenario also (Table 3).

Table 3

Literacy Rates in India (1951-2001)

Census year	*Persons*	*Males*	*Females*	*Male-female Gap in Literacy rates*
1951	18.33	27.16	8.86	18.30
1961	28.30	40.40	15.35	25.05
1971	34.45	45.96	21.97	23.98
1981	43.57	56.38	29.76	26.62
1991	52.21	64.13	39.29	24.84
2001	64.84	75.85	54.16	21.69

The Incidence of Poverty

As discussed in the previous parts of the paper, Article 39 pleads for an equal status of women, but the real situation shows pernicious state of affairs. The gap between male and female literacy rate has widened as compared to the gone times. Where increase in literacy rates is a salubrious phenomenon, there only the increase of this gap puts a constraint on the ovations. Article 39 also directs the government to equalize the economic disparities and livelihood demarcations between rich and poor sections of the population. But again it seems to be an eyewash if a gauge is rendered to the estimates of incidence of poverty in India. Table 4 shows the very related statistics and puts another question mark in front of the socialistic policies of the government.

Table 4

Estimates of Incidence of Poverty in India

Year	*Poverty Ratio (per cent)*			*Number of poor (million)*		
	Rural	*Urban*	*Combined*	*Rural*	*Urban*	*Combined*
1977-78	53.1	45.2	51.3	264.3	64.6	328.9
1983	45.7	40.8	44.5	252.0	70.9	322.9
1987-88	39.1	38.2	38.9	231.0	75.2	307.1
1993-94	37.3	32.4	36.0	244.0	76.3	320.3
1999-00	27.1	23.6	26.1	193.2	67.1	260.3
2007*	21.1	15.1	19.3	170.5	49.6	220.1

* "Poverty Projection for 2007" Tenth Five-Year Plan Documents.

As shown in Table 4, poverty has reduced to a large extent, but the common masses doubt this claim because a large number of ordinary people have never experienced the participation in the process of data collection for the Census. Many of the families and other social units and their real status remain unrecorded in the data. Though poverty has declined at the macro-level, there are wide rural-urban and inter-state disparities in the improvement pattern. In 1999-2000 Bihar and Orissa continued to be the two poorest states. In 1999-2000, 20 states and Union Territories had poverty ratios below the national average. A partial improvement in case of states like Andhra Pradesh, Gujarat, Karnataka, Kerala, Maharashtra, Punjab and West Bengal cannot satisfy the suffrage of the afflicted population. The major motive behind discussing the scene of education, health and poverty lies in expressing the actual implementation scale of Article 39 of the Directive Principles of State Policies.

Moving a little ahead, Article 41 is another unit enumerated in the Directive Principles, which facilitates the common masses by providing another comfortable condition to survive. It requires that, "the state shall within the limits of economic capacity and development, make effective provisions for securing the rights to work, to education and to public assistance in cases of unemployment, old age, sickness and disablement and in other cases of undeserved want". The principle enshrined in Article 41 holds its reflections in Article 45 also. Article 45 requires that, "the state shall endeavour to provide within a period of 10 years from the commencement of this Constitution, free and compulsory education for all children until they complete the age of fourteen years". As far as the issue of providing primary education is concerned, it was garlanded by the legislature. The parliament passed the 86th Constitutional Amendment Act, 2002 to make elementary education a Fundamental Right for children in the age group of 6-11 years. Along with these steps, leading to fruition, mid-day meal scheme was also introduced in August 1995. During 2002-03 on the basis of enrolment data furnished by states/UTs, 28.37 lakh million tonnes of food grain has been allocated for 10.36 crore children as on 31 March; 21.77 lakh million tonnes (76.72%) of food grain has been lifted. This scheme has certainly been implemented; but at present, 29 states/UTs are providing meals fully/partially to about 5.78 crore children which is just 54.8 per cent of the targeted 10.57 crore children.

Provisions of Primary Education

The number of primary schools increased from 6.39 lakh in 2000-01 to 6.64 lakh in 2001-02. The number of upper primary schools increased from 2.06 lakh in 2000-01 to 2.19 lakh in 2001-02. The discussion which deserves a space here is about the enrolment rate of students in these primary schools and further the gender gap institution in this enrolment. During 2000-01 and 2001-02 the growth rate of enrolment for girls at the elementary level was higher than that of boys. Participation of girls at all levels of school education has improved appreciably over the years but still huge gap can be noticed among states/in Gross Enrolment Ratio (GER) at primary/upper primary level. Though the drop-out at the elementary education level has decreased in the recent years, but still it is relatively high, specially in case of girl students. It was 39.9 per cent and 56.9 per cent at the primary and upper primary level in 2001-02 respectively. The reasons behind this drop-outs could be excessive household burdens, malnutrition, partial treatment by parents, son preference, etc. Whatever the reasons may be, the situation of a girl child in case of primary educational institution is not safe, because sexual abuse is another controversial issue, burning as a forest fire in government schools and further defaming teacher-pupil relationship. All this show that in documents and papers, the shadow of the requirements laid by Directive Principles of State Policies can be visualized but still their internalization is far off in case of attitudinal approach of the individuals who need to promote the social values for a common good. This was all about evaluating the context of the scenario of primary education. Another content demanding a civic thought is the right to work. This right ought to be provided without any discrimination of gender, age and social status as per the guidelines entombed in Directive Principles. Along with which it is required that the administration ensures to provide assistance to the public in case of any conscious or unconscious deprivation rendered thereon.

Right to Work

According to the 58th round (July-December 2004) survey of NSSO, the female workforce participation rate in rural areas declined to 281 per thousand as compared to 299 in the 55th Round (July 1999-2000). In urban areas, it increased marginally from 139 to 140. There is another discrimination in context of nature of work deployed to both rural and urban women. In rural areas women are mostly engaged primarily in agricultural activities, animal husbandry and other related works. And in urban areas a significant proportion of women workers are employed in the unorganized sectors such as household industries, petty trade and services, building and construction activities, etc. The differentiation between these activities also exposes the dominated and dominating factor respectively. The fields in which females work in rural areas are male dominating hence, women acquire a secondary status which is dominated by masculine decisiveness. On the other hand, the works which females undertake in urban areas instil confidence and zeal in them. Choosing rural or urban areas to take birth is something involuntary for females, even then mandatory socio-economic circumstances are imposed upon women; which in fact hinder an open feminine participation in work. The 'work' phenomenon is dependent upon the literate rates to a large extent. The proportion of women in organized sector employment is higher in states with higher female literacy rates. Employment of women in the organized sector (both public and private) as on March 31, 2002 was 4.95 million, which constituted 18.1 per cent of the total organized sector employment in the country, compared to 17.9 per cent in 2001. The distribution of women employees across the industries reveals that community, social and personnel services sector employed 56.5 per cent of women workers followed by manufacturing (20.6%), agriculture and allied occupation (9.4%) and finance, insurance, and business (5.2%). It can be authentically inferred that the employment of women in organized or unorganized sector depends upon their access to educational provisions and skill-development training. Even prior to this, individual attitude is a very important instrument to bring about occupational equity in both the genders. Until and unless the families themselves start treating female child at par with that of male child, the implementation of Directive Principles of States Policies for women welfare is not possible. It has been analysed that gender discrimination is attributed to almost all the social services, though intentionally or unintentionally.

Children and Work

The youngest demographic segment, i.e., children are always a major concern for the cause of protection, security and welfare because child health and security is a barometer for other areas of

Human Development (HDR, 2005). Directive Principles along with the Fundamental Rights entailed in Part IV and Part III of the Indian Constitution emphatically aim at securing them. Article 24 provides that, "No child below the age of fourteen years shall be employed to work in any factory or mine or engaged in any other hazardous employment". Supreme Court reinforced the prowess of this article in a judgement. In people's *Union for Democratic Rights* v. *Union of India* (AIR, 1982); Supreme Court asserted that the prohibition contained in Article 24 could be plainly and indubitably enforced against everyone, whether state or private individuals. In apposition to Article 41, Article 42 also impliedly protects children from occupational atrocities and direct the government to step ahead for children's development. Safety, security and development of children has always been a targeted aim of the Indian government because it has been morally insisted by directive principles of state policies and legally enforced by the fundamental rights of Indian Constitution. Still the situation needs a thorough analysis and a management approach.

According to the Census 2001, there are 1.25 crore working children in the age group of 5-14 as compared to the total child population of 25.2 crore of which 1.07 crore working children are in the age group of 10-14. Though the relative ratios to the total child population are lesser but the statistics as such are alarming. The Government of India adopted a National Policy on Child Labour in 1987; which forwarded a three fold strategy, viz (i) legal action plan, (ii) general development programmes, and (iii) project based action plans. Keeping in view the third fold of the policy, the government has adopted two schemes (a) National Child Labour Project Scheme (NCLP) and (b) Grant-in-Aid to voluntary organizations for taking up action oriented programmes in the field of rehabilitation of child labour. At present, there are 1000 NCLPs which cover 2.11 lakh working children and protect them from any hazardous, dangerous or poisonous toil of the industries or other economic units, in which they are employed. Tenth Plan further aims at an addition of 150 NCLPs. Grant-in-Aid scheme beholds targets of a higher liability by providing financial assistance to the suffering working children and these schemes cover those areas also, which are out of functionary aspect of the NCLPs. Though a lot of contributive efforts have been initiated for this very purpose, but still the data shows a disenchanted version. It has been over three decades that extreme steps have been taken to check child labour, but still contentment in lieu is a target in least proximity. The related statistics confer a nebulous adoption of Directive Principles of State Policies along with an unobligatory administrative approach of the Indian government.

Till the point of discussion, some imminent articles of the Indian Constitution have been referred for an analysis. An attempt has been made to present both 'the ought to be' and the 'present' situations in an elaborative manner. Coming back to the title of the paper it is important to discuss the impact of real and mythological implementation and adoption of the Directive Principles of State Policies on the modern interpretation dedicated to the concept of development. Because until and unless the rules, laws, legislations or directions of the government do not pace up with the ongoing social change, all administrative efforts collapse into the realm of non-effectivity.

Contemporary Conceptualization of Development

It is crucial to refer to the contemporary conceptualization of development because 'development' is a process that has experienced multiple transformation in the recent years. Earlier it was interpreted in mere economic terms, but now it laminates many other aspects of life, for instance, environment, society, education and all over welfare of individuals. In fact, new development is said to be eternal if it is 'sustainable'. The term 'sustainable development' was coined at the Cocoyoc Declaration on 'environment and development' in 1970. This form of development has been advocated for, in many events like Stockholm Declarations (1972); Brudtland Commission Report (1987) and many more. Sustainability is the most needed criterion for development. It implies that any benefit to present generation mankind must not incur any loss to the future generation and on the other side, development is sustainable if it incorporates all the chores of survival. To bring about a sustained society the paradigm of development needs to be economically viable and environment friendly. It implies that the social environment must be improvised into desirable direction

(Vyas, 1996). Though the term 'sustainability' was not popular at the time when the Constitution was framed, but still the impressions are inscribed in many parts of the Indian Constitution. Directive Principles of State Policies provide directions to efficaciously maintain the systems of education, health, occupation and many other social services. In fact this is the expected pattern in which sustainability can be brought about. This shows that these principles aimed at achievement of sustainable development but the framers of the Constitution could not probably realize the need to use this term. In the modern world, progress and development are not limitized to economic aspects, rather social and human development are the combined aims. Providing elementary education and reducing illiteracy rates, improving health facilities, securing comfortable conditions for work, installing secularism, equalizing gender gaps, uplifting environmental standard, etc., are some of the important indicators of sustainable development; but no doubt all must be accomplished simultaneously. A reductionist or a selective approach hinders the drive towards the goal of a resilient progress. The major drawback in the present complex world is that if economy develops, it leads to environmental degradation (Kumar, 2002). If literacy rates are increased, it leads to an increase in gender discrepancies in the data; if heath sector is aimed at to be improved, the remote areas and the areas affected with higher morbidity are deprived of. Hence, all these angles need to be considered to cultivate an equilibrium. Unless and until all the pillars of society are not plastered, the administration cannot acquire a connotation with the aspirations of the masses.

Conclusion

Directive Principles of State Policies have internalized all those motives, which the people in India desire to relish. Government has made innumerable efforts to attain these goals, but still the situation is not absolutely satisfactory. The evidence is presented in the preceding statistical references. However, the reason behind this failure is the non-enforceable status, of Directive Principles of State Policies. There might have been some cause for which the framers of the Constitution did not give 'enforceability' to these principles; but now this unjustifiable status has become the bone of contention for a present developmental process. Though Fundamental Rights confer many belligerent and enforceable rights to Indians, but directive principle possess many such germane social provisions which, if implemented would create an authentic welfare democracy in India. Providing suggestion is easier than producing action, so it may not be practical to make these directions justifiable by law courts so in such a situation, more schemes, projects and programmes should be formulated which incorporate larger number of public into welfare targets. And moreover, already executed schemes and projects must be evaluated on socio-economic basis so that the pitfalls can be checked. Concludingly, with due respect to the Directive Principles of State Policies it can be said that they hold an 'elderly' position in the Indian Constitution and administration just as an old aged person holds in an Indian family; who has a strong say in the family but still obeying his directions is a sweet will of the members.

Select References

AIR 1982 SC 1473. Also see *Labourers working on Salal Hydro-project* v. *State of J & K*, AIR, 1984, SC. 177.

Anand, A.S. (2005), "The Constitutional Model of Equality and Fraternity" in *Quest for Human Rights* by Mohammad Shabhir, Rawat Publication, Jaipur.

Brown, R. Lester (2005), *Plan B: Rescuing a Planet under Stress and a Civilization in Trouble*, Orient Longman, Hyderabad.

C.A.D., III, pp. 494-95.

Documents of Tenth Five-Year Plan, *Poverty Projection for 2007.*

Economic Survey (2003-2004), Government of India.

Human Development Report (2004), The Government of Punjab (Under the auspices of UNDP).

Human Development Report (2005), *International Cooperation at a Crossroads: Aid, Trade and Security in an Unequal World,* Oxford Press, New Delhi.

Kumar, Arvind (2002), *Environmental Pollution and Agriculture*, Efficient Offset Printers, New Delhi, (pp. 477-482).

Kumar, Narinder (1997), *Constitutional Law of India,* Pioneer Publication, New Delhi.

United Nations Development Programme, Human Development Report (HDR), 1995 and 2003.

Vyas, S. Vijay (1996), "Environmental Policies and Policy Implementation in India", in *Environment and Development* by M.S. Rathore, Rawat Publications, Jaipur.

23

Statistical Analysis of Crimes against Women, Children, Incest and Foeticide

JAWED USMANI AND TARIQ WALI

Given the current trends of urbanization in India spurred by free play of market forces in concert with other significant factors, operating under globalized economy, certain gender-based crimes against women and children have registered a steep rise over the past decade or so. Going by the official data released recently by the Union Home Ministry (2005), the proportion of IPC crimes committed against women to the total IPC crimes registered, have increased continually during the last 5 years from 7 per cent in 1999 to 8.4 per cent. Analysis of the data reveals that the aggregate number of crimes against women in 2004 significantly increased by 9.8 per cent over the previous year. Torture cases (58,121) increased by 14.6 per cent over the previous year while cases involving molestation (34,567) have registered a hike by 4.9 per cent over the previous year. Crimes against women in mega cities have also gone up by almost 5 per cent over the national average. Even the rarely reported cases of incest also stood at a dismal 505 cases (NCRB data).

That women face violence, directly and indirectly, at every stage of their lives, is further indicated by extension of threat to the female sex even before their birth takes place. Such a grim reality is evident by the increasing trends of female foeticide through sex-based selective abortions, rampant despite legislation in certain parts of India. Extrapolation by expected and actual sex ratio analysis by some workers suggest a close to 100 million baby girls are simply missing as aborted foetuses the world over. Demographic data (Census 2001) subjected to similar analysis point out over 5 per cent of the female population in India as similarly missing.

Detailed analysis based on the latest primary data, trends, their interpretations and new developments vis-à-vis gender based crimes, female foeticide, and child sexual abuse discussed in the paper will be presented by the author.

To begin with, the Platform for Action of the Fourth World Conference on Women held in Beijing, China in 1995 defines the term "violence against women" as any act of gender-based violence that results in or is likely to result in, physical, sexual or psychological harm or suffering to women, including threats of such acts, coercion or arbitrary deprivation of liberty, whether occurring in public or private life. Accordingly, violence against women encompasses but is not limited to the following: (a) physical, sexual and psychological violence occurring in the family, including battering, sexual abuse of female children in the household, dowry-related violence, marital rape, female genital mutilation and other traditional practices harmful to women, non-spousal violence and violence related to exploitation; (b) physical, sexual and psychological violence occurring within the general community, including rape, sexual abuse, sexual harassment and intimidation at work, in educational institutions and elsewhere, trafficking in women and forced prostitution; and (c) physical, sexual and psychological violence perpetrated or condoned by the state, wherever it occurs.

Other acts of violence against women enumerated in the same document include violation of the human rights of women in situations of armed conflict, in particular, murder, systematic rape, sexual slavery and forced pregnancy. Acts of criminal violence against women also include terrorism, forced sterilization and forced abortion, coercive use of contraceptives, female foeticide/prenatal sex selection and female infanticide.[1]

Gender-based crimes including violent crimes committed against women pose an unprecedented threat to women's lives across the globe[2] with our own country, India being no exception to the emerging global trends of high crime rates.[3]

Alarming rise in crimes against women in India is borne out by the document containing official statistics, released recently by National Crime Records Bureau (NCRB), the governmental body under Union Ministry of Home Affairs, Government of India. The document, Crime in India – 2004, contains, inter alia, the returns received by the NCRB, filed by all states of India including the Union Territories pertaining to the registered crimes committed against women during the year 2004.

Given the current trends of urbanization in gender-biased social structure of India, spurred by free play of market forces in concert with other significant factors under globalized economy, certain gender-based crimes against women and children have registered a significant spurt over the past decade or so.

In this paper the authors have mainly concentrated upon the latest incidence, crime rates, trends, victimology and growth rates of certain gender-based crimes like rape, incest, kidnapping and abduction, dowry deaths, sexual harassment, and importation of girls along with updated data on female foeticide in India. The authors have also given snapshot data concerning these crimes that occur in 35 mega cities during the year 2004 with population of over one million as per the 2001 Census of India. An attempt has also been made here, for the first time, to link such cluster of gender based crimes to urbanicity even as the authors seek to analyse the increase in crime rates to urban social stress originally postulated as a key factor in causation of social pathology rooted in such aberrant social phenomena.

Materials and Methods

The National Crime Records Bureau (NCRB) database of crimes in India, maintained since 1953 up to 2004, was obtained and thoroughly analysed in order to gather data pertaining to certain crimes against women and children, namely, rape, dowry deaths, molestation, sexual harassment, cruelty by husband and relatives, importation of girls, and incest. Incidence of these crimes was tabulated for trends analysis as also to find a pattern, if any, serving as a significant link with urbanicity.

Crime rates were calculated as the number of registered crimes per 1,00,000 mid-year population for the reference year. Similarly, the snapshot data analysis for 2004 was done for a few of such crimes committed in 35 mega cities having population of over one million as per 2001 Census of India. Primary data regarding crimes against children (2004) were also obtained and analysed from the NCRB Database. Data pertaining to prevailing sex ratio (2003) of number of girls for 1,000 boys, released by office of Registrar-General, India in October 2003 were compared to the 2001 Census of India data (Paper 1 of 2001), as collaborated wherever called for by latest available facts and figures from literature reviewed by the authors to make this study updated to the utmost extent possible.

Observations and Findings

Crimes Against Women

Disconcertingly enough, the proportion of crime against women has alarmingly deteriorated over the past many years in spite of the existence of a number of special legislations enacted to provide protection to women. Evidently, women continue to be victims of a cluster of crimes. Although women, as such, may be victims of any of the crimes such as homicides, robbery, cheating and so on, only the crimes that are directed specifically against women are characterized under the rubric of Crimes Against Women (CAW); and classified accordingly in NCRB Database (Table 1 and 2).

Incidence of CAW in 2003 was 1,40,601 with Crime Rate (CR) at 13.2 per lakh while it came up in 2004 to 1,5433 with CR at 14.2 per lakh. While any one crime against women as per 2004 figures, is registered in India every 3 minutes; one rape case is reported in every 29 minutes (faster by 6 minutes; as it was 1 in 35 minutes in 2003); one incident of dowry death every 75 minutes; one molestation case registered every 15 minutes; one eve-teasing/

sexual harassment case occurs every 53 minutes; one kidnapping/ abduction takes place every 23 minutes and one instance of cruelty by husband and relatives is reported every 9 minutes. Besides, one crime against children is reportedly committed every 36 minutes, predominantly against the girl child. The proportion of IPC crimes committed against women to the total IPC crimes registered, have increased continually during the last 5 years from 7 per cent in 1999 to 8.4 per cent.

Rape Cases

Total number of rape cases registered in 2004 was 18,233 with all-India crime rate of 1.7. Exceeding the national CR were 13 states and 4 UTs. Among 35 mega-cities, Delhi city reported 30.3 per cent (457 out of 1,510) of total rape cases in all mega cities while Madhya Pradesh with a huge figure 2,875 (15.8%) reported rape cases, was ranked first amongst the states followed by West Bengal with 1,475 cases (8.1%) and Uttar Pradesh with 1,397 cases (7.7%) with Maharashtra marginally trailing by 1,388 cases (7.6%). Ten cities with highest percentile contribution in rape cases included – Delhi city (30.3%), Mumbai (12.4%), Indore (4.9%), Jabalpur (4.4%), Pune (4.2%), Jaipur (3.7%), Hyderabad (3.7%), Ludhiana (3.2%), Bhopal (3.1%) and Nagpur (2.7%) (Table 3 and 4).

Incest Cases

Incest is defined as a deviant carnal intercourse between close blood relations of prohibited degree. It is defined in Alska Statutes Section 450 (Chapter 41) Offences Against the Person as "a person commits the crime of incest if, being 18 years of age or older, that person engages in sexual penetration with another who is related, either legitimately or illegitimately".

Further, incest being a crime against the ordains of nature between close blood relatives, is a highly stigmatized offence and taboo in most societies. In India, the IPC does not describe an offence of incest as such though many cases are booked under Section 377 IPC. This may be due to the fact that a range of marital relationships of different kinds and modes are prevalent amongst various cult religions and sects of Indian population. Cases like grievous hurt, murder and suicide arising out of incestuous relationships are, at times, brought before law.[4] As such, incest cases are, as a rule, under-reported in India on account of associated stigma and taboos against them in society. Incest incidence according to a survey conducted by certain civil society organization (CSO) was found to be surprisingly high and was held as the most common form of sexual abuse of the children in Indian households. It is estimated that at least 25 per cent of the adult population is molested sexually violated before the age of 16 years with at least 27 million adult survivors of this form of sexual abuse.[5]

Total number of incest cases as per NCRB data stood at 505 (with 506 victims) in 2004 as against 309 cases in 2003 with an alarming increase of 63.4 per cent. Out of these 506 victims of incest, some 189 cases were up to less than 18 years while 250 cases belonged to age group 18-30 years while 67 cases were aged more than 30 years with top five states reporting incest cases were (1) Chattisgarh (78); (2) Punjab (65); (3) Madhya Pradesh (63); (4) Rajasthan (39); and (5) Tamil Nadu (36 cases). In mega cities, Delhi (14); Mumbai (131); Bangalore and Lucknow (6 each), followed by Ahmedabad (5), Chennai and Bhopal (4 each). In all, out of the 64 total reported cases of incest (12.7%) in 35 mega cities with 42 victims below 18 years of age and 22 victims with an age group of 18-30 years (Table 5 and 6).

Crimes in Mega Cities

The term 'mega city' refers to cities having population of over 10 lakhs (1 million). The number of such cities has increased from 23 in 1991 to 35 in 2001.

Beset with typical problems such as unchecked migration, illegal settlements, diverse socio-cultural disparities, uneven distribution of incomes, etc., the mega cities are facing increased criminal activities, organized groups, gangsters, professional criminals and even youth and juveniles find crime as an outlet and short cut for a lavish life in mega cities.

For want of the mid-year population estimates for the year 2004 for these 35 mega cities, the actual Census population of these cities for the year 2001 is used for calculating the crime rates.

The population of these 35 mega cities constitutes nearly 10 per cent of the country's total population.

Crime Profile

A close to 27.8 per cent of population lives in urban areas as per 2001 Census. The present study does not aim at finding a complete urban crime pattern in the country but restricts to only 35 mega cities. This study is confined to certain crimes under IPC only.

Crimes under the Indian Penal Code (IPC) Incidence

All India... 18,32,015 (Mega Cities... 3,09,929; Share: 16.9 per cent) A total of 3,09,929 cognizable crimes under the IPC were reported in 35 mega cities during 2004 as compared to 2,91,246 crimes during 2003, thereby reporting an increase of 6.4 per cent. At the national level, this increase was 6.8 per cent over previous year 2003.

Crime Rates (IPC)

All India... 168.8 Mega cities... 287.3 The average rate of crime in Urban agglomeration centres at 287.3 was much higher than the country's crime rate of 168.8. The crime rate for each city is compared with the corresponding crime rate of the domain state in Table 7.

Crime rate (IPC) in cities was generally higher than the corresponding crime rate of domain state. In case of Chennai and Surat alone, the crime rate was somewhat lower than that of the respective state. In case of Kolkata city, the crime rate (around 82) was almost equal to that of domain state, West Bengal (82.6). In case of Mumbai city (179.9), the crime rate was slightly higher than that of Maharashtra (173.3). Following the national trend of increase in crime rate by 5.0 per cent (from 160.7 in 2003 to 168.8 in 2004), the crime rate in cities has also increased by 6.4 per cent (from 270.0 in 2003 to 287.3 in 2004).

Rising Trends of Female Foeticide in India

Speaking of crime against children, some 14,423 crimes were registered in 2004 as against 11,633 in 2003 as per the latest NCRB data with increase in CR from 1.1 in 2003 to 1.3 in 2004. The

NCRB data make it clear that the incidents of foeticide in general increased by 50.9 per cent during 2004 (86 cases) over 2003 (57 cases).

As if this was not enough, it is evident (Table 8) that certain states already below the child sex ratio at national level have, in recent years, further registered the dismal deterioration in this regard ratio. One recent survey by the Punjab Deputy Commissioner done in Nai Majara (Punjab) of children in the 0-1 age group did reveal the most awful figure of ratio 437:1000, far lower than Punjab state itself. Even, some 16 villages in Punjab do have sex ratios like 500:1000.[6]

That women face violence directly and indirectly at every stage of their lives, is further indicated by extension of threat to the female sex even before their birth takes place. Such a grim reality is evident by the increasing trends of female foeticide through sex-selective abortion that is rampant in certain parts of India despite legislation.

A meticulous global demographic analysis of actual and expected sex ratios shows that about 100 million girls are missing from the world over are dead.[7] It is estimated that 10 million foeticides had occurred in India during the last 20 years and just 77 cases registered in the last 4 years in India under the Pre-conception and Pre-natal Diagnostic Techniques (Regulation, and Prevention of Misuse) Act, 1994 with only 2 convictions so far. Demographic data (Census 2001) subjected to similar analysis point out over 5 per cent of the female population in India as similarly missing.[8]

This fatal flaw both of our socio-political system and law-enforcing agencies bodes ill for our country, and therefore it urgently calls for a serious review and correction at appropriate level.

Discussion

The foregoing crime data analysis and trends regarding certain key crimes committed against women and children, in general, and particularly, in mega city, associated urban milieu serve to highlight not only the ongoing abuse and brazen violation of human rights of women and children but also indirectly point out the role of growing urbanization to render such a violation to epidemic proportions. Our present study serves to collaborate and confirm similar studies done by other workers,[9,10,11] who have hinted at the urban crisis as a factor, for urbanization has led to a massive increase in behavioural disturbance especially associated with breakdown of families, including abandonment of and violence to spouses, children, and the elderly as well as depressive, psycho-somatic and anxiety disorders. It was also suggested that social deviance could be traced to many of the underlying social processes accompanying urbanization including competition, anomie, class conflict, accommodation, and assimilation. As the current phase of urbanization in India is spurred and driven by globalization, there is a gross mismatch of material and social infrastructure vis-à-vis the escalating popular aspirations, identity crisis, overcrowding, and heightened demands caused by mass media and urban locales. This fact, as we submit, should not be lost sight of when we are encountering such cluster of crimes reaching epidemic proportions. There is, we posit, a significant link of urban social stress that serves to explain as a key factor in causation of social pathology rooted in such a spurt in crimes against women and children reaching epidemic proportions in recent times.

Table 1

Crime Against Women (All India) Since the Year 1999 up to 2004

S.No.	*Year*	*Total Cases of Crime Against Women*
1.	1999	1,35,771
2.	2000	1,41,373
3.	2001	1,43,795
4.	2002	1,47,678
5.	2003	1,40,601
6.	2004	1,54,333

Source: India, Ministry of Home Affairs, NCRB (2006), Crime in India – 2004, New Delhi (Table redrawn and modified by authors)

Table 2

Incidents of Certain Crime Against Women During 1999-2004 and Percentage Variation in 2004 Over 2003

S. No.	Crime Head	Year						Percentage variation in 2004 over 2003
		1999	2000	2001	2002	2003	2004	
1.	Rape	15468	16496	16075	16373	15847	18233	+15%
2.	Kidnapping & Abduction	15962	15023	14645	14506	13296	15578	+17.1%
3.	Dowry Death	6699	6995	6851	6822	6208	7026	+13.2%
4.	Torture	43823	45778	49170	49273	50703	58121	+14.6%
5.	Molestation	32311	32940	34124	33943	32943	34567	+4.9%
6.	Sexual Harassment	8858	11024	9746	10155	12325	10001	–18.8%
7.	Importation of Girls	1	64	114	76	46	89	+93%
Total (All Crimes Against Women)		135771	141373	143795	143034	140601	154333	+9.8%

Source: India, Ministry of Home Affairs, NCRB (2006), Crime in India – 2004, New Delhi (Table redrawn and modified by the authors).

Table 3

Rape Cases: Trends Analysis with Corresponding Crime Rates

S.No.	Year	Total No. of Rape Cases (All India)	Mid-Year/Actual Population Base (in lakhs)	Crime Rate (CR)
1.	1971	2,487	5481.6	0.45
2.	1981	5,409	6833.3	0.79
3.	1991	10,410	8463.9	1.22
4.	1992	11,708	–	–

Contd.

Contd.

5.	1993	12,218	–	–
6.	1994	13,208	–	–
7.	1995	13,754	–	–
8.	1996	14,846	–	–
9.	1997	14,330	–	–
10.	1998	15,151	–	–
11.	1999	15,468	–	–
12.	2000	16,496	–	–
13.	2001	16,075	10,286.1	1.56
14.	2002	16,373	–	–
15.	2003	15,847	–	–
16.	2004	18,233	10,856.0	1.67

Source: India, Ministry of Home Affairs, NCRB (2006), Crime in India-2004, New Delhi (Table redrawn and modified by the authors).

Table 4

Rape Crimes: Offenders' Identity

1.	**Total Number of Rape Cases Reported from 28 States: 15,058**	
(i)	Parents/close family members were alleged offenders	488
(ii)	Relatives as alleged offenders	1,009
(iii)	Neighbours as alleged offenders	5,092
(iv)	Other known persons as alleged offenders	8,469
2.	**Total Number of Cases Reported from 7 UTs: 561**	
(i)	Parents/close family members were alleged offenders	17
(ii)	Relatives as alleged offenders	24
(iii)	Neighbours as alleged offenders	266
(iv)	Other known persons as alleged offenders	252
3.	**Total Number of Cases Reported from 35 Mega Cities: 1,383**	
(i)	Parents/close family members were alleged offenders	64
(ii)	Relatives as alleged offenders	74
(iii)	Neighbours as alleged offenders	609
(iv)	Other known persons as alleged offenders	636

Source: India, Ministry of Home Affairs, NCRB (2006), Crime in India – 2004, New Delhi (Table redrawn and modified by the authors).

Table 5

Top 10 States/UTs and Cities Ranked on the Basis of Incidence of Crimes Against Women in 2004 (All India)

Rank order	*States/UTs*	*Cities*
1.	Andhra Pradesh (12.3)	Delhi (City) (16.3)
2.	Uttar Pradesh (10.0)	Hyderabad (9.7)
3.	Madhya Pradesh (9.9)	Bangalore (5.91
4.	Rajasthan (8.5)	Mumbai (5.8)
5.	Maharashtra (7.9)	Vijayawada (5.4)
6.	West Bengal (7.2)	Ahmedabad (5.0)
7.	Tamil Nadu (6,0)	Chennai (4.2)
8.	Bihar (5.2)	Jaipur (4.0)
9.	Kerala (4.2)	Kolkata (3.3)
10.	Gujarat (4.0)	Kanpur (3.1)

Source: India, Ministry of Home Affairs, NCRB (2006), Crime in India – 2004, New Delhi (Table redrawn and modified by the authors).

Table 6

Top 10 States/UTs and City Ranked on the Basis of Percentage Contribution to All Crimes Against Women in India (Rate of Total Cognizable Crimes in parentheses)

Rank order	*States/UTs*	*Cities*
1.	Delhi (24.1)	Vijayavada (109.5)
2.	Andhra Pradesh (24.0)	Faridabad (57.7)
3.	Madhya Pradesh (23.5)	Agra (35.9)
4.	Rajasthan (21.7)	Indore (35.8)
5.	Assam(20.2)	Hyderabad (35.7)
6.	Tripura (20.0)	Jaipur (35.2)
6.	Jammu & Kashmir (20.0)	
7.	Kerala (19.7)	Jabalpur (31.1)
8.	Chandigarh (19.3)	Meerut (30.3)
9.	Haryana (19.1)	Bhopal (29.3)
10.	Chattisgarh (17.0)	Asansol (27.8)

Source: India, Ministry of Home Affairs, NCRB (2006), Crime in India – 2004, New Delhi (Table Redrawn and Modified by the authors).

Table 7

IPC Crime Rate: Mega Cities v. *Domain States*

S. No.	City	Rate of Crime (IPC)	
		City	Domain State
1.	Agra	260.6	73.2
2.	Ahmedabad	388.4	197.3
3.	Allahabad	147.7	73.2
4.	Amritsar	119.1	100.7
5.	Asansol	97.3	82.6
6.	Bangalore	501.6	207.9
7.	Bhopal	843.2	304.4
8.	Chennai	193.6	259.4
9.	Coimbatore	264.9	259.4
10.	Delhi	380.6	351.0
11.	Dhanbad	162.2	110.5
12.	Faridabad	298.4	174.4
13.	Hyderabad	340.9	201.3
14.	Indore	728.2	304.4
15.	Jabalpur	572.5	304.4
16.	Jaipur	569.0	255.9
17.	Jamshedpur	199.9	110.5
18.	Kanpur	168.3	73.2
19.	Kochi	498.6	315.4
20.	Kolkata	81.4	82.6
21.	Lucknow	277.9	73.2
22.	Ludhiana	182.9	100.7
23.	Madurai	264.8	259.4
24.	Meerut	212.4	73.2
25.	Mumbai	179.9	173.3
26.	Nagpur	401.2	173.3
27.	Nasik	226.2	173.3
28.	Patna	445.0	122.4
29.	Pune	286.3	173.3

Contd.

Contd.

30.	Rajkot	433.0	197.3
31.	Surat	147.0	197.3
32.	Vadodara	372.1	197.3
33.	Varanasi	128.5	73.2
34.	Vijayavada	757.6	201.3
35.	Visakhapatnam	239.4	201.3
Total (Cities/All India)		287.3	168.8

Source: India, Ministry of Home Affairs, NCRB (2006), Crime in India – 2004, New Delhi (Table redrawn and modified by the authors).

Table 8

Missing Women: States with Most Adverse Child Sex Ratio (Females per 1000 males)

S.No.	*State*	*2003 with Rank*	*2001 with Rank*
1.	Punjab	776(1)	793 (1)
2.	Himachal Pradesh	803 (2)	897 (4)
3.	Haryana	807(3)	820 (2)
4.	Uttar Pradesh	853 (4)	916 (6)
5.	Rajasthan	855 (5)	909 (5)
6.	Bihar	861 (6)	938 (7)
7.	Gujarat	862(7)	878 (3)
	India	883	927

Source: Office of the Registrar-General, Figures released in October 2003

Notes

1. United Nations (1995): *Draft Platform for Action,* The Fourth World Conference on Women: Action for Equality, Development and Peace, 1995 (E/CN.6/1995/L.17), New York
2. Shephered, J.P. and Farrington, D.P. (1995): "Preventing Crime and Violence", *BMJ,* 310: pp. 271-72
3. US Bureau of Justice Programs (2004): National Crime Victimization Survey (NCVS) Report; available at

http://www.ojp.usdoJ.qoy/bjs. The report says that in 2004, US residents age 12 or older experienced approximately 24 million crimes, according to NCVS with 21 per cent (5.2 million) were crimes of violence. Also, for 1,000 persons age 12 or older, there occurred 1 rape/sexual assault; 2 assaults with injury and 2 robberies. Further, urban residents had higher violence victimization rates, followed by suburban resident rates. Rural residents had the lowest rates. Added to that, every two minutes, somewhere in America, someone is sexually assaulted with minorities/blacks more at higher risk (2003).

4. Ramachandran, A. and Chandran M.R. (1997): *A Short Text Book of Forensic Medicine and Toxicology,* i.e.; AIPD, Chennai, p. 92.
5. Chandran, S. (2003): "Incest the Most Common Form of Child Abuse" accessed from www.thesouth-asian.com (Feb. 2003 News letter)
6. Dogra, C.S., (2006): "Death Becomes Her", *Outlook*, Feb 20-27, 2006, XLVI(8), pp. 66-76.
7. Fathalla, M.F. (1994): "The one hundred million missing women are dead: Let it Happen Never Again", *Int Gynecol Obstet,* 1994; 46; pp. 101-4
8. Dogra, C.S. (2006): *op. cit.,* p. 76.
9. Kleinman, A. (1991): "Preface" in *Psychological Aspects of Depression* (eds. J. Backer and A. Kleiman), LFA, London.
10. Park, et al., (1995): *The City,* University of Chicago Press, Chicago, IL.
11. Vlachav, D. and S. Galea (2002): "Urbanization, Urbanicity and Health", *Journal of Urban Health,* 79(4); supplement 1.

(drstwali@rediffmail.com)

24

Uniform Civil Code

A Politico-Judicial Analysis

AJAI KUMAR

Article 44 of Indian Constitution lays emphasis to secure Uniform Civil Code for its citizen throughout the territory of India.[1] This article forms a part of the Directive Principle of State Policy and simply enjoins the state to enact a Uniform Civil Code. It possesses two characteristics. Firstly, it is not enforceable in any court, so its obedience or implementation cannot be secured through judicial proceeding. Secondly, it is fundamental in the governance of the country and it shall be the duty of the state to apply these principles in making laws.[2] The object of the Uniform Civil Code in India has been to achieve national unity and integrity through communal harmony. The fundamental duties mandating that every citizen of India must have a duty "to promote harmony and the spirit of common brotherhood amongst all the people of India transcending religious, linguistic and sectional diversities".[3] Uniform Civil Code is also a medium through which the people belonging to heterogeneous elements come to united into a Nation as such. It will also further fraternity and unity/integrity of nation.

The idea of Uniform Civil Code was at first introduced into the national political debate in the year 1940 when a demand for such a code was made by the National Planning Committee appointed by the Congress.[4] The subcommittee for the 'Women's Role' in a planned economy was specifically directed to study the role women would play in the future independent India, and it presented its report to the National Planning Committee in August, 1940.The report advocated for the enactment of a Uniform Civil Code. It envisaged the proposed Uniform Civil Code to be an optional code to begin with, which could gradually replace the different personal laws followed by various religious communities. However, other resolutions by the subcommittee and the National Planning Committee indicated that the members of these committees did not think that the enactment of a Uniform Civil Code was a feasible idea. By 1940, a few leaders of the All India Women's Conference were also demanding the enactment of a Uniform Civil Code. However, the Charter of Women's Right prepared by the All India Women's Conference mentioned the right of women to have reforms made in personal laws but did not extend the claim of Uniform Civil Code.

The directive to enact a Uniform Civil Code in the Constitution was included as a result of the efforts of Mr. Minoo Masani, as a member of subcommittee on Fundamental Right, he moved a resolution on 28 March, 1947, that the state should be made responsible to enact a Uniform Civil Code in order to break down the barriers between various communities.[5]

Mr. Minoo Masani, Mr. Hansa Mehta, Ms. Rajkumari Amrit Kaur and Dr. Ambedkar voted in favour of the inclusion of the clause of the Uniform Civil Code, but the majority of the subcommittee voted against its inclusion on the grounds that it was beyond the scope of Fundamental Rights. However, when it was decided that the rights were to be divided into justiciable Fundamental Rights and non-justiciable Directive Principles, the subcommittee agreed to make an enactment of the Uniform Civil Code as Directive Principle.[6]

The first legislative attempt in this respect was indicated in the Constituent Assembly. It was the Constituent Assembly in which the idea of Uniform Civil Code was legally mooted in India. After the deliberation, the subcommittee on Fundamental Rights decided to recommend that though Uniform Civil Code was highly desirable but it was applicable entirely on voluntary basis.[7] But this recommendation was not unanimous and three members of the sub-committee namely Mr. Minoo, Masani, Ms. Rajkumari Amrit Kaur and Mr. Hansa Mehta recorded their dissent.[8] Whereas Sri Mohammed Ismail Sahib wanted to add a proviso to Article 35 (draft form) that, "provided that any group, section or community of people shall not be obliged to give up its own personal law in case it has such a law".[9] He argued that the right of people to follow their own personal law was among the Fundamental Rights. Sri Naziruddin Ahmed wanted to add another proviso, "provided that personal law of any community which has been guaranteed by the statute shall not be changed except with the previous approval of the community ascertained in such manner as the union legislature may determine by law." Another amendment in Article 35 was proposed by Sri Mahboob Ali Baig Sahib Bahadur, "provided that nothing in this article shall affect the personal law of the citizen". Other member Sri B. Poker Sahib Bahadur who supported the motion moved by Sri Mohamed Ismail Sahib proposed to add a different proviso, i.e., "provided that any group, section or community of people shall not be obliged to give up its own personal law in case it has such a law". Sri Hussain Imam (another member of Constituent Assembly) contented that for a big country like India having diversified population, the Uniform Civil Code is not feasible. Attempts of dilution of this provision could not find favour with the Constituent Assembly.

In the Constituent Assembly, few members came in support of Uniform Civil Code while countering the opposite arguments Sri K.M. Munshi argued that Article 35 is not against Article 19 (draft form) because under Article 19 the state may regulate secular activities or may bring social reform or social welfare. Sri Alladi Krisnaswami Ayyar also argued in support of Uniform Civil Code as a progressive system which may include all the good aspects of various personal laws. Dr. Ambedkar in his speech supported the view of Sri Munshi and Sri Ayyar. He refuted the argument that the validity of Uniform Civil Code for a big and diverse country like India is not possible on the ground that India has already one law covering almost every aspect of human relationship except marriage and succession.

The controversy arose in the Constituent Assembly is not set at rest till date and continues with Indian judiciary in different flavour. The Supreme Court and different High Courts in their various decisions have no express uniform views on the point of desirability of Uniform Civil Code. In few cases too much importance is given to it by Supreme Court and an urgent need has been shown for enacting Uniform Civil Code by Parliament whereas in few cases the Supreme Court has shown reluctant attitude on this point and has avoided the issue either by holding that time is not ripe for enacting Uniform Civil Court or by saying that it is within the domain of Parliament and judiciary is unable to resolve the problem. In few cases, the Supreme Court has avoided this issue by siding it away from main issue. A few observations by the Supreme Court in different cases indicating its inconsistent behaviour:

In *State of Bombay* v. *Narasu Appa Mali*,[10] the validity of the Bombay Prevention of Hindu Bigamous Marriage Act, 1946 was challenged on various grounds in the proceedings before Bombay High Court arising out of criminal prosecutions under the Act and one of the grounds which is relevant for our present purpose, was taken in the following manner. It was urged that the provisions of the Hindu law and Muslim law (religious law), providing polygamy for the male but strict monogamy for the females, were violative of the provision of equality and discriminatory on the ground of sex as contained in Article14 and Article 15 of the Constitution of India and, therefore, the relevant provisions of the personal laws of both the Hindus and Muslims became void and inoperative from the commencement of the Constitution. As a result, both the Hindus and Muslims became equally liable and punishable under Section 494 of I.P.C., for contracting bigamous marriage. But the impugned Bombay Act singled out the Hindu only and made the offence of bigamy under the Act graver and more serious than Section 494 of I.P.C., by making it cognizable, non-compoundable and also by defining the expression a bit more wide under the Act. The question has been considered with appreciable depth by Division Bench consisting of two most eminent judges, Chief Justice Chagla and

Justice Gajendradadkar. Chief Justice Chagla in his judgment observed:

> "Now, it is an historical fact that both the Muslims and the Hindus in this country have their own personal laws which are based upon their respective religious texts and which embody their own distinctive evolution and which are coloured by their own distinctive backgrounds. Article 44 itself recognize separate and distinctive personal laws because it lays down as a directive to be achieved that within a measurable time India should enjoy the privilege of a common Uniform Civil Code applicable to all its citizens irrespective of race and religion."[10a]

In the year 1985, the Supreme Court had delivered two important decisions on the point of Uniform Civil Code, The first famous decision was in *Mohd. Ahmed Khan* v. *Shah Bano Begam.*[11] The case was before the five judges bench consisting of Chief Justice Y.V. Chandrachud, Justice D.A Desai, Justice O. Chinnappa Reddy, Justice E.S. Venkataramiah and Justice Ranganath Mishra. The judgment was delivered by Chief Justice Y.V. Chandrachud on behalf of himself and on behalf of the rest four judges. The petitioner went to Supreme Court through special leave and relief was prayed to quash the maintenance order passed by the High Court of Madhya Pradesh against the petitioner husband. This order was passed by High Court on the revision application filed by the respondent – wife. Honourable Chief Justice Y.V. Chandrachud put the issue for consideration in this case as – does Muslim personal law impose no obligation upon the husband to provide for maintenance of his divorced wife? Is the law so ruthless in its inequality that, no matter how much the husband pays for the maintenance of his divorced wife during the period of iddat – absolves him forever from the duty of paying adequately so as to enable her to keep her body and soul together? Is there any provision in the Muslim Personal Law under which a sum is payable to the wife 'on divorce'?[12]

On the above discussion we may conclude that neither relief was praved for Uniform Civil Code nor the issue was before the court on Uniform Civil Code in this case. The case was exclusively based on maintenance laws. In spite of these facts, Chief Justice Y.V. Chandrachud had expressed regret,

> "the Article 44 of our Constitution has remained a dead letter. There is no evidence of any official activity for framing a Common Civil Code for the country. A Common Civil Code will help the cause of national integration by removing desperate loyalties to laws which have conflicting ideologies It is the state which is charged with the duty of securing a Uniform Civil Code for citizen of the Country and unquestionable, it has the legislative competence to so do. We understand the difficulties involved in brining persons of different faith and persuasions on a common platform. But a beginning has to be made if the Constitution is to have any meaning. Inevitably, *the role of the reformer has to be assumed by the courts* because: it is beyond the endurance of sensitive minds to allow injustice to be suffered when it is so palpable. But piecemeal attempts of the courts to bridge the gap between personal laws cannot take place of a Common Civil Code. Justice to all is a far more satisfactory way of dispensing justice than justice from case to case".[13] (Emphasis added)

After seventeen days of this decision another judgment was delivered by the Supreme Court on the point of Uniform Civil Code[14] in *Ms. Jorden Diengdeh* v. *S. Chopra.*[15] The case was before the Division Bench. The judgment was delivered by Justice O. Chinnappa Reddy for himself and on behalf of Justice R.B. Mishra. The relief prayed by petitioner in this case was to declare her marriage as nullity. Her marriage was solemnized with a Sikh male (respondent) under the Indian Christian Marriage Act,1872. The ground on which declaration was sought was impotency of husband though the husband was capable of achieving erection and penetration. The Supreme Court had made a survey of all divorce laws prevailing at the time in India like – The Indian Divorce Act. 1869, the Special Marriage Act, 1954, the Hindu Marriage Act, 1955, the Parsee Marriage and Divorce Act, 1936 and the Dissolution of Muslim Marriage Act,1939. The Court concluded that law relating to judicial separation, divorce and nullity of marriage is far, far from uniform. Surely, the time has now come for complete reform of law of marriage and make a uniform law applicable to all people irrespective of religion or caste. It appears to be necessary to introduce irretrievable breakdown of marriage and mutual consent as ground of divorce in all cases.[16] The Supreme Court had made a suggestion that time has come for the intervention of the legislature in these matters to provide for a uniform code of marriage and divorce. The court directed that a copy of this order might be forwarded to the Ministry of Law and Justice for such action as they might deem fit to take.[17]

In year 1993, the issue of Uniform Civil Code was again for consideration before Supreme Court in *Maharshi Avadesh* v. *Union of Indian.*[18] Three prayers were made by petitioner before the Division Bench consisting of Justice K. Jayachandra Reddy and Justice G.N. Ray. The first prayer was to issue a writ of mandamus to the respondents to consider the question of enacting a common Civil Code for all citizens of India. The second prayer was to declare Muslim Women (Protection of Rights on Divorce) Act, 1986 as void being arbitrary and discriminatory. The third prayer was to direct respondent not to enact Shariat Act. The Supreme Court held that these are all matters for legislature and the court cannot legislate on these matters. It is important to note that in this case the petitioner specifically prayed for issue of direction to respondent for enactment of Uniform Civil Code which was refused by the court.

A famous decision of Supreme Court is *Sarala Mudgal* v. *Union of India*[19] which came out in the year 1995, wherein, the Supreme Court reconsidered the issue of Uniform Civil Code. Four petitions were filed under Article 32 of the Constitution. The first writ petition included the petition of the president of 'Kalayani', a registered society working for the welfare of needy families and in distress and petition of Ms. Meena Mathur for punishment of her husband under 494 of I.P.C.[20] The second writ was filed by Ms. Sunita alias Fathima to whom Mr. Jitendra Mathur was married. He was the husband of earlier petitioner Ms. Meena Mathur, who after having converted into Muslim religion married with the second petitioner Ms. Sunita. She was actually claiming maintenance. Her problem was as to under which personal law she may claim maintenance because she had also converted into Muslim religion from Hindu. The third writ petition was filed by Ms. Geeta

Rani. She was married with Mr. Pradeep Kumar according to Hindu rites. Her husband after being converted into Muslim religion married with another lady Ms. Deepa. She was claiming remedy for declaration of her husband's second marriage as void. The fourth writ petition was being filed by Ms. Sushmita Ghosh. She had prayed that her husband be restrained from entering into second marriage with Ms. Vinita Gupta. Her husband had also embraced Islam.

It is very important to note that in this case no petitioner prayed before the court for issue of direction to Government of India for enacting Uniform Civil Code. The case was before the Division Bench of apex court consisting of Justice Kuldip Singh and Justice R.M. Sahai.[21] Justice Kuldip Singh had also pointed out that the question for the consideration in this case was whether a Hindu husband married under Hindu law, by embracing Islam, can solemnize second marriage? Whether such a marriage without having the first marriage dissolved under the law, be a valid marriage with the first wife who continues to be a Hindu? Whether the apostate husband would be guilty of the offence under Section 494 of the I.P.C.[22]

On the point of Uniform Civil Code, Justice Kuldip Singh had referred two earlier above-mentioned decisions of this court in cases – *Mohd Ahmed Khan* v. *Shah Bano Begam*[23] and *Ms. Jorden Diengdeh* v. *S.S. Chopra*[24] and after tracing political history of India concluded that the government till date had been wholly remiss in its duty of implementing the constitutional mandate under Article 44 of Constitution of India. He requested the Government of India through Prime Minister of the country to have a fresh look at Article 44 and endeavour to secure Uniform Civil Code. He further issued the direction to Government of India through Secretary, Ministry of Law and Justice to file an affidavit in this court in August, 1996 indicating therein the step taken and effort made, by Government of India toward securing a Uniform Civil Code.

Justice R.M. Sahai while delivering concurring judgment agreed in principle with Justice Kuldip Singh on point of desirability of a Uniform Civil Code. He pointed out that pattern of debate, even today is the same as was voiced forcefully by the member of minority community in the Constituent Assembly. The argument of one party in the case was is that non-implementation of the provisions contained in Article 44 amounts to grave failure of Indian democracy, whereas other side claimed that the code may cause dissatisfaction and disintegration. He emphasized that government may consider feasibility of appointing a committee to enact Conversion of Religion Act immediately to check the abuse of religion by any person. The Act should provide that every citizen who changes his religion cannot marry another wife unless he divorces his first wife.

Correctness of principles laid down in Sarala Mudgal[25] case was examined by the Supreme Court in *Ahmedabad Women Action Group* v. *Union of India*[26] and further being explained in *Lily Thomas* v. *Union of India*[27] In Ahmedabad Women Action Group[28] case, three writs were filed as Public Interest Litigation. In first writ petition, the prayers were made by petitioner to declare law of polygamy amongst Muslim which emphasized the power of Muslim husband to declare unilateral talak, Muslim Women (Protection of Rights on Divorce) Act,1986 and inheritance law of Shia and Sunni as void. Second writ petition contained the prayer to declare Sections 2(2), 5(ii) and (iii), 6 and Explanation of Section 30 of Hindu Succession Act,1956, Section 2 of Hindu Marriage Act,1955, Section 3(2),6 and 9 of the Hindu Minority and Guardianship Act,1956 and power of Hindu male for testamentary disposition as void offending Article 14 and 15 of the Constitution, In third writ petition, the petitioner prayed to declare Sections 10 and 34 of Indian Divorce Act,1869 (old provisions) and Sections 43 to 46 of the Indian Succession Act, 1925 as void. Though in all three writ petitions, prayers were not directly concerned with the issue of Uniform Civil Code but indirectly called for making uniformity in personal law. The Supreme Court held that these writ petitions did not deserve disposal on merit because they involve issues of state policies with which the court will not originally have any concern. The remedy lies somewhere else and not by knocking the door of the court. Again a case where the prayer was for uniform laws in the field of family law, but refused by the court.

Lily Thomas v. *Union of India*[29] was another case of bigamous marriage wherein Smt. Sushmita Ghosh w/o Sri G.C. Ghosh filed the writ petition stated that she was married with Sri G.C. Ghosh in accordance with Hindu rites on May 10, 1984 and was living happily at Delhi. Later on her husband converted himself into Islam religion with objective to have remarriage with another women Miss Vanita Ghosh. The petitioner prayed for the following relief:

1. The honourable Court by an appropriate writ, order or direction, declare polygamous marriages by a Hindu and a non-Hindu after conversion to Islam religion are illegal and void.
2. The court issue appropriate directions to respondent no. 1 and 2 to carry out suitable amendments in Hindu Marriage Act, 1955 so as to curtail and forbid the practice of polygamy.
3. The court issue appropriate direction to declare that where a non-Muslim male gets converted to the 'Muslim' faith without any real change of belief and merely with a view to avoid an earlier marriage or enter into second marriage, any of such marriage entered into by him after conversion would be void.
4. The court also issue appropriate direction to respondent no. 3 restraining him from entering into any marriage with Miss. Vanita Gupta or any other women during the subsistence of his marriage with the petitioner.

The judgment was delivered by Division Bench consisting of Justice Shagir Ahmed and Justice R.P. Sethi. Justice Sethi after referring *Sarla Mugdal's* Case,[30] Shah *Bano Begum* Case,[31] *Ahmedabad Women Action Group* Case[32] *Maharshi Avadesh* Case,[33] *Pannalal Banishlal Patti* Case[34] on a point of Uniform Civil Code and *P.M. Ashwathanarayana Setty* Case,[35] *Keshvanand Bharti* Case,[36] came on conclusion that this court has no power to issue directions for enforcement of the Directive Principle of State Policy of the Constitution including Article 44. They do not create any justifiable right in favour of any person. Honourable Justice Sethi had also made a remark that no direction appeared to have been issued by this court for the purpose of having Uniform Civil Code within the meaning of Article 44 of the Constitution. Justice Kuldip Singh in his judgment *(Sarla Mugdal* Case)[37] only requested the government to have a fresh look at Article 44 in the light of words used in that Article. Whereas Justice Sahai in his concurring but separate judgment only suggested the ways and means, if deemed proper, for implementation of the aforesaid Directives, Justice Saghir Ahmed observed, "I agreed with Justice Sethi that any direction for the enforcement of Article 44 of the Constitution could not have been issued by only of the Judge in *Sarla Mugdal* case."[38] In fact, *Sarla Mugdal's* case was considered by this court in *Ahmedabad Women Action Group* Case[39] and was held that the question regarding the desirability of enacting a Uniform Civil Code did not directly arise in *Sarla Mugdal* Case.[40]

Before *Ahmedabad Women Action Group* Case, in the year 1996 another important pronouncement of the Supreme Court appeared in *Pannalal Bansilal Patel* v. *State* of *A.P.*[41] The fact of the case was not relating to marriage and divorce law. The validity of few sections of A.P. Charitable Hindu Religious and Endowment Act, 1987 were challenged in this case. The case did not directly involve the question of Uniform Civil Code and the relief was also not prayed by the petitioner in this connection but observation of Justice K. Ramaswami is relevant:

> "In a pluralist society like India in which people have faith in their respective religions, beliefs or tenants propounded by different religions or their offshoot, the founding fathers, while making the Constitution, were confronted with problems to unify and integrate people of India professing different religious faiths, born in different castes, sects or subsects in the society speaking different language and dialects in different regions and provided a secular Constitution to integrate all sections of the society as a united Bharat. The Directive Principle of the Constitution themselves visualize diversity and attempted to foster uniformity among people of different faiths. *A uniform law, though highly desirable, enactments thereof in one go perhaps may be counter-productive to unity and integrity of the nation.* In a democracy governed by rule of law, gradual progressive change and order should be brought about. Making law or amendment to a law is a slow process and the legislative attempts to remedy where the need is felt most acute. It would, therefore, be inexpedient and incorrect to think that all laws have to be made uniformly applicable to all people in one go."

Lastly and finally, the recent verdict of the Supreme Court in year 2003 the issue of Uniform Civil Code and its desirability was raised once again in *John Vallamattom* v. *Union of India.*[42] The case was considered by three judges bench consisting of Chief Justice V.N. Khare, Justice S.B. Sinha and Justice Dr. A.R. Lakshman. The first petitioner was a Christian priest belonging to religious denomination of Roman Catholics. The second petitioner was also a member of the Christian community. Both petitioners were aggrieved by the discriminatory treatment meted out to the members of the Christian community under the Indian Succession Act, 1925 by which they were practically prevented from bequeathing property for religious and charitable purposes. This had led them to file this writ petition by which the constitutional validity of section 118 of Indian Succession Act,1925 was being challenged The section lays down special procedure for bequeathing any property to religious and charitable uses by a Christian having any near relative. The will is required to be bequeathed by testator not less than twelve month before his death and deposited within six months from its execution in safe custody as provided by law. The petitioner argued that the section is violative of Article 14 and 15 of the Constitution because:

1. it discriminates against a Christian vis-à-vis non-Christian.
2. it discriminates against religious and charitable use of property vis-à-vis other use.
3. it discriminates against a Christian having a nephew, niece or nearest relative vis-à-vis a Christian having no such relative.
4. It discriminates against a Christian who dies within twelve months of execution of the will of which he has no control.[43]

This analysis makes it clear that the petitioners never prayed for direction to legislature for enacting Uniform Civil Code. Chief Justice V.N. Khare was the only judge out of three judges who pointed out the necessity of a Common Civil Code and its relevance to the cause of national integrity by removing the contradictions based on ideologies. In the wording of Chief Justice Khare:

> "the aforesaid two provisions viz., Article 15 and 44 show that the former guarantees religious freedom whereas the latter divests religion from social relations and personal law. It is no matter of doubt that marriage, succession and the like matters of a secular character cannot be brought within the guarantee enshrined

under Article 25 and 26 of the Constitution. Any legislation which brings succession and like matters of secular character within ambit of Article 25 and 26, a suspect legislation. It is a matter of regret that Article 44 of the Constitution has not been given effect to Parliament is still to step in for framing a Common Civil Code in the country. A Common Civil Code will help the cause of national integration by removing the contradictions based on ideologies".[44]

This discussion indicates that the issue of Uniform Civil Code has been agitated and re-agitated in the Supreme Court of India several times. But at the same time when it is raised by the petitioner, the Supreme Court either ignored it or side tracked it as secondary issue. Actually, it has become a political issue with which judiciary is very often confronted and has always found herself helpless to enter in this field. This issue is essentially in the legislative domain and requires a public debate to form any acceptable public opinion.

Notes

1. Article 44 – "The state shall endeavour to secure for its citizen a Uniform Civil Code throughout the territory of India".
2. M.P. Singh, (ed.) V.N. Shukla's, *Constitution of India*, 298 (9th ed. 1994).
3. Article 51-A of Constitution of India.
4. See, A. Parashar, *Women and Family Law Reforms in India,* pp. 230-235(1992).
5. Minutes of the Meeting of the subcommittee on Fundamental Rights, 28 March, 1947 in Shiva Rao, B., *The Framing of India's Constitution,* 128(1968 Vol. 11).
6. Ibid. at 134-136 (30 March, 1947).
7. Shiva Rao, *The Framing of India's Constitution,* 1968 Vol. II Select Documents, 206, Tripathi, Bombay, Referring to Debate of 19 April, 194.
8. Ibid. at 173.
9. Vol. VII Constituent Assembly Debate at 540.
10. AIR 1952 Bom. 84.

10a. Ibid. at 87.
11. AIR 1985 S.C. 945.
12. Ibid. at 947 (Para 3).
13. Ibid. at 954 (Para 32).
14. The judgment in *Mohd. Ahmed Khan* v. *Shah Bano Begum* was delivered on 24 April, 1985 whereas *Ms. Jorden Diendeh* v. *S.S. Chopra* was delivered on 10 May. 1985.
15. AIR 1985 S.C.935.
16. Ibid. at 940.
17. Ibid. at 941.
18. 1994 Supp.(1) 713.
19. AIR 1995 S.C. 1531.
20. Ibid. at 1533.
21. Ibid.
22. Ibid., at 1 532.
23. AIR 1985 S.C.945.
24. AIR1985 S.C.935.
25. AIR 1995 S.C. 1531.
26 AIR 1997 S.C.3614.
27. AIR 2000 S.C. 1650.
28. AIR 1997 S.C.3614.
29. AIR 2000 S.C. 1650.
30. AIR 1995 S.C.1531.
31. AIR 1985 S.C.945.
32. AIR 1997 S.C.3614.
33. 1994 Supp.(I) S.C.C.713.
34. AIR 1996 S.C. 1023.
35. AIR 1989 S.C. 100.
36. AIR 1973 S.C. 1481.
37. AIR 1995 S.C.1531.
38. Ibid.
39. AIR 1997 S.C. 3614.
40. AIR 1995 S.C. 1531.
41. AIR 1996 S.C.W. 507.
42. AIR 2003 S.C. 2902.
43. Ibid. at 2908.
44. Ibid. at 2913.

Contributors

Abha Kulshreshtha, Advocate, Delhi High Court, New Delhi.

Ajai Kumar, Associate Professor, Law School, BHU, Varanasi.

Anis Ahmad, Assistant Professor, Faculty of Law, M.D. University, Rohtak.

B.C. Nirmal, Professor of Law, Banaras Hindu University, Varanasi.

C. Chellappan, Former Member, National Commission of Scheduled Castes/Scheduled Tribes, New Delhi.

D.S. Somashekhar, Professor of History, Tunga Mahavidyalaya, Thirthahalli, Shimoga, Karnataka.

Fasahat Shamoon, Research Fellow, Department of Sociology & Social Work, AMU, Aligarh.

Iqbal Ali Khan, Professor of Law, AMU, Aligarh.

Jasleen Kewlani, Assistant Professor, Department of Law, Rajeev Gandhi National University of Law, Patiala.

Javanshir Majido, Third Secretary, Embassy of Azerbaijan in India, New Delhi.

Jawed Usmani, Professor & Chairman, Department of Forensic Medicine & Toxicology, JN Medical College, AMU, Aligarh.

Lalita Parihar, Professor of Law, University of Jammu, Jammu.

Mohammad Shabbir, Professor of Law (Ambedkar Chair Professor of Law), Dr. Ambedkar Chair of Legal Studies & Research, Department of Law, AMU, Aligarh.

Mohd. Zafar Mahfooz Nomani, Associate Professor of Law, Aligarh Muslim University, Aligarh.

Mohammad Momin, Associate Professor, Department of Law, University of Burdwan, Burdwan.

Mushtaq Ahmad, Advocate on Record, Supreme Court of India, New Delhi.

Noor Aziah Mohd. Awal, Associate Professor, Faculty of Law, University of Kebangsaan, Bangi, Selangor, Malaysia.

P.K. Mathur, Associate Professor, Department of Sociology & Social Work, AMU, Aligarh.

Parminder Kaur, Assistant Professor, Department of Sociology, Master Tara Singh College, Ludhiana.

Rattan Singh, Associate Professor, Department of Law, Guru Nanak Dev University, Amritsar.

S.K. Varshney, Professor of Law and Director, Lucknow. Law School, Lucknow University, Lucknow.

Shakeel A. Samdani, Associate Professor, Department of Law, AMU, Aligarh.

Shaukat Ali, Professor of Law, Faculty of Law, MJP Rohilkhand University, Bareilly.

Shavi Sharma, Assistant Professor, Department of Law, University of Jammu, Jammu.

Sushma Yadav, Ambedkar Chair Professor of Social Justice, IIPA, New Delhi.

Tariq Wali, Department of Forensic Medicine & Toxicology, JN Medical College, AMU, Aligarh.

Zafar A. Khan, Research Officer, Dr. Ambedkar Chair of Legal Studies & Research , Department of Law, AMU, Aligarh.